D0027495

THE CAMBRIDGE COMPANION TO

MUḤAMMAD

As the Messenger of God, Muḥammad stands at the heart of the Islamic religion, revered by Muslims throughout the world. *The Cambridge Companion to Muḥammad* comprises a collection of essays by some of the most accomplished scholars in the field who are exploring the life and legacy of the Prophet. The book is divided into three parts, the first charting his biography and the milieu into which he was born, the revelation of the Qur'ān, and his role in the early Muslim community. The second part assesses his legacy as a lawmaker, philosopher, and politician. In the third part, chapters examine how Muḥammad has been remembered across history in biography, prose, poetry, and, most recently, in film and fiction. Essays are written to engage and inform students, teachers, and readers coming to the subject for the first time. They will come away with a deeper appreciation of the breadth of the Islamic tradition, of the centrality of the role of the Prophet in that tradition, and, indeed, of what it means to be a Muslim today.

Jonathan E. Brockopp is associate professor of history and religious studies at Pennsylvania State University. A specialist on early Islamic legal texts, he has written widely on Islamic law, ethics, and comparative religions. His books include *Early Mālikī Law: Ibn ʿAbd al-Ḥakam and His* Major Compendium of Jurisprudence (2000); *Judaism and Islam in Practice: A Sourcebook* (2000, coauthored with Jacob Neusner and Tamara Sonn); and two edited volumes on Islamic ethics. His article "Theorizing Charismatic Authority in Early Islamic Law" (2005) advances a new theory for understanding the role of Muḥammad in Islamic history.

CAMBRIDGE COMPANIONS TO RELIGION

This is a series of companions to major topics and key figures in theology and religious studies. Each volume contains specially commissioned chapters by international scholars that provide an accessible and stimulating introduction to the subject for new readers and nonspecialists.

Other titles in the series

AMERICAN JUDAISM
Edited by Dana Evan Kaplan

KARL BARTH
Edited by John Webster

THE BIBLE, 2ND EDITION
Edited by Bruce Chilton

BIBLICAL INTERPRETATION
Edited by John Barton

DIETRICH BONHOEFFER
Edited by John de Gruchy

JOHN CALVIN
Edited by Donald K. McKim

CHRISTIAN DOCTRINE
Edited by Colin Gunton

CHRISTIAN ETHICS
Edited by Robin Gill

CHRISTIAN PHILOSOPHICAL THEOLOGY
Edited by Charles Taliaferro and Chad V. Meister

JONATHAN EDWARDS
Edited by Stephen J. Stein

FEMINIST THEOLOGY
Edited by Susan Frank Parsons

THE JESUITS
Edited by Thomas Worcester

JESUS
Edited by Markus Bockmuehl

LIBERATION THEOLOGY
Edited by Chris Rowland

MARTIN LUTHER
Edited by Donald K. McKim

MEDIEVAL JEWISH PHILOSOPHY
Edited by Daniel H. Frank and Oliver Leaman

MODERN JEWISH PHILOSOPHY
Edited by Michael L. Morgan and Peter Eli Gordon

POSTMODERN THEOLOGY
Edited by Kevin J. Vanhoozer

Continued after the Index

THE CAMBRIDGE COMPANION TO

MUḤAMMAD

Edited by Jonathan E. Brockopp
Pennsylvania State University

CAMBRIDGE
UNIVERSITY PRESS

CAMBRIDGE UNIVERSITY PRESS
Cambridge, New York, Melbourne, Madrid, Cape Town, Singapore,
São Paulo, Delhi, Dubai, Tokyo

Cambridge University Press
32 Avenue of the Americas, New York, NY 10013-2473, USA

www.cambridge.org
Information on this title: www.cambridge.org/9780521713726

© Cambridge University Press 2010

This publication is in copyright. Subject to statutory exception and to the provisions of relevant collective licensing agreements, no reproduction of any part may take place without the written permission of Cambridge University Press.

First published 2010

Printed in the United States of America

A catalog record for this publication is available from the British Library.

Library of Congress Cataloging in Publication data

The Cambridge companion to Muhammad / edited by Jonathan E. Brockopp.
p. cm. – (Cambridge companions to religion)
Includes bibliographical references and index.
ISBN 978-0-521-88607-9 (hardback) – ISBN 978-0-521-71372-6 (pbk.)
1. Muhammad, Prophet, d. 632 – Biography – History and criticism I. Brockopp, Jonathan E., 1962– II. Title. III. Series.
BP75.3.C36 2010
297.6′3 – dc22 2009039058

ISBN 978-0-521-88607-9 Hardback
ISBN 978-0-521-71372-6 Paperback

Cambridge University Press has no responsibility for the persistence or accuracy of URLs for external or third-party Internet Web sites referred to in this publication and does not guarantee that any content on such Web sites is, or will remain, accurate or appropriate.

JKM Library
1100 East 55th Street
Chicago, IL 60615

This book is dedicated to
Gerhard Böwering,
scholar, teacher, and friend

Contents

List of figures

List of maps

Notes on contributors

Asma Afsaruddin is professor of Islamic studies in the Department of Near Eastern Languages and Cultures at Indiana University, Bloomington. Her research focuses on the religious and political thought of Islam, Qur'ān and *ḥadīth*, Islamic intellectual history, and gender. She is the author or editor of four books, including *Excellence and Precedence: Medieval Islamic Discourse on Legitimate Leadership* (2002) and *The First Muslims: History and Memory* (2008). Afsaruddin is currently completing a book manuscript about competing perspectives on *jihād* and martyrdom in premodern and modern Islamic thought. Her research has won funding from the Harry Frank Guggenheim Foundation and the Carnegie Corporation of New York.

Shahzad Bashir is associate professor of religious studies and Director of the Abbasi Program in Islamic Studies at Stanford University. He is the author of *Messianic Hopes and Mystical Visions: The Nūrbakhshīya between Medieval and Modern Islam* (2003), *Fazlallah Astarabadi and the Hurufis* (2005), and the forthcoming *Bodies of God's Friends: Sufis in Persianate Islamic Societies*. His current projects involve evaluations of rhetorical strategies utilized in Islamic historical and hagiographical literature.

Jonathan E. Brockopp is associate professor of history and religious studies at Pennsylvania State University. A specialist on early Islamic legal texts, he has written widely on Islamic law, ethics, and comparative religions. His books include *Early Mālikī Law: Ibn ʿAbd al-Ḥakam and His Major Compendium of Jurisprudence* (2000), *Judaism and Islam in Practice: A Sourcebook* (2000, coauthored with Jacob Neusner and Tamara Sonn), and two edited volumes on Islamic ethics. His article "Theorizing Charismatic Authority in Early Islamic Law" (2005) advances a new theory for understanding the role of Muḥammad in Islamic history.

Carl W. Ernst is a specialist in Islamic studies, with a focus on West and South Asia. His published research, based on the study of Arabic, Persian, and Urdu, has been mainly devoted to the study of Islam and Sufism. His publications include *Following Muhammad: Rethinking Islam in the Contemporary World* (2003), *Sufi Martyrs of Love: Chishti Sufism in South Asia and Beyond* (2002, coauthored with Bruce Lawrence), and *Guide to Sufism* (1997). He is now William R. Kenan Jr. Distinguished Professor of Religious Studies at the University of North Carolina at Chapel Hill.

Anna M. Gade is a Southeast Asianist who specializes in modern religious and social change in Muslim Asia and is associate professor of religious studies at the University of Wisconsin, Madison. She is author of *Perfection Makes Practice: Learning, Emotion, and the Recited Qur'an in Indonesia* (2004), a study of a revitalization movement in Qur'ānic education and performance based on fieldwork in South Sulawesi. She has also carried out ethnographic research in Cambodia to explain intersections of religion and development among contemporary Muslims. She recently completed a new book on the Qur'ān.

Robert Gleave is professor of Arabic studies at the University of Exeter, United Kingdom. He works mainly in the area of Islamic legal theory (*uṣūl al-fiqh*) and in particular the development of Twelver Shīʿī Law and the theory of legal interpretation in Islamic law. His books include *Inevitable Doubt: Two Theories of Shīʿī Jurisprudence* (2000) and *Scripturalist Islam: The History and Doctrines of the Akhbārī Shīʿī School* (2007). His current project is an examination of interpretation and linguistic meaning in Islamic jurisprudence.

Frank Griffel is professor of Islamic studies at Yale University, publishing in the fields of Islamic law, Muslim theology, and Muslim intellectual history. In addition to *Apostasie und Toleranz im Islam* (2000), he is the author of *Al-Ghazālī's Philosophical Theology* (2009), a detailed study on the life and thought of the influential Muslim theologian al-Ghazālī (d. 1111). In 2007, he received a Carnegie Fellowship to support his current research on the way that Aristotelian philosophy (*falsafa*) was integrated into Muslim theology.

Amir Hussain is professor in the Department of Theological Studies at Loyola Marymount University in Los Angeles, where he teaches courses on world religions. His specialty is the study of Islam, focusing on contemporary Muslim societies in North America. He is active in the Canadian Society for the Study of Religion and the American Academy of Religion (where he is co-chair of the Contemporary Islam Group and serves on the steering committee of the Religion in South Asia Section). He is on the editorial boards of *Contemporary Islam: Dynamics of Muslim Life* and *Comparative Islamic Studies*. In 2008, he was made a Fellow of the Los Angeles Institute for the Humanities. His most recent book is an introduction to Islam for North Americans titled *Oil and Water: Two Faiths, One God* (2006).

Marion Holmes Katz is associate professor of Middle Eastern and Islamic studies at New York University. She specializes in issues of Islamic law, gender, and ritual. She has written *Body of Text: The Emergence of the Sunni Law of Ritual Purity* (2002) and *The Birth of the Prophet Muhammad: Devotional Piety in Sunni Islam* (2007). She is currently working on a history of women's mosque access.

Michael Lecker is professor of Arabic at the Institute of Asian and African Studies of Hebrew University. He is the author of more than three dozen articles on early Islamic history, focusing primarily on the life of Muḥammad, many of which have been collected in his *Jews and Arabs in Pre- and Early Islamic Arabia* (1998). More recent publications include *The "Constitution of Medina": Muhammad's First Legal Document* (2004) and *People, Tribes and Society in*

Arabia around the Time of Muhammad (2005). For his recent work on prosopography, visit http://michael-lecker.net.

Joseph E. Lowry is associate professor in the Department of Near Eastern Languages and Civilizations at the University of Pennsylvania. He has published articles on Islamic legal theory and medieval and modern Arabic literature. His books include a coedited volume in memory of George Makdisi, *Law and Education in Medieval Islam* (2004), and *Early Islamic Legal Theory: The* Risāla *of Muḥammad ibn Idrīs al-Shāfiʿī* (2007). He is currently working on several articles and coediting a volume of studies in Arabic literary biography covering the period from 1350 to 1850.

Uri Rubin is professor of Arabic and Islamic studies at Tel-Aviv University. His publications on the Qurʾān, Qurʾān exegesis (*tasfīr*), and early Islamic tradition (*sīra* and *ḥadīth*) include a Hebrew translation of the Qurʾān (2005); *The Eye of the Beholder* (1995); *Between Bible and Qurʾān* (1995); and numerous articles on Muḥammad, Qurʾānic exegesis, the pre-Islamic history of Mecca and the Kaʿba, and the sanctity of Jerusalem as reflected in the Qurʾān and its exegesis.

Walid A. Saleh is associate professor of religion at the University of Toronto. He is a specialist on the Qurʾān and its interpretation (*tafsīr*) and on Islamic apocalyptic literature. He is the author of *The Formation of the Classical Tafsir Tradition* (2004) and *In Defense of the Bible* (2008). He is currently working on an introduction to *tafsīr* studies.

Abdulkader Tayob is professor of religious studies at the University of Cape Town. He has published extensively on the history of religious movements and institutions in South Africa and on the study of religion as a discipline. He now works on Islam and public life in Africa and the contemporary intellectual history of Islam. His publications include the widely used *Islam, a Short Introduction* (1999); *Islam in South Africa: Mosques, Imams and Sermons* (1999); and *Religion in Modern Islamic Discourse (2009).*

John V. Tolan works on the history of religious and cultural relations between the Arab and Latin worlds in the Middle Ages. He has taught in universities in North America and Europe and is currently professor of history at the University of Nantes and director of the Maison des Sciences de l'Homme Ange Guépin. His books include *Petrus Alfonsi and His Medieval Readers* (1993), *Saracens: Islam in the Medieval European Imagination* (2002), *Sons of Ishmael: Muslims through European Eyes in the Middle Ages* (2008), and *Saint Francis and the Sultan: The Curious History of a Christian-Muslim Encounter* (2009).

Introduction

JONATHAN E. BROCKOPP

Muḥammad is the world's most popular name for boys. The king of Morocco, the director general of the International Atomic Energy Agency, and the president of Egypt are all named Muḥammad, and when the famous boxer Cassius Clay became a Muslim, he was given the name Muhammad Ali. If there is a Muslim family in the world that does not have a brother, grandfather, or uncle named Muḥammad, they almost certainly have a relative who has been given one of the Prophet's other names: Muṣṭafā', Aḥmad, or al-Amīn. One also finds the names Muḥammadī ("Muḥammad like") and Muḥammadayn ("double Muḥammad"). These habits of naming are indicative of a popular devotion to the Prophet that enhances, and in some cases overwhelms, the historical limits of the man who died more than fourteen centuries ago.

The fact of this devotion should not surprise. The popular veneration of Muḥammad is quite similar to that offered to Jesus, the Buddha, and countless other religious figures around the world. Yet time and again – whether in reaction to Salman Rushdie's novel *The Satanic Verses* or to cartoons in the Danish newspaper *Jyllands-Posten* – Muslims' reactions in defense of their prophet have caught non-Muslims off guard. There are many reasons for this gap in understanding, but three concern me here. First, although Jesus and the Buddha have overwhelmingly positive reputations in contemporary Western civilization, that of Muḥammad is decidedly more mixed. Second, many readers are simply unaware of the breadth and depth of devotion to Muḥammad in Muslim societies as evidenced in the riches of Persian literary traditions, rituals surrounding the celebration of his birthday, modern poetry, music festivals, and more. But the third, and perhaps most important, reason for this misunderstanding has to do with the unique role of the Prophet Muḥammad in Islamic religious history.

Muḥammad is much more than a man who died more than 1,400 years ago; he is the central animating figure of the Islamic tradition. He is imitated in virtually every act of ritual, leadership, devotion to

God, morality, and public comportment. Muslims pray in just the way that Muḥammad did, and the Ṣūfī quest for unity with God is based on Muḥammad's own journey to heaven. Some Muslim men seek to dress and wear their hair as the Prophet did, and some Muslim women seek to dress as did his wives. To carry out these actions, Muslims study the life of their prophet to perfect their own religious practice. But every act of reading is also one of interpretation, and imitation is no rote repetition but a creative adaptation to current circumstances. We could even say that Muslims continue to define Muḥammad as they reread and apply the events of his life to their own time and place.

It is fair to suggest that Muḥammad would be amazed at the Islam of today. He was an Arab and perceived of himself as a prophet to the Arabs, yet less than a fifth of the world's Muslims speak Arabic today. Muslim rituals and practices, from Indonesia to the Americas, incorporate tradition and modernity in an almost-bewildering variety. Yet almost all Muslims use some Arabic phrases in prayer, including recitation of the Qurʾān in its original language, though they may not understand the meaning of the words. Further, scholars of Muslim history must master the Qurʾān and the earliest Islamic literary sources, all of which are written in Arabic. To learn about Muḥammad, then, first requires an imaginary journey into the time and space of Arabia some fourteen centuries ago.

Muḥammad was born, lived, and died in Arabia, or more specifically, in the part of western Arabia we call the Ḥijāz. This is a strip of mountains with a coastal plain that parallels the Red Sea and receives a small amount of rainfall (about four inches) each year, just enough to support small animal herds and, in the lowland oases and the highland plateaus, some agriculture. Archeological evidence tells us of lively cultural centers in the south and north of the Arabian Peninsula, but we still have much to learn about the area where Muḥammad was born. His hometown of Mecca was probably an important trading town, with a religious cult centering on the Kaʿba, a shrine that would later become the physical center of Islam. Caravans of camels were apparently organized both north to Syria and south to Yemen, as well as east to Iraq, but local trade was probably also important.

The religious world of the Ḥijāz likely reflected that of the surrounding regions, where local traditions lived side by side with various forms of Christianity, Judaism, and Zoroastrianism. What little we know about these local traditions, often called paganism or polytheism, comes largely from later Islamic sources. These inform us that Meccans venerated many different gods and goddesses, some of them representing qualities of strength or of fate, whereas others represented natural forces.

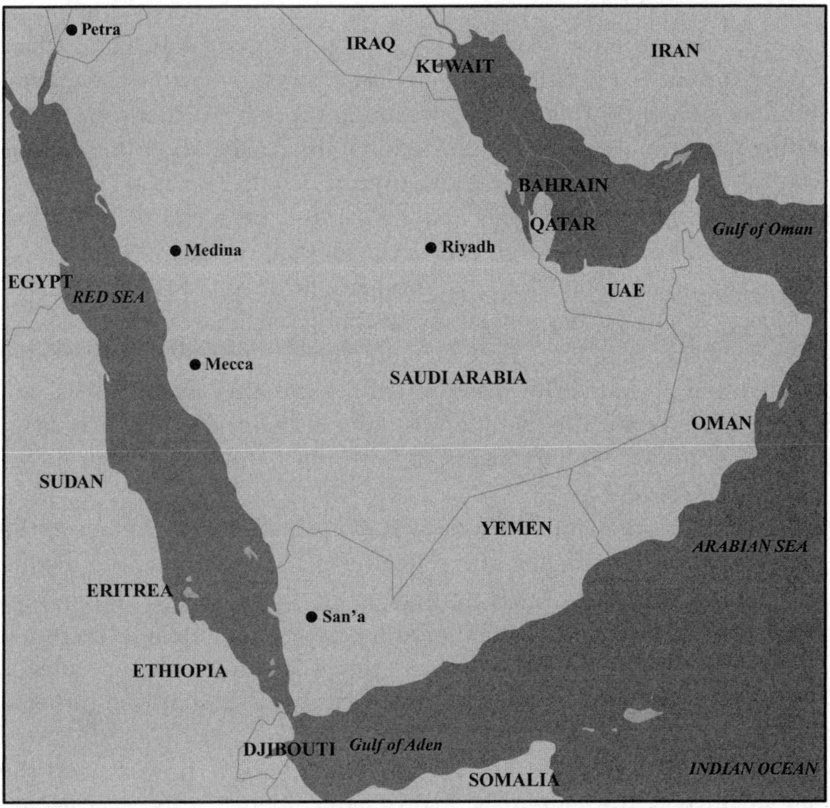

Map 1. Map of the Arabian Peninsula, showing the location of Mecca and Medina.

The name Allāh was known to them, however, as that of a high god who had especial control of weather and ships at sea (Q 29:63–5; 31:31–2). As for other religions, it must be recalled that Arabia was quite distant from the centers of those cults, and that Christianity, Judaism, and Zoroastrianism were all undergoing significant shifts in their identity during this period. Therefore, the adherents of those traditions, who made their way to the Ḥijāz for one reason or another, may have had beliefs and practices quite different from what we might normally associate with the versions of those religions that have been transmitted to us.

THE LIFE OF MUḤAMMAD

Just as we depend on internal sources for our knowledge of early Christianity and Buddhism, so also we are entirely dependent on Islamic sources for Muḥammad's own history, especially the most significant events of his life. These tell us that Muḥammad was born to ʿAbd Allāh and Āmina, perhaps in the year 570 CE. Most biographers emphasize the miraculous events associated with his conception and birth, such as the appearance of a mystical light on his father's brow before conception and the emerging of this light from Āmina's womb. Further signs of his calling are recorded in his childhood, including a visitation from angels who split open his breast to remove from it the black spot of sin. These are some of the hints that this man had already been chosen by God to be his special servant and to receive the Qur'ān, the last of God's revelations to humankind. Before that moment, however, Muḥammad lived in Mecca, and like many inhabitants of that town, he was involved with organizing caravans. For a time he worked for a wealthy widow named Khadīja, and his industriousness caught her eye; they were married and started a family together. So life was quite ordinary when, at the age of forty (in 610 CE), Muḥammad began meditating in a cave high in the hills outside of Mecca.

During these meditations, he was overwhelmed by a vision of the angel Gabriel commanding him, "Recite!" This event changed his life forever, and he began, slowly, to understand that God had chosen him for a special mission. From that point forward, Muḥammad's life would be caught up with the persistent, at times unpredictable, appearance of revelations from God, revelations that would eventually be gathered together to make up the Qur'ān.

Muḥammad's life is, in many ways, inseparable from that of the Qur'ān. Just as the Qur'ān is traditionally divided into Meccan and Medinan phases, so also Muḥammad's life may usefully be separated into two periods: the first from 610 to 622, from the time he first received revelation until his flight (*hijra*) from Mecca to Yathrib (later called Medina), and the second from 622 until his death in 632. This break is significant in many ways and is marked by the fact that Muslims begin their calendar in 622, the year that the new Muslim community was founded in Yathrib.

In terms of the Qur'ān, the Meccan and Medinan phases mark a difference in language, content, and style. For example, a typical seven-verse sample (Q 80:17–23) from the Meccan period reads like this:

> May humankind perish! How ungrateful!
> Of what things did He create them?
> Of a drop of fluid
> He created them, and determined them,
> then He made the path easy for them,
> then makes them to die, and buries them,
> then, when He wills, He raises them.

In pithy language, the Qur'ān reprimands humankind for being ingrates. The audience for these short verses is universal, and the scope reaches from conception to resurrection; further, the Arabic is punctuated with rhythmic language and rhymes. In contrast, here are three verses (Q 2:183–5) typical of the Medinan period:

> O you who believe! The Fast is prescribed for you, just as it was prescribed for those who were before you – perhaps you will be aware!
>
> Days numbered – but if anyone is sick, or on a journey, then a number of other days, and for those who are able to fast, a redemption by feeding a poor person. But those who willingly do the better, so it is better for them, and should you fast it is better for you, if you only knew.
>
> The month of Ramaḍān, in which the Qur'ān was sent down as a guidance to people, and as clear signs of guidance and salvation. So those of you who witness the month should fast it. As for the one who is sick, or on a journey, then a number of other days. God desires ease for you, not hardship; and that you complete the number, and magnify God according to that to which He has guided you, perhaps you will be grateful.

In these Medinan verses the scope is narrower. Instead of all humankind, a specific group of believers is addressed and given the task of fasting. Whereas the Meccan verses invoke the natural world and speak of its ultimate end in apocalyptic terms, the Medinan verses are often interested in providing a community with order and rules. What ties them together is the command to remember God's activities (e.g., creation, revelation) and to be grateful for them. This is only one example of the complex relationship between the two styles of writing, but the distinctions here form a striking parallel to the stories we have of the Prophet. During the Meccan period, we are told that the Prophet was caught up in an adversarial relationship with the population of Mecca, which largely rejected his preaching. The strong exclamations in the first excerpt seem especially suited to this crowd. In contrast, the Prophet found a receptive community in Medina, one that needed to differentiate itself from surrounding communities of Jews, pagans, and, outside of Medina, Christians.

To some Western scholars, the relationship between the Qur'ān and Muḥammad seems too convenient, as if stories of the Prophet's life were designed to explain differences found in the Qur'ān. For the Meccan period, the problem is complicated by the fact that the Qur'ān is the only writing we possess that derives from that period. All the rest – histories of the period, biographies of the Prophet, interpretation of the Qur'ān – was written down long after the Arab conquest of the Sassanid empire and the southern half of the Byzantine Empire (632–645 CE) and certainly after Muḥammad's successes in Medina. As several contributors to this volume point out, Muḥammad's doubts in his early mission (as described in the Qur'ān) were hard to understand given the almost-unbelievable expansion of Islam after his death. Although some histories dutifully record the Prophet's despair, others gloss over those weak moments in favor of a more triumphant picture, one that fits better with his ultimate success.

Nonetheless, all the sources agree on this basic outline of events: After his first experience of receiving the revelation, Muḥammad took three years before he began preaching publicly. During that time, he discussed these incidents with his wife, Khadīja, who helped him understand the nature of the supernatural events. All agree that she was the first to believe in his mission, though there is a significant dispute about who among the men was first: his cousin and eventual son-in-law ʿAlī, his freedman Zayd b. Ḥāritha, his friend Abū Bakr, or several others. The members of this intimate circle are worth noting, especially his wife, Khadīja; his daughter, Fāṭima; his cousin, ʿAlī; and his friend Abū Bakr, as their examples are precedent setting for Muslims, and their names are often mentioned in this volume. But it is also worth noting that this close circle did not include his influential uncles, though the precise role of Abū Ṭālib, Muḥammad's protector after his father and grandfather died, is disputed. Abū Ṭālib did, however, continue to extend his protection to Muḥammad, even after his nephew (Muḥammad) and son (ʿAlī) rejected the religion of their fathers.

One may wonder, however, to what extent either Muḥammad or the earliest sūras of the Qur'ān demanded a rejection of pre-Islamic religious practices. After all, the verses quoted herein demand that "He" has ultimate authority over life and death but do not explicitly deny the existence of other divine powers. (In contrast, later sūras of the Qur'ān are quite clear in their rejection of polytheism or, in the language of the Qur'ān, of "ascribing partners to God.") One indication that Muḥammad may have sought reconciliation early in his career is the event now known as the Satanic Verses. The story, as told to us by the historian Abū Jaʿfar al-Ṭabarī (d. 310/922–923[1]), goes that Muḥammad

[1] In the field of Islamic studies, it is common to use "double dating." The first year refers to the Muslim calendar, which begins with the Prophet's flight (or *hijra*) from Mecca

wished so fervently for reconciliation with the religion of his forebears that when Satan whispered false verses in his ears, he mistook them for true revelation.

Whether true or not, the story points to an increasing animosity between Muḥammad and his Meccan audience, an animosity discussed at length by Walid A. Saleh in Chapter 1 and illustrated by an emigration of some of Muḥammad's followers from Mecca to the Christian kingdom of Abyssinia and by a boycott against Muḥammad's clan. Tradition has also preserved many stories of both Muḥammad's and his followers' suffering, especially after the deaths of Abū Ṭālib and Khadīja in 619.

With the loss of his protectors, Muḥammad was openly mocked in Mecca and forced to look outside the town for support. Numerous verses in the Qurʾān, said to come from this period, seem to console Muḥammad, encouraging him to be patient. This is also the time when most sources say that this verse (Q 17:1) was revealed:

> Glory be to Him who transported His servant by night from the sacred mosque to the farthest mosque, which We have surrounded with blessing, in order to show him one of Our signs.

This verse, of especial importance to Ṣūfīs, is the scriptural basis for Muḥammad's Night Journey, in which God transported him to Jerusalem. This event is often combined with the *miʿrāj*, Muḥammad's ascent into heaven, where he spoke with God face-to-face. Early historians disagreed on when, precisely, these trips occurred, but their connection to a period of persecution is psychologically satisfying: in Muḥammad's time of trouble, God granted him a vision that marked his special place among the prophets.

MUḤAMMAD IN MEDINA

Eventually, Muḥammad left Mecca, negotiating safe passage for him and for his followers to the oasis of Yathrib, some two hundred miles to the north. This *hijra*, the emigration of Muslims from Mecca to Yathrib in 622, was a turning point for the early community. Yathrib would come to be known as Medina (Ar. *madīnat al-nabī*, "the city of the Prophet"), and there hundreds converted to the new religion; when the Prophet died there in 632, he left behind thousands of believers.

We know much more about Muḥammad's ten years in Medina than about his time in Mecca. In addition to the Qurʾān, we have the accounts

to Medina; it is sometimes marked by the symbol AH (*anno hegira*). The second date refers to the Common or Christian Era (CE).

transmitted by his ever-increasing cohort of followers. It is also worth noting, however, that although the key events of Mecca were interior (Muḥammad's first revelations, his response to his mission and to the Meccan resistance, his Night Journey), the key events of Medina were public (community organization, several significant battles, and many minor raids). Public events not only have more witnesses but also conform to known patterns of human social behavior. Medina was also home to a diverse community of social and religious groups, and Muḥammad's increasing stature brought him into negotiations with even more such groups in the surrounding territory. As a result, we often have competing accounts of single events, thus reflecting the different interests of those groups.

Unlike Mecca, Medina did not have a single town center but rather a variety of settlements strewn across an area of some twenty square miles. As Michael Lecker discusses in Chapter 3, we know a good deal about who occupied which areas of land because of recorded disputes over prestige (in providing land for the Prophet, for example) and other sources, such as histories of Medina, that do not belong to the traditional biographical literature. From these accounts we know that Medina had two key Arab tribes, the Aws and the Khazraj, which were split into a number of clans. In addition, there were other tribal groups in the oasis, including several Jewish tribes; they were Arabic speakers and fully integrated into the political and economic life of the oasis, but we know little of their precise religious practices or of what contact, if any, they had with the larger Jewish communities of Palestine and Iraq.

Ostensibly, Muḥammad's arrival (traditionally on the twelfth of Rabīʿ al-Awwal, year 1 of the *hijra* [September 24, 622]), was meant to provide some central leadership to the various warring elements of the oasis. That he did, but he also brought along a further division, one that would prove decisive for Medina's future. From Mecca, Muḥammad was accompanied by numerous followers (known as *muhājirūn*, "those who had undertaken the *hijra*"), all of whom were believers in his message. These were largely settled among the Medinan believers of the Aws and Khazraj tribes, a group sensibly known as the helpers (Ar. *anṣār*). Although the *muhājirūn* and the *anṣār* were united in faith, they were divided by tribal and other loyalties. The negotiation of those loyalties, and the relationship of the believers with the other inhabitants of Medina, is the subject of a curious document that Western historians have dubbed the Constitution of Medina (see the appendix to Chapter 3).

The Medinan verses of the Qurʾān give us an insight into the social complexity of this community. There are lengthy disputes with Jews and Christians, collectively known as the People of the Book (Ar. *ahl al-kitāb*), on theological matters, ranging from the nature of God to the nature of Jesus. There is extensive regulation of family matters: marriage, divorce, manumission of slaves, and treatment of children. There are descriptions of ritual cleansing, exhortations to pray and remember God, and rules of warfare. These last have received a good deal of attention, and rightfully so, as the transformation of *jihād* (from struggling against persecution in Mecca to taking up arms in Medina) coincides with the establishment of the community in Medina.

It is clear that the *hijra* from Mecca to Medina did not end the hostile relations between Muḥammad and his hometown. The Battle of Badr (2/624) is the most important of these early skirmishes. While trying to raid a Meccan caravan, Muḥammad and about three hundred of his followers ran into a larger Meccan military force instead. The Muslims decided to stay their ground and fight, surprisingly winning the day. The event is celebrated in the Qurʾān, with God reminding the Muslims that He was behind their victory. Curiously, this animosity with the Meccans roughly coincides with a change in the prescribed prayer direction, one that put Mecca, not Jerusalem, at the center of the Muslim world. At the same time, verses are revealed that incorporate certain pre-Islamic practices, such as the pilgrimage to Mecca, into Islamic worship. In these ways, Islam was further differentiated from the practices of Jews and Christians.

The battles with the Meccans continued; some of these were barely survived by the Muslims (Uḥud in 3/625), and others were a draw (Battle of the Trench in 5/627). During this period, Muḥammad perceived the Jewish tribes in Medina to be a threat – they did not support his policies of war and refused to succumb to Muḥammad's leadership. He banished one tribe after another, finally besieging the last significant tribe, the Qurayẓa, after the Battle of the Trench. In a brutal judgment, several hundred men of the tribe were executed and the women and children were enslaved. That this was a political and not a purely religious persecution seems evident from the fact that other, smaller groups of Jews remained in Medina.

The Battle of the Trench proved a turning point, emboldening Muḥammad to expand his influence among the Bedouin tribes to the north of Medina. In the year 6/628, he concluded the Treaty of Ḥudaybiyya with the Meccans, allowing Medinans to perform the pilgrimage rites in Mecca without fear of reprisals. Muḥammad then undertook the first two conquests of his career: Khaybar (7/629) and Mecca (8/630). Khaybar was a rich oasis largely inhabited by Jews, and

Muḥammad's negotiation of that conquest (in which Jews would maintain their rights to their lives, religious practices, and land in exchange for recognizing Muslim authority) was a key precedent for the conquest of Byzantine and Sassanid territory after his death. At the conquest of Mecca, Muḥammad explicitly forbade his followers from killing any Meccans who stayed in their homes; the historian Ibn Isḥāq (d. 150/767) records that only four Meccans were killed.

In the last three years of his life, Muḥammad devoted himself to consolidating his control over central Arabia through diplomacy and warfare. Having seen his rise to power, many surrounding leaders were anxious to curry his favor, sending emissaries to Medina. Muḥammad also led a sizable military force (our sources say thirty thousand men) to the Byzantine border town of Tabūk. The battle was not decisive, however, and it would not be until after Muḥammad's death that Muslim forces would successfully defeat a contingent of the Byzantine army. It is possible, however, to overestimate the extent of Muḥammad's influence in Arabia. Even up to his death there remained significant opposition to his rule both within Medina and without.

In the year 10/632, Muḥammad undertook his "farewell pilgrimage," accounts of which have been preserved by his Companions. His death a few months later was devastating to this early community. The believers were dismayed, and many left the new faith to return to their old ways. Eventually, leadership was unified under one of Muḥammad's close Companions, Abū Bakr, who was called a caliph, a deputy or a follower, of the Prophet. Abū Bakr was an old man, however, and at his death two years later, ʿUmar b. al-Khaṭṭāb, another early Companion of the Prophet, but one with more ambition, took over leadership of the community. It was under ʿUmar and his successors that the conquests of surrounding territory began in earnest. Within a few decades, two of the world's major empires, the Byzantine and the Persian, would lose much of their territory to this new Arab-Islamic movement, a movement that gained strength with every successful conquest.

This early movement also survived enormous challenges. Numerous groups rejected the authority of the caliphs, including the partisans (Ar. *shīʿa*) of ʿAlī, who believed that leadership of the community should remain within the Prophet's own family. Significant civil wars were fought in 656, 660, and 680. Perhaps even more surprising is that this movement maintained a separate identity and did not lose itself among the powerful cultural influences of the major world empires it conquered. After all, empires do not disappear overnight, and neither were the early conquests missions of wanton destruction. Tax structures, bureaucracies, and property ownership were all maintained as they were found, and the populace was not forcibly converted. The millions of Christian Copts in Egypt today attest to this fact, and Lebanon is still almost half Christian. Although the military conquests were an event of remarkable swiftness, the bureaucratic and cultural conquests were a much longer process. Slowly, the language of bureaucracy began to change from Greek to Arabic. The Roman denarius and Greek drachma became the Arab dinar and dirham, and the emperor's visage was gradually replaced with the statements "There is no God but God" and "Muḥammad is the Messenger of God." Muḥammad's name was thereby stamped into the consciousness of this community sixty years after his death.

SOURCES FOR THE LIFE OF MUḤAMMAD

The coin depicted below is symbolic of the difficulties faced by researchers who seek to understand this earliest period of Islamic history. On the one hand, this coin is tangible evidence of Muḥammad's life and legacy; it, along with ancient Qur'ān manuscripts also from this period, forms irrefutable evidence of the early Muslim community. On the other hand, gold coins and fine manuscripts can be produced only by a wealthy and powerful state, one that has clear political interests in maintaining a certain sense of the past. For information from Muḥammad's own period, we must turn to a difficult set of literary sources – histories, biographies, and legal texts. The earliest of these may go back to the first century of Islam, but even these did not reach their final form until the full flowering of Arabic literature, almost two hundred years after the Prophet's death. Although these sources are rich with information, they also contain contradictory voices and even fabrications, as the memories of the Prophet's Companions were recalled for subsequent generations. As Michael Lecker argues, there are pearls of specific details in this sea of information, but the process of distinguishing fact from falsehood is quite controversial.

The earliest compilers, Ibn Isḥāq, al-Wāqidī (d. 207/823), Ibn Sa'd (d. 230/845), and al-Bukhārī (d. 256/870), worked hard to include accurate accounts, but they were also remarkably tolerant of contradiction, fearing more the omission of an important story than the cacophony of Companion voices. An early biography, therefore, reads somewhat like a postmodern novel, with multiple accounts of single events all packed next to one another. The *Sīra* of Ibn Isḥāq, for example, includes two accounts of Muḥammad's chest being split open, one when he was a child in the care of a Bedouin nursemaid and the other when he was an adult, before being sent on the Night Journey. He makes no effort to reconcile the two or to say that one or the other is false. Yet the difference

Figure 1. Umayyad coin with Muḥammad's name, dated 78/697–698. Bildarchiv Preussischer Kulturbesitz/Art Resource, New York.

is significant. In one, Muḥammad is made pure long before taking up his prophetic mission; in the other, the splitting of the chest is a spiritual preparation for his journey to heaven. Scholars have responded to this contradictory information in numerous ways. Early Muslim scholars argued over whether Muḥammad's Night Journey was a bodily journey or merely a spiritual one. Early modern Christian writers called Muḥammad a fraud for claiming to have achieved this impossible act, whereas writers in the early twentieth century saw this journey as a fiction created by devoted followers.

WESTERN SCHOLARSHIP ON MUḤAMMAD'S LIFE

Fifty years ago when Maxime Rodinson first published *Mahomet*, he prefaced his book with an apology for adding yet one more study of Muḥammad to a world already full with "a very great number of biographies of the prophet of Islam." As John V. Tolan describes in Chapter 11, the study of Muḥammad in Europe goes back several hundred years. But Rodinson needed only to look at the first half of the twentieth century to find significant works of scholarship produced by Muḥammad Ḥusayn Haykal, W. Montgomery Watt, Frants Buhl, Tor Andrae, and others. Although it is easy to dismiss some of these texts as "Orientalist" and therefore unworthy of attention, this is a mistake. These early twentieth-century authors engaged the primary sources with care, bringing new insights into these complicated texts. In the case of Tor Andrae, for example, his comparison of emergent Islamic with Ebionite religious texts produces remarkable insights, though he was perhaps overly influenced by the notion of parallels among religious traditions. Similarly, Rodinson has been taken to task for explaining away Muḥammad's prophetic experiences as epilepsy, yet his astute observations on the role of ideology and social relationships in the early Muslim community cannot be easily dismissed.

In the past fifty years, scholars have tended to shy away from sweeping treatments of Muḥammad's life, leaving to writers such as Karen Armstrong and Hans Küng the task of reconciling Muḥammad's story with modern life. The appearance of Michael Cook's *Muhammad* in 1986 is remarkable for its exception to this trend, yet it also is arguably less a biography of Muḥammad than it is a study of problems facing anyone who would write such a biography. Instead, Western scholars have either retreated into specific, narrow studies or rejected the search for the historical Muḥammad altogether. The first of these trends seeks to refine the work already done by the great scholars of the past. A specific event from the Prophet's life or a relevant text passage is subjected to close scrutiny. The scholars carrying out this work bring enormous erudition to their tasks, but their work, published in such journals as *Oriens* and *Jerusalem Studies in Arabic and Islam*, is not accessible to a general reading public. This is, in part, by design. First, it takes a significant mastery of texts to understand the point of the research in the first place, and second, there is little support for such work, either in the Muslim world or outside of it. More than ever, universities are under pressure to demonstrate relevance, making it significantly harder to fund scholars to devote years of their lives to mastering difficult languages and texts.

Such scholars are also under pressure by the second trend, the rejection of any search for the historical Muḥammad. The meaning of this phrase, "the historical Muḥammad," was once seen as self-evident. It meant the empirical data of Muḥammad's life as a man, apart from any supernatural claims by him or his followers. Although the original notion might have been to weed out the ideological (i.e., religious) convictions of Muḥammad's followers from their accounts of his life, it is now well understood that there can be no ideologically free account of such a man. As John Tolan points out, scholars have very often used their research as a foil for working out their own polemical agendas. In hopes of avoiding this trap, many have simply abandoned the task of understanding Muḥammad in his own world, seeking rather to understand the ways in which his followers have perceived him. The focus, they argue, should be on who Muslims say Muḥammad was, not on who scholars say he was.

To be sure, some non-Muslim scholars still remain blithely unaware of the influence their research can have on the Muslim world. Others seem openly antagonistic toward Islam or religious belief altogether. Yet it is a mistake to abandon historical-critical analysis of the texts for one simple reason: if we do not understand the earliest accounts of

Muḥammad's life, then we cannot know how later writers changed and adapted those accounts. In other words, we need to identify the earliest layers of biographical writing if we are to trace out the ways that later authors utilize this information; only then can we assess the work of interpretation undertaken by those later authors.

ORGANIZATION OF THIS BOOK

The Cambridge Companion to Muḥammad is designed to represent current trends in the scholarly study of Muḥammad's life and legacy. It is split into three sections: "Muḥammad in His World," "Muḥammad in History," and "Muḥammad in Memory." The first section gives essential background on the social and political landscape of Arabia before Muḥammad's appearance on the world stage. It focuses on specific events in his life, from the Meccan and Medinan periods, and subjects our sources for these events to historical-critical analysis. The second section moves to the literature and culture produced in the premodern era (750–1453), focusing on the influence of Muḥammad's example in this period. Separate chapters (on law, Ṣūfism, ritual, personal piety, philosophy and politics) explore the ways that Muḥammad was held to be the ideal example for Muslims in all areas of society. The final section moves to the early modern and modern periods, analyzing poems, theological and literary texts, and even songs and images, to elucidate the ways that the Prophet is remembered – by Muslims and non-Muslims alike – up to our own time.

The contributors to this volume all hold university appointments and all are devoted teachers. As such, they write with intellectual rigor and uncommon clarity of thought. Although it is our intention that this volume will help advance scholarly study, the book is designed to be read by nonspecialists. Read in aggregate, the chapters of this book should give readers a clear sense of who Muḥammad was and some insight of his meaning for Muslims today and in the past.

In the opening chapter of the first section, Walid Saleh provides a brief survey of Arabian history, beliefs, and practices before the rise of Islam, quickly moving on to the way that Muḥammad was received as a prophet among the Arabs. His analysis combines a close reading of Qurʾānic passages with the earliest biographical sources and shows how Muḥammad addressed Arab expectations while also laying the foundation for their future conquest of the Sassanid and much of the Byzantine empires. The next chapter, by Uri Rubin, continues Saleh's analysis of the relationship of the Qurʾān to the Prophet's biography, focusing on one key episode during Muḥammad's Meccan period: the splitting of the moon. Early Muslim writers understood this event as a miracle and developed it into one of the most memorable images of Muḥammad, one still popular among Muslims today. Rubin discusses this interpretation in light of Muḥammad's preaching in Mecca, where he was primarily a warner of apocalyptic events. This view of Muḥammad is in stark contrast to Muḥammad's Medinan period as described by Michael Lecker. In his chapter, Lecker takes advantage of competing, often contradictory, accounts of Muḥammad's life in Medina to find small, solid pieces of data on which we can begin to build a firm sense of Muḥammad the man. Like Rubin, Lecker focuses on an event of seeming insignificance – Muḥammad's acquisition of land in Medina – to illustrate Muḥammad's standing after the *hijra*. At the end of his chapter, he includes a translation of a key document from this period known to Western scholars as the Constitution of Medina.

The chapters of the first section have much to say about how we read early sources for Muḥammad's life, especially the Qur'ān and the biographical literature (Sīra). They are concerned with capturing a sense of how Muḥammad was regarded during his own lifetime, before the development of Islam into a world phenomenon. The subsequent section, however, concerns sources written long after the story of Muḥammad's life had been written. What we see in that section is the ways that authors of the period (750–1453) emphasized different aspects of Muḥammad's life and personality as they sought to incorporate his life into Muslim rituals and institutions, providing an example of emulation to their audiences.

The first chapter in the second section, by Joseph E. Lowry, shows the process by which Muḥammad came to be understood as the ideal lawgiver. Muḥammad's example, known as his *sunna* (literally, "the well-worn path"),was made manifest through a specific narrative form known as a *ḥadīth*. But as Lowry demonstrates, not all early Muslims agreed that Islamic law should be based on the words and deeds of the Prophet; nor was there agreement as to how one gets from prophetic precedent to applied law. Some of these arguments continue today, but the study of Muḥammad's *ḥadīth* remains a central aspect of Islamic learning. In Chapter 5, Robert Gleave addresses another problem posed by the *ḥadīth*: how does imitation of the Prophet's actions translate into Muslims' everyday practices? The *ḥadīth*s, after all, preserve much more than the way the Prophet prayed or led the troops into battle; they also contain advice on hygiene, medical treatments, and other personal matters. Gleave points out that a number of fine distinctions were developed to help pious believers sort through this vast array of information, but he also elucidates the theological issues that are intimately bound up with the view of Muḥammad as having a special relationship to God, the divine lawgiver.

The precise nature of Muḥammad's relationship to God was further developed by early Ṣūfīs, as discussed in Carl Ernst's chapter. According to Ṣūfī theologians, Muḥammad's right to serve as an exemplar for human action is based not merely in history but also on a cosmic relationship between Muḥammad and God, known as the Muḥammadan reality. Sūfī writers described this relationship in eloquent and poetic language, but this perception also profoundly affected their worldview and their ritual activities on a daily basis.

Special devotion to the person of Muḥammad is by no means limited to Ṣūfī practitioners. As Marion Holmes Katz makes clear in her chapter, Muslims for centuries have engaged in pious acts of imitation that place the Prophet at the heart of Islamic ritual activity. The most obvious example is that of ritual prayer, which is carried out in precise imitation of the Prophet's actions, but there are many other examples. Katz focuses on one of these important rituals, the celebration of the Prophet's birth (*mawlid*), which is still commemorated today. As Katz points out, the *mawlid* celebration is a time to focus particularly on God's love in sending Muḥammad to humankind and on Muḥammad's love for his followers.

The final two chapters of the second section move us from the day-to-day imitation of the Prophet to attempts to develop political and philosophical systems on the basis of his example. In Chapter 8, Frank Griffel outlines the efforts of Muslim philosophers and theologians to reconcile Greek speculation on the nature of prophecy with their knowledge of Muḥammad's example. As Griffel points out, these philosophers developed an astute analysis of dreams, intuition, and prophecy, and the ways that these human capacities connected both prophets and ordinary human beings to the divine. Just as the philosophers sought to reconcile their notions of science with prophecy, so also political theorists looked to Muḥammad for their notions of ideal leadership. As Asma Afsaruddin points out in Chapter 9, these theorists seized on two important notions: precedence and excellence. The first regards closeness to the Prophet, in terms of belief but also in terms of family relationships, as a key requirement of just leadership of the community. The second seeks to define moral excellence by means of the Prophet's own example. Although the issue of just leadership of the community has obvious implications for Muslims today, the arguments that Afsaruddin outlines depend heavily on proper interpretation of the Prophet's biography.

The third section of this book elucidates the continued importance of the Prophet's biography in the prose, poetry, and song of the early modern and modern periods. Following the rapid expansion of the Muslim world in the early modern period, and the rise of scholarship on Islam in Europe, this section draws from a much larger geographical canvas. For example, Shahzad Bashir opens the section by looking at three examples of devotional literature from Iran and Central Asia in the early modern period. Much more than panegyrics glorifying the Prophet, these are complex texts that offer us important insights into the piety of the time. In analyzing this literature, Bashir finds sensitive consideration of themes such as the relationship of miracles and belief, devotion, and the mystical path.

In the early modern period, however, the Prophet was much more than simply a figure of devotion; he was also a symbol of threat to Europeans. As discussed by John V. Tolan, European scholars, animated first by the Crusades and then by the invasion of European territory by the Ottoman armies, depicted the Prophet as a bloodthirsty profligate. But Tolan argues that this was by no means the only view of Muḥammad available to Europeans of the time. Especially as the study of Arabic and Islamic history developed in the West, scholars produced more complex and at times even irenic images of Muḥammad.

Tolan's chapter brings us up to the modern period, where increased literacy and electronic media have led to an explosion of reflections on Muḥammad's life by Muslims. As Anna M. Gade points out, the influence of Western methods of scholarship and literary criticism on the Muslim world is significant. Bookstalls in Indonesia, for example, feature translations of biographies by W. Montgomery Watt and Martin Lings alongside that of the Egyptian scholar Muḥammad Ḥusayn Haykal. Karen Armstrong's books have also been widely translated and are available throughout the Muslim world. Gade sees two significant trends in this modern writing: a commitment to historical authenticity and an emphasis on moral emulation. The first of these often results in skepticism toward supernatural events, and as such, they represent a break from premodern biographies that highlighted those events. The second, however, is a clear continuation of the emphasis on moral excellence found through the biographical tradition.

In the last chapter of this section, Amir Hussain discusses the influence of the Prophet on the media of a new generation: novels and popular music, the Internet, and film. Focusing primarily on North America, Hussain begins with a recent example of a very old genre, a praise poem to the Prophet Muḥammad. This song, by Yusuf Islam, the former Cat

Stevens, is just one instance of a broader creative movement to express pious devotion to Muḥammad. Hussain then continues to discuss the role of images, both positive and negative, in the Muslim world. As is evident from Hussain's chapter, and from the illustrations that accompany this book, Muslims have used the arts to express their love for the Prophet throughout the centuries. Although some authorities have decried any depiction of the Prophet as possibly idolatrous, most accept poems, songs, and even images if their purpose is to increase faith. These images emphasize a major theme of this book: Muslim devotion to the Prophet has taken on a wide variety of forms.

In the epilogue to this book, Abdulkader Tayob situates this collection of essays in the broader history of scholarly study of Muḥammad, raising key questions about how we study the great figures of the past. His essay is a keen reminder that all reading of the past is an act of interpretation, of balancing evidence, and of making historical artifacts speak to modern audiences. As such, readers should regard this collection not as the final judgment of scholarship on the life and meaning of Muḥammad but rather as a companion to further study. But there is more: Tayob argues that our time is marked by a trend toward humanizing the Prophet Muḥammad, a process that takes on different meanings for different groups. But the result of this process is the continued relevance of Muḥammad into the future, for both Muslims and non-Muslims alike.

Finally, a book such as this is registers many debts. Above all, I thank my collaborators for devoting such significant energies to this project and for graciously responding to my many queries and comments on their chapters. All have my gratitude, but conversations with Amir Hussain, Anna Gade, Michael Lecker, Walid Saleh, and Abdulkader Tayob helped me sharpen my ideas and greatly improved the book. Michael Lecker in particular offered many useful comments and corrections to my introduction. I must also mention Jane Dammen McAuliffe, editor of *The Cambridge Companion to the Qurʾān*, who gave me both timely guidance and also an outstanding template on which to base this book. At Cambridge University Press, Marigold Acland offered sage advice at every stage of the book's production, and her assistant Sarah Green saved me many hours securing permissions for the images in this book. At Aptara, Larry Fox and his team have my thanks for their patience and attention to detail. And as always, Paula Droege has been my constant companion, listening, encouraging, and reflecting.

Part I

Muḥammad in his world

1 The Arabian context of Muḥammad's life

WALID A. SALEH

Mecca, the city where Muḥammad was born, lies in the middle of the Arabian Peninsula, an immense expanse of land abutting the territories of the most ancient civilizations. Larger than India or Europe, the Arabian Peninsula is almost 1.5 million square miles.[1] Mostly a desert, apart from the southwestern highlands of Yemen, and devoid of any rivers or easily accessible fresh water, Arabia was impenetrable and impossible for armies to march through. It was also an inhospitable and unprofitable land; with no agricultural base to tax, Arabia was spared the avarice of imperial authorities until the struggle between Byzantium and Sassanid Iran became global and drew Arabia into its orbit.[2] Arabia was thus peculiarly unique: in proximity to the most centralized empires ever to exist in the ancient world, yet never under the direct control of any.

By Muḥammad's time, the Arabian Peninsula was nevertheless experiencing the pressure of the two major empires on its sides, the Byzantine Empire to the north, comfortably Christian if riven by Christological controversies, and the religiously diverse Sassanid Empire to the east, reviving its ambition to take control of the eastern parts of the Mediterranean from Byzantium. Caught in bitter, long, draining wars, the two empires were polarizing the Near East and pulling all of it into the fight. Any native political dynasties and kingdoms – in Yemen or on the borders with Syria and Iraq – were by then either abolished by the two empires or under the indirect control of either Constantinople or Iran. Each of the two empires experimented with bribery and vassal kingdoms to check the predatory raids of the nomads into the cultivated area of the

1 For a detailed study of the topography and ancient history of Arabia, see Robert G. Hoyland, *Arabia and the Arabs: From the Bronze Age to the Coming of Islam* (London: Routledge, 2001).

2 For economic activities and the involvement of imperial powers, see Michael Lecker, "Muḥammad at Medina: A Geographical Approach," *Jerusalem Studies in Arabic and Islam* 6 (1985): 29–62; G. W. Heck, "Gold Mining in Arabia and the Rise of the Islamic State," *Journal of the Economic and Social History of the Orient* 41 (1999): 364–95. Exploiting Arabia was not governance, however.

Fertile Crescent, and each sought to use the nomads of Arabia as auxiliary troops to their own advantage, yet immediate direct governance was never fully carried out. Arabia was an anomaly in this sense, impossible to fully integrate in the political structures of the region and impossible to ignore. There was no indication that Arabia would ever play a major role in the ongoing imperial struggles of the region. Nothing in the long history of the Near East pointed to what was to come.[3]

Muḥammad's achievements were thus accomplished despite the limitations of his environment. Not only was he born outside the two empires; he was born in the periphery of Arabia itself, in the Ḥijāz region, not in Yemen or on the eastern shores of the Persian Gulf or in the areas adjacent to Iraq and Syria, the usual sites of cultural activities. The Ḥijāz area was the most inaccessible part of Arabia to the empires, an area that seemed anarchic, with no discernible political structure when seen from Constantinople or Ctesiphon. Yet the usual picture of Arabia as untouched by its surroundings is misleading: Arabia was part of its late antique setting, part of the cultural landscape of the area; even its paganism, embattled as it was becoming, was still part of the lay of the land.[4]

The Arabs were not the ignorant lot that later Islamic tradition would like us to believe. They knew Rome, and they knew Ctesiphon. They were actually in the process of being fully absorbed into the high culture of the area; it was only a matter of time, one might have predicted, until they would convert to either Christianity or, less likely, to Judaism. Muḥammad, in a way, almost single-handedly reversed the historical trend, and he reshaped not only Arabia but also the ancient Near East in his own image. Muḥammad brought late antiquity to a surprising culmination.

Another important aspect of Arabia at that moment is that its inhabitants considered themselves ethnically related, a race connected somehow by blood and the Arabic language. Its peripheral position to its surroundings and the homogeneous ethnic composition of Arabia are perhaps the most determining aspects of the environment of Muḥammad. For this immense expanse of land to be disunited or ungoverned is not exceptional – steppes were usually impossible to subsume under imperial rule – yet for this expansive area to be linguistically and ethnically more or less homogeneous, even when religiously diverse, was

3 The most lucid and comprehensive account of Arabia in relationship to Rome and Iran is by Peter Brown, *The Rise of Western Christendom*, 2nd ed. (London: Blackwell, 2003). He heavily depends on Garth Fowden's pioneering work, see note 8 *infra*.

4 For a detailed assessment of what we know of the Ḥijāz area, see the detailed review of literature and the study by James E. Montgomery, "The Empty Ḥijāz," in *Arabic Theology, Arabic Philosophy, from the Many to the One: Essays in Celebration of Richard M. Frank*, ed. James E. Montgomery (Leuven: Peeters, 2006), 36–97.

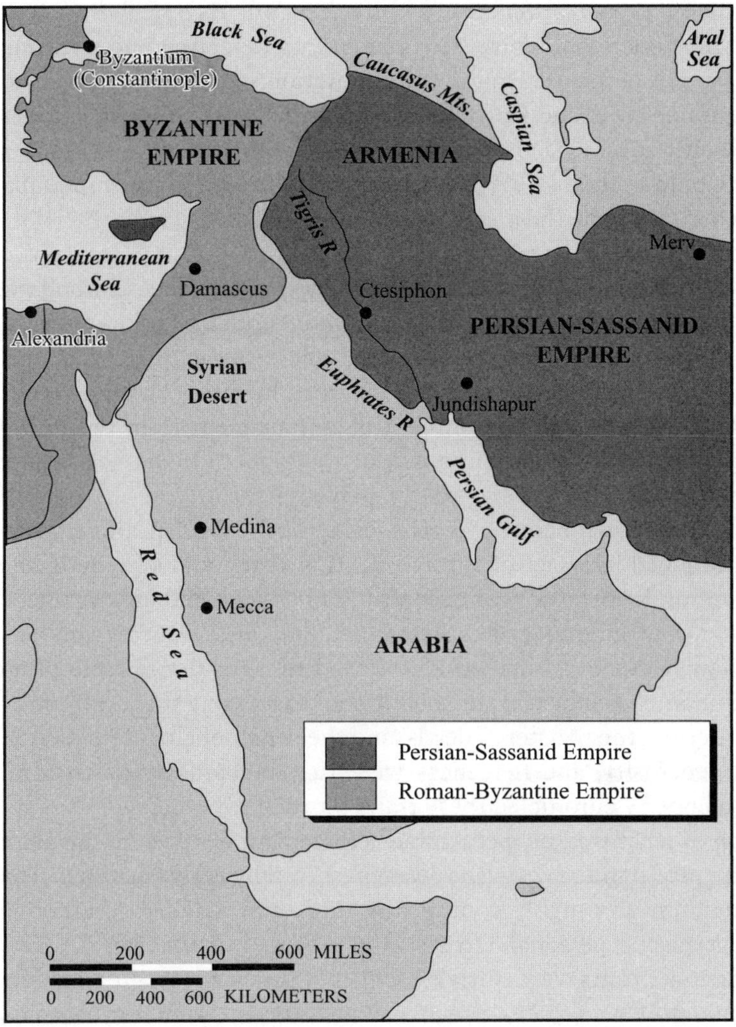

Map 2. The Arabian Peninsula, showing important population centers.

remarkable. Muḥammad was born into a tribe in a tribal city in a sea of tribes, so to speak, but he belonged already to a relatively homogeneous landscape, which he would come to reshape.

The basic form of social organization in Arabia was the tribe, a putatively blood-related group that acted as a social, economic, and military unit. The cohesiveness of the tribe was essential for its survival. Loyalty to the tribe was a matter of utmost pride to its members; loyalty was not a coerced sentiment but rather the virtue that defined tribespeople. This was a unique political structure to belong to – it was not conducive to stable political organization but was very dynamic. As a freeborn member of a tribe, one would have been reared in a fiercely proud tradition of fighting and defiance. Honor and reputation, courage and generosity, love of one's kin and fealty to the ancestors were the cornerstones of one's constitution. Defiance was thus a defining character. Such a member would be impossible to integrate into a tax-imposing imperially controlled system like the ones in the areas adjacent to Arabia. Freedom from subservience and loyalty to the tribe were such that any larger political structures were constructed through temporary alliances among the more or less equal tribes, alliances that were kept and broken by each tribe at will. Yet inner Arabia, the land where Muḥammad grew up, never knew a complex political structure until he arrived on the scene.

In the impoverished environment of Arabia, apart from the riches of the Syrian Desert, the Iraqi border, or the Yemeni highlands, where wealth was easy to come by, poetry played a major role in the cultural landscape. Even before the appearance of the Qur'ān, there was a highly developed language of communication that could be used in the whole land of Arabia and was universally cherished and cultivated. In fact, as James Montgomery has stated, "Arabic *qaṣīda* poetry is a necessary though by no means sufficient condition for the miracle of an Arabic Qur'ān."[5] Poetry was the medium for expressing the ideals of the social structure, the register of deeds, and the bearer of glory. Eloquence, courage, generosity, and fierceness were the standards one strived to attain, and poetry chronicled these traits for each tribe.

Much of what we know of Arabia before Islam is based on the analysis of the pre-Islamic poetry that was preserved by early Muslims. The poetic medium was highly complex by then, and it reflected a heroic ethos that placed personal virtues at the center of the world.[6] Two complementary traits were cultivated: *ḥilm* ("forbearance," "reasonableness") and *jahl* ("arrogance," "overbearing haughtiness of a tribal man, the spirit of stubborn resistance against all that shows the slightest sign of injuring their sense of honour or destroying the traditional way of life"[7]). In the face of the tragic life, there was a heroic stance. One defied everything in defense of one's tribe and honor. The poetry portrays the tribal Arab as unbowed and unbent, fearful of nothing.

Garth Fowden had these various cultural overlays in mind when he assessed the significance of the rise of Islam: "The Islamic Empire

[5] Ibid., 97.

[6] The most accessible introduction to pre-Islamic poetry is Michael A. Sells, *Desert Tracings* (Middletown, CT: Wesleyan University Press, 1989).

[7] Toshihiko Izutsu, *Ethico-Religious Concepts in the Qur'ān* (Montreal: McGill University Press, 2002), 27.

was implicit in late antiquity, but nothing quite like it had ever been seen before."[8] The same could be said about the life of Muḥammad as it came to be told by Muslims in the *Sīra*, the literature written about Muḥammad by his companions and followers. His life mirrored the expectations one would find in the biographies of holy men from late antiquity and fashioned them in a uniquely Arabic fashion. Foreshadowings, miraculous birth, protected childhood, visions, miraculous deeds, a band of followers, and an affinity with the cosmos were all woven together to present a life superior to any presented before and able to measure to that of Moses, Jesus, and Alexander the Great. Muḥammad's life was presented in universal terms, reflecting the universalism of the late antique culture that Muslims came to inherit. His life was considered the culmination of history, understood by Muslims to be the history of Rome and Iran combined. Muḥammad's life was the meaning of the human history that started with Adam and culminated in the coming of Islam. The ambitions of Rome pale before the heights early Muslims ascribed to Muḥammad.

For the past 150 years historians have been trying to unearth the historical Muḥammad, and in many respects, this endeavor is continuing.[9] It is clear, however, that the political career of Muḥammad as presented by the *Sīra* is historically far more reliable than the *Sīra*'s presentation of his birth, early childhood, and life before he became a public figure. Yet these mythical parts of his biography, the early phase when he was not yet a prophet, came eventually to symbolize the meaning of his life and career; in this sense, myth was far more able to capture the significance of Muḥammad's career than were the mere concrete historical triumphs.[10] It is interesting that, to medieval Muslims, Muḥammad's life was mainly seen through its cosmic, symbol-laden events, which invariably were mythically constructed, and not through its more mundane historical parts. His quasi-miraculous birth would loom larger than any event; his trip to heaven (*miʿrāj*), his communion with the cosmos, and his supernatural qualities came to play a far more significant role when his story was retold. The ethical realm of his character was also emphasized: Muḥammad was the prophet of mercy. The celebration of

8 Garth Fowden, *Empire to Commonwealth: Consequences of Monotheism in Late Antiquity* (Princeton, NJ: Princeton University Press, 1993), 138.

9 For a review of the literature, see F. E. Peters, *Muhammad and the Origins of Islam* (Albany: State University of New York Press, 1994); Harald Motzki, ed., *The Biography of Muḥammad: The Issue of the Sources* (Leiden: Brill, 2000).

10 One of the most engaging studies of the role of myth in the biography and life of Muḥammad is Jaroslav Stetkevych's *Muḥammad and the Golden Bough: Reconstructing Arabian Myth* (Bloomington: Indiana University Press, 1996).

Figure 2. A modern poster showing Muḥammad (*upper right*) and his connection to previous prophets, with Adam at the root of the tree. From Richard Johan Natvig's Muslim poster collection, University of Bergen.

Muḥammad's life eventually took place on his birth date, and the *mawlid* was a hymnal celebration of what the universe experienced when he was born.[11]

THE BIOGRAPHY OF MUḤAMMAD

The biography of Muḥammad is told not in the Qur'ān but rather in a biography written by Ibn Isḥāq (d. 150/767) a hundred years or more after Muḥammad's death.[12] It is a rather sprawling narrative. The English translation of Ibn Isḥāq's original text occupies eight hundred pages. Already there is a definite structure apparent in the telling, a structure that cuts through much of early Islamic narratives: the before and the after of the *hijra*. The life of Muḥammad and, more important, the meaning of the Qur'ān were mapped onto this decisive moment: his migration from Mecca to Medina in 622 CE. Such was the significance of this event that history began with it, to the extent that his immediate followers would look back and reckon an Islamic calendar that started with this event. The life of Muḥammad was not only fashioned by how the early generation of his followers understood its significance, however. Already we can see the pull on Muḥammad's life by paradigms established in the cultures that surrounded Arabia: he has to measure up to the narratives of Moses and Jesus, even though it is his political career in Medina that was deemed the most important. As such, the biography saw to it that Muḥammad's birth and childhood and death were elevated to be consistent with events in the last ten years of his life. There were thus tensions in the *Sīra of Muḥammad* that reflected the different demands of competing paradigms.

The work of Ibn Isḥāq grew out of an already active literary tradition that was attempting to record the life of Muḥammad. The heroic Muḥammad was the first to be celebrated, and all evidence points to the fact that early Muslims kept the memory of his deeds as a military leader and as the head of the community in Medina. His exploits were recorded in what we call *maghāzī* literature.[13] Soon, this truncated

[11] For an early miracle, see Chapter 2 in this volume. For celebration of the Prophet's birthday, see Chapter 7 in this volume; see also N. J. G. Kaptein, *Muḥammad's Birthday Festival: Early History in the Central Muslim Lands and Development in the Muslim West until the 10th/16th Century* (Leiden: Brill, 1993); Marion Katz, *The Birth of the Prophet Muhammad: Devotional Piety in Sunni Islam* (London: Routledge, 2007).

[12] Ibn Isḥāq, *The Life of Muhammad: A Translation of Isḥāq's Sīrat Rasūl Allāh*, trans. A. Guillaume (Oxford: Oxford University Press, 1955).

[13] See J. M. B. Jones, "The Chronology of the Maghāzī – A Textual Survey," *Bulletin of the School of Oriental and African Studies* 19 (1957): 245–80.

telling of Muḥammad's life was unsatisfactory. A more linear and complete life was presented, and this chapter is dedicated to the early part of his life as portrayed in the *Sīra* and historical literature written by Muslims.

NARRATIVES OF THE BIRTH OF MUḤAMMAD AND HIS EARLY CHILDHOOD

We know that Muḥammad was an orphan, and the Qur'ān, in a rare reference to Muḥammad's early life, mentions this fact as well as his poverty (Q 93:6–11). He was born in Mecca to the tribe of Quraysh, to a branch of the family called the Banū Hāshim. They were a noble lineage, like all of the Quraysh tribe, but they were not the wealthiest of the tribe. The *Sīra* presents Muḥammad's father as possessing a light on his forehead, a light apparent to many, especially to other women, that disappears after he sleeps with Āmina, his wife. Like many motifs in the *Sīra*, the light can function on many symbolic levels, from its mere contrast with darkness to the Gnostic notions. It is this adroit use of symbols that made the *Sīra* a potent medium. Eventually, Muḥammad's essence was tied to a preexistent light, the first entity to be created by God, and to his stature as the perfect human being.[14] The light was also connected to visions that Muḥammad's mother saw while pregnant. A light would shine from her belly that lit up Syria – rather far away from Mecca. A voice ordered her to dedicate the newly born child to the One God and to name him Muḥammad.[15]

Another important aspect of Muḥammad's birth is that Jews, Christians, Zoroastrians, and pagan Arabs predicted his coming. Each was represented in the *Sīra* by an episode that had a rabbi, a priest, a son of a Magi priest, or a soothsayer predicting the birth of an important individual. In this sense, every denomination (from the Near East) was bearing witness to his coming. Bearing witness to Muḥammad's greatness and prophetic future is a constant theme in the *Sīra*. As a child, he was inspected, and the signs of his prophetic career were verified by experts, who were invariably Christians. The most famous episode is the encounter of the boy Muḥammad with a Christian monk who inspected him for the sign of prophecy, a seal between the blades of the

[14] For the symbolism of light and its use by Muslims in relation to Muḥammad, see Chapter 6 in this volume; see also Uri Rubin, "Pre-existence and Light: Aspects of the Concept of Nūr Muḥammad," *Israel Oriental Studies* 5 (1975): 62–119.

[15] Ibn Isḥāq, *Life of Muhammad*, 69.

shoulders.[16] These were also ominous encounters, for the *Sīra* represents the boy Muḥammad as always in danger of losing his life, and only the protection of his God would see to it that he be saved and safe. Judaism, Christianity, and Zoroastrianism were in danger of losing their preeminence, and their representatives in the *Sīra* were evidently not happy with the coming of this new prophet.

Much of the casting of the story of the early life of Muḥammad has the purpose of elevating it to the realm of the mysterious. It was also tied to a universal plan for the salvation of humanity. It was not an ordinary life, and the people around him were made aware of his larger-than-life character. His wet nurse, his servant, his employer (and future wife), and his uncles all at different times were made witnesses to Muḥammad's extraordinary powers. Chief among the strategies used to elevate his life was the portrayal of its affinity with the cosmos: the inanimate world was made to respond to Muḥammad as if it were animate. Thus, a cloud would follow him in his travel to shade him. The rocks would moan for him, and the world responded to his commands.

Perhaps the most enigmatic of the episodes that the *Sīra* recounts is the episode of the opening of Muḥammad's chest. Two mysterious angelic figures, and there are also reports that they were two birds, abducted the child Muḥammad (Ibn Isḥāq repeats this story at a later point, when Muḥammad was an adult), opened his chest, and performed a ritual of cleansing of his heart. Muḥammad, we are made to understand, was rendered pure or, theologically worded, infallible. The story has been studied extensively, and its shamanistic resonance has been noticed by scholars.[17] It plays a central role in the presentation of Muḥammad in the *Sīra*; fully human yet substantially different, this is not deification but a transformation of essence all the same. Moreover, this episode connects the Muḥammad of the *Sīra* to the Muḥammad of the Qur'ān, as it is usually recounted in interpretations of Q 94:1.

In contrast to these miracle stories from Ibn Isḥāq, the Qur'ān is emphatic about what I would call the mundane character of the human Muḥammad. He is a messenger, a warner, a guide, a deliverer of a message, but he is emphatically a *bashar*, a human being. The Christological background for this humbleness is deafening, a humbleness that soon early Muslims would shed. He is certainly not a miracle worker in the Qur'ān, and many of the arguments in the Qur'ān attempt to redefine miracles and resist the temptation of performing miracles as

16 Ibid., 79–82.

17 Harris Birkeland, *The Legend of the Opening of Muhammad's Breast* (Oslo: Avhandlinger utgitt av det Norske Videnskaps-Akademi i Oslo, 1955).

vindication of prophecy. Yet the *Sīra* is replete with a miraculous and miracle-working Muḥammad. The *Sīra*, as expected, coming as it does after the Qur'ān, gets the upper hand. The Muḥammad we have is fashioned by the *Sīra*, and a remapping of the Qur'ān is carried out on the miraculous presentation of the *Sīra*. Thus, for example, the physical seal of prophecy, a birthmark that Muḥammad is supposed to have had on his body, which the Christian monk inspected, is connected to the Qur'ānic concept of the seal of prophets, a title given to Muḥammad in Q 33:40. The *Sīra* thus is emphatic about the role of mythology in presenting the significance of Muḥammad, and if the Qur'ān was not so obliging in this regard, it was made to be; key words in enigmatic Qur'ānic verses were tied to major mythical narratives, and as such, the *Sīra* stood buttressed by the Qur'ān.

The shadow of the historical Muḥammad is, however, not far from the picture presented by Ibn Isḥāq. A decent youth with a good reputation, Muḥammad comes across as a respectable member of his community, if not part of the elite. He is willing to settle down and marry a widow, who clearly made the first move. In a sense, the sensible Muḥammad is quite on display. It is against this background that the swelling tide of transformation that Muḥammad experienced is presented. He was as surprised with his prophetic experience as his people were at first bemused. It is not so much its shocking effect on his tribe that mattered but its effect on him. Both the *Sīra* and the Qur'ān agree that Muḥammad was initially pained by his role as a messenger, as a public figure with a call.[18] This is, of course, a familiar trope, the prophet who is unwilling to carry out his mission, but in the case of Muḥammad, there was the added layer of a prophet who came to a people who did not abide by the paradigm he was presenting himself in, a prophecy with a divine message. The Arabs were not expecting a prophet, and they were not in the habit of listening to them, or according them authority, moral or political.

But if the Qur'ān is slight on the details of Muḥammad's life during this period, it is quite explicit about the reaction of the Arabs to his preaching. In numerous passages, the Qur'ān reports their words verbatim before responding; it did not help that what animated Muḥammad was incomprehensible to the Arabs. Muḥammad was already speaking a discourse that was alien to them; not that they did not know the fables of the old (*asāṭīr al-awwalīn*), as they called the stories of Jews and

[18] See Uri Rubin, "The Shrouded Messenger: On the Interpretation of al-muzzammil and al-muddaththir," *Jerusalem Studies in Arabic and Islam* 16 (1993): 96–230.

Christians, but to be affronted by the claims of a prophetic mission sent to them was too much to bear (Q 38:4). Why did he not minister to them in a foreign language, they quipped, as his entire message seemed alien to their pagan world (Q 41:44)? A prophet is good for Jews and Christians (Q 6:156). Why did not his God send an angel instead? He would have been more reliable (Q 6:8–9). Why was Muḥammad chosen in the first place? Certainly a more renowned or noble Meccan individual was possible (Q 43:31). Is Muḥammad not surely confused (Q 43:31)? Perhaps he is a poet, like many a poet before him (Q 21:5). A priest, one of us, who is having visions (Q 52:29). Perhaps possessed, by the many *jinn*s roaming the desert. But why a prophecy when such things were not for the Arabs? In this sense, his opponents were as cruel as they were accommodating: trying to see him as having an Arabic experience, one that they could accept. What they were not willing to concede is authority to his voice, even though Muḥammad was genuinely unaware – at first – of the connection between prophetic claims and political authority (Q 52:40; 88:22; 38:86). Prophecy entailed power, and the Meccans were not going to be pushed around, despite the reassurances of Muḥammad that he was not after power.

MUḤAMMAD'S PROPHETIC EXPERIENCE

The *Sīra* presents Mecca at the time of the coming of Muḥammad as clearly aware of the shortcomings of paganism. Sensible individuals span out in the world in search of truth. The *Sīra* tells the story of four such inquisitive individuals[19]; each is trying to find the true religion, and most end up converting to Christianity. However, we are also introduced to the concept of a monotheistic original religion, an ur-religion, the faith of Abraham, the *ḥanafīya*.[20] The proud Meccan Arabs ended up rediscovering this faith, the faith that their ancestors used to profess – after all, the *Sīra* presents the Arabs as descendants of Abraham through Ishmael. There are several ways in which the notion of an original religion of the Arabs functions; the most significant is, it seems, its attempt to mitigate the severity of the break with the past. Muḥammad does come across in the Qur'ān as a mere bringer of old tides, nothing the Jews and the Christians did not have. Apparently, it was what the Arabs at one time also had, but no more, the Sīra claims. The Arabs were once

[19] Ibn Isḥāq, *Life of Muhammad*, 98–103.

[20] For a detailed study of the *ḥanafīya*, see Uri Rubin, "Ḥanafiyya and Kaʿab – An Inquiry into the Arabian Pre-Islamic Background of Dīn Ibrāhīm," *Jerusalem Studies in Arabic and Islam* 13 (1990): 85–112.

the followers of the religion of Abraham, and Muḥammad is bringing that religion back.

Clearly, the *Sīra* is taking its cue from the Qur'ān when it argues that the stumbling block for the Pagans was the break with the past. There was a profound sense of scandal about what Muḥammad wanted the Meccans to do: forsake their fathers – which, in the scale of things, was far more disturbing than wanting them to forsake their gods. By connecting Muḥammad to the *ḥanafīya*, this pristine, pure monotheistic religion, the *Sīra* presents Muḥammad as accommodating the Meccans, allowing them to feel that they were still honoring their fathers and, at the same time, escaping the religions of their feared neighbors: Muḥammad was asking them to become neither Christians or Jews but something very similar.

Muḥammad, the *Sīra* insists, was himself dissatisfied with the situation of his city. He took to contemplation and would scale the mountains around Mecca to be alone and reflect on the state of his town. He had turned forty by the time that things escalated. He started having dreams that always came true. He also started to be greeted by rocks and trees – or at least to hear greetings, then to turn only to find trees and rocks. In a sense, the inanimate world was already aware of his rank as a prophet. His first prophetic experience took place in a cave. The *Sīra* informs us, while recounting the events of his first prophetic experience, that Muḥammad's mission was universal, meant for all humankind. The outcast of Mecca was sent to humanity, and at no time does the *Sīra* forget to emphasize that. As we can see, all these details raise suspicion: forty is the age of perfection, and the cave is a reminder of Plato's cave, and it was too early in his mission to make a claim to universalism. The *Sīra* is presenting the significance of the events concomitant with their telling.

As mentioned previously, the first angelic vision happened when Muḥammad was asleep in a cave on a mountain. The angel Gabriel brought with him a book and ordered Muḥammad to read. Having ordered Muḥammad to read three times, Muḥammad finally responded, "*Mā anā bi-qāri'?*" ("What should I read?"). Gabriel then recites what is considered the first section to be revealed of the Qur'ān (Q 96:1–5).[21] Another understanding of the event is to take Muḥammad's response to mean that he was not able to read. Hence, what he was telling Gabriel was "I can't read" instead of asking "What should I read?" The Arabic

[21] On this Sūra, see Uri Rubin, "Iqra' bi-smi Rabbika . . . ! Some Notes on the Interpretation of Sūrat al-ʿalaq (VS. 1–5)," *Israel Oriental Studies* 13 (1993): 213–30.

phrase is ambivalent enough to mean both. At first, this seems rather inconsequential. Is the *Sīra* claiming that Muḥammad is overwhelmed by the experience, or is it claiming that he is illiterate? Soon it would become apparent that the notion of an illiterate Muḥammad was fundamental in the presentation of the prophetic character of Muḥammad. The Arabs were not Gentiles (*ummīyūn*) as the Qur'ān insisted (Q 62:2); they were illiterate (*ummīyūn*) as the *Sīra* now understands the word; the same word means something different from its Qur'ānic usage. The purest illiterate of the Arabs was, of course, Muḥammad. Unable to write, he could not have forged the Qur'ān.[22]

The narratives of the *Sīra* of Ibn Isḥāq are usually homogeneous, and we are not offered alternative parallel stories to the version presented. But the broader tradition has preserved a rich amount of material that offers alternative variations of almost every event from Muḥammad's early life. The study of the variant versions of an episode has added immensely to our understanding of how different groups of Muslims saw and understood the career of Muḥammad.[23]

The Qur'ān, in this instance, has recorded what appears to be a reference to the same event, Muḥammad's first vision. Sūra 53, the only instance of a vision mentioned in the Qur'ān, clearly indicates that what Muḥammad saw was God himself and not Gabriel. In either case, the vision was overwhelming and so profound that its main effect was to convince Muḥammad of his mission. The figure filled the horizon. What Muḥammad experienced was also a revelation, a *waḥī*. In this sense, the most important aspect of Muḥammad's experience was the receiving of a coherent verbal revelation that he felt compelled to proclaim. Whatever was the nature of the experience, its verbal echo was the most important result, and Muḥammad was soon keenly aware of a message being delivered to him.

The *Sīra* and the tradition on the whole, including the Qur'ān, do not record any other vision of the divine as such, apart from a vision of God in the ascension story (*miʿrāj*), a vision that is attested only outside the Qur'ān. The narratives mostly present Muḥammad's experience as auditory, a trance that usually resulted in a new revelation that was

[22] On the term *ummī*, "gentile" or "illiterate," see Isaiah Goldfeld, "The Illiterate Prophet (nabī ummī): An Inquiry into the Development of a Dogma in Islamic Tradition," *Der Islam* 57 (1980): 58–67.

[23] Perhaps the most important studies carried out on these episodes are by Harris Birkeland, Rudi Paret, M. J. Kister, and Uri Rubin. See especially Uri Rubin's *The Eye of the Beholder: The Life of Muḥammad as Viewed by the Early Muslims* (Princeton, NJ: Darwin Press, 1995).

proclaimed to his followers. What is interesting about this revelation, which was called Qurʾān, is its self-referential nature, its constant cross-referencing of motifs and themes. As such, the compositional coherency of Muḥammad's revelation is quite striking.

THE AUDACITY OF PROPHECY

Much later in the career of Muḥammad, in Medina, during the famous Battle of the Trench (5/627), Muḥammad is supposed to have uttered some words that demonstrate the quality of the man. This was the nadir of his military career, Medina was besieged, and the situation was critical. There was every indication that the end of the saga of Muḥammad was at hand. Mecca amassed a large army in an attempt finally to eliminate Muḥammad. Eventually, the trenches dug by the Muslims successfully defended the city, and the army of Mecca, made up mostly of nomadic tribes, could not sustain the siege for more than a month. Thwarted in their effort, they could not conquer the city, but neither were they defeated, having hardly any casualties. Yet Muḥammad saw a shift in the balance of power: seeing the armies of his enemies retreat, he said, "Now we will raid them and they will not raid us."[24] A prediction that proved all too true. Mecca lost its nerve and soon Muḥammad proved invincible. A historian is, of course, justified in raising doubts about the historicity of this statement, although the strategic nature of the utterance points to a cold, measured military analysis of the situation and not a prophecy. But whether true or fictitious, it sums up Muḥammad's command of his environment. Even at his weakest, he seemed to see through the fog to formulate his next step. The Meccans did not lack in resolve; they simply were no match for him. Even when he misjudged them, Muḥammad was willing to radically alter his strategy. The Meccans proved themselves adaptable to change and willing to learn, but they were slower; there is no doubt about who was the revolutionary visionary in this story.

Muḥammad started his prophetic career in Mecca, which he had to leave after almost a decade of preaching, and the accounts of his departure make clear that only a handful of Quraysh members followed him to Medina. The pagans were not deserting their gods for a prophet (Q 38:6). As such, there is no escaping the conclusion that Muḥammad's mission in Mecca was a failure. His arguments, style, and preaching all

[24] From the *Ṣaḥīḥ* of al-Bukhārī, chapter on the *maghāzī* as quoted in my *In Defense of the Bible* (Leiden: E. J. Brill, 2008), 181.

proved in vain. Why did his stint in Mecca fail? Was there a way that it could have succeeded? These questions are raised to understand fully the rhetorical nature of the Qurʾānic revelation – because the Qurʾān is all that is left for us of his preaching to his Meccan fellow tribespeople. In what way did the Qurʾān understand the environment it was preaching to, and in what way did it refuse to accommodate it? The answer, of course, will always remain truncated, for paganism did not survive to write its point of view.

The *Sīra* presents Muḥammad as desperately hoping for an accommodation with his tribe. The event that depicts such willingness to accommodate is the episode of the Satanic Verses. The episode is famous, and here I give the minimum outline of the story. Muḥammad is supposed to have praised the three goddesses of the Meccans in his Qurʾān, only to have the verses removed the next day, claiming that the verses were whispered by the devil himself. Instead, a scathing ridicule was offered of these false gods.[25] Apart from this one-day lapse, which was excised from the text, the Qurʾān is simply unrelenting, unaccommodating, and outright despising of paganism. Rudi Paret, in his study of one of the shortest of sūras in the Qurʾān (Q 109), brilliantly captures the resolve of Muḥammad to demarcate himself from his tribespeople.[26] The gulf between the two was insurmountable. The two systems were mutually exclusive. As one verse states: "They wished you would relent, they would then have relented" (Q 68:9). But of course neither did, and the belligerence escalated.

The voice preaching in the Qurʾān is thus uncompromising. It brooks no dissent with its fundamental message: one God, a destruction of the world, a resurrection of the dead, and a judgment of deeds. Humans were to humble themselves before the Lord, act fearfully, and observe a code of behavior dictated by God and not by the honor of the tribe. The pagans kept complaining that Muḥammad was ridiculing their reason, insulting their ancestors, and pitting kin against kin. In every respect, Muḥammad was contravening the very foundations of the moral world of his city. He even had the audacity to proclaim a new history, a before-and-after

[25] For the literature on this episode, see Shahab Ahmed, "Ibn Taymiyyah and the Satanic Verses," *Studia Islamica* 87 (1998): 67–124.

[26] Rudi Paret, "Sure 109," *Der Islam* 39 (1964): 197–200, where he states that the *sūra* sounds like a call for a war ("Sie klingt wie ein Kampfruf," 200). All the scholarship of Paret is in German, and its diffusion in Qurʾānic studies in the English-speaking world has been minimal. This is unfortunate because he is one of the giants of the German school of Qurʾānic studies. I am in the process of translating his magisterial *Mohammed und der Koran*, the most lucid analysis of Muḥammad's career through the data in the Qurʾān.

him – a *jāhiliyya*, the time of the tribal ethos that he came to put an end to. He compared them to cattle, made fun of their respect for their ancestors. He declared blood ties useless. A solidification of Muḥammad's message was accompanied by a realization of the futility of conversion, and soon the Qurʾān is resigned to the new reality: those who saw the light converted; those who did not will live to see the damnation of God. It is almost a relief, because now the discursive nature of his preaching is far more pronounced. The Qurʾān has more time to elaborate on the points of contention, both aware of the futility of any arguments and insistent on arguing its own point of view.

In this regard, Muḥammad was preaching above the heads of the Meccans; it is not clear when he came to the conclusion that his mission to his city was a failure, but he must have done so or else he would not have prepared a way out. The radical uncompromising voice of the Qurʾān must, then, reflect this realization: because all is lost, only the full articulation of the truth is to really matter. The Qurʾān was not anymore interested in converting the pagans so much as reading a judgment against them. It also wanted to make sure that the small band of believers could sustain the misery of their isolation (Q 6:51–2). There were moments when the Qurʾān did not even care to explain itself to Muḥammad – we have to remember that rhetorically the Qurʾān addresses Muḥammad, and the Qurʾān is a persona in the dialogue. The Qurʾān, quoting Muḥammad regretting the complicated situation he is in, reproaches him: "If you do not like the gulf separating you from them, why not fly into the heavens, or bore a tunnel into earth" (Q 6:35). A miracle is not worth his enemies' weight, even if miracles were what God had granted before.

A MECCAN MANIFESTO

Sūra 6 in the Qurʾān is, in many respects, a summation of most of the arguments of the Meccan Qurʾān. It is, in my opinion, the last manifesto of Muḥammad in Mecca, radically uncompromising and yet careful to reargue each point of the whole mission. Rhetorically, it fashions a unity by making Muḥammad utter the same prayer, more or less, at the beginning and at the end of the Sūra. Muḥammad is ordered to recite it at the beginning of the Sūra (Q 6:14) and once again at the very end of the Sūra, this time making sure that Abraham is mentioned as the ancestor of this faith (Q 6:161–4). This is, moreover, the same prayer of Abraham that is narrated in the middle of the Sūra (Q 6:78–9). The prayer is the essence of Muḥammad's message: a radical monotheism and surrender to the One God. Remarkably the story of the conversion of Abraham is the only narrative in this long chapter, a rather stark departure from the practice of the Qur'ān, which usually narrates biographies from the lives of other prophets. The Qur'ān here has resigned itself and simply lists the prophets' names instead of their stories. In essence, there is one message, and it is what Abraham believed in, and all the prophets after him preached the same message (Q 6:83–90).

The bone of contention in the Sūra is the demand for a miracle to vouchsafe the veracity of Muḥammad's mission. In this regard, the arguments of the pagans are unimpeachable: Muḥammad had made it a point to connect himself to Moses and Jesus, had praised their miracle working as a sign of God; it is only natural that the Meccans should ask for the same. It is this demand for a miracle that becomes the backbone of Sūra 6 (and, as a matter of fact, of much of the anxiety of the rhetorical arguments in the Qur'ān); at each interval a specific demand is mentioned, only for the challenge to be rejected. What would prevent the Meccans from claiming that the miracle is not sorcery (Q 6:7)? A materialization of a miracle is, the Qur'ān declares, tantamount to carrying out God's chastisement. To force God's hand is to incur His wrath simultaneously (Q 6:8). They are simply incapable of seeing or hearing or understanding; they deny every sign and argue instead with Muḥammad, mockingly calling the Qur'ān the fables of the old (Q 6:25).

The Qur'ān then invokes God as a witness for its own veracity, calling itself by its own name, the Qur'ān, a revelation sent to warn the Meccans that there is only one God and that worshiping other gods beside him will only cause damnation (Q 6:19). Earthly life is declared a frivolous game, a nothing compared to the life to come (Q 6:32), in the face of Meccan insistence that the only real life is this one (Q 6:29). God is certainly capable of producing a miracle for Muḥammad, but they are ignorant not to know that (Q 6:37); God is already manifest in the world, and His chastisement will come to prove His will. Once more the nature of prophecy is adumbrated: prophets are messengers with good tidings and warnings; they are not empowered beyond that, they have no riches or treasures, and they are not kings; they follow what is revealed to them (Q 6:48–52). It is God who is the master of the world; He Will judge – indeed, if judgment was at Muḥammad's will, he would have brought it –, but God is not willing to let a human judge other humans, a clear sign of God's mercy (Q 6:54, 58). Nonetheless, God's chastisement will come all the same, and an unrelenting horror awaits those who refuse to abide by God's message.

After a long foray into what is licit and what is not, the Sūra then sums up the moral commands of the Meccan Qur'ān (Q 6:151–2); the Qur'ān is declared a book like the book of Moses, despite the Meccans' protestation that only the two sects (meaning Jews and Christians) were known to have such books (Q 6:156). But God will come with His angels, and then nothing will benefit those who were unwilling to believe (Q 6:158). It is clear that Sūra 6 is not envisioning a polity or a community of believers as such, or if it did, not for the Muslims. The call is for a personal conversion and personal responsibility. Muḥammad had realized the limits of his mission in Mecca.

CONCLUSION: MUḤAMMAD THE PROPHET IN LATE ANTIQUITY

Muḥammad was not only a product of his environment; like a classic revolutionary character, he was also capable of transcending his limitations. In a tribal pagan environment, he dared to preach a salvific religion, a high imperial cult – and monotheism was then the cult of an empire – and he wanted to end the barbarism of the Arabs. The Arabs were to be made similar to the peoples of the empire, the *Rūm*, the Romans up north, with a book, and part of the legacy of Abraham. It is not insignificant that Muḥammad was rooting for the Romans in their wars with Sassanid Iran (Q 30:1–5). It is also worth noting that Alexander the Great became part of the salvific history of the Qurʾān: empire building and monotheism are one (Q 18). Muḥammad wanted to bring Rome to Arabia and, having been too successful, ended up taking Arabia to Rome.

Further reading

Brown, Peter. *The Rise of Western Christendom*. 2nd ed. London: Blackwell, 2003.

Fowden, Garth. *Empire to Commonwealth: Consequences of Monotheism in Late Antiquity*. Princeton, NJ: Princeton University Press, 1993.

Izutsu, Toshihiko. *Ethico-Religious Concepts in the Qur'ān*. Montreal: McGill University Press, 2002.

Motzki, Harald, ed. *The Biography of Muḥammad: The Issue of the Sources*. Leiden: Brill, 2000.

Peters, F. E. *Muhammad and the Origins of Islam*, Albany: State University of New York Press, 1994.

Stetkevych, Jaroslav. *Muḥammad and the Golden Bough: Reconstructing Arabian Myth*. Bloomington: Indiana University Press, 1996.

2 Muḥammad's message in Mecca: warnings, signs, and miracles

URI RUBIN

In the previous chapter, Walid Saleh describes the many portents from Muḥammad's early life that set the stage for his ultimate role as prophet to Arabia. Such miraculous events are said to have continued throughout the Prophet's life, confirming his mission and demonstrating his personal connection to God. The present chapter looks more closely at the differences between the two major sources for Muḥammad's life, namely the Qur'ān, on the one hand, and the extra-Qur'ānic sources, on the other hand. The latter include the compilations of *tafsīr* (Qur'ānic exegesis), Sīra (Muḥammad's biography), and *ḥadīth* (tradition). The comparative analysis will focus on Muḥammad's image as emerging in his Meccan period, which stretches from the moment when he first received revelation, through his first attempts at preaching God's warning and promise to the people of Mecca, and up to their final rejection of him. This rejection resulted in Muḥammad's flight (*hijra*) to the oasis of Yathrib, later to be known as Medina.

When we read the Qur'ānic Meccan passages alone, without benefit of post-Qur'ānic interpretation, Muḥammad emerges as a mortal prophet who still has no miracle other than the Qur'ān, the book he received from God over the last twenty-two years of his life, first in Mecca (610–622 CE) and then in Medina (622–632). Muḥammad appears in these passages as a man who both warns of the oncoming Judgment Day and brings God's message of mercy. But in the post-Qur'ānic sources, a different Muḥammad emerges; these sources move away from the mortal Qur'ānic warner toward an ideal hero whom later generations of devoted believers have shaped and read back into the Qur'ān by means of its exegesis.

The basic differences between the Qur'ānic Muḥammad and the post-Qur'ānic one will be brought out in this essay by looking closely at one event, the splitting of the moon. This event is referred to in two verses of the Qur'ān (54:1–2) that form part of Qur'ānic eschatology, but when later on the same event is discussed in the post-Qur'ānic literature, it is already transformed from an eschatological sign into a historical miracle. This transformation indicates that the post-Qur'ānic literature is already aware of the worldly triumph that Muḥammad experienced after his *hijra* to Medina, and hence it is able to read back this post-*hijra* triumph into the Meccan period and place the splitting of the moon within the historical context of Muḥammad's worldly success. But let us begin the discussion with the Qur'ānic Meccan sūras, reading them for their own sake.

THE QUR'ĀNIC WARNER

The earliest Qur'ānic passages (i.e., those revealed to Muḥammad during his Meccan period[1]) employ tactics of warning and good tidings that are designed to support the Qur'ānic monotheistic campaign. These passages warn the unbelievers of God's chastisement while promising divine reward to the believers. Accordingly, Muḥammad is styled a *nadhīr* ("warner") and a *bashīr* ("announcer of good tidings").

Muḥammad's function as a warner is essential to his prophetic mission from the very outset. Already Sūra 74, fourth according to ʿAṭāʾ al-Khurāsānī's order of revelation (see note 1), opens with a request that Muḥammad "rise and warn." Further on, the Sūra describes the horrors of hell and the fate of the unbelievers in its flames. The gardens of Paradise that await the righteous are also depicted, and it is asserted that the sinners are denied access to it because they have not believed in the Day of Judgment. The same twofold message is conveyed in Sūra 92, which appears shortly after Sūra 74 on the list of Meccan *sūras*. In these revelations, Muḥammad's religious campaign is focused on the eschatological sphere and conveys the strong feeling that the Last Judgment is very near.

The addressees of the Qur'ānic eschatological warnings are defined in Q 6:92 as the inhabitants of Umm al-Qura ("Mother of Cities")

[1] The division of the Qur'ān into Meccan and Medinan sūras is based on traditions containing lists of sūras arranged according to their order of revelation. One of the earliest available lists is by ʿAṭāʾ al-Khurāsānī (Syrian, d. 135/753), who ascribes it to Ibn ʿAbbās. The list was preserved by Muḥammad b. Ayyūb b. al-Ḍurays (d. 294/906) in his *Faḍāʾil al-Qurʾān*, ed. Ghazwat Budayr (Damascus: Dār al-Fikr, 1987), 33–4. For later sources in which this list appears, see Neal Robinson, *Discovering the Qur'ān: A Contemporary Approach to a Veiled Text*, 2nd ed. (Washington, D.C.: Georgetown University Press, 2003), 69. Even if one does not take these lists as historical, they are still relevant to anyone interested in the manner in which the early Muslims remembered Muḥammad's prophetic career. See further Gerhard Böwering, "Chronology and the Qur'ān," in *Encyclopaedia of the Qur'ān*, ed. Jane Dammen McAuliffe (Leiden: Brill, 2001–2006), 1:316–35.

and those around it. The same applies to Q 42:7, where Muḥammad is requested to warn Umm al-Qurā and those around it by means of the Arabic Qurʾān that has been revealed to him and to give warning of the Day of Gathering (*yawm al-jamʿ*) when "a party shall be in Paradise and (another) party in the Blaze."

The inhabitants of Umm al-Qurā (i.e., Mecca) are the Quraysh, Muḥammad's own tribe, who are mentioned by name in Sūra 106. This Meccan chapter (twenty-eighth in ʿAṭāʾ al-Khurāsānī's order) reveals another level of Muḥammad's role as a warner. The first two verses of the Sūra mention the "winter and summer caravans" of the Quraysh, which seem to be taken as a sign of divine benefaction, from which the Quraysh must draw a monotheistic conclusion and "worship the Lord [i.e., Allāh] of this House" (i.e., the Kaʿba) (v. 3). He deserves to be worshipped because he is the one who "has fed them against hunger and has made them secure from fear" (v. 4). This statement contains a hidden threat to the Quraysh: if they do not worship Allāh, they are liable to suffer hunger and killing (i.e., to lose their hegemony in Arabia, which had been given them by Allāh and not by any other deity). In further Meccan passages, they are requested to remember the fate of ancient mighty towns in Arabia that were likewise destroyed by God (e.g., Q 46:27). In Q 41:13, the fate of the Quraysh is explicitly linked to that of the extinct generations. Muḥammad tells them, "I have warned you of a scourge like the scourge of ʿĀd and Thamūd." The bitter end of these ancient generations is expounded in the Qurʾānic "punishment stories."[2]

The punishment awaiting the Quraysh is the result of their sinful conduct, the nature of which is made clear by the manner in which they are referred to throughout the Qurʾān. They are often designated as "idolaters" (*mushrikūn*, lit. "those who associate"). This refers to their polytheistic tenets and especially to their belief in God's associates or partners (*shurakāʾ*) who are considered his offspring.[3] The same Meccan polytheists are also referred to as "unbelievers" (*kāfirūn*, lit. "those who disbelieve"), which pertains to their rejection of God's signs as brought to them by Muḥammad.[4]

The warning of an earthly calamity as inherent in Sūra 106, as well in the punishment stories, is complementary to the eschatological

[2] See David Marshall, "Punishment Stories," in McAuliffe, *Encyclopaedia of the Qurʾān*, 4:318–22.

[3] The Qurʾān mentions by name three of God's alleged daughters: Allāt, al-ʿUzzā, and Manāt (Q 53:19–21).

[4] See Camilla Adang, "Belief and Unbelief," in McAuliffe, *Encyclopaedia of the Qurʾān*, 1:218–26.

warnings addressed to the same audience in the other Meccan sūra. These chapters elaborate on the idea of the oncoming judgment, and especially on the role of Allāh as the ultimate judge between believers and unbelievers (e.g., Q 32:25; 39:46; 40:12). Belief in the Day of Judgment is declared an article of faith (e.g., Q 70:26), and it is stressed that one must always check one's deeds while being fearful of standing God's trial in the hereafter (e.g., Q 29:5). Disbelief in the Last Judgment and in the inevitable appearance before God the judge entails divine wrath and chastisement in the flames of hell (e.g., Q 6:31; 30:8–9; 32:10–12; 74:46; 82:9; 83:10–12; 95:7; 107:1).

The Last Judgment, according to early Meccan revelations, will be preceded by cosmic disasters, as is stated, for example, in Q 81:1–13: the sun shall be covered, the stars shall be thrown down, the mountains shall be moved away, the pregnant camels shall be left untended, the wild animals shall be mustered, the seas shall be set on fire, the heaven shall be stripped off, and so on. Or as described in Q 82:1–4: heaven shall become cleft asunder, the stars shall become dispersed, the seas shall swarm over, and the graves shall be overthrown (see also Q 84:1–5; 99:1–5; 101:1–5). Sometimes mention is made of devastating events pertaining to the sun and the moon in particular: the moon shall be eclipsed, and the sun and the moon shall be "brought together" (Q 75:7–9). In this case, the calamity marks the onset of resurrection (Q 75:1–5), which means that the ideas of resurrection and judgment overlap in the Qurʾān.[5]

Such calamities are already described in a biblical apocalypse. In Joel 2:30–1 [3:3–4 in the Hebrew Bible] God says: "I will show portents in the heavens and on the earth; blood and fire and columns of smoke. The sun shall be turned to darkness and the moon to blood, before the great and terrible day of the Lord comes." The same recurs in the New Testament,[6] and later on the Qurʾān has embedded these eschatological warnings into the Arabian context of Muḥammad's antipolytheistic campaign.

The beginning of the Last Judgment is frequently referred to as the Hour (*al-sāʿa*). The Meccan passages (and occasionally the Medinan ones) assert that it is inevitable (Q 18:21; 40:59) and that one must not doubt it (Q 43:61). Whoever denies the Hour shall be in hell (Q 25:11). Indeed, the believers "go in fear of it" (Q 42:18), yet the unbelievers refuse to

[5] For which, see Maurice Borrmans, "Resurrection," in McAuliffe, *Encyclopaedia of the Qurʾān*, 4:434–5.

[6] Joel's apocalypse is quoted in Acts 2:19–20. And see further Matthew 24:29: "Immediately after the suffering of those days, the sun will be darkened, and the moon will not give its light; the stars will fall from heaven, and the powers of heaven will be shaken" (see also Mark 13:24–5).

believe that it will ever come (Q 34:3; 41:50; 45:32). It is expected to occur within a short time (e.g., Q 16:77; 42:17) and suddenly (Q 6:31; 12:107; 21:40; 47:18; 43:66), but God will not disclose exactly when (Q 7:187; 20:15; 31:34; 33:63; 41:47; 43:85; 79:42–6).

Similar allusions to the unknown hour already occur in the New Testament but in a specific Christian context,[7] which the Qurʾān has reshaped and built into Muḥammad's discourse with his Arab polytheistic interlocutors.

When the Hour comes, "they who are in error . . . shall know who is in more evil plight and weaker in forces" (Q 19:75), because on that day, the "vain-doers" shall perish (Q 45:27). Furthermore, "the Hour is their promised time, and the Hour shall be most grievous and bitter" (Q 54:46).

The Hour is sometimes alluded to with various ominous designations, such as "the Clatterer" (*al-qāriʿa*, Q 101:1–3), "the Enveloper" (*al-ghāshiya*, Q 88:1), "the Imminent" (*al-āzifa*, Q 40:18; 53:57), "the Shocking Event" (*al-wāqiʿa*, Q 56:1), and "the Great Predominating Calamity" (*al-ṭāmmatu l-kubrā*, Q 79:34).

One eschatological cataclysm that marks the Hour is the splitting of the moon, which is mentioned in Sūra 54 (al-Qamar), thirty-sixth according to ʿAṭāʾ's list. It is here that a comparative reading of the Qurʾān and the extra-Qurʾānic sources reveals significant aspects of the changing interpretation of Muḥammad's prophetic message in Mecca, and especially his progress from a mere mortal warner to something else.

THE QURʾĀNIC MOON PASSAGE

The moon passage (Q 54:1–2) reads:

ٱقْتَرَبَتِ ٱلسَّاعَةُ وَٱنشَقَّ ٱلْقَمَرُ The Hour is at hand and the moon is

وَإِن يَرَوْا۟ آيَةً يُعْرِضُوا۟ وَيَقُولُوا۟ سِحْرٌ split. And if they see a sign they turn

مُّسْتَمِرٌّ aside and say: transient enchantment.[8]

[7] Matthew 24:36: "But about that day and hour no one knows, neither the angels of heaven, nor the Son, but only the Father" (see also Mark 13:32).

[8] On this passage and the myths that have evolved around it, see, e.g., Tor Andrae, *Die Person Muhammeds in Lehre und Glauben seiner Gemeinde* (Stockholm: P. A. Norstedt, 1918), 55–7; Annemarie Schimmel, *And Muhammad Is His Messenger: The Veneration of the Prophet in Islamic Piety* (Chapel Hill: University of North Carolina Press, 1985), 69–71. On the controversy in modern Islam concerning the authenticity of the traditions, see Gautier H. A. Juynboll, *The Authenticity of the Tradition Literature: Discussions in Modern Egypt* (Leiden: E. J. Brill, 1969), 145–7.

THE ESCHATOLOGICAL CONTEXT

The splitting of the moon seems to allude to a partial lunar eclipse,[9] one of several that could be seen in Mecca before Muḥammad's *hijra* to Medina (i.e., between 610 and 622 CE).[10] But what is meant here is no mere astronomical observation. The juxtaposition of the Hour and the splitting of the moon indicates that the lunar eclipse is taken as a warning of the oncoming eschatological cataclysm.

The eschatological implication of the eclipse is intensified by the vocabulary of the passage. The verb *inshaqqa,* which is a figurative description of the partial concealment of the full moon, recurs in other Meccan eschatological passages, in which it signifies the literal splitting of heaven on the Day of Judgment. In Q 69:16, it is stated that "heaven shall be split [*wa-'nshaqqat*], for on that day it shall be frail." The same is stated in the passages of Q 84:1 (*inshaqqat*), and in Q 25:25 (*tashaqqaqu*), as well as in the Medinan passage of Q 55:37 (*inshaqqat*). The same cataclysm is described in verbal forms derived not only from the Arabic root SH-Q-Q but also from the root F-Ṭ-R (Q 73:18; 82:1).

From this eschatological function of *inshaqqa* it may be inferred that the splitting of the moon in the moon passage also bears an eschatological connotation, although here it is only a figurative preview of the imminent literal splitting of the moon as well as of the entire heavens.

SIGNS

The eclipsed or split moon is defined in the moon passage as a "sign" (*āya,* pl. *ayāt*). This puts the eclipse on a par with a series of other visual signs that are adduced in the Meccan sūras to display the overall powers of Allāh as the one and only God who has created the universe and controls it. These are natural signs that are celestial as well as terrestrial. They are revealed in God's giving all creatures rain and making seed grow and providing food of all kinds, or in creating the skies and the sun and the moon and the stars, or in making the sea with its fruits and the ships sailing in it. The Qur'ān states that all these are signs for those who can understand (Q 16:10–16).

Although the foregoing signs illustrate God's bounty, the split moon is a sign that should be a reminder of the approaching Day of Judgment.

[9] This has already been suggested before. For details, see Rudi Paret, *Der Koran: Kommentar und Konkordanz* (Stuttgart: Verlag W. Kohlhammer, 1971), 495.

[10] The list of all lunar eclipses is available at the NASA Eclipse Web site, at http://eclipse.gsfc.nasa.gov/JLEX/JLEX-AS.html.

The unbelievers, however, ignore the visual signs, and as pointed out in the moon passage, for them even a lunar eclipse is nothing but a passing illusion. Other Qur'ānic passages indicate that they demand different kinds of visual signs, ones that would go against the ordinary course of nature (i.e., miracles). A list of their requested miracles is provided in several Meccan passages. To believe in Muḥammad's warnings, they need to see an angel descending to assist him or a treasure that will be sent down to him (Q 6:8–9; 11:12; 15:7; 23:24; 25:7–8, 21). Alternatively, they demand to see if the Prophet can cause a fountain to gush forth from the earth for them, or produce a garden of palms and grapes in the midst of which he should cause rivers to flow forth, or cause the sky to come down on them in pieces, or bring God and all his angels face-to-face with them, or produce a golden house, or ascend into heaven and bring down with him a book they can read (Q 17:90–3; see also Q 74:52).

The miraculous signs they demand should resemble those brought by previous prophets (Q 21:5), which means that the Prophet must perform those miraculous deeds as known from the stories about Moses and Jesus, and of which the Qur'ān itself is aware.[11]

But Muḥammad cannot produce such miraculous signs because no prophet can produce a sign without God's permission (Q 13:38; 14:11; 40:78). Moreover, Muḥammad would not be able to produce the signs demanded of him even if he descended through a tunnel into the center of the earth or ascended on a ladder into heaven (Q 6:35). Furthermore, the miraculous signs, says the Qur'ān, did not prevent the previous nations from rejecting their own prophets (Q 17:59). Therefore, all the Prophet can say is, "The signs are only with Allāh, and I am only a plain warner [*nadhīr mubīn*]" (Q 29:50). The Qur'ānic text itself – that is, the verbal signs that the Prophet recites – should be sufficient for his foes (Q 29:51).

Muḥammad's failure to produce the visual signs demanded by his foes runs parallel to the assertion that he is just a mortal of flesh and blood (*bashar*) (Q 17:93; 18:110; 41:6), not an angel; he is one who does not know the unseen (Q 6:50; 7:188; 11:31 [here about Noah]).

On account of his mortality, all the plain warner can do is adduce natural signs, like a lunar eclipse, which testify to God's omnipotence and are derived from the material cosmos that is always there for people

[11] The miracles that are attributed to Moses revolve around his rod and his "white hand" (Q 7:107–8, 117; 20:69; 26:32–3, 45). His rod helps him strike water from the rock (Q 2:60; 7:160) and split the sea (Q 26:63). Jesus creates a living bird out of clay, heals the blind and the leprous, and raises the dead and knows the unseen (Q 3:49; 5:110).

to observe. There lies the visual proof of his monotheistic message as well as of the imminent Hour.

SIḤR – "ENCHANTMENT"

But the Qur'ān informs us in the Meccan sūras that even if the unbelievers see each and every sign in the world, they will not believe (Q 6:25; 7:146, cf. 10:96–7). This is why they also refuse to correctly interpret cosmic phenomena like an eclipsed sun or moon. As stated in the moon passage, they reject the vision of the eclipsed moon as "enchantment" (*siḥr*), which means that they impute to Muḥammad an attempt to bewitch and manipulate them into believing that the phenomenon is a portent of the Hour. In fact, the Meccan unbelievers reject any sign they see by claiming that it is mere *siḥr* (Q 37:14–15).

Muḥammad's Meccan foes dismiss as *siḥr* even the verbal signs recited to them, and especially the Qur'ānic eschatological warnings, including the idea of resurrection (Q 11:7). They claim that he tries to bewitch them and make them believe that he speaks the word of God, although he is just an ordinary human being like themselves (Q 74:24–5; see also Q 21:2–3; 34:43; 43:30; 46:7).

THE POST-QUR'ĀNIC WARNER

As we turn from the Qur'ān to the post-Qur'ānic sources, we realize that some traditions still preserve Muḥammad's Qur'ānic image, portraying him as a mortal warner whom God does not provide with any miraculous signs to help him persuade his audience. Certain canonical *ḥadīth* collections contain a tradition on the authority of the Companion Abū Hurayra in which Muḥammad is said to have stated that every prophet has been given a sign of the kind that could make people believe (*mā mina l-anbiyā'i nabiyyun illā u'ṭiya mina l-āyāt mā mithluhu āmana 'alayhi l-basharu*), whereas all Muḥammad has been given is a revelation (*waḥy*) from God. Muḥammad goes on to express his hope that on the day of resurrection the number of his believers will exceed that of any other prophet.[12]

This tradition is still aware of the gap separating the Qur'ānic Muḥammad from the previous prophets who, unlike him, were aided by miracles. But the tradition turns the Qur'ān itself into a sign that

[12] E.g., Bukhārī, *Ṣaḥīḥ*, *Faḍā'il al-Qur'ān* [section 66]: *Bāb kayfa nazala l-waḥyu* [chapter 1].

surpasses that of any other prophet; by force of it, Muḥammad will have in the hereafter the greatest number of believers.

THE ESCHATOLOGICAL INTERPRETATION OF THE MOON PASSAGE

As for the post-Qur'ānic *tafsīr* of the moon passage, here, too, some traditions keep to the Qur'ānic image of Muḥammad as a mortal warner aided by no miracles. This applies to those exegetical traditions that take the splitting of the moon as a lunar eclipse prefiguring eschatological cataclysm.

For example, ʿAbd al-Razzāq (d. 211/827) has recorded in his *Muṣannaf* a tradition traced back to ʿIkrima (d. 105/723), the Medinan *mawlā* of Ibn ʿAbbās. ʿIkrima relates that once in Muḥammad's time the moon was eclipsed (*kasafa l-qamaru*) and the people said, "A spell has been cast over the moon" (*suḥira l-qamar*). Thereupon the Prophet recited the first verse of the moon passage: "The Hour is at hand and the moon has been split."[13]

In this version, Muḥammad is still the mortal warner who can only adduce visual signs from the material cosmos, in this case, an alarming lunar eclipse that was seen in Mecca. The inner eschatological context of the Qur'ānic moon passage is fully preserved, and the verb *inshaqqa* is still just a figurative prediction of the eschatological cataclysm.

LITERAL SPLITTING

Other post-Qur'ānic interpretations that are found in the early *tafsīr* sources also preserve the eschatological connotation of the moon passage, yet they reveal an ever-growing tendency to release Muḥammad of his human limitations. They produce a new Muḥammad, one who not only warns but also provides the miraculous signs that attest to the truth of his warning. In these traditions, the celestial phenomenon itself is not just an incidental lunar eclipse that looks like splitting but rather an intentional splitting apart of the moon. The verb *inshaqqa* is transformed here from figurative to literal, and the event changes from a sign that Muḥammad merely interprets into a miracle of the most powerful kind. This transformation is noticeable in the earliest available *tafsīr* compilations.

[13] ʿAbd al-Razzāq b. Hammām al-Ṣanʿānī, *al-Muṣannaf*, ed. Ḥabīb al-Raḥmān al-Aʿẓamī (Beirut: al-maktab al-Islāmī, 1970), 3:104–5 (no. 4941).

Muqātil b. Sulaymān (d. 150/767) begins his commentary on the moon passage saying that the Hour is the resurrection (*al-qiyāma*). He then states that there are three portents of the Hour: the prophetic emergence (*khurūj*) of Muḥammad,[14] the "smoke" (*al-dukhān*; see Q 44:10[15]), and the splitting of the moon. This explanation, which joins the splitting of the moon with the two other events signaling the approaching Hour, preserves the eschatological sense of the passage. Yet Muqātil immediately proceeds to tell a story that provides the occasion of revelation (*sabab al-nuzūl*) that places the splitting of the moon into history: Muḥammad's Meccan adversaries asked him to show them a sign (*āya*), and thereupon the moon was split in two halves (*niṣfayn*). The Meccans said that this was the act of sorcerers (*ʿamal al-saḥara*). Eventually, the two halves were reunited into one (*ilta'ama*).[16]

In this account, the moon not only is split apart, which turns the verb *inshaqqa* from figurative to literal, but the event itself no longer happens by chance but rather on demand. Muḥammad meets the challenge set by his adversaries, which implies superhuman powers. Consequently, the charge of *siḥr* that comes as a reaction to the miraculous sign changes from mental enchantment of the mind into actual magic.

In ʿAbd al-Razzāq's *Tafsīr*, the verb *inshaqqa* is also perceived in its literal sense. Here various versions of what supposedly happened are recorded on the authority of some prominent Companions of the Prophet.[17] The Baṣran Companion Anas b. Mālik (d. ca. 91/709–95/713) tells us that the people of Mecca asked the Prophet for a sign and then the moon was split in two. Although nothing is new here compared with what we have already seen in the work of Muqātil, several versions that are traced back to the Medinan/Kūfan Companion ʿAbdallāh b. Masʿūd (d. 32/652–53) add some local color to the spectacle. This Companion embraced Islam in Mecca at a very early stage of Muḥammad's career, which makes him an eyewitness to the event. In one version, Ibn Masʿūd assures us that he saw the moon split apart, so much so that he could

14 This reflects traditions to the effect that Muḥammad's prophetic emergence occurred when the Hour was just about to come. See, e.g., Muḥammad b. Jarīr al-Ṭabarī, *Tārīkh al-rusul wa-l-mulūk*, ed. M. J. De Goeje et al. (Leiden: E. J. Brill, 1879–1901), 1: 12–13.

15 In this verse, the Prophet is requested to expect a day on which "heaven shall bring a manifest smoke covering the people." The eschatological connotation of the smoke is borne out by the previous passage from Joel.

16 Muqātil b. Sulaymān, *Tafsīr al-Qur'ān*, ed. ʿAbdallāh Maḥmūd Shiḥāta, 5 vols. (Cairo: al-hay'a l-Miṣriyya al-ʿāmma li-l-kitāb, 1979), 4:177.

17 ʿAbd al-Razzāq al-Ṣanʿānī, *Tafsīr al-Qur'ān*, ed. Muṣṭafā Muslim Muḥammad, 3 vols. (Riyadh: maktabat al-rushd, 1989), 2:257.

Figure 3. "Muḥammad Splits the Moon," an illustration from a *Falnameh* (Persian book of prophecies), in the Dresden State Library. SLUB Dresden/Deutsche Fotothek.

see Mount Ḥirāʾ between its two halves. In another version, he says that one part of the moon was seen above Mount Abū Qubays and the other above Mount al-Suwaydāʾ. These mountains are located in the vicinity of the Kaʿba, and thus the miracle adds to the sacredness of the local Meccan geography. This geographical specification also serves to authenticate the splitting of the moon as a historical event. Nevertheless, the eschatological connotation of the happening is also maintained, as one of Ibn Masʿūd's versions concludes with Muḥammad's statement: "Just as you have seen the two halves of the split moon, so is true what I have told you about the approaching Hour."[18]

These traditions have been provided with *isnāds* considered sound (*ṣaḥīḥ*), which made them acceptable to authors of canonical *ḥadīth* compilations. For example, al-Bukhārī (d. 256/870) dedicated special chapters to the splitting of the moon in which he assembled various versions of Ibn Masʿūd as well as of other Companions.[19]

ESCHATOLOGY VERSUS HISTORY

Despite the widely accepted perception of the moon passage as alluding to a historical splitting apart of the moon above the mountains of Mecca, further texts reveal attempts at depriving the event of its claimed place in history. This is evinced by some linguistic explanations that insist on reading the form *inshaqqa* as denoting the future, thus preserving the purely eschatological context of the passage. Al-Thaʿlabī (d. 427/1035) records in his *Tafsīr* the interpretation of ʿUthmān b. ʿAṭāʾ al-Khurāsānī (d. 155/751), who says on the authority of his father that *inshaqqa* means *sa-yanshaqqu* ("will be split").[20] Al-Māwardī (d. 450/1058) adds some more details, saying that the moon will be split after the second blast of the trumpet (*al-nafkha al-thāniya*), which is a stage in the process of resurrection (cf. Q 39:68). He also provides the observation of al-Ḥasan al-Baṣrī (d. 110/728) to the effect that, had the moon been split in the past, everyone would have seen it (and remembered it, which was not the case).[21]

These interpretations reflect efforts to get around what could be considered the irrationality of the literal splitting in its supposed historical

[18] For additional versions on the authority of Ibn Masʿūd and others, with a splitting just as literal, see Muḥammad b. Jarīr al-Ṭabarī, *Jāmiʿ al-bayān fī tafsīr al-Qurʾān* (Cairo: Būlāq, 1323/1905; reprinted in Beirut, n.p., 1972), 27:50–1; citation is from the Būlāq edition. The localities above which the two parts of the moon are seen include Minā, another prominent station of the pilgrimage to Mecca.

[19] Bukhārī, *Ṣaḥīḥ, Tafsīr* [65]: *Bāb wa-ʾnshaqqa l-qamar* (Q 54:1); *Manāqib al-Anṣār* [section 63]: *Bāb inshiqāq al-qamar* [chapter 36].

[20] Abū Isḥāq Aḥmad b. Muḥammad al-Thaʿlabī, *al-Kashf wa-l-bayān ʿan tafsīr āy al-Qurʾān*, ed. Abū Muḥammad b. ʿĀshūr and Naẓīr al-Sāʿidī (Beirut: dār iḥyāʾ al-turāth al-ʿArabī, 2002), 9:160.

[21] al-Māwardī, *al-Nukat wa-l-ʿuyūn fī tafsīr al-Qurʾān*, ed. ʿAbd al-Maqṣūd b. ʿAbd al-Raḥīm (Beirut: dār al-kutub al-ʿilmiyya, 1992), 5:409.

setting.[22] In contrast, exegetical maneuvers were exercised to rule out the possibility of reading the verb *inshaqqa* in the future tense and to maintain the historicity of the splitting. In a *qirāʾa* ("variant reading") attributed to Ibn Masʿūd, the verb *inshaqqa* is preceded by *qad*, so that the meaning can only be "[the moon] was already split [in Muḥammad's time]."[23]

Furthermore, Ibn Masʿūd is said to have added the splitting of the moon to a list of four other events that the Qurʾān mentions with reference to the calamities of the Day of Judgment. But in Ibn Masʿūd's tradition, the five events are said to have already come about in Muḥammad's lifetime (*khamsun qad maḍayna*).[24] One of the other four on the list is the (event of) the smoke (Q 44:10), which, as seen previously, was defined by Muqātil as a portent of the Hour. But in Ibn Masʿūd's tradition, the smoke is presented as an event of the past, which brings to mind a series of occurrences described in traditions recorded in the *tafsīr* sources regarding the smoke passage. These traditions depict a prolonged drought and famine that God has inflicted on the Meccans as punishment for their opposition to Muḥammad. The famine, which causes a smokelike haze that dims the eyes, begins miraculously, as soon as Muḥammad prays to God asking him to bring down on the Quraysh seven years of drought like those suffered by the Egyptians in Joseph's time.[25] This exposition detaches the smoke from the context of the Hour and transforms this event, together with the splitting of the moon and other incidents on Ibn Masʿūd's list, from eschatological signs into historical miracles.

[22] Another interpretation, which likewise tries to avoid the literal sense of *inshaqqa*, takes this verb as a metaphor connoting "to become apparent" (*waḍuḥa l-amru wa-ẓahara*) or signaling the "splitting apart of the cover of darkness that has concealed the moon" (*inshiqāqu l-ẓulmati ʿanhu*). No explanation is provided, however, as to the implication of such an interpretation on the significance of the moon passage. See Māwardī, *Nukat*, 5:409.

[23] Ṭabarī, *Tafsīr*, 27:51. The same reading was reportedly used by the Medinan/Kūfan Companion Ḥudhayfa b. al-Yamān (d. 36/656) in a Friday sermon about the approaching Hour. See Hūd b. Muḥakkam al-Huwwārī, *Tafsīr kitāb Allāh al-ʿAzīz*, ed. Belḥāj Sharīfī (Beirut: dār al-gharb al-Islāmī, 1990) 4:250–1. See also Ṭabarī, *Tafsīr*, 27:51; Ibn Kathīr, *al-Bidāya wa-l-nihāya* (Beirut: maktabat al-maʿārif, 1974), 4:75.

[24] The remaining three are the (event of) "that which shall cleave" (*al-lizām*, Q 25:77), the (event of) the "seizing" (*al-baṭsha*, Q 44:16), and the (victory of) the Rūm (Q 30:2–3). See Ṭabarī, *Tafsīr*, 27:51. This tradition recurs in the canonical *ḥadīth* collections; see, e.g., Bukhārī, *Ṣaḥīḥ*, *Tafsīr* [65], on Q 25:77.

[25] On the traditions about the famine and Muḥammad's prayer, see Uri Rubin, "Muhammad's Curse of Muḍar and the Blockade of Mecca," *Journal of the Economic and Social History of the Orient* 3 (1988): 249–64; Heidi Toelle, "Smoke," in McAuliffe, *Encyclopaedia of the Qurʾān*, 5:64–5.

The historicity of the splitting of the moon is also endorsed in traditions attributed to Ibn ʿAbbās, as recorded in al-Ṭabarī's (d. 310/923) *Tafsīr*. He is reported to have said about the moon passage: "This has already come to pass [*dhāka qad maḍā*]. It occurred before the *hijra*, when the moon was split till its two [separate] halves could be seen."[26]

The reinterpretation of the Meccan eschatological warnings – such as the splitting of the moon and the smoke – reflect a new post-Qurʾānic perception of Muhammad's career before the *hijra*. His life has now become part of a sacred history that already fulfills in this world many of God's warnings as well as promises. This new outlook indicates that the post-Qurʾānic literature looks at Muḥammad's Meccan period from a new perspective; it is already aware of the worldly triumph that Muḥammad experienced after his *hijra* to Medina, which resulted in his message expanding to the rest of the world. The post-Qurʾānic sources read back this post-*hijra* triumph into the Meccan period and remove the splitting of the moon and the smoke from the eschatological context of the Hour, relocating them in the historical sphere of Muḥammad's worldly career. In their new historical context, these events function as miracles marking the divine aid and protection under which Muḥammad's life proceeds.

A NEW PRE-*HIJRA* HISTORY

The splitting of the moon, once detached from the context of the Hour and perceived as a historical event demonstrating Muḥammad's supernatural abilities, could be grafted onto the specific accounts of Muḥammad's pre-*hijra* period that were eventually retold as part of a glorious history of a continuous success. This literary progression took place at a secondary stage, as proved by a comparative reading of the earliest descriptions of Muḥammad's confrontation with his Meccan opponents and their later reshaped versions.

[26] Ṭabarī, *Tafsīr*, 27:51. The same view was recorded on the authority of al-Ḍaḥḥāk b. Muzāḥim (Khurāsānī, d. 102/720). See ibid., 52. In another version of Ibn ʿAbbās, the splitting of the moon is linked together with two other events that are said to have already happened: the "defeat of the hosts" (Q 54:45: *sa-yuhzamu l-jamʿu*) and the opening of the "gate of severe chastisement" (Q 23:77: *ḥattā idhā fataḥnā ʿalayhim bāban dhā ʿadhābin shadīd*). See Jalāl al-Dīn al-Suyūṭī, *al-Durr al-manthūr fī l-tafsīr bi-l-maʾthūr* (Cairo: Būlāq, 1869; repr., Beirut: Dār al-Maʿrifa, n.d.), 6:134 (from Ibn Mardawyahi; citation is from the Būlāq edition). These are again two Meccan warnings of eschatological chastisement that the exegetical traditions have transformed into an allusion to the historical disaster that the Quraysh were about to incur in the Battle of Badr (2/624). See the commentaries on Q 23:77; 54:45.

For example, Ibn Isḥāq (d. 150/768), author of one of the earliest available biographies of Muḥammad, has recorded a tradition of Ibn ʿAbbās describing a meeting that took place in the first stages of Muḥammad's public activity in Mecca. The tradition provides a list of Arab leaders of the Meccan opposition to Muḥammad (among them Abū Sufyān, al-Walīd b. al-Mughīra, and Abū Jahl) who have summoned Muḥammad. He arrives full of hope that the leaders have decided to join him, only to find out that they accuse him of a series of transgressions against their most sacred religious and moral values. They offer him money to make him stop preaching or medical treatment for his "madness." Muḥammad replies that he is not expecting a reward because his mission is only to bring good tidings and be a warner. The leaders then say that, because they are short of land and water and livelihood, they would like Muḥammad to call on his lord to remove the mountains that shut them in and straighten out the land for them and open up rivers in it like those in Syria and Iraq. They also request that he resurrect their forefathers for them, and especially Quṣayy, to see if they confirm Muḥammad's religious message. If he can accomplish it, they will know that he is truly God's messenger. But Muḥammad only repeats his former reply; namely, he has been sent only to deliver God's good tidings and warnings. This is also the reply he makes when the leaders demand to see an angel aiding him and making gardens and castles and treasures for him, or to let the heavens be dropped on them in pieces, and so on, because he seems to them an ordinary mortal.[27]

This account is based on the Qurʾānic pattern of the conflict with the unbelievers. Although the latter demand miraculous signs, the Prophet insists that he is a mere mortal messenger of God whose only mission is to warn. But when the story of the same encounter is retold in a later version, Muḥammad's conduct is already decisively different. This version, too, is attributed to Ibn ʿAbbās and is recorded in the *Dalāʾil al-nubuwwa* by Abū Nuʿaym al-Iṣfahānī (d. 430/1038). It is formulated as an occasion of revelation (*sabab al-nuzūl*) of the moon passage. As in the former version, the leaders, whose names are specified, ask for a miraculous sign, but this time they say to him: "If you speak the truth, let the moon be split in two for us, and let one half be above Abū Qubays and the other above Quʿayqiʿān" (these two mountains are near the hills of the Ṣafā and the Marwa, in the vicinity of the Kaʿba). Muḥammad asks

[27] ʿAbd al-Malik b. Hishām, *al-Sīra al-nabawiyya*, ed. Muṣṭafā al-Saqqā, Ibrāhīm al-Abyārī, and ʿAbd al-Ḥāfiẓ Shalabī (Beirut: dār iḥyāʾ al-turāth al-ʿArabī, 1971), 1: 315–18.

God to produce what they have asked for, and the moon is indeed split as they demanded, and Muḥammad tells them: "Behold!"[28]

In the present version, a new Muḥammad emerges who, unlike the one described in Ibn Isḥāq, is no longer the passive persecuted mortal warner who fails to meet the challenge of his foes. Now he is already the capable hero who, when put to the test, immediately produces – with God's help – whatever is requested of him, even a split moon. In this setting, the event is no longer a portent of the Hour but rather a miraculous weapon designed to assist Muḥammad in his earthly confrontations with the unbelievers.

The splitting of the moon is deprived of its eschatological context and functions as a worldly weapon in yet another front of Muḥammad's campaign, the Jewish one. A relatively late tradition to that effect is again traced back to Ibn ʿAbbās. It relates that the Jewish rabbis (*aḥbār al-yahūd*) came to the Prophet and asked for a miracle to believe in him. Thereupon the Prophet asked his Lord for a sign, and then he showed them the moon being split. It became two moons, one above the hill of the Ṣafā and the other above the Marwa (both in the vicinity of the Kaʿba). This lasted from the afternoon until nightfall. The Jews, however, rejected the sign as *siḥr*.[29]

In this version, the miraculous splitting of the moon, though taking place in Mecca, has acquired a typical Medinan setting, because the conflict with the Jews broke out only after Muḥammad's *hijra* to Medina. Thus, the Meccan period has again won a Medinan touch. As for Muḥammad, here, too, he is capable of producing a miracle on demand, whereas the Jews are typically the obstinate unbelievers who will not accept even the clearest sign of Muḥammad's powers. This provides a retrospective justification of their bitter fate.

POLITICAL APPLICATIONS

As is the case with any significant event in Muḥammad's *Sīra*, having served as an eyewitness to the splitting of the moon became a matter of prestige that was employed for political purposes. Furthermore, because the splitting of the moon took place in pre-*hijra* times,

[28] Abū Nuʿaym al-Iṣfahānī, *Dalāʾil al-nubuwwa*, ed. Muḥammad Qalʿajī and ʿAbd al-Barr ʿAbbās (Beirut: dār al-nafāʾis, 1986), 279–80 (no. 209). See also Suyūṭī, *al-Durr al-manthūr*, 6:133 (from Abū Nuʿaym's *Ḥilyat al-awliyāʾ*); Ibn Kathīr, *Bidāya*, 3:119–20.

[29] Suyūṭī, *al-Durr al-manthūr*, 6:133–4 (from Abū Nuʿaym).

a Muslim whose presence on the scene was documented could boast of his early conversion to Islam.

A version that has been applied to the well-known controversy between Sunnīs and Shīʿīs over the succession to the Prophet mentions the name of Abū Bakr, the first caliph after Muḥammad. It is ascribed to Mujāhid (d. 104/722) and relates that, when the moon was split, Muḥammad said: "Abū Bakr, behold!"[30] Thus, the miraculous splitting became a sign designed especially for Abū Bakr to observe, as if to welcome his conversion to Islam and exhibit his senior status among the first Companions, which in turn makes him the most worthy of them to be a caliph after the Prophet.

In contrast, Companions venerated by the Shīʿīs won their own praiseworthy place in the traditions about the moon, one of them being Ḥamza b. ʿAbd al-Muṭṭalib, Muḥammad's paternal uncle. He was considered among the Shīʿīs as the "lord of the martyrs."[31] His name occurs in a tradition recorded by al-Māwardī in which the moon is split only because Ḥamza has asked the Prophet for a sign to strengthen his belief in him. This takes place as soon as Ḥamza has embraced Islam out of rage at Abū Jahl, the leader of the Meccan opposition to Muḥammad.[32]

Moreover, ʿAlī himself, who according to the Shīʿīs ought to have been Muḥammad's first successor, is said to have been present on the scene. In a version recorded in al-Majlisī's *Biḥār al-anwār*, ʿAlī declares, "The moon was split while we were with the Prophet."[33] Another Shīʿī version plants the event in the well-known scene of the meetings at al-ʿAqaba on the eve of Muḥammad's *hijra* from Mecca to Medina. This version appears in the *Tafsīr* of al-Qummī (d. 307/919) and is related on the authority of the *imām* Jaʿfar al-Ṣādiq (Abū ʿAbdallāh, d. 148/765). He says that the people present at the meeting asked Muḥammad to split the moon to prove that God was with him. The angel Gabriel descended and told Muḥammad that God had put everything under his command. So Muḥammad ordered the moon to split apart, and when it did, Muḥammad, together with all "our *shīʿa*," bowed down in gratitude. Thereupon the audience asked that the moon be united again and it was.

30 Ṭabarī, *Tafsīr*, 27:51–2.

31 See Frederik Leemhuis, "Ḥamza b. ʿAbd al-Muṭṭalib," in McAuliffe, *Encyclopaedia of the Qurʾān*, 2:400–1.

32 Māwardī, *Nukat*, 5:409.

33 Muḥammad Bāqir al-Majlisī, *Biḥār al-anwār* (Tehran; repr., Beirut: muʾassasat al-wafāʾ, 1983), 17:350.

Then they asked that the moon be split again and it was.[34] In this version, the terms of the miracle are subject to the whims of the Shīʿīs, which demonstrates their importance in the eyes of God.

MUḤAMMAD AND THE PROPHETS

Post-Qurʾānic Muslims needed a hero who could be venerated not only for the Qurʾān that had been revealed to him but also for his extraordinary personality and unusual abilities. The Qurʾān could not remain Muḥammad's only substitute for miracles performed by previous prophets (see earlier herein the tradition of Abū Hurayra), and similar miraculous signs had to be attributed to him as well. The splitting of the moon was only one of those miracles, and soon numerous others became the subject of traditions that were circulated and recorded in the various sources of *tafsīr*, *sīra*, and *ḥadīth* and later on collected in the compilations of *dalāʾil al-nubuwwa* ("proofs of prophethood"). What makes the splitting of the moon unique, though, is its position as one of the very few miracles that could be read into an explicit Qurʾānic statement.

This miracle eventually served Muslim authors in their attempts to turn Muḥammad into the greatest prophet ever sent by God. For this purpose, they created an inventory of Muḥammad's miracles and undertook a systematic comparison between them and those of the previous prophets, thus proving that his miracles surpassed those of any other prophet. A whole chapter dedicated to such a comparison (*muwāzāt*) is found in al-Khargūshī's (d. 406/1015) *Sharaf al-Muṣṭafā*. Concerning the splitting of the moon, he writes: "They say: 'God gave Moses [the miracle] of the splitting of the sea, and the sea belongs to the kingdom of the earth and the regions of this world.' We say [to them]: '[God] provided Muḥammad with the splitting of the moon, and the moon belongs to the lights of the celestial sphere [*anwār al-falak*], and this is more convincing in the field of miracles [*ablagh fī bāb al-iʿjāz*].'"[35]

Ibn Kathīr (d. 774/1373), too, compares the miracles of Muḥammad with those of the other prophets, and in a chapter dedicated to the miracles of Moses, he refers to the hand of Moses that he inserted into his

[34] ʿAlī b. Ibrāhīm al-Qummī, *al-Tafsīr* (Beirut: muʾassasat al-aʿlā li-l-maṭbūʿāt, 1991), 2:318–19.

[35] Abū Saʿd ʿAbd al-Malik b. Abī ʿUthmān al-Khargūshī, *Sharaf al-muṣṭafā*, ed. Nabīl al-Ghamrī (Mecca: dār al-bashāʾir al-Islāmiyya, 2003), 4:300.

bosom and it came out "white without evil," a miracle that was designated as one of the arguments from God to Pharaoh (Q 28:32). Ibn Kathīr states that this is not as great as the splitting of the moon that God gave to Muḥammad. The moon was split when the Prophet pointed his hand at it, and it was divided in two pieces, one appearing beyond Mount Ḥirā' and the other in front of it. Ibn Kathīr adds that there is no doubt that this miracle is greater and more illustrious and magnificent and clear than any other miracle, and its impact is also broader and more apparent and greater.[36] In Ibn Kathīr's statement, Muḥammad's hand has become a magic instrument that surpasses the white hand of Moses. Not just his hand but his forefinger in particular feature in one of the traditions as causing the moon to split.[37]

These attempts at demonstrating Muḥammad's superiority to Moses indicate that the latter, though a Muslim prophet according to the Qur'ān, retained a Jewish identity in the mind of the believers, which made it necessary to assert his inferiority to Muḥammad and thus bring out the superiority of the Islamic *umma* over the non-Muslim monotheistic communities.

CONCLUSION: THE NEW MUḤAMMAD

The foregoing discussion has detected a progression from signs to miracles, from eschatology to history, from the figurative description to the literal one. These levels add up to the transformation of Muḥammad from a human messenger to a supernatural hero. This process was the result of the popular need of the post-Qur'ānic society for a hero with whom one could identify even after the death of the historical Muḥammad. Muḥammad could become the needed hero thanks to the historical victories that he had won together with his Companions. The military achievements in Medina after the *hijra* and the successful spread of Islam outside of Arabia enabled the Prophet to go on living in the minds of the devoted believers as a new Muḥammad, a person blessed with powers that he still lacked in the Qur'ān and that bridged the gap between him and the previous prophets. This new Muḥammad was eventually read into the pre-*hijra* history of the Prophet, as seen in the exegesis of the moon passage. There he no longer has to apologize for being just a plain warner; with the miracles that God enables him to

36 Ibn Kathīr, *Bidāya*, 6:277.
37 Ālūsī, *Rūḥ al-maʿānī*, 27:75.

perform, he can meet any challenge and even make the moon split on demand.

This new Muḥammad became the one on whom the Muslim scholars achieved consensus, and as put already by Goldziher:

> It is one of the most curious phenomena in the development of Islam to observe the ease with which orthodox theology also adapts itself to the needs of popular belief, though this entails open contradiction to the unambiguous teaching of the Koran. The power of *ijmāʿ* here scored one of its biggest triumphs in the whole system of Islam, insofar as the belief of the people succeeded in penetrating into the canonical conception of the Prophet, and, so to speak, forcing it to make him into a fortuneteller, worker of miracles, and magician.[38]

In their yearning for a new Muḥammad, the Muslim exegetes, Sunnīs and Shīʿīs alike, were determined to maintain the historicity of the splitting of the moon and preserve its literal sense. They disapproved of any attempt at a rationalistic interpretation of the Qurʾānic moon passage and deplored whoever tried to suggest as much. For example, al-Māwardī states that the opinion of the majority of the public (*al-jumhūr*) that accords with the manifest meaning of the Qurʾān (*ẓāhir al-tanzīl*) is that the moon was split in Muḥammad's time.[39] The Shīʿī exegete Muḥammad b. al-Ḥasan al-Ṭūsī (d. 460/1067) states that whoever denied the historicity of the splitting of the moon and interpreted the moon passage as referring to the eschatological future – as did al-Ḥasan al-Baṣrī, and as maintained by the scientist Abū Zayd al-Balkhī (d. 322/934) – has abandoned the *ẓāhir* of the Qurʾān (i.e., its manifest meaning), because *inshaqqa* clearly stands for the past. Al-Ṭūsī also asserts that the Muslims are unanimous that the moon was split apart, and no notice should be taken of whoever denied it.[40] The Ṣūfī-oriented exegete Abū l-Qāsim al-Qushayrī (d. 465/1072) states, too, that the Muslims are unanimous that the moon was split.[41]

38 Ignaz Goldziher, *Muslim Studies (Muhammedanische Studien)*, ed. and trans. S. M. Stern and C. R. Barber (London: George Allen and Unwin, 1967–1971), 2:261.

39 Māwardī, *Nukat*, 5:409.

40 Muḥammad b. al-Ḥasan al-Ṭūsī, *al-Tabyān fī tafsīr al-Qurʾān*, ed. Aḥmad al-ʿĀmilī (Beirut: dār iḥyāʾ al-turāth al-ʿArabī, n.d.), 9:443.

41 Abū l-Qāsim al-Qushayrī, *Laṭāʾif al-ishārāt*, ed. Ibrāhīm Basyūnī (Cairo: al-hayʾa l-Miṣriyya l-ʿāmma li-l-taʾlīf wa-l-nashr, 1971), 6:61.

Under the impact of this consensus, the previously mentioned tradition of ʿIkrima, which implies that the verb *inshaqqa* is a figurative representation of a lunar eclipse, is also rejected. The Muslim scholars are convinced that *inshaqqa* denotes literal splitting, and therefore Ibn Kathīr defines ʿIkrima's tradition as a "peculiar exposition" (*siyāq gharīb*). He maintains that an actual splitting did occur, which at best may have coincided with an eclipse of the moon.[42] He also reports that the split moon was observed in India and that a memorial monument was erected there, bearing the date of the event.[43] As late as the nineteenth century, al-Ālūsī (d. 1270/1853) declares that "the philosophers" have denied the splitting from the very outset but that their arguments are "weaker than the house of a spider."[44]

Today "scientific" proofs of the splitting based on telescopic photos of the moon's surface are provided at various Islamic Web sites, and the controversy over the validity of these "proofs" still goes on.[45] This testifies to the unceasing urge of generations of pious Muslims to sustain Muḥammad's superiority over the rest of the prophets.

Further reading

Gril, Denis. "Miracles." In McAuliffe, *Encyclopaedia of the Qur'ān*, 3:392–9.

Horovitz, Josef. "The Growth of the Mohammed Legend." *Muslim World* 10 (1920): 269–78. (Reprinted in Uri Rubin, ed. *The Life of Muḥammad*. Vol. 4 of *The Formation of the Classical Islamic World*. Aldershot, U.K.: Ashgate, 1998.)

Khān, Gabriel Mandel. "Magic." In McAuliffe, *Encyclopaedia of the Qur'ān*, 3:245–52.

McAuliffe, Jane Dammen, ed. *Encyclopaedia of the Qur'ān*. 6 vols. Leiden: Brill, 2001–2006.

Nagel, Tilman. *Mohammed – Leben und Legende*. Munich: Oldenbourg Wissenschaftsverlag, 2008.

Netton, Ian Richard. "Nature as Signs." In *McAuliffe, Encyclopaedia of the Qur'ān*, 3:528–36.

Rubin, Uri. *The Eye of the Beholder: The Life of Muḥammad as Viewed by the Early Muslims (A Textual Analysis)*. Princeton, NJ: Darwin Press, 1995.

"Muḥammad." In McAuliffe, *Encyclopaedia of the Qur'ān*, 3:440–58.

42 Ibn Kathīr, *Bidāya*, 6:76.

43 Ibid., 3:120; 6:77.

44 Abū l-Faḍl Shihāb al-Dīn al-Ālūsī, *Rūḥ al-maʿānī* (repr., Beirut: dār iḥyāʾ al-turāth al-ʿArabī, n.d.), 27:76.

45 A Google search under "<انشقاق القمر>" yields the relevant results. See, e.g., http://ar.wikipedia.org/wiki/%D8%A7%D9%86%D8%B4%D9%82%D8%A7%D9%82_%D8%A7%D9%84%D9%82%D9%85%D8%B1.

"Prophets and Prophethood." In McAuliffe, *Encyclopaedia of the Qur'ān*, 4:289–307.
Schimmel, Annemarie. *And Muhammad Is His Messenger: The Veneration of the Prophet in Islamic Piety*. Chapel Hill: University of North Carolina Press, 1985.
Smith, Jane I. "Eschatology." *In McAuliffe, Encyclopaedia of the Qur'ān*, 2:44–54.

3 Glimpses of Muḥammad's Medinan decade

MICHAEL LECKER

Over the centuries, Muslims have compiled a large number of biographies about the Prophet Muḥammad, including both mainstream biographies and less well-known or almost-forgotten ones. However, no meaningful study of Muḥammad's life can be carried out on the basis of biographies alone, because valuable evidence is often found in other sources such as Qur'ān exegesis and collections of poetry.

From the very beginning, the story of Muḥammad's life has been a battlefield of competing claims. The huge literary output about him is made up of thousands of conflicting accounts originating with the Companions of Muḥammad and their offspring, who were eager to secure for themselves and their fathers a place in history. We do not know why a certain account was accepted in the mainstream literature while other accounts were pushed aside. Conflicts and contradictions also abound because early Islamic society was divided along tribal, political, ideological, and regional lines, and hence cannot be expected to have adopted a unified version regarding Muḥammad's life. Members of northern and southern tribes (according to Arabian genealogical theory), Umayyads, ʿAbbāsids, Shīʿīs, Khārijīs, Syrians, Medinans, and Iraqis had their own versions regarding events in Muḥammad's life, not to mention legal and exegetical prejudices that were also at work. For example, it is unrealistic to expect Muḥammad's tribe (the Quraysh of Mecca that rejected him) and the *anṣār* (the "helpers" of Medina who sheltered him) to preserve the same versions of Muḥammad's *hijra*. Unsurprisingly, the accounts of the *hijra* found in the biographies can be traced predominantly to these *anṣār*.

Historians usually consider conflicts and contradictions as an obstacle, but they are also a blessing. Conflicts shed light on the social and political context in which the biographies were created by pointing out disputed matters and identifying the parties involved.

APOLOGETIC, SELF-CENSORSHIP, AND COMBINED REPORTS

Our source material becomes even more challenging when we take into account several context-related characteristics. Apologetic is fairly widespread, indicating that the society in which the early biographies came into being was keenly interested in how Muḥammad's followers and adversaries were portrayed. For example, as I have discussed elsewhere, relatives of the Medinan opposition leader Abū Qays ibn al-Aslat (d. 622 CE) were very creative in "correcting" his image.[1]

Self-censorship similarly points to the social and political context of the early biographies. In his introduction to the biography of the Prophet, Ibn Hishām (d. 218/833) admits that he censored materials received from Ibn Isḥāq (d. 150/767), "the mention of which was abominable," and those materials that might have distressed some people.[2]

Also, combined reports belong here. A combined report is created by pasting together passages on a certain event taken from several often-conflicting accounts. As Ignaz Goldziher has shown, Ibn Shihāb al-Zuhrī (d. 124/742) applied this technique in the generation that preceded Ibn Isḥāq to a sensitive account: it dealt with the scandal known in Sunnī tradition as the lie (*al-ifk*), namely the rumors about an alleged relationship between Muḥammad's young wife ʿĀʾisha and a certain Bedouin.[3] Admittedly, those who transmitted historical accounts had more lenient standards on transmitting reports than, say, the doctors of law; yet the combined-reports technique created new accounts altogether and made it possible to circumvent passages that might have distressed some people.

Conflicts, contradictions, apologetic, self-censorship, and the use of combined reports indicate that Muḥammad's early biographies were products of their time, as were, of course, the informants and compilers who created them. These persons did not adhere to the principles and methods employed by modern historians. Chronology, the sequence of events, and the integrity of their accounts were less important for them than was the message they sought to convey. In other words,

1 See appendix B in Michael Lecker, *Muslims, Jews and Pagans: Studies on Early Islamic Medina* (Leiden: E. J. Brill, 1995), 154–5.

2 This poses an intriguing challenge for future researchers, who may be able to determine what Ibn Hishām omitted by employing sources that quote Ibn Isḥāq's uncensored accounts, thereby clarifying the difference in the attitudes of the two compilers.

3 Gautier H. A. Juynboll, "Ṣafwān b. al-Muʿaṭṭal," in *Encyclopedia of Islam*, ed. Hamilton A. R. Gibb et al., 2nd ed. (Leiden: E. J. Brill, 1960–2004), 8:819; Everett K. Rowson, "Gossip," in *Encyclopaedia of the Qurʾān*, ed. Jane Dammen McAuliffe (Leiden: E. J. Brill, 2001–2006), 2:343–4.

Muḥammad's biographies should not be classified as history books. Rather, they are repositories of accounts arranged around certain themes. However, after a careful scrutiny and in combination with evidence from many other sources, these accounts can sometimes guide us toward a better understanding of Muḥammad's life.

From a Western historian's point of view, the biographies of Muḥammad have serious shortcomings: the amount of solid facts they include is small, and they rarely enlighten us with general overviews of the state of affairs at any given point in time. This confers on the biographies an unrealistic air, as if their creators deliberately detached them from the historical realities on the ground. The solid facts and general overviews were already missing in the original accounts that lie at the basis of the biographies and could not be added at a later stage because their compilers only sifted and edited the original accounts.

But it must also be noted that, among Muslims, the popularity of Muḥammad's biographies is based not on the historical evidence that they include but on their didactic, edifying, propagandistic, and entertaining features that address the needs of readers and listeners on various educational, psychological, and artistic levels. Had it not been for those features, the biographies would have been forgotten or marginalized long ago.

THE NEW POLITICS

Arabian society at the time of Muḥammad was tribal. Several tribes are particularly prominent in Islamic history – not through their military strength or battlefield exploits but through their role in Muḥammad's life. His own tribe, Quraysh, probably controlled Mecca in the decades preceding the *hijra*, although it was not necessarily the largest tribe there. In Medina there were six main tribes. The Balī tribe (of the tribal federation Quḍāʿa) was the main influence among the earlier Arab settlers. Many of the Balī were converted to Judaism during their long sojourn with the Jews. At the time of Muḥammad, the Balī groups that were scattered throughout Medina were the clients of the more recent Arab settlers, namely the brother tribes of Aws and Khazraj or the *anṣār*. The Khazraj that were stronger than the Aws were Muḥammad's relatives – a basic fact of immense importance in his life: his grandfather ʿAbd al-Muṭṭalib was the son of a Khazrajī woman. Starting with the agreement between Muḥammad and the *anṣār* on the eve of his *hijra* and throughout his Medinan period, the Khazraj provided Muḥammad with much more support than the Aws did.

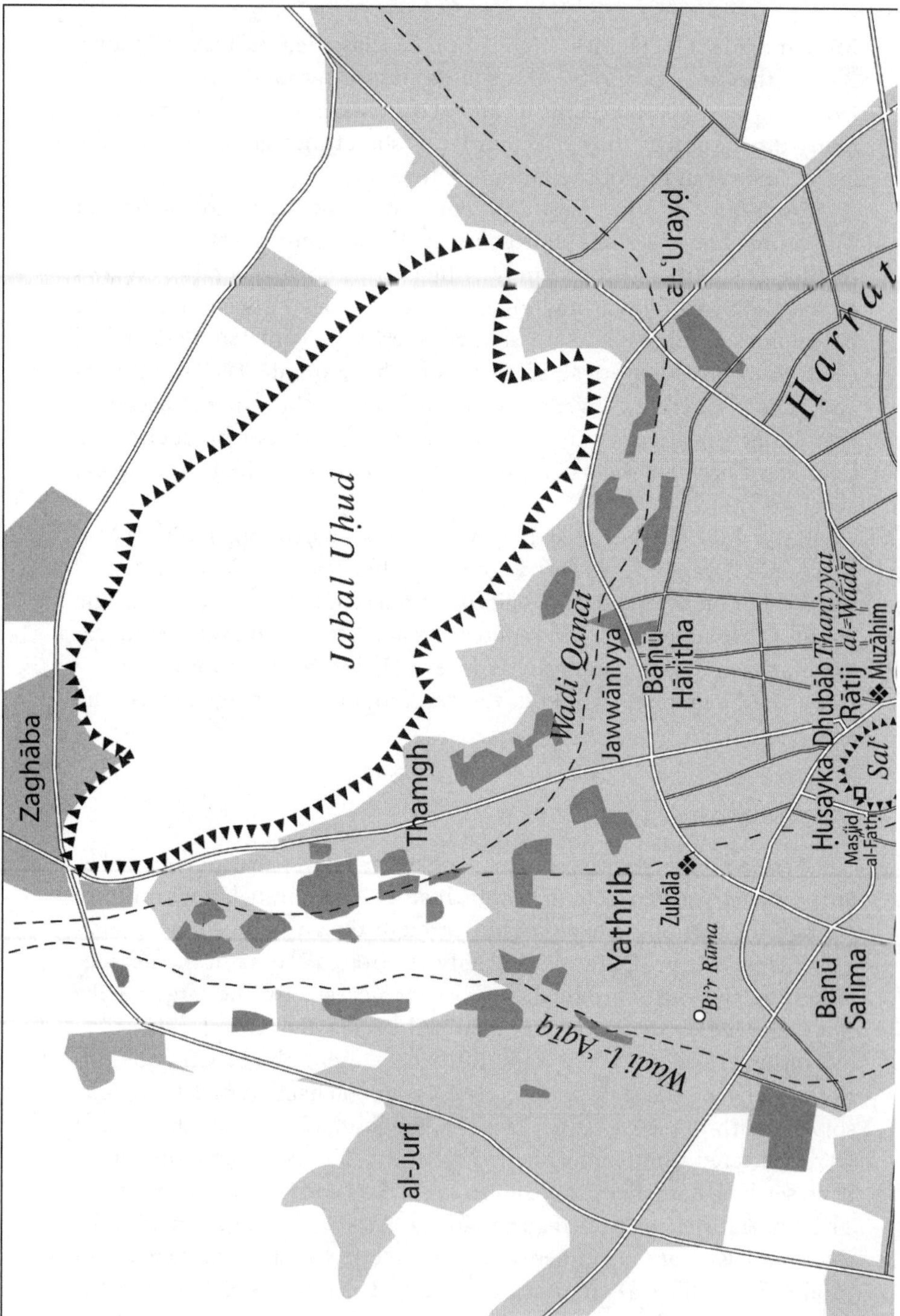
Zaghāba
Thamgh
Jabal Uḥud
Wadi Qanāt
Jawwāniyya
Banū Ḥāritha
al-ʿUrayḍ
Ḥarrat
Thaniyyat al-Wadāʿ
Muzāḥim
Dhubāb
Rātij
Salʿ
Ḥusayka
Masjid al-Fatḥ
Yathrib
Zubāla
Biʾr Rūma
Banū Salima
Wadi l-ʿAqīq
al-Jurf

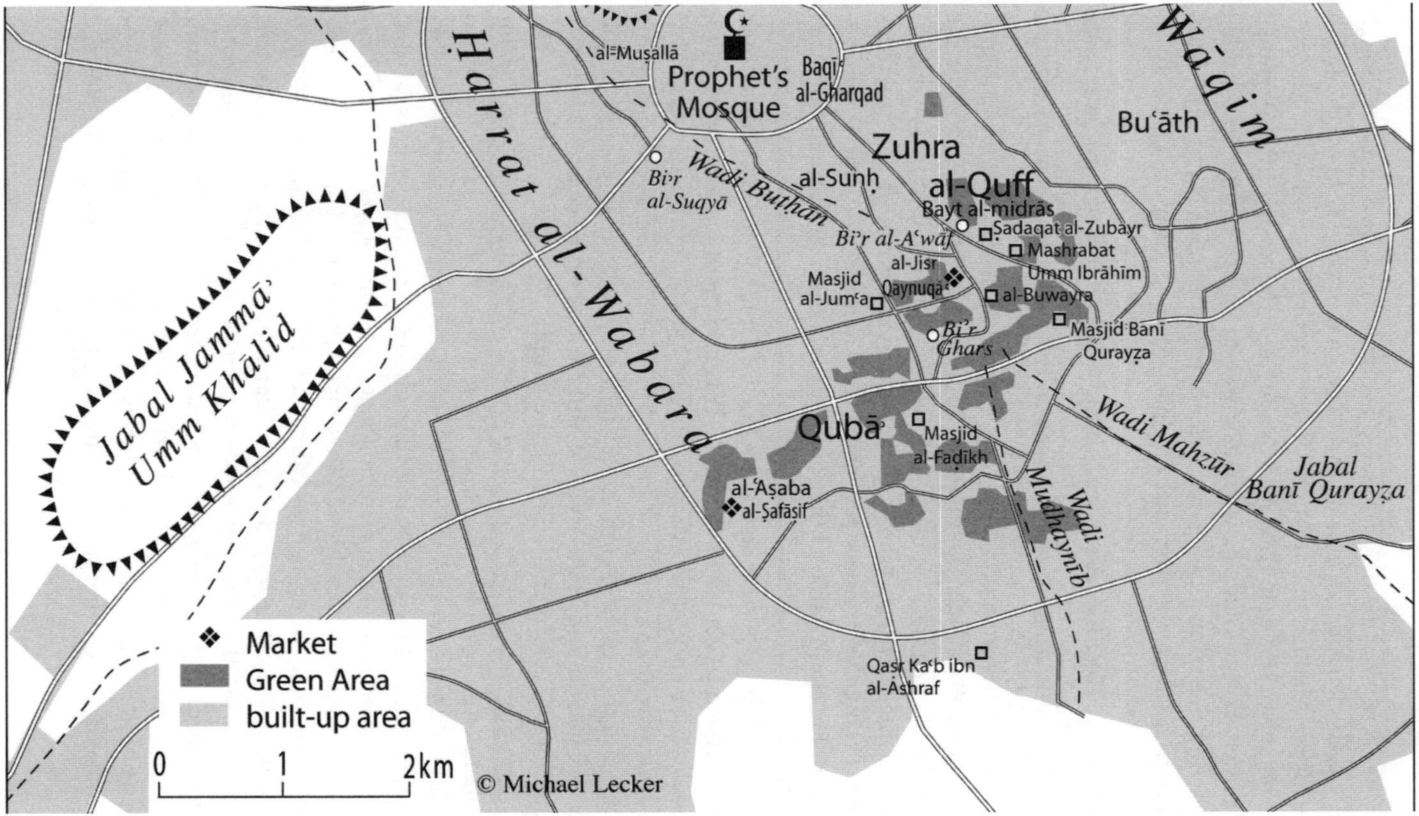

Map 3. A map of Medina, showing both modern roads and the sites of settlements in Muḥammad's time.

As shown in this map,[4] Medina is divided into two distinct though not clearly demarcated areas: Lower Medina, or the *sāfila*, in the north and Upper Medina, or the *ʿāliya*, in the south. The Arab tribe Khazraj, one branch of the Arab tribe Aws (Nabīt), and the Jewish tribe Qaynuqāʿ inhabited Lower Medina, whereas three branches of the Aws (called Aws Allāh) and the two large Jewish tribes Banū l-Naḍīr and Banū Qurayẓa lived on the east side of Upper Medina, or more precisely, in the case of the former, between Upper and Lower Medina. A fifth branch of the Aws (ʿAmr ibn ʿAwf) lived in the town of Qubāʾ on the west side of Upper Medina. The Naḍīr, and probably other tribes as well, owned property such as fields, orchards, and fortresses in other parts of Medina.

Among the many Jewish tribes that lived in Medina, we can similarly discern an older population and a more recent one. Most of the tribes, including the large tribe of Qaynuqāʿ, belonged to the older Jewish settlement, whereas the Naḍīr and Qurayẓa were more recent settlers besides being the strongest Jewish tribes. Their position among the Jewish tribes is comparable to that of the Aws and Khazraj among the Arab tribes.

It has been argued that, even before he came to Medina, Muḥammad had intended to get rid of the Jews. This argument is based on the presumed occurrence of the word *yahūd*, or "Jews," in the account of his agreement with the *anṣār* before the *hijra*. But the text is corrupt at this point, and the *yahūd* do not appear in the account at all (Arabic philology still plays a role in the study of Muḥammad's life because the texts – including the edited ones – are often corrupt).

The previously mentioned agreement with the *anṣār* secured for Muḥammad a basis for preaching his religion. But he did not come to Medina as an arbiter and peacemaker between the two *anṣār* tribes, Aws and Khazraj, as the two tribes had already started a process of reconciliation before his arrival and were no longer in a state of war. Although it is true that several private blood vengeance accounts had not yet been settled, the general situation was calm. Nevertheless, Muḥammad's struggle to gain control of Medina was longer and harder than some assume, because he faced formidable opposition from the Jews on the one hand and the pagan tribal leaders on the other hand. The political and military position of the main Jewish tribes is often misunderstood because of a garbled passage that misled Julius Wellhausen and many others in his wake. In its corrupt form, the passage has it that when Muḥammad

4 The map was drawn by Mrs. Tamar Soffer. I wish to express my gratitude to Daoud Stephen Casewit for his invaluable comments on an earlier draft of the map.

came to Medina, the Muslims were the dominant military factor as the owners of weapons and fortresses, whereas the Jews were the clients of the Aws and Khazraj. In its correct form, the passage states that the Jews were the owners of fortresses and weapons and the allies (not the clients) of the Aws and Khazraj.[5]

The Naḍīr and Qurayẓa blocked the expansion of Islam into the east side of Upper Medina. Whatever setbacks the two tribes suffered in the generations that preceded the *hijra*, by Muḥammad's time they had regained their former strength or most of it. This is demonstrated by the Battle of Buʿāth several years before the *hijra* in which the Aws, following their alliance with the Naḍīr and Qurayẓa, had the upper hand over the stronger Khazraj. The latter had been weakened, it is true, by the withdrawal of their strongest leader ʿAbdallāh ibn Ubayy.

Muḥammad also faced the hostility of tribal leaders from both the Aws and Khazraj. But the lack of internal solidarity among the *anṣār* gave him some maneuvering space: there were conflicts between the Aws and Khazraj (who were no longer in a state of war), among their branches, and as we shall see, even within the branches themselves. Also with regard to the Jews, Muḥammad had some maneuvering space as a result of conflicts between the Naḍīr and the Qurayẓa.

One of the tribal leaders hostile to Muḥammad was the previously mentioned ʿAbdallāh ibn Ubayy. Prior to the *hijra*, he had probably been the strongest leader among the Khazraj. A somewhat-vague account has it that he was nearly crowned as king (i.e., of the Khazraj). He was probably backed by the Jews who were grateful to him for his withdrawal from the Battle of Buʿāth.

In all, Muḥammad's takeover of Medina or of most of it – to the extent that one can speak of a takeover in tribal society – took several years. He achieved this by neutralizing its social and political system for a period that was long enough for him to gain the upper hand over his Jewish and pagan rivals. The agreement misleadingly referred to in Orientalist jargon as the Constitution of Medina (see its translation in the appendix to this chapter) was a major breakthrough. This agreement, concluded during his first year in Medina, was basically between the Medinan *anṣār* and the Meccan *muhājirūn*.[6] It has two sections, one addressing the *muʾminūn* (literally, "believers") and the other addressing the Jewish participants whose rights and duties were different from those

[5] See, e.g., Ibn Shabba, *Akhbār al-Madīna*, ed. ʿAlī Muḥammad Dandal and Yāsīn Bayān (Beirut: Dār al-kutub al-ʿilmiyya, 1417/1996), 1:252.

[6] The identity of the participants is further defined by the precise meaning of the terms *muʾmin* and *muslim*.

of the *mu'minūn*. The main Jewish tribes Naḍīr, Qurayẓa, and Qaynuqāʿ are not listed among the participants for the simple reason that they were not part of it. Muḥammad did conclude treaties with the main tribes, but they were mere nonbelligerency treaties. Among the Jewish participants, there was only one independent Jewish tribe, the Thaʿlaba ibn al-Fiṭyawn that lived in Zuhra, the town of the Naḍīr (though their participation did not spare them from expulsion some two years later). The other Jewish groups listed in the agreement were small groups of obscure origin.

On the face of it, the agreement upheld the tribal system of Medina. But in reality, families – and needless to say, tribal groups – were split between those who followed Muḥammad (i.e., the *mu'minūn*) and all the others. For example, the agreement stipulated regarding blood vengeance – the very cement of the *ʿaṣaba* or the nuclear group made of male agnates: "A *mu'min* will not kill a *mu'min* in retaliation for a non-believer and will not aid a non-believer against a *mu'min*" (clause 15).

The *mu'minūn* are hereby separated from their own brothers who had not yet become *mu'minūn*. The old blood vengeance bonds with their male agnates were replaced by bonds with their fellow *mu'minūn* regardless of their tribal affiliation. This was a major turning point. If a *mu'min* does not kill a *mu'min* from another tribe to retaliate the murder of his own brother who was still a nonbeliever, this means that Muḥammad's community provided its members with far more than common belief. Each new *mu'min* weakened his tribal group and of course its leader. The tribal leaders who were Muḥammad's rivals were unprepared for this challenge, and indeed for the new politics introduced by the farsighted prophet. Julius Wellhausen and many in his wake assumed that the agreement included the whole population of Medina, but in reality, at the time of its conclusion, most of the people of Medina, both Jews and pagans, were not part of it.

PEARLS IN A VAST SEA

Among the thousands of details, we sometimes come across facts of crucial importance – pearls in a vast sea – which can help form a sound foundation for the study of Muḥammad's life, together with a large number of facts regarding markets, orchards, fields, fortresses – and, of course, biographical details relating to the people surrounding Muḥammad. One of these pearls concerns Muḥammad's acquisition of land in Medina.

Shortly after his arrival at Medina (still called Yathrib at that time), Muḥammad became the owner of an orchard called al-Ḥashāshīn and a large plot of land in the town of Zuhra. Zuhra is described elsewhere as the town of the Jewish tribe Naḍīr,[7] although it was also inhabited by other groups. Zuhra and other towns in Medina were almost forgotten after the advent of Islam because their plots were divided among Muḥammad's Companions from among the *muhājirūn* of Quraysh and their offspring, and hence became called after their new owners. Muḥammad reportedly found the land in Zuhra that had been the property of people from the towns of Rātij and Ḥusayka. The former owners had been expelled before Muḥammad's arrival, leaving behind them a large tract of land. More precisely, most of them had been expelled shortly before his arrival, whereas some of them relinquished their land after his arrival. This indicates that the developments that followed the *hijra* possibly increased the pressures on Muḥammad's neighbors, who had to choose between some form of cooperation with him and exile.

Typically, we do not owe this detailed account of Muḥammad's land in Zuhra to the acumen of a medieval historian but to ancillary evidence found in a dispute between the *anṣār* of Medina and the *muhājirūn* of Quraysh regarding the first charitable endowment (*ṣadaqa*) in Islam, namely whether it belonged to Muḥammad or to the future caliph ʿUmar. The details about Muḥammad's land are adduced to support the claim of the *muhājirūn* that the first endowment was ʿUmar's: Muḥammad had given ʿUmar a plot of land, and the latter bought an adjacent plot of land from certain Jews. Muḥammad told ʿUmar – who obviously owned a large estate – to declare his property a charitable endowment.[8]

Muḥammad's orchard al-Ḥashāshīn can be associated with two Jewish tribes. The Qaynuqāʿ had two fortresses near al-Ḥashāshīn,[9] but it may have belonged to the Naḍīr: it is reported that the orchards that Muḥammad took from the Naḍīr were Ḥashāshīn, Mazāriʿ, and Ibil.[10]

7 Thaʿālibī, *Tafsīr* (*al-Jawāhir al-ḥisān fī tafsīr al-qur'ān*) (Beirut: al-Aʿlamī, n.d.), 9:267: "wa-kānū bi-qarya lahum yuqālu lahā Zuhra."

8 Samhūdī, *Wafā' al-wafā*, ed. Qāsim al-Sāmarrā'ī (London: al-Furqān, 1422/2001), 4:192: "sa'alnā ʿan awwal man ḥabbasa fī l-islām," etc.

9 Samhūdī, *Wafā'*, 4:221. See also p. 239, s.v. "Ḥishshān: wa-l-Ḥashāshīn bi-ṣīghat al-jamʿ ayḍan bi-manāzil Banī Qaynuqāʿ." In previous studies of mine, I have vocalized this place-name with a *shadda*, al-Ḥashshāshīn. I now realize that the *shadda* is probably superfluous.

10 Samhūdī, *Wafā'*, 3:406: "kānat amwāl rasūli llāh ṣlʿm min amwāl Banī l-Naḍīr Ḥashāshīn wa-Mazāriʿ wa-Ibil." The place-name Ibil can also be read as Ublā with an *alif maqṣūra*. Its location is unknown. The Mazāriʿ ("fields") were probably located in al-Jurf, where several *mazāriʿ* were called after their Muslim owners; Samhūdī, *Wafā'*, 5:452 (index). This assumption is supported by corroborating evidence: as

Although some ambiguity regarding the former owners of al-Ḥashāshīn remains,[11] an association with the Naḍīr or the Qaynuqāʿ is possible because al-Quff, the town of the Qaynuqāʿ in which the *bayt al-midrās* (the Jewish "house of study") was located, was close to Zuhra, the town of the Naḍīr. Zuhra must have been a large town with a bustling business center: it reportedly had three hundred Jewish goldsmiths (*ṣāʾigh*).[12] This detail is yet another pearl that sheds light on a reality that is otherwise hidden from us because non-Arabs or non-Muslims tend to be invisible in the literature and because Muḥammad's economic activities were not of great interest for the medieval scholars who recorded and transmitted the accounts of his life.

we shall see, Muḥammad had a field in al-Jurf, and the Naḍīr leader Kaʿb ibn al-Ashraf had a field there: he refers in a verse to *baṭn al-Jurf* or "al-Jurf Valley" as his property; al-Suhaylī, *al-Rawḍ al-unuf*, ed. ʿAbd al-Raḥmān al-Wakīl (Cairo: Dār al-Kutub al-ʿIlmiyya, 1387/1967–1390/1970), 5:416. Indeed, Yāqūt, *Muʿjam al-buldān*, s.v. "al-Jurf," links Kaʿb's verse to this specific place. In al-Maqrīzī, *Kitāb al-mawāʿiẓ wa-l-iʿtibār fī dhikr al-khiṭaṭ wa-l-āthār*, ed. Ayman Fuad Sayyid (London: Furqān, 1422/2002), 1:257, l. 20, we find: "aqṭaʿa rasūlu llāh ṣlʿm l-Zubayr arḍan fīhā nakhl min amwāl Banī l-Naḍīr wa-dhakara annahā arḍ yuqālu lahā l-Jurf" (from Hishām ibn ʿUrwa [ibn al-Zubayr], from his father). But the text is probably garbled: it was Abū Bakr who granted al-Jurf to al-Zubayr; al-Balādhurī, *Futūḥ*, ed. M. J. de Goeje (Leiden: E. J. Brill, 1863–1866), 21: "anna l-nabī ṣlʿm aqṭaʿa l-Zubayr arḍan min amwāl Banī l-Naḍīr fihā nakhl wa-anna Abā Bakr aqṭaʿa l-Zubayr l-Jurf" (from Hishām ibn ʿUrwa, from his father). See also Ibn Saʿd, *al-Ṭabaqāt al-kubrā* (Beirut: Dār Ṣādir-Dār Bayrūt, 1380/1960–1388/1968), 3:104.

11 As we have just seen, Muḥammad's land in Zuhra had belonged to people from the towns of Rātij and Ḥusayka.

12 See also Majd al-Dīn al-Fīrūzābādī, *al-Maghānim al-muṭāba fī maʿālim Ṭāba*, ed. Ḥamad al-Jāsir, Riyadh: Yamāma, 1389/1969: Zuhra: "mawḍiʿ bi-l-Madīna bayna l-ḥarra wa-l-sāfila qāla l-Zubayr ibn Bakkār kānat Zuhra aʿẓam qarya bi-l-Madīna wa-kāna bihā jummāʿ mina l-yahūd wa-qad bādū wa-kāna fīhā thalāthumiʾat ṣāʾigh." Ibn al-Najjār, *al-Durra al-thamīna fī taʾrīkh al-Madīna*, ed. Muḥammad Zaynhum Muḥammad ʿAzb (Cairo: Maktaba al-Thaqāfa al-Dīniyya, 1416/1995), 35, has "wa-kānat Zuhra min aʿẓam qurā l-Madīna wa-kāna fīhā thalāthumiʾat ṣāniʿ mina l-yahūd." But instead of *ṣāniʿ*, read: *ṣāʾigh*. Ibn al-Najjār is quoted in M. Gil, *In the Kingdom of Ishmael* (Tel Aviv: Tel Aviv University, 1997) (in Hebrew), 1:10 (English version, *Jews in Islamic countries in the Middle Ages* (Leiden: E. J. Brill, 2004), 10. In both books, read *ṣāʾigh* instead of *ṣāniʿ*. See also Lecker, "Muḥammad at Medina: A Geographical Approach," *Jerusalem Studies in Arabic and Islam* 6 (1985): 41. Cf. G. W. Heck, "Gold Mining in Arabia and the Rise of the Islamic State," *Journal of the Economic and Social History of the Orient* 41 (1999): 371, who fails to mention the common denominator of the three groups of craftsmen he lists: "Al-Samhūdī indicates that there were more [? – M. L.] than three hundred jewelry smiths in the Medinese suburb of al-Zuhrah alone. Indeed, they and the goldsmiths of Fadak and Khaybar were regionally renowned for the quality of their craftsmanship." It must be added that the names Zayyid b. Thābit and Ḥuwayṭib b. ʿAbd al-Ghazza that appear earlier on the same page are corrupt – this is quite unusual in a high-quality journal.

Zuhra almost disappeared from the literature after the advent of Islam. Yet a rare reference to it as a town that was still there after the *hijra* is found in a tradition of the type called "the proofs of the veracity of Muḥammad's prophethood" (*dalāʾil al-nubuwwa*): a *jinnī* is quoted as saying that when Muḥammad left his hometown and came to the land of palm trees and fortresses (*nakhīl wa-āṭām*, i.e., Medina), he was between Zuhra and Yathrib.[13] Yathrib in this context is the town of Yathrib, not the cluster of towns that was also called Yathrib before Islam.

Besides the palm orchard al-Ḥashāshīn, Muḥammad had a field in al-Jurf that is located in the ʿAqīq Valley northwest of Medina.[14] Again, we are indebted for this detail not to the acumen of a medieval historian but to the dispute regarding the legitimacy of handling agriculture as opposed to *jihād*: those who supported agriculture referred to the fact that Muḥammad himself was engaged in it. On the whole, the sources are not generous with regard to details about practical aspects of Muḥammad's activity, which makes research even more challenging. One thing is certain: the more we learn about the geography of pre- and early Islamic Medina, the better we understand the evidence about Muḥammad's life.

In addition to landed property, diplomacy, and politics, there are also small details about Muḥammad's trade activities that have been preserved and ought to be given greater priority in the study of his life. After all, Muḥammad was a former merchant, and several of his leading Companions were famous for their business skills. In particular,

[13] Ibn Kathīr, *al-Bidāya wa-l-nihāya* (Beirut: Dār iḥyāʾ al-turāth al-ʿArabī, 1412/1992–1413/1993), 2:425–6; "between Zuhra and Yathrib" also appears correctly in Suyūṭī, *al-Khaṣāʾiṣ al-kubrā*, ed. Harrās (Cairo: Dār al-kutub al-ḥadītha, 1387/1967), 1:465. "Between Mecca and Yathrib" in Ibn Ḥajar, *al-Iṣāba fī tamyīz al-ṣaḥāba*, ed. al-Bijāwī (Cairo: Dār nahḍat Miṣr, 1392/1972), 3:309, is *lectio facilior*.

[14] M. J. Kister, "Land Property and *Jihād*," *Journal of the Economic and Social History of the Orient* 34 (1991): 300–1; Sarakhsī, *Sharḥ kitāb al-kasb li-l-Shaybānī*, ed. ʿAbd al-Fattāḥ Ghudda (Ḥalab: Maktab al-maṭbūʿāt al-Islāmiyya, 1417/1997), 80: "wa-ʾzdaraʿa rasūlu llāh ṣlʿm bi-l-Jurf" (the Messenger of Allāh raised seed-produce for himself in al-Jurf); Sarakhsī, *al-Mabsūṭ* (Cairo: Maṭbaʿat al-saʿāda, [1324]–1331), 23:2. The early historian of Medina, Ibn Zabāla, reports that Muḥammad's field (*mazraʿa*) in al-Jurf was called al-Zayn; Samhūdī, *Wafāʾ*, 4:313. The verb *izdaraʿa* is linked elsewhere to irrigation by camels, and one assumes that they were also used by Muḥammad; see Balādhurī, *Ansāb al-ashrāf*, 4:i, ed. Iḥsān ʿAbbās (Beirut 1400/1979, 516): "kāna Marwān qadi zdaraʿa bi-l-Madīna fī khilāfat ʿUthmān ʿalā thalāthīna jamalan." The Companion ʿAbd al-Raḥmān ibn ʿAwf employed twenty camels to irrigate his land in al-Jurf, and the produce sufficed to feed his family for a whole year; Ibn ʿAsākir, *Taʾrīkh madīnat Dimashq*, ed. al-ʿAmrawī (Beirut: Dār al-fikr, 1415/1995–1419/1998), 35:305: "wa-kāna yazraʿu bi-l-Jurf ʿalā ʿishrīna nāḍiḥan wa-kāna yudkhilu qūt ahlihi min dhālika sana." Earlier in the same report, read *al-Naqīʿ* instead of *al-Baqīʿ*. For ʿAbd al-Raḥmān working in his field in al-Jurf, see Ibn ʿAsākir, *Dimashq*, 68:119–20.

Muḥammad's relationship with Jewish tribes in Medina is illuminated through paying attention to these details. Before the expulsion of the Jewish Qaynuqāʿ in 624, Muḥammad had made an attempt to create a market of his own within their market. His attempt was frustrated by the intervention of the Naḍīr leader Kaʿb ibn al-Ashraf. (We already know that the towns of these Jewish tribes were adjacent to one another.) The details regarding the market of Muḥammad shed light on Muḥammad's economic strategy. One of the accounts relevant to this affair runs as follows:

> When the Messenger of God wanted to establish for Medina a market [i.e., a market of his own; Medina already had several markets], he came to the market of the Banū Qaynuqāʿ, stamped its ground with his foot and said: "This is your market, let it not be narrowed and let no rent be taken in it."[15]

The competition with the Qaynuqāʿ must be associated with their siege and expulsion from Medina following Muḥammad's victory over the Meccans in the Battle of Badr (2/624). The Qaynuqāʿ were more vulnerable than the Naḍīr and Qurayẓa on two accounts: they lived in Lower Medina, where Muḥammad established himself among his relatives and close supporters from the Khazraj, and they had an alliance with one of the Khazraj branches, namely the ʿAwf ibn al-Khazraj.

The Qaynuqāʿ affair offers a rare insight into Medinan politics at the time of Muḥammad. Two tribal leaders of the ʿAwf ibn al-Khazraj were the guarantors of the alliance with the Qaynuqāʿ. One of them was the previously mentioned ʿAbdallāh ibn Ubayy and the other was the younger ʿUbāda ibn al-Ṣāmit. The two were the leaders of subgroups within the ʿAwf ibn al-Khazraj. ʿUbāda's announcement that he abandoned his alliance with the Qaynuqāʿ in favor of an alliance with Muḥammad spelled doom for the Qaynuqāʿ. They were now totally exposed, as the subgroup led by ʿAbdallāh ibn Ubayy would not fight against ʿUbāda's subgroup to protect them; that would have been suicidal. The Qaynuqāʿ had lost even before their siege began. Following their capitulation, their men were almost beheaded, but ʿAbdallāh ibn Ubayy forced Muḥammad to spare them and let the tribe go into exile. ʿUbāda's change of heart is the real story behind the demise of the Qaynuqāʿ.[16]

[15] Ibn Shabba, *Akhbār al-Madīna*, 1:183. Cf. M. J. Kister, "The Market of the Prophet," *Journal of the Economic and Social History of the Orient* 8 (1965): 272–6.

[16] In most of Muḥammad's biographies, this down-to-earth crucial development gives way to a preposterous story according to which the war started after a woman had been disgraced in the market of the Qaynuqāʿ.

The expulsion of the Qaynuqāʿ opened new horizons for Muḥammad's trade, although the Naḍīr and Qurayẓa still engaged in large-scale international trade. Muḥammad now attempted to divert Mecca's trade to Medina. This was the background for agreements that he concluded with several Bedouin tribes in the vicinity of Medina. Another indication of his attempts is found in a report relating to two Christian traders from Palestine:

> Tamīm al-Dārī and ʿAdī ibn Baddāʾ were both Christians. In the Jāhiliyya they used to trade with Mecca and stay there for long periods. When the Prophet made the *hijra*, they shifted their trade to Medina.[17]

The expulsion of the Naḍīr (4/626) and the massacre of the Qurayẓa (5/627) removed the obstacles blocking the expansion of Muḥammad's influence into the east side of Upper Medina. On the west side, namely in the town of Qubāʾ, Muḥammad gained a foothold much earlier, namely at the time of the *hijra*. The Qurayẓa were allied with the Aws, and most closely so with the three Aws branches that lived on the east side of Upper Medina (Aws Allāh). After Qurayẓa's demise, the three branches that had lost their mainstay converted to Islam.

Economic interests, such as property and trade, were certainly part of Muḥammad's rise to power, but diplomacy and politics also contributed immensely to his success, and the policies he laid down helped make Islam a world religion and a world power. Again, these aspects of Muḥammad's activity are often marginalized, because the sources understandably give precedence to the prophetic and spiritual aspects of his activity. Although many details regarding his diplomacy and politics are still vague, some progress can be achieved. For example, many letters of Muḥammad to individuals and tribes were preserved thanks to the recipients and their offspring. For them, the original letters were precious relics and sometimes proofs of title to the territories mentioned or demarcated in them. Only many years later did the letters find their way to the literature.

One case of successful diplomacy should be referred to in some detail. The Ḥudaybiyya Treaty (6/628) was concluded between Muḥammad and the Meccan pagans on the fringes of Mecca's sacred area (*ḥaram*) some two years before the conquest of Mecca. The text of the treaty

[17] Suyūṭī, *al-Durr al-manthūr* (Beirut: Dār al-kutub al-ʿilmiyya, 1421/2000), 2:603 (Q 5:106): "kāna Tamīm al-Dārī wa-ʿAdī ibn Baddāʾ rajulayni naṣrāniyyayni yattajirāni ilā Macca fī l-jāhiliyya wa-yuṭīlāni l-iqāma bihā fa-lammā hājara l-nabi ṣlʿm ḥawwalā [printed: *ḥawwala*] majtarahumā ilā l-Madīna."

is found in the biographies in more than one version, but one is baffled by Muḥammad's concessions during the negotiations that led to the conclusion of the treaty. The only authority that provides a satisfactory explanation for the concessions is not a specialist on Muḥammad's biography but the legal expert Sarakhsī (d. 483/1090), for whom the concessions form a legal precedent. According to him, the Ḥudaybiyya nonbelligerency treaty indicates that it is legitimate for a ruler to accept humiliating terms if they are for the general good. This is borne out by the example of Muḥammad himself, who agreed at Ḥudaybiyya to return to the pagans every Muslim from among them who would come to him: "There was between the people of Mecca and the people of Khaybar a conspiracy [*muwāṭa'a*] that if the Messenger of God marches on one of the parties, the other party would raid Medina [that is located between Mecca and Khaybar]. So he made a non-belligerency agreement with the people of Mecca in order to be secure from their side when he marches on Khaybar."[18] In other words, Muḥammad's trophy was Khaybar and not any other concession made by the Meccan pagans. The fact that Khaybar was conquered shortly afterward speaks for itself.

After Khaybar, Muḥammad's prime target was Mecca, which he managed to conquer in 8/630, having been attacked in Medina twice by Meccan-led tribal coalitions. Muḥammad's diplomatic skills were essential in convincing many of Mecca's Bedouin allies to shift their loyalties to him. There is rich evidence about the tribal coalition amalgamated by Muḥammad against Mecca, because the expedition against Muḥammad's hometown was often the only chance of tribal leaders to obtain companion status and a place in the story of Muḥammad's life. The conquest of Mecca came after Muḥammad and his archenemy Abū Sufyān, who had led the tribal coalitions against Medina, drew closer to each other. Muḥammad even married one of his former enemy's daughters. Some details of these developments survived despite the general reluctance of the sources to deal with the political and diplomatic aspects of Muḥammad's activity.

CONCLUSION

The reconstruction of Muḥammad's life is a major challenge for modern research. It requires not only ingenuity and courage but also

[18] The first modern scholar to draw attention to Sarakhsī's crucial account was Muḥammad Ḥamīdullāh, at that time at the Faculty of Law at the Osmania University in Hyderabad, in his *Muslim Conduct of State* (Hyderabad: Government Central Press, 1941–1942), 165–6; Michael Lecker, "The Ḥudaybiyya-Treaty and the Expedition against Khaybar," *Jerusalem Studies in Arabic and Islam* 5 (1984): 1–11.

patience and some philological skills, considering the many textual pitfalls. We still do not understand the literature on Muḥammad's life. It is clear, however, that it must be studied in its social and political context: every false claim is useful in the versions game, the rules of which are still unknown.

We may never find out who said what to whom on this or that occasion. But we should be able to reconstruct without fanfare an outline of Muḥammad's life that can withstand all but the most extreme scholarly criticism. The fruit of this research will come in shades of gray representing different grades of probability; a black-and-white approach is not nuanced enough to reflect the complexity of the evidence. The historical Muḥammad is there waiting to be discovered. We only have to discern the crucial evidence and put aside - for the time being - the masses of insignificant details.

APPENDIX: THE SO–CALLED CONSTITUTION OF MEDINA (IN IBN ISḤĀQ'S VERSION)[19]

1. This is a compact from Muḥammad the prophet between the *mu'minūn* and *muslimūn* of Quraysh and Yathrib and those who join them as clients, attach themselves to them and fight the Holy War with them.
2. They form one people to the exclusion of others.
3. The *muhājirūn* from Quraysh keep to their tribal organization and leadership, co-operating with each other regarding blood money [and related matters] and ransoming their captives according to what is customary and equitable among the *mu'minūn*.
4. The Banū ʿAwf keep to their tribal organization and leadership, continuing to co-operate with each other in accordance with their former mutual aid agreements regarding blood money [and related matters], and every sub-group ransoms its captives according to what is customary and equitable among the *mu'minūn*.
5. The Banū l-Ḥārith keep to their tribal organization and leadership, continuing to co-operate . . . [the formula in paragraph 4 is repeated].
6. The Banū Sāʿida keep to their tribal organization and leadership, continuing to co-operate . . .
7. The Banū Jusham keep to their tribal organization and leadership, continuing to co-operate . . .
8. The Banū l-Najjār keep to their tribal organization and leadership, continuing to co-operate . . .

[19] This is an updated version of the translation in Michael Lecker, *The Constitution of Medina: Muhammad's First Legal Document* (Princeton, NJ: Darwin Press, 2004).

9. The Banū ʿAmr ibn ʿAwf keep to their tribal organization and leadership, continuing to co-operate . . .
10. The Banū l-Nabīt keep to their tribal organization and leadership, continuing to co-operate . . .
11. The Banū l-Aws keep to their tribal organization and leadership, continuing to co-operate . . .
12. The *mu'minūn* shall not neglect to give [aid] to a debtor amongst them [who is not entitled to support according to tribal law, but will aid him] according to what is customary in matters of ransom or blood money.
13. No *mu'min* shall make an alliance with an ally of another *mu'min* to the exclusion of the latter.
14. The god-fearing *mu'minūn* are against whosoever of them demands an excessive sum of blood money or desires a gift of injustice, sin, transgression, or evil among the *mu'minūn*. They shall all unite against him even if he is the son of one of them.
15. A *mu'min* will not kill a *mu'min* in retaliation for a non-believer and will not aid a non-believer against a *mu'min*.
16. The protection of Allāh [as extended by the *mu'minūn*] is unvarying, [and hence] the least of them is entitled to grant protection that is binding for all of them.
17. The *mu'minūn* are each other's allies to the exclusion of other people.
18. The Jews who join us as clients will receive aid and equal rights; they will not be wronged, nor will their enemies be aided against them.
19. The peace of the *mu'minūn* is unvarying, [and hence] a *mu'min* will not make peace to the exclusion of another *mu'min* in fighting in the cause of Allāh, except on the basis of equality and equity between them.
20. Each raiding party that raids with us will take turns with each other.
21. The *mu'minūn* will fully retaliate on each other's behalf in the case of death or injury incurred while fighting in the cause of Allāh.
22. The god-fearing *mu'minūn* guarantee the best and most upright fulfilment of this [treaty].
23. A polytheist will not grant protection to any property or to any person of Quraysh, nor will he intervene between them [viz. the property or person] and a *mu'min*.
24. Should anyone murder a *mu'min* arbitrarily, and should undisputed evidence of this murder exist, he will be slain in retaliation, unless the agnatic kin of the deceased is appeased [with blood money]. All

the *mu'minūn* are [united] against him and it is not permissible to them not to act against him.

25. It is not permissible to *a mu'min* who acknowledges what is in this treaty and believes in Allāh and the Last Day to support a murderer or give him shelter. Upon whoever supports him or gives him shelter is the curse of Allāh and his wrath on the day of resurrection, and neither repentance nor ransom will be accepted from him.
26. Whatever you differ about should be brought before Allāh and Muḥammad.
27. The Jews share expenditure with the *mu'minūn* as long as they are at war.
28. The Jews of Banū ʿAwf are secure from the *mu'minūn*. The Jews have their religion and the *muslimūn* have theirs. [This applies to] their allies and their persons. But whoever acts unjustly and sins will only destroy himself and his agnates.
29. The Jews of Banū l-Najjār have the same [rights] as the Jews of Banū ʿAwf.
30. The Jews of Banū l-Ḥārith have the same [rights] as the Jews of Banū ʿAwf.
31. The Jews of Banū Sāʿida have the same [rights] as the Jews of Banū ʿAwf.
32. The Jews of Banū Jusham have the same [rights] as the Jews of Banū ʿAwf.
33. The Jews of Banū l-Aws have the same [rights] as the Jews of Banū ʿAwf.
34. The Jews of Banū Thaʿlaba have the same [rights] as the Jews of Banū ʿAwf. But whoever acts unjustly and sins will only destroy himself and his agnates.
35. The Jafna are a tribal group of the Thaʿlaba and are on a par with them.
36. The Banū l-Shuṭayba have the same [rights] as the Jews of Banū ʿAwf.
37. The righteous man will restrain the sinner.
38. The allies of the Thaʿlaba are on a par with them.
39. The nomadic allies of the Jews are on a par with them.
40. No-one of them [viz. of the Jews' nomadic allies] may go out [of Medina] without Muḥammad's permission.
41. There is no refraining from retaliation for a wound.
42. He who kills [someone entitled to security] kills himself and his agnates, unless he [viz. his victim] acted unjustly.
43. Allāh guarantees the most righteous fulfilment of this [treaty].

44. Incumbent upon the Jews is their expenditure and upon the *muslimūn* theirs.
45. They will aid each other against whosoever is at war with the people of this treaty.
46. There is among them sincere advice and counsel.
47. The righteous man will restrain the sinner.
48. A man will not betray his client; aid will be provided to him who has been wronged.
49. The *jawf* of Yathrib is a *ḥaram* for the people of this treaty.
50. The protected neighbor is like one's self, as long as he does not cause damage or act sinfully.
51. No protection will be granted without the permission of the parties to this treaty.
52. Every murder [or another major crime] or dispute between the people of this treaty from which evil is to be feared should be brought before Allāh and Muḥammad.
53. Allāh guarantees the truest and most righteous fulfilment of the clauses of this treaty.
54. No protection will be granted to Quraysh nor to whoever supports them.
55. They [viz. the participating parties] undertake to aid each other against whosoever attacks Yathrib.
56. If they [the Jews] are called [by the other parties to the treaty] to conclude and accept [?] an agreement, they will conclude and accept [?] it; and if they [the Jews] call for the same, it is incumbent upon the *mu'minūn* to give it them, with the exception of those fighting for religion. Everybody should pay their share at their own expense [?].
57. The Jews of Aws, their allies and their persons, have the same standing as the people of this treaty, together with the righteous and sincere of the people of this treaty.
58. The righteous man will restrain the sinner.
59. He who offends, offends only against himself.
60. Allāh guarantees the most loyal and most righteous fulfilment of this treaty.
61. This compact does not intervene to protect an unjust man and a sinner.
62. He [of the Jews] who goes out [opting not to participate in the compact] is safe and he who stays is safe, except he who acts unjustly and sins.

63. Allāh is the protector of him who is righteous and god-fearing and so is Muḥammad, the Messenger of God.
64. The most worthy of them [the Jews] to participate in this treaty are the righteous and sincere.

Further reading

Buhl, Frants, and Alford T. Welch. "Muḥammad." In *Encyclopaedia of Islam,* edited by Hamilton A. R. Gibb et al. 2nd ed. 12 vols. Leiden: E. J. Brill, 1960–2004, 7:360–76.

Chabi, Jacqueline. "Mecca." In *Encyclopaedia of the Qur'ān*, edited by Jane Dammen McAuliffe. 6 vols. Leiden: E. J. Brill, 2001–2006, 3:337–41.

Motzki, Harald, ed. *The Biography of Muhammad: The Issue of the Sources.* Leiden: E. J. Brill, 2000.

Raven, W. "Sīra." In *Encyclopaedia of Islam,* ed. Hamilton A. R. Gibb et al. 2nd ed. 12 vols. Leiden: E. J. Brill, 1960–2004, 9:660–3.

Rubin, Uri, ed. The Life of Muhammad. Vol. 4 of *The Formation of the Classical Islamic World.* Aldershot, U.K.: Ashgate, 1998.

Schöller, Marco. "Medina." In *Encyclopaedia of the Qur'ān*, ed. Jane Dammen McAuliffe, 6 vols. Leiden: E. J. Brill, 2001–2006, 3:367–71.

Part II

Muḥammad in history

4 The Prophet as lawgiver and legal authority

JOSEPH E. LOWRY

Among Muḥammad's many sobriquets is that of lawgiver, *al-shāriʿ*. Although the term is ambiguous and can also refer to God, Muḥammad is deemed worthy of this epithet because of his role in transmitting the two revelatory textual sources that form the basis of Islamic law: Qurʾān and Ḥadīth. The Qurʾān is the word of God but transmitted through Muḥammad's experience of revelation and first uttered by Muḥammad. Muḥammad is, thus, the immediate, though not the ultimate, source of Qurʾānic revelations. However, Ḥadīth, the corpus of traditions from the Prophet, although it is divinely inspired, represents Muḥammad's own, direct contribution to the material sources of Islamic law.

Qurʾānic legislation is mostly terse, elevated in style, limited to relatively few legal topics, and of modest proportion. By contrast, traditions from the Prophet display a range of literary styles, treat numerous areas of the law (and much besides), and amount to a vast corpus of texts.

EARLY REFERENCES TO MUḤAMMAD AS A LEGAL AUTHORITY

The Qurʾān neither describes a specifically legislative role for Muḥammad nor systematically connects him with its legislation. In a few Qurʾānic passages, Muḥammad is connected with the enunciation of norms. But such passages exhibit no obvious recurring structural or rhetorical features, the legal doctrines implicated are diverse, and Muḥammad's precise function with regard to such norms is neither regular nor clarified. For example, Muḥammad is twice connected with allusions to biblical commandments but in very different literary settings.[1] Most Qurʾānic legislation does not, however, expressly

[1] See Q 6:151–3 and 60:12. On commandment lists and the Decalogue in the Qurʾān, see Keith Lewinstein, "Commandments," in *Encyclopaedia of the Qurʾān*, ed. Jane Dammen McAuliffe. 6 vols. (Leiden: Brill, 2001–2006), (hereinafter *EQ*) 1:365–7; Sebastian Günther, *"O People of the Scripture! Come to a Word Common to You and Us*

involve Muḥammad. The Qur'ān's interpreters, in contrast, understood the Qur'ān's recurrent pairings of God and God's messenger (*rasūl*), in which obedience to both is said to lead to salvation, as suggesting at least Muḥammad's political authority and as implying his legislative authority:

> Those who obey God and His messenger will be admitted by Him to gardens, through which rivers flow, but those who turn away – He will punish them most painfully. (Q 48:17)[2]

Several passages have also been understood to refer to Muḥammad as an arbitrator of disputes:

> No, by your Lord, they will not believe until they make you the judge (*ḥattā yuḥakkimūka*) concerning what is in dispute between them, and then they will not find in their souls any difficulty in what you decide but will submit readily. (Q 4:65)[3]

Such passages may reflect that Muḥammad was viewed by his early followers as a *ḥakam*, an arbitrator, or as a *kāhin*, a soothsayer who exercised an oracular function and pronounced decisions in a rhyming prose that seems stylistically related to the Qur'ān's early Sūras. These comparisons were not welcome,[4] yet Muḥammad is specifically named to serve as arbitrator in the so-called Constitution of Medina (translated in the appendix of Chapter 3). This seemingly authentic document regulates the rights and responsibilities of Muḥammad's followers and various Medinan groups with regard to ransoming prisoners, fixing compensation or retaliation in tort cases, forming alliances, granting asylum, and conducting defense. Twice the document refers to Muḥammad's role

(Q. 3:64): The Ten Commandments and the Qur'an," *Journal of Qur'anic Studies* 9, no. 1 (2007): 28–58; Joseph E. Lowry, "When Less Is More: Law and Commandment in *Sūrat al-An'ām*," *Journal of Qur'anic Studies* 9, no. 2 (2007): 22–42.

2 Alan Jones, trans., *The Qur'ān* (Cambridge, U.K.: Gibb Memorial Trust, 2007). For a survey of passages that refer to Muḥammad, see Uri Rubin, "Muḥammad," *EQ* 3:440–58.

3 See also Q 4:59; 5:42–3; 33:36.

4 That such comparisons were unwelcome can be seen in Qur'ānic passages denying an oracular source of inspiration for Muḥammad's pronouncements. See, e.g., Q 15:6, in which he is accused by those who disbelieve (*alladhīna kafarū*) of being *majnūn*, that is, possessed by a *jinn* or genie, a supernatural being considered the source of inspiration for poets and *kāhins*. The Qur'ān denies that Muḥammad is a poet at Q 21:5 and denounces poets in the last few lines of sura 26.

as arbitrator of disputes arising under it, using language reminiscent of a Qur'ānic formulation.[5]

THE EMERGENCE OF THE ḤADĪTH AS EMBODIMENT OF THE PROPHETIC SUNNA

Over the course of the second century AH (eighth century CE), a class of experts in religion emerged concerned with determining how to live one's life in accordance with God's will. The historical contours, social background, and intellectual dimensions of their emergence remain obscure in important respects, but some of their debates over authority, doctrine, and piety have survived and grant us insight into formative moments in the Islamic intellectual and religious traditions. It seems probable that the model of the Prophet loomed large for these early scholars in their efforts to discover and elaborate norms, but the earliest preserved legal literature reflects competing views of legal and Prophetic authority.

An early ʿAbbāsid bureaucrat, Ibn al-Muqaffaʿ (d. ca. 139/757), complains about the proliferation of *sunna*s as a cause of legal diversity. What he means by this term is not, however, entirely clear. He accuses unnamed persons of advocating "adherence to the Sunna" (*luzūm al-sunna*) and of including practices with no *sunna* behind them as part of the Sunna (*fa-yajʿal mā laysa lahu sunna sunna*). A *sunna* is an instance of normative behavior, that is, a practice or precedent to be emulated.[6] Later scholars would call the totality of Muḥammad's normative practice the Prophetic Sunna, literally, the path traveled by Muḥammad that Muslims are invited (or expected) to follow in their own lives.[7] It is not

[5] Paragraphs 26 and 52 in Lecker's translation in Chapter 3 of this volume. Muṣṭafā al-Saqqā et al., eds., *Al-Sīra al-nabawīya li-Ibn Hishām* (Cairo: al-Ḥalabī, 1955), 1:503, 2:10–11, 504, 2:5–6. The Arabic phrase, "maradduhu ilā Allāh... wa-Muḥammad" is similar to Q 4:59 (*raddūhu ilā allāh wa'l-rasūl*). On this complex document as a whole, see Michael Lecker, *The "Constitution of Medina"* (Princeton, NJ: Darwin Press, 2004).

[6] I use the word *sunna* to refer to individual instances of exemplary (and especially prophetic behavior) and the word *Sunna* to refer to the totality of Muḥammad's normative practice. This reflects Arabic usage, in which both words can mean either a single instance or the collective sum total of such instances. In turn, normative practice is expressed by individual traditions called a *ḥadīth* ("narrative") or less often a *khabar* ("report"). I use the word *ḥadīth* to refer to individual narratives and the word Ḥadīth to refer to the corpus as a whole, as in the corpus of prophetic *ḥadīth*s.

[7] From the term *sunna* is formed the adjective Sunnī, which refers both to the majority sect of Muslims and implicitly identifies non-Sunni Muslims as somehow less faithful

clear, however, that Ibn al-Muqaffaʿ refers here solely to the Sunna of Muḥammad, as he suggests that true *sunna*s would go back to "the age of God's Messenger or the Imams of Guidance after him."[8] Other early jurists seem equally eclectic in their choice of exemplary authorities. For example, a collection of ninety-three legal traditions on inheritance attributed to the Kūfan jurist Sufyān al-Thawrī (d. 162/778) contains only seven that report Prophetic dicta.[9] The earliest preserved law book, which exists in several recensions, is the *Muwaṭṭaʾ* of Mālik b. Anas (d. 179/795). Although Mālik frequently cites Prophetic Ḥadīth, he viewed actual Medinan practice as a more authoritative source of doctrine, suggesting that, for him, such practice embodied a truer record of the Sunna than did *ḥadīth*s.[10]

In the early third century AH (ninth century CE), two figures emerged whose activities contributed substantially to cementing the role of Prophetic Ḥadīth in Islamic thought and practice: Muḥammad b. Idrīs al-Shāfiʿī (d. 204/820) and Aḥmad ibn Ḥanbal (d. 241/855). Al-Shāfiʿī, a jurist who studied with Mālik (and many others), sought to demonstrate that the Ḥadīth were, by divine design, the sole legislative supplement to the Qurʾān. This point had far-reaching implications that he enunciated in four principles: (1) the Sunna was contained entirely within the Prophetic Ḥadīth; (2) the Ḥadīth, together with the Qurʾān, constituted the entirety of revelation; (3) the law was grounded entirely in revelation; and (4) all revealed texts could be subjected to hermeneutical procedures

to the example of the Prophet. The adjective Sunni originates in the Arabic phrases *ahl al-sunna* ("people of the Sunna") and *ahl al-sunna wa'l-jamāʿa* ("the people of the Sunna and the Collective"), which are connected with the rise of the Ḥadīth and with conceptions of early Islamic political history. See Laura Vecca Vaglieri, "Sulla Origine della Denominazione 'Sunniti,'" in *Studi Orientalistici in onore di Giorgio Levi della Vida* (Rome: Istituto per l'Oriente, 1956): 573–85; G. H. A. Juynboll, "Sunna," in *Encyclopedia of Islam*, ed. Hamilton A. R. Gibb et al., 2nd ed., 12 vols. (Leiden: E. J. Brill, 1960–2004), (hereinafter *EI*²), 9:878.

8 See his *Risāla fī al-ṣaḥāba*, ed. Muḥammad Kurd ʿAlī, in *Rasāʾil al-bulaghāʾ* (Cairo: Maṭbaʿat Lajnat al-Taʾlīf wa'l-Tarjama wa'l-Nashr, 1954), 126–7; Charles Pellat, ed. and trans. (French), *Ibn al-Muqaffaʿ: Conseilleur du Calife* (Paris: Maisonneuve, 1976), 40–5. See also Joseph E. Lowry, "The First Islamic Legal Theory: Ibn al-Muqaffaʿ on Interpretation, Authority, and The Structure of the Law," *Journal of the American Oriental Society* 128, no. 1 (2009): 25–40. Ibn al-Muqaffaʿ, a member of the political elite, may not have been in close touch with currents in religious thought.

9 I rely on the count of the editor of this short text. Hans-Peter Raddatz, "Frühislamisches Erbrecht nach dem Kitāb al-Farāʾiḍ des Sufyān aṯ-Ṯaurī," *Die Welt des Islams* 13 (1971): 26–78 (Ar. text 34–46), at 59, 70.

10 The authoritativeness of such practice is the principle that distinguishes Mālik and his followers from other schools of legal thought. For the Mālikī distinction between *ḥadīth* and *sunna*, see Yasin Dutton, *The Origins of Islamic Law* (Richmond, VA: Curzon, 1999), 168–77.

for the purpose of deriving legal doctrine. These four principles came eventually to underlie all Sunnī legal thought. The reduction of the Sunna to *ḥadīth* texts (as opposed, for example, to a local practice such as that of Medina, or to the opinions of a revered authority) also provided a major impetus for the collection and formal study of such texts, both for their own sake and with a view toward norm creation and norm elaboration, and gave rise to what has been called a text-based epistemology.[11]

The incorporation of the Prophetic Sunna into legal argument generated hermeneutical problems, mostly stemming from apparent doctrinal inconsistency between the Qurʾān and individual *ḥadīth*s. Al-Shāfiʿī systematized several hermeneutical procedures to resolve such inconsistencies, and the effectiveness of these techniques formed an important part of his argument that the Qurʾān and Sunna constituted an interlocking, seamless whole: the Prophetic Ḥadīth might restate or echo Qurʾānic legislation or add optional detail, Ḥadīth might explain matters left unspecified in Qurʾānic legislation, or they might legislate completely independently of the Qurʾān. By portraying the law as a well-designed series of rationally explainable interactions between the Qurʾān and the Sunna, the role of the Sunna was made to seem not only integral but absolutely indispensable to the structure of the law.[12]

Aḥmad ibn Ḥanbal, like al-Shāfiʿī, emphasized the singular importance of the Ḥadīth for determining the details of the law. Aḥmad's personal piety, however, rooted in an immediate concern for salvation, a moderate austerity, and a profound moral seriousness and scrupulosity, provided the prime impetus for his own collection and study of the Ḥadīth. Aḥmad assembled an enormous collection of Prophetic *ḥadīth*s and contributed substantially to the development of scientific criteria for the evaluation and selection of *ḥadīth*s. His legal opinions (*masāʾil*) were also collected, yet when asked to opine on legal matters, he might humbly admit that he did not know the answer. Aḥmad's combination of vast expertise in the Ḥadīth and his personal example made him a hero of the early Ḥadīth movement, an image enhanced by his persecution at the hands of the state.[13] Although al-Shāfiʿī's significance has been emphasized in much secondary literature, scholars increasingly point

[11] This helpful term is from Brannon Wheeler, *Applying the Canon in Islam* (Albany: State University of New York Press, 1996), 43–58.

[12] Joseph E. Lowry, *Early Islamic Legal Theory* (Leiden: Brill, 2007), 23–59.

[13] On Aḥmad generally, see Christopher Melchert, *Ahmad ibn Hanbal* (Oxford: Oneworld, 2006); on his piety, see also Michael Cooperson, *Classical Arabic Biography* (Cambridge: Cambridge University Press, 2000), 107–17; Christopher Melchert, "The Piety of the Ḥadīth Folk," *International Journal of Middle East Studies* 34 (2002): 425–39.

to Aḥmad's importance as a foundational figure in the formation of the Sunnī worldview.[14]

That Aḥmad and al-Shāfiʿī both valued the collection and use of Prophetic Ḥadīth made them allies against two groups: certain Iraqi jurists who relied on legal reasoning as much or even more than on revelatory authority and certain rationalist theologians who argued that God acted according to a rationally ascertainable concept of the good, knowable independent of revelation. Such differences were neatly summed up in the polemical labels *ahl al-ḥadīth* (partisans of Ḥadīth), *ahl al-ra'y* (partisans of human reasoning in law), and *ahl al-kalām* (rationalist theologians). But reality was more complex. Al-Shāfiʿī, for all his insistence on the importance of the Ḥadīth and his express criticisms of rationalist jurisprudence and theology, is clearly fully committed to virtuoso uses of human reason in legal interpretation.

The increasing importance of the Ḥadīth in legal argument was not uncontroversial. Rationalist theologians mounted epistemological challenges to the authority of the Ḥadīth based on doubts about its authenticity and probity. Scripturalists expressed concern that a corpus of (especially written) Ḥadīth would compete with the Qur'ān. The attempt to hold a written scripture and an oral tradition as separate recalled similar distinctions made in rabbinic thought. Such disputes over the Ḥadīth intersected a major cultural transformation of the ninth century CE, the rise of books and private reading, which impinged on a set of social practices connected with oral instruction and instructional authority.[15]

These controversies notwithstanding, it seems likely that a range of factors – social, pietistic, theological, possibly even political – came together to contribute to the receptivity of early Muslims to the emergence of the Ḥadīth. In comparison with the Qur'ān, a linguistically and literarily highly complex text presupposing a very advanced knowledge of Arabic, the Ḥadīth, with its concrete portrayal of Muḥammad and

[14] E.g., Melchert, *Ahmad ibn Hanbal*, who suggests, perhaps, that modern scholarship, in its preference for al-Shāfiʿī over Aḥmad, has to some extent replicated the prejudices of some premodern jurists. On this point, see also Scott Lucas, *Constructive Critics, Ḥadīth Literature, and the Articulation of Sunnī Islam* (Leiden: Brill, 2004).

[15] On Muslim scripturalism, see Michael Cook, "ʿAnan and Islam: The Origins of Karaite Scritpuralism," *Jerusalem Studies in Arabic and Islam* 9 (1987): 161–82; and now Aisha Y. Musa, *Ḥadīth as Scripture* (New York: Palgrave Macmillan, 2008). It should be noted that both Mālik and al-Shāfiʿī allow for the recording of Ḥadīth in writing. Mālik, *al-Muwaṭṭa'* (rec. al-Shaybānī), ed. ʿA. W. ʿAbd al-Laṭīf (Beirut: Dār al-Qalam, n.d.), 330, no. 936; al-Shāfiʿī, *al-Risāla*, ed. Aḥmad Muḥammad Shākir (Cairo: al-Ḥalabī, 1940), para. 1001.

those around him, and its dominantly narrative and frequently aphoristic character, provided a responsive, human gateway into Islam, especially for non-Arabic-speaking Muslims, or prospective converts, at the margins of Muslim territories. This appeal to the margins may be connected with the fact that most compilers of authoritative Ḥadīth collections and many key Ḥadīth scholars were of Iranian or Central Asian background.[16]

In addition, early Muslim political history is fraught with conflict over legitimacy. The model of the Prophet was usefully remote and malleable for those who invoked it in the service of political agendas, like the ʿAbbāsids, who styled themselves as "the acceptable rulers from the Prophet's family" (*al-riḍā min āl al-bayt*; see Chapter 9). The figure of the Prophet could thus be made to represent an ideal of bygone communal unity whose imminent recapture had a powerful appeal. The theology and pietism of the early partisans of the Ḥadīth, too, may have emphasized the model of the Prophet as a usefully remote source of authority that transcended the often painful political disunity and asserted impiety of earthly rulers and political contenders. In this regard, perhaps the Shīʿī focus on the authority of the Imāms represents a similar longing, both for a world more in line with an imagined unity in the primeval Muslim community and for a solitary figure to imbue with supreme religious authority.

THE CLASSICAL COLLECTIONS AND THEIR CANONIZATION

From the mid-third century AH (the ninth century CE) to the early fourth century AH (the tenth century CE), *ḥadīth*s were gathered into several important compilations. Six of these became the basis for nearly all subsequent study and legal use of the Ḥadīth, and two of the six came to be regarded as paramount in authority. A few earlier collections survive and a few important later collections were made as well. All such collections belong to subgenres that are often indicated by the titles of the works themselves: *ṣaḥīḥ*, *sunan*, *musnad*, and *muṣannaf*. The two most authoritative such collections have the title *ṣaḥīḥ*, a term that signifies "authentic" in the context of the Ḥadīth. The title *sunan* (plural of *sunna*) refers simply to a collection of Prophetic *sunna*s as expressed by Ḥadīth. The term *musnad* ("supported," i.e., by an *isnād*) refers to

[16] See Richard W. Bulliet, *Islam: The View from the Edge* (New York: Columbia University Press, 1994), esp. 23–36.

a collection that includes chains of transmitters. Finally, a *muṣannaf* ("compilation") is a collection of traditions arranged by legal topic, in the manner of a treatise on Islamic law, and it may contain *ḥadīth*s that report the views of persons other than the Prophet. Irrespective of their titles, most such collections were organized by legal topic.

Mālik's *Muwaṭṭa'*, the earliest preserved comprehensive work of Islamic law, is not devoted solely to *ḥadīth*s, but it does contain 1,720 traditions, about half of which go back to the Prophet. The earliest preserved collection of *ḥadīth*s, the *Musnad* of al-Ṭayālisī (d. 204/819, probably edited by a student), contains 2,767 Prophetic *ḥadīth*s transmitted from 281 Companions. Two younger contemporaries of al-Ṭayālisī, ʿAbd al-Razzāq al-Ṣanʿānī (from Sanaa, d. 211/826) and Ibn Abī Shayba (d. 235/849), produced voluminous *muṣannaf*s containing tens of thousands of mostly non-Prophetic reports (*āthār*, sing. *athar*), such as opinions of Muḥammad's Companions, their Successors, and especially legal opinions of early Muslim authorities who lived after the Successors. The fact that Ibn Abī Shayba transmits many of these non-Prophetic reports from al-Ṭayālisī suggests that the surviving work of the latter originally contained much non-Prophetic material. A particularly highly regarded collection is the massive *Musnad* of Aḥmad ibn Ḥanbal, arranged by transmitter and containing upward of thirty thousand *ḥadīth*s. Another important early *Musnad* was put together by al-Dārimī (d. 255/869). But the two works that tower above all others in authority are the *Ṣaḥīḥ* collections by al-Bukhārī (d. 256/870) and Muslim ibn al-Ḥajjāj (d. 261/875).

The two *Ṣaḥīḥ*s, as they are known, differ in plan and scope, though both are arranged by legal topic. Muslim prefaces his with an introduction in which he explains his goals and methods, but al-Bukhārī does not. Al-Bukhārī repeats individual *ḥadīth*s, but Muslim does so much less frequently. Accordingly, Muslim's work contains only about 4,000 *ḥadīth*s, whereas al-Bukhārī's contains 7,275, including repetitions (said, like many such works, to have been culled from several hundred thousand). Finally, it is noteworthy that al-Bukhārī relies on 434 transmitters not cited by Muslim, and Muslim uses 625 transmitters not found in al-Bukhārī. Four other works, together with those of al-Bukhārī and Muslim, constitute the six main Ḥadīth collections used by Sunnīs. The compilers of the remaining four are Ibn Māja (d. 273/887), Abū Dā'ūd (d. 275/889),[17] al-Tirmidhī (d. 279/892), and al-Nasā'ī (d. 303/915), and their works all have the title *Sunan* (al-Tirmidhī's compilation is also

[17] Confusingly, al-Ṭayālisī is also named Abū Dā'ūd.

called *al-Jāmiʿ al-ṣaḥīḥ*, or *The Authentic Collection*).[18] Important later compilations include the *Sunan* of al-Dāraquṭnī (d. 385/995), the *Sunan* of al-Bayhaqī (d. 458/1066), and the *Maṣābīḥ al-sunna* (*Lanterns of the Sunna*) of Ibn al-Farrāʾ al-Baghawī (d. 516/1122), which became popular in a reworked form titled the *Mishkāt al-maṣābīḥ* (*The Lanterns' Niche*) by al-Khaṭīb al-Tabrīzī (fl. 738/1337).

Although all six of the standard collections, together with various earlier and later ones, constitute the foundational works of Sunnī Ḥadīth literature, the canonization of the two *Ṣaḥīḥ*s of al-Bukhārī and Muslim affirmed the authority of the Prophetic Ḥadīth for all Sunnīs. This process, which began roughly with the death of Muslim (in 261/875) and lasted about two centuries, involved intensive study of and familiarization with the works of Muslim and al-Bukhārī: identifying the two compilers' methodologies, determining the identities of all their transmitters, and noting the occurrence of repetitions of individual *ḥadīth*s. Derivative works were produced, as well as critical assessments that identified additional *ḥadīth*s that should have been included but were not, problematic *ḥadīth*s that were included, or transmitters who seemed not to belong. These activities were carried on locally for nearly a century in Iran among disciples of the two scholars before spreading to Baghdad. The works of al-Bukhārī and Muslim came gradually to be seen not only as foundational sources of law but also as communal sites of study and critical reflection. Thus, the two *Ṣaḥīḥ*s gradually came to be endowed in the Sunnī *imaginaire* with an enhanced, almost-transcendent authority, and it is tempting to see the process by which they acquired this authority as more or less parallel to, and indeed partly constitutive of, the emergence of mature Sunnism.[19]

The widespread commitment to the preservation and study of the corpus of Prophetic Ḥadīth was a hallmark of Sunnism. Shīʿism developed an analogous body of literature, but it more often reported dicta of the Shīʿī Imāms than those of the Prophet, and the dicta of the Prophet were always reported via an Imām. The theological reason behind this difference is that only the Imāms have the supernaturally

[18] Facts and figures on these various compilations may be found in John Burton, *An Introduction to the Ḥadīth* (Edinburgh: Edinburgh University Press, 1994), 119–30; Muḥammad Zubayr Ṣiddīqī, *Ḥadīth Literature*, rev. ed. (Cambridge, U.K.: Islamic Texts Society, 1993), 43–75; Muḥammad Abdul Rauf, "*Ḥadīth* Literature – I," in *Arabic Literature to the End of the Umayyad Period*, ed. A. F. L. Beeston et al. (Cambridge: Cambridge University Press, 1983), 271–88; Ibn Khaldūn, *The Muqaddima*, trans. Franz Rosenthal (Princeton, NJ: Princeton University Press, 1967), 2:447–63.

[19] On this process in general, see Jonathan Brown, *The Canonization of al-Bukhārī and Muslim* (Leiden: Brill, 2007).

endowed, esoteric knowledge to correctly interpret God's will, whether as expressed in the Qur'ān or through Prophetic dicta. Thus, it is primarily the Imāms' dicta that require collection and study. Also, the Companions, heroes of Sunnism and the primary transmitters of the Prophetic Ḥadīth, collectively failed to recognize the claims of the Imāms to leadership of the Muslim community; thus, they could not be considered, as they were in Sunnism, trustworthy sources of Ḥadīth. The four main collections of Shīʿī Hadīth (more usually called *akhbār* by Shīʿīs) are (1) *al-Kāfī fī ʿilm al-dīn* (*The Sufficient [Book] of Religious Knowledge*) of al-Kulaynī (d. 329/939); (2) *Man lā yaḥḍuruhu al-faqīh* (*[The Book for] Those Who Have no Access to a Jurist*) of Ibn Bābūya (d. 381/991); (3) *Tahdhīb al-aḥkām* (*The Good Arrangement of Rulings*) by the noted scholar al-Ṭūsī (d. 460/1067); and (4) *al-Ibtiṣār fīmā ukhtulifat minhu al-akhbār* (*Perceiving the Inconsistencies among Reports*), also by al-Ṭūsī. All four works are organized by legal topic.[20]

The other major sectarian division in Islam, the Khārijīs, of whom today there remains only the subdivision called Ibāḍīs (limited to areas of Oman and North Africa), also had a complex attitude toward the Ḥadīth. This stemmed from their belief that some of Muḥammad's Companions had become corrupt after the rule of the first two caliphs, and from the general scripturalist attitude of the Khārijīs. Their own most authoritative Ḥadīth collection, *al-Jāmiʿ al-ṣaḥīḥ*, also called *Musnad al-Rabīʿ b. Ḥabīb*, was given final form by Yūsuf b. Ibrāhīm al-Warjlānī (d. 571/1174). It contains 1,005 Prophetic Ḥadīth and overlaps considerably with the standard Sunnī collections. The Baṣran Successor Jābir b. Zayd (d. between 94/711 and 102/722) is their most important transmitter and recognized as a transmitter by Sunnīs.[21]

THE FORMAL STUDY OF THE ḤADĪTH

The latter fifth century AH (eleventh century CE) marked the beginning of a distinctive Islamic scholasticism, characterized by the

[20] For a modern introduction to Shiite Ḥadīth scholarship, see ʿAbd al-Hādī al-Faḍlī, *Introduction to the Ḥadīth*, trans. Nazmina Virjee (London: ICAS Press, 2002); on the Shiite collections in general, see the excellent overview by Robert Gleave, "Between *Ḥadīth* and *Fiqh*: The 'Canonical' Imāmī Collections of *Akhbār*," *Islamic Law and Society* 8, no. 3 (2001): 350–82.

[21] On early Khārijī scripturalism, see Patricia Crone and F. W. Zimmerman, *The Epistle of Sālim ibn Dhakwān* (Oxford: Oxford University Press, 2001), 291–4. Sunnis considered the Khārijīs heretics. See the creed attributed to Abū Zurʿa and Abū Ḥātim, two important late-ninth-century Ḥadīth scholars, in Binyamin Abrahamov, *Islamic Theology* (Edinburgh: Edinburgh University Press, 1998), 55 (art. 26). On Ibāḍī Ḥadīth, see generally J. C. Wilkinson, "Ibāḍī Ḥadīth: An Essay in Normalization," *Der Islam* 62 (1985): 231–59.

professionalization of the religious scholars, due in large part to the economic opportunities created by the emergence of mature institutions of religious instruction. Instruction in the Ḥadīth formed a regular part of the curriculum in such institutions, including especially *madrasas* (law colleges), and continued to be important in the informal scholarly networks that remained equally responsible for the transmission of religious learning. Some scholastic institutions were founded solely for the purpose of studying the Ḥadīth.[22] A scholarly literature about the various aspects of Ḥadīth study – the "science [or sciences] of Ḥadīth" (*ʿilm* [or *ʿulūm*] *al-ḥadīth*) – had evolved as part of the process of the canonization of the two *Ṣaḥīḥ*s, and its origins reached, in some instances, back into the scholarly writings of the third century AH (ninth century CE).

Early trends in Ḥadīth study culminated in an important assessment of eighth- and ninth-century transmitters by Ibn Abī Ḥātim al-Rāzī (d. 317/938), the *Kitāb al-jarḥ wa'l-taʿdīl*. The technical terms contained in its title – *jarḥ* and *taʿdīl* – refer to the rejection and approval, respectively, of Ḥadīth transmitters and thus designate a critical component of the science of Ḥadīth criticism. In addition, the introduction (*taqdima*) to this voluminous work comprises an important early theoretical and historical introduction to Ḥadīth study in general.[23] Other important general introductions to the science of Ḥadīth included the *Kitāb maʿrifat ʿulūm al-ḥadīth* (*The Book of Knowledge of the Sciences of Ḥadīth*) by the renowned Ḥadīth scholar al-Ḥākim al-Naysābūrī (d. 405/1014)[24] and the *Muqaddimat Ibn al-Ṣalāḥ* (*Ibn al-Ṣalāḥ's Introduction*) by Ibn al-Ṣalāḥ al-Shahrazūrī (d. 643/1245).[25]

The science of Ḥadīth sought to elaborate and apply the criteria for determining a given *ḥadīth* text's authenticity that had been developed in, and through, the study of the two *Ṣaḥīḥ*s. This was accomplished by categorizing individual transmitters, chains of transmitters, and the texts of individual *ḥadīth*s themselves. Individual transmitters

[22] On formal institutions of Ḥadīth instruction, see George Makdis, *The Rise of Colleges* (Edinburgh: Edinburgh University Press, 1981), 32–4, 210–14.

[23] On which, see Eerik Dickinson, *The Development of Early Sunnite* Ḥadith *Criticism* (Leiden: Brill, 2001).

[24] Ed. Muʿaẓẓam Ḥusayn (Beirut: al-Maktab al-Tijārī li'l-Ṭibāʿa wa'l-Tawzīʿ wa'l-Nashr, 1966?). A shorter introductory work by this author is translated into English, *al-Madkhal ilā maʿrifat al-Iklīl* (*Introduction to the Iklīl*): James Robson, ed. and trans., *Introduction to the Science of Tradition* (London: Luzac, 1953). On al-Ḥākim's life and works, see J. Brown, *Canonization*, 154–84.

[25] Also known as the *Kitāb maʿrifat anwāʿ ʿilm al-ḥadīth* (*The Book of Knowledge about the Varieties of the Science of Ḥadīth*): *Muqaddimat Ibn al-Ṣalāḥ . . .*, ed. ʿĀ'isha bt. ʿAbd al-Raḥmān (Bint al-Shāṭi') (Cairo: Dār al-Maʿārif, 1989). This work is now translated into English by Eerik Dickinson as *An Introduction to the Science of the Ḥadīth* (Reading, MA: Garnet Press, 2005).

fell into several categories, ranging from the absolutely trustworthy to the thoroughly unreliable. It should be noted that many women became important and respected transmitters, especially in the earliest period and again after the canonization of the two *Ṣaḥīḥs*.[26] *Isnāds*, too, were carefully categorized in regard to their completeness or lack thereof and the different kinds of gaps that they might contain. The *ḥadīths* themselves were classified to a great extent on the basis of the foregoing criteria but sometimes also on the basis of content, as *ṣaḥīḥ* ("sound," "authentic"); *ḥasan* ("good," "acceptable"); and *ḍaʿīf* ("weak"), which last comprised subcategories such as *shādhdh* (having an unusual *matn*) and *mawḍūʿ* ("forged," this last classification being especially related to content-based criticism).[27]

The identification and evaluation of all the collectors and transmitters of *ḥadīths* in the early centuries of Islam involved the formulation of criteria for evaluating the likelihood and quality of transmission between individuals as well the development of a list of the most important early scholars of Ḥadīth. Such lists gave a framework to the analysis of *isnāds* and thus helped to construct an account of the heroes whose painstaking labors ensured the careful transmission of the Prophet's legacy for subsequent generations. Such persons (e.g., Aḥmad b. Ḥanbal) were clearly distinguished in the works of the Ḥadīth scholars from jurists who excelled at legal reasoning (e.g., al-Shāfiʿī).[28]

These efforts were also connected with a much more massive project of the Ḥadīth literature, the scrutiny of all collectors and transmitters throughout the centuries in *kutub al-rijāl* ("books on men"), a vast prosopographical literature that carefully characterized the probity, scholarly ability, and relevant biographical details of thousands of scholars and transmitters. This literature perhaps begins with the *Kitāb al-ṭabaqāt* (*Book of Generations*) of Muḥammad Ibn Saʿd (d. 230/845) and includes *al-Tārīkh al-kabīr* (*The Great History*) by al-Bukhārī, the *Kitāb al-jarḥ*

[26] See Ṣiddiqī, *Ḥadīth Literature*, 117–23; Asma Sayeed, "Shifting Frontiers: Women and Ḥadīth Transmission in Islamic History (First to Eighth Centuries)," Ph.D. diss. (Princeton University, 2005); Muhammad Akram Nadwi, *Al-Muhaddithat: The Women Scholars of Islam* (London: Interface Publications, 2007).

[27] Many of these terms are already found in the writings of al-Shāfiʿī, who discusses them using what appears to be a preexisting technical vocabulary. Melchert, *Ahmad ibn Hanbal*, 50, proposes that al-Shāfiʿī may have learned such technical terms from Aḥmad b. Ḥanbal.

[28] Al-Ḥākim al-Naysābūrī lists twenty-three such heroes and expressly contrasts them with the masters of legal reasoning. *Kitāb Maʿrifat ʿulūm al-ḥadīth*, 63–85. For comparable (though shorter) lists, see Lucas, *Constructive Critics*, 127–51; J. Brown, *Canonization*, 51–2; Dickinson, *Development*, 49–51.

wa'l-ta'dīl of Ibn Abī Ḥātim, and many, many more, including substantial compilations from the scholastic period by such major Ḥadīth scholars as al-Dhahabī (d. 748/1348) and Ibn Ḥajar al-ʿAsqalānī (d. 852/1449). These works form a key part of a larger so-called biographical literature in Arabic that catalogs the careers of scholars of all kinds and provides a major source for modern scholarship.

The scholastic period witnessed the production of definitive commentaries on the two *Ṣaḥīḥ*s, including important ones on al-Bukhārī by Ibn Ḥajar al-ʿAsqalānī and on Muslim by al-Nawawī (d. 676/1277). The maturation of the science of Ḥadīth also allowed smaller, popularizing collections to be made for private, devotional, or introductory study by nonspecialists. Al-Nawawī compiled two short works in particular that deserve mention, *al-Arbaʿūn al-Nawawīya* (*al-Nawawī's Forty [Ḥadīth]*), and *Riyāḍ al-ṣāliḥīn* (*Gardens of the Righteous*).[29]

Scholasticism was very much driven by the formal study of Islamic law. The science of legal theory, *uṣūl al-fiqh* (lit., "the bases of the law"), which thrived in the scholastic environment, sought to lay out in a systematic way the philosophical and theological foundations according to which Islamic law was formulated – the Ḥadīth were treated extensively within this framework. The primary task of Islamic legal theory is to achieve a precise understanding of God's legislative intent through a careful literary and theological analysis of the Qurʾān and Prophetic Ḥadīth, using a variety of hermeneutical techniques. A fundamental assumption of this science is that, although God wishes his commands and prohibitions to be known with precision, most answers to legal questions depend on fallible human essays in interpretation and so remain provisional. Legal theorists were thus obsessed with epistemology and in particular with drawing a precise distinction between certain knowledge (*ʿilm*) and merely probable knowledge (*ẓann*) of God's rulings (*aḥkām*); merely probable knowledge was sufficient to generate legal obligations.

This overt concern with epistemology and the careful recognition of inherent uncertainty in God's law led Islamic legal theory to develop its own somewhat pessimistic classification of Ḥadīth. *Mutawātir ḥadīth*s, which had multiple lines of transmission in the generation of the Companions, were the most probative and engendered certain knowledge. However, only very few *ḥadīth*s met this high standard; most were instead categorized as *akhbār āḥād* (sing. *khabar al-wāḥid*), which

[29] For English translations of both, see *An-Nawawi's Forty Ḥadīth*, trans. Ezzidin Ibrahim and Denys Johnson-Davies (Chicago: Kazi Press, 1995); *Gardens of the Righteous*, trans. Muhammad Zafrulla Khan (London: Curzon Press, 1975). The latter also includes verses from the Qurʾān.

exhibited only a single line of transmission at the Companion level and so provided only probable assurance of the correct ruling. A middle category evolved in tandem with the canonization of the two *Ṣaḥīḥs*, that of *mashhūr* ("well known," widely accepted by Ḥadīth scholars), which in effect raised the epistemological status of many *aḥād ḥadīth*s. Later theorists also developed a concept of *tawātur maʿnawī*, a group of *ḥadīth*s that could collectively be considered *mutwātir* because they expressed the same idea but differed only in their wording. These epistemologically rigorous classifications, though theoretically important for understanding the probabilistic bent of Islamic legal thought, did not interfere with the use of Ḥadīth as a source of legal rules or with the attraction of Ḥadīth study more generally.[30]

ḤADĪTH, REFORM, AND MODERNITY

Pronounced textualist trends in Islamic law and theology – generally styled as revivalist or reformist – emerged across the eighteenth and nineteenth centuries and into the twentieth.[31] These currents exhibited a complex relationship to the Prophetic Ḥadīth, combining a renewed interest in the figure of the Prophet and in Prophetic Ḥadīth as sources of guidance with an enhanced critical sensibility in regard to the potential uses of the Prophet and the Ḥadīth. The proponents of several such reformist strands placed the Ḥadīth squarely at the center of Islamic thought and practice. In so doing, they sought to bypass premodern structures of juristic authority – principally the four Sunnī schools of legal thought (*madhhab*, pl. *madhāhib*) – on the grounds that such structures, through the weight of their own institutional agendas and legacies, had become ends in themselves and had begun to interfere with scholars' and believers' direct access to the Qurʾān and Prophetic precedents. A key principle relied on by the schools, submission to the interpretive authority of master jurists within a school (*taqlīd*), was denounced, and the duty (of scholars) to engage in independent legal research and reasoning (*ijtihād*) based directly on the Qurʾān and Prophetic *ḥadīth*s, without institutional interference, emphasized.

[30] On *mashhūr* traditions, see J. Brown, *Canonization*, 183–94; Wael Hallaq, *A History of Islamic Legal Theories* (Cambridge: Cambridge University Press, 1997), 65–6. On the approach of *uṣūl al-fiqh* to the Ḥadīth in general, see Aron Zysow, "The Economy of Certainty: An Introduction to the Typology of Islamic Legal Theory," Ph.D. diss. (Harvard University, 1984), 11–84.

[31] The field of Islamic studies has faced challenges in conceptualizing the routes taken by Islamic thought to modernity. See Ahmad Dallal, "The Origins and Objectives of Islamic Revivalist Thought, 1750–1850," *Journal of the American Oriental Society* 113 (1993): 341–59.

One important factor in the desire to return to the sources and skirt the strictures of scholastic and other institutions was the rise of strong, bureaucratically adept states beginning in the sixteenth century. These states – the Ottomans in Anatolia, southeastern Europe, and many Arab regions; the Safavids in Iran; and the Mughals in India – exercised growing control over religious institutions, and the trend of state involvement in and interference with the affairs of religious scholars increased continually right through the colonial period and into the age of modern nation-states. The transfer of religious institutions from the private to the public spheres is one of the major transformations undergone by Islam as it entered the early modern and modern eras.

The renewed emphasis on the Ḥadīth, which in some cases came to be described as Salafī for its asserted reliance on the model practice of the earliest generations of pious Muslims (*al-salaf al-ṣāliḥ*), had roots in such premodern thinkers as the great Ḥanbalī jurist and theologian Ibn Taymīya (d. 728/1328), the Ẓāhirī jurist and theologian Ibn Ḥazm (d. 456/1064), and the previously mentioned Aḥmad b. Ḥanbal. Important concomitants of this attitude were (often) trenchant critiques of popular religious practices associated with Ṣūfism and (less often, and paradoxically) occasional caution and even ambivalence toward the Ḥadīth.

Muḥammad b. ʿAbd al-Wahhāb (d. 1792), namesake of the Wahhābīs and active in Arabia, is one of the best-known figures who exemplified this trend. Such developments were not limited to Sunnīs, however, and extended also even to Zaydī Shīʿī scholars in Yemen. Zaydīs, like all Shīʿīs, were suspicious of the Sunnī Ḥadīth collections for their lack of interest in the Shīʿī Imāms and their use of transmitters who were hostile to the Imāms' claims. However, Zaydīs had also begun to use Sunnī Ḥadīth (selectively) as early as the twelfth century CE, and Zaydī scholars such as Muḥammad b. Ibrāhīm Ibn al-Wazīr (d. 840/1436) and Ibn al-Amīr al-Ṣanʿānī (d. 1768 or 1769) exhibited an increasingly positive attitude toward the Sunnī Ḥadīth collections. This traditionalist current in Zaydism culminated in the towering figure of Muḥammad al-Shawkānī (d. 1834), who criticized the Sunnī *madhāhib*; rejected *taqlīd*; and insisted on his authority to practice *ijtihād* by directly consulting the Qurʾān and, surprisingly for a Shīʿī jurist, the Sunnī Ḥadīth collections.[32]

In India, too, reform-minded thinkers emphasized the authority of the Ḥadīth. Shāh Walī Allāh (d. 1762), who studied Ḥadīth in the Ḥijāz in

[32] Bernard Haykel, *Revival and Reform in Islam* (Cambridge: Cambridge University Press, 2003), 41, 76; J. Brown, *Canonization*, 314–18. In this regard, al-Ṣanʿānī's thought foreshadowed that of Muḥammad al-Albānī (d. 1999), who championed the use of Ḥadīth but also insisted on the right to conduct de novo critical reexaminations of transmitters and of individual *ḥadīth*s. J. Brown, *Canonization*, 321–34.

his youth, argued that the doctrines of the *madhāhib* were subordinate to what could be derived directly from the Prophetic Sunna.[33] Walī Allāh was responding in part to the deemphasis of the Qurʾān and the Ḥadīth in the so-called *dars-i niẓāmī*, the popular seminary curriculum developed in the early eighteenth century by scholars associated with the Farangī Maḥall family of Lucknow that put rationalist subjects such as Arabic grammar, logic, philosophy, mathematics, rhetoric, law, and theology at the center of higher religious studies.[34] Interestingly, Walī Allāh's emphasis on the authority of the Ḥadīth led him (like Mālikī jurists but unusually in the context of Indian Ḥanafism) to privilege the *Muwaṭṭaʾ* of Mālik over the two *Ṣaḥīḥ*s, although he also effectively prohibited criticism of the two *Ṣaḥīḥ*s, holding that anyone who impugned them be considered a heretic.[35]

Walī Allāh's impact ran in various directions in relation to the Ḥadīth, which remained central to the concerns of nineteenth-century Indian *ʿulamāʾ*.[36] Sayyid Aḥmad Barelwī (d. 1831), one of many disciples of Walī Allāh's sons,[37] urged exclusive reliance on the Qurʾān and Prophetic Sunna as part of a reformist agenda that included criticism of popular religious practices, involved anti-Shīʿī agitation, and culminated in the attempt to carve out a Muslim state by waging *jihād* against the Sikhs. In his case, the return to the Prophet's model went beyond an emphasis on Ḥadīth as a source of law and extended to a reenactment of key moments from Muslim sacred history.[38] Other intellectual descendants of Walī Allāh founded seminaries, such as the Dār al-ʿUlūm in Deoband (established in 1867 with further branches

[33] Delhi gained recognition as a center of Ḥadīth study, with ties to the Ḥijāz, in the lifetime of ʿAbd al-Ḥaqq al-Dihlāwī (d. 1052/1642), though the study of so-called rational sciences was prominent in the Mughal period. Barbara Metcalf, *Islamic Revival in British India* (Princeton, NJ: Princeton University Press, 1982), 19.

[34] Metcalf, *Islamic Revival*, 31. The rationalist tendency of this curriculum may have reflected the onset of a wider, and growing, intellectual orientation in this period. See Khaled El-Rouayheb, "Opening the Gate of Verification," *International Journal of Middle East Studies* 38, no. 2 (2006): 263–81. As far back as Aḥmad b. Ḥanbal, proponents of the Ḥadīth had consciously opposed the elitism of their rationalist counterparts, and it is tempting to interpret this cleavage along shifting socioeconomic lines. See Peter Gran, *Islamic Roots of Capitalism: Egypt, 1760–1840*, 2nd ed. (Syracuse, NY: Syracuse University Press, 1998), lvi–lvii.

[35] On Walī Allāh in general, see Daniel Brown, *Rethinking Tradition in Modern Islamic Thought* (Cambridge: Cambridge University Press, 1996), 22–5; J. Brown, *Canonization*, 318–21; Metcalf, *Islamic Revival*, 35–43.

[36] Muhammad Qasim Zaman, *The Ulama in Contemporary Islam* (Princeton, NJ: Princeton University Press, 2002), 12.

[37] Metcalf, *Islamic Revival*, 47–8.

[38] Metcalf, *Islamic Revival*, 52–63; D. Brown, *Rethinking Tradition*, 25, 27.

and affiliates founded in the later nineteenth and twentieth centuries). The Deobandis returned to the *dars-i niẓāmī* but reversed its emphases, putting study of the Qurʾān and above all the Ḥadīth and the six chief collections at the curriculum's center.[39] Of special interest in the Indian context is the appearance of the Ahl-i Ḥadīth movement (in the second half of the nineteenth century), which traced its roots back through Barelwī to Walī Allāh and to al-Shawkānī. Its name obviously harks back to the *ahl al-ḥadīth* of the eighth and ninth centuries.[40]

It is tempting to link these reformist currents with responses to European colonialism, but al-Shawkānī, for example, showed no interest in the European colonial threat. Both Walī Allāh's interest in Ḥadīth and Sayyid Aḥmad Barelwī's *jihād* against the Sikhs arose in the context of the collapse of Mughal political authority.[41] In contrast, the emergence of the Deoband movement was occasioned in part by the failure of the 1857 uprising against the British, and the attendant curricular emphasis on Ḥadīth likely was seen as a necessary religious reform – a return to fundamentals – in the face of political domination by non-Muslims.[42]

For the Egyptian reformers Muḥammad ʿAbduh (d. 1905) and his student Rashīd Riḍā (d. 1935, widely regarded as a founding figure of modern Salafism), the critical reevaluation of the Ḥadīth formed part of their response to perceptions of Western technological, political, and cultural domination. ʿAbduh and Riḍā celebrated the Prophet and his Companions as models of flexibility and rational problem solving who laid the religious foundations of a culturally superior, technologically advanced civilization – premodern Islamic civilization. They emphasized the early Muslims' deployment of reason, not their careful obedience to precedent. Thus, both ʿAbduh and Riḍā and were cautious in accepting individual *ḥadīth*s and suggested that any non-*mutawātir* tradition be scrutinized, not merely accepted for having been declared *ṣaḥīḥ*. By defining as carefully as possible all matters not directly governed by the Qurʾān and Sunna, they saw themselves as leaving maximum scope for *ijtihād*, an

39 They also taught Ḥanafī law and accepted the authority of the *madhhab* structure inclusive of *taqlīd*. Qasim Zaman, *Ulama*, 70; Metcalf, *Islamic Revival*, 87–8, 100–2, 125–36, 141.

40 They rejected the *madhāhib* and became embroiled in controversy with other Ḥadīth-friendly intellectual currents, such as the Deobandis. Metcalf, *Islamic Revival*, 264–96; D. Brown, *Rethinking Tradition*, 27–30.

41 Metcalf, *Islamic Revival*, 35, 62. However, the emphasis on Ḥadīth study gradually evolved among Walī Allāh's successors into responses to colonialism such as, for example, issuing *fatwā*s directly to private individuals to bypass colonial legal structures that incorporated aspects of Islamic law. Such *fatwā*s often privileged direct reliance on Ḥadīth over doctrines of the *madhāhib*. Metcalf, *Islamic Revival*, 48–52.

42 Metcalf, *Islamic Revival*, 87–8.

approach that they viewed as true to that of the earliest generations of Muslims, including the Prophet and his Companions.

Neither ʿAbduh nor Riḍā was in any sense 'anti-Ḥadīth.' Rather, both urged direct interpretive engagement with the Ḥadīth (especially of the *aḥād* variety) to elicit the "true" Sunna, which could be checked against the more certain principles found in the Qur'ān. This was because they viewed the most important precedent of Muḥammad and his Companions as their capacity for innovation, not the individual innovations whose solutions were reported as discrete *ḥadīth*s.[43] Theirs was one approach along a spectrum that ranged from the analytically cautious to the historical relativist.

Representative of the latter, for example, were the Ahl-i Qur'ān, a breakaway movement within the Ahl-i Ḥadīth, members of which held that the Ḥadīth concerned only the immediate historical situation of the Prophet and that only the Qur'ān contained a transcendental message of timeless relevance.[44] Some modernists such as Fazlur Rahman (d. 1988) sought more subtle ways to limit the precedential force of Muḥammad's actions as recorded in *ḥadīth*s. Rahman held that the Qur'ān contains both "universal and concrete" statements, the former having a transcendent value and the latter being "specific injunctions" of "a specific nature" that are "too specific to be termed 'laws' in the strict sense."[45] The Sunna represents Muḥammad's application of transcendent Qur'ānic principles to concrete historical situations and thus consists of nonbinding (but instructive) instantiations, in the form of *ḥadīth*s, of universal principles. This approach preserves the Qur'ān, the authority of the Sunna, and the historical validity of the Ḥadīth but also neutralizes the Ḥadīth as legal authority for the present.[46] Such views potentially limit the place of the Prophet in modern legal discourse. They can perhaps be seen as resting on distinctions made already by the premodern legal theorist al-Qarāfī (d. 684/1285), who argued that only Muḥammad's acts in his capacity as master jurist (*muftī*) had precedential value; his administrative and narrowly judicial pronouncements were less legally relevant.[47] However, in Rahman's case, one senses a

[43] Albert Hourani, *Arabic Thought in the Liberal Age, 1798–1939* (Cambridge: Cambridge University Press, 1983), 146–7; D. Brown, *Rethinking Tradition*, 37, 41; G. H. A. Juynboll, *The Authenticity of the Tradition Literature* (Leiden: Brill, 1969), 15–23; J. Brown, *Canonization*, 305–6.

[44] Both groups evolved into quasi-sectaries, as manifested in their appearance and ritual practice. Metcalf, *Islamic Revival*, 267, 289; D. Brown, *Rethinking Tradition*, 38–9.

[45] Fazlur Rahman, *Islam*, 2nd ed. (Chicago: University of Chicago Press, 1979), 69.

[46] Ibid., 68–71 and chap. 4 generally; see also D. Brown, *Rethinking Tradition*, 102–6.

[47] Shihāb al-Dīn al-Qarāfī, *Kitāb al-Furūq*, ed. M. A. Sarrāj et al. (Cairo: Dār al-Salām, 2001), 1:346–50 (*al-farq al-sādis wa'l-thalāthūn*).

more general discomfort with premodern formulations of Islamic law, whose raw materials consist mostly of Ḥadīth. For him, Muḥammad's importance lies in his attempts to discover and apply the spirit of the Qurʾān, not in the specific precedents that he set in a contingent historical situation.[48]

Apart from the engagement of early modern and modern Muslim thinkers with the continuing relevance of the Ḥadīth, the corpus, as the embodiment of the Prophetic Sunna, retains considerable symbolic value. Article 1 of the 1992 Saudi Arabian Basic Law of Government (*al-niẓām al-asāsī liʾl-ḥukm*) provides, "The Kingdom of Saudi Arabia is an Arab and Islamic state. Its constitution [*dustūr*] is the Book of God . . . and the Sunna of His Messenger."[49] This formulation, though perhaps unlikely to engender a searching exploration of the Ḥadīth as the basis for a modern constitution among Saudi jurists, nevertheless shows how mere reference to the Prophet's Sunna is still perceived as having a powerful legitimating function in such a conspicuously modern context as constitution drafting.

CONCLUSIONS

The emergence of the Ḥadīth in early Islam heralded (or reflected) an intense focus on the person of the Prophet as a source of legal authority, a focus that could perhaps also be found in contemporaneous trends in conversion, personal piety, early asceticism, early mysticism, sectarian formations, and even political propaganda. The ensuing reduction of Prophetic precedents to texts that could be applied to a given fact situation had lasting effects on the character of all Islamic legal thought. As texts, the *ḥadīth*s could be analyzed, subjected to hermeneutical procedures, compared and contrasted with the Qurʾān, and contested by using all the tools of Islamic legal reasoning. The size and complexity of the Ḥadīth corpus also meant that any given *ḥadīth* could be opposed by adducing another *ḥadīth* that embodied a contrary principle. Moreover, the critical rigor of premodern Muslim Ḥadīth scholarship was an implicit concession to the potential inauthenticity of some *ḥadīth*s in circulation, and this concession, in combination with early skepticism about the Ḥadīth among some jurists and theologians, left its mark on

[48] A description of some modern Muslims' outright hostility to the Ḥadīth may be found in Musa's *Ḥadīth as Scripture*, 83–109.

[49] Royal Decree A/90 (27 Shaʿbān 1412). I have relied on the Arabic text found on the Web site of the Saudi Ministry of Foreign Affairs, at http://www.mofa.gov.sa/Detail.asp?InSectionID=1747&InNewsItemID=24887 (last accessed November 19, 2008).

Islamic legal epistemology. The legal interpretation of a given *ḥadīth* was, accordingly, always contestable and rarely certain.

Early controversies notwithstanding, the Muslim community – Sunnīs, Shīʿīs, and Khārijīs – gradually achieved a measure of consensus on the importance of preserving the Prophet's legal precedents as embodied in the Ḥadīth. Although the Ḥadīth and the legal role of the Prophet remain important for all Islamic legal thought, the controversies and diversity of views that characterized the early reception of the Prophetic Ḥadīth have reemerged to a degree over the course of the early modern and modern periods. Particularly remarkable is the resilient ability of individual *ḥadīth*s, and of the corpus as a whole, to survive such potentially aggressive scrutiny, both from proponents and from detractors. Along with the enduring attraction of the figure of the Prophet, this ability surely contributed to their preeminent status as a basic source of Muslim thought and practice.

Further reading

al-Bukhārī, Muḥammad b. Ismāʿīl. *Ṣaḥīḥ al-Bukhārī*. 9 vols. Translated by M. M. Khan. Chicago: Kazi Press, 1976–1979.

Ibn Rushd. *The Distinguished Jurist's Primer*. 2 vols. Translated by I. A. K. Nyazee. Reading, MA: Garnet Press, 1996.

Melchert, Christopher. "How Ḥanafism Came to Originate in Kufa and Traditionalism in Medina." *Islamic Law and Society* 6 (1999): 318–47.

Motzki, Harald. *The Origins of Islamic Jurisprudence: Meccan Fiqh before the Classical Schools*. Translated by Marion Katz. Leiden: E. J. Brill, 2002. (See esp. xi–49.)

Muslim b. al-Ḥajjāj. *Ṣaḥīḥ Muslim*. 4 vols. Translated by ʿA. Ḥ. Ṣiddiqī. Lahore: Sh. Muhammad Ashraf, 1971.

Schacht, Joseph. *The Origins of Muhammadan Jurisprudence*. Oxford: Clarendon Press, 1950.

Schoeler, Gregor. *The Oral and the Written in Early Islam*. Translated by Uwe Vagelpohl. London: Routledge, 2006.

Weiss, Bernard. *The Spirit of Islamic Law*. Athens: University of Georgia Press, 1998.

5 Personal piety

ROBERT GLEAVE

The collections of sayings and actions of the Prophet Muḥammad record his life in the minutest detail, including the Prophet's advice about the benefits of hair care:

> The Prophet said: "Combing [one's hair] expels infectious diseases and moisturizing expels misery."
>
> The Prophet forbade brushing one's hair two times in a day.
>
> The Prophet said, "Good hair is God's *kiswa* [the cloth covering of the Kaʿba in Mecca] – so treat it with respect."[1]

According to most Muslim theologians and jurists, Muḥammad provided the community with an example (*sunna*). *Sunna* contains not only stipulations (rules that the community must follow) but also, more generally, advice about the execution of basic life skills, including personal hygiene. The Muslim tradition's assessment of most of the statements and actions described in the foregoing reports (and many other descriptions of everyday actions) is that they do not, in themselves, give rise to formal religious obligations (*wājibāt*). Believers who do not follow the Prophet's regulations (and, say, brush their hair more than twice a day) are not committing a major sin or misdemeanor. They are, however, missing out on a chance to perform acts of personal piety.

Premodern collections of *ḥadīth*s are infused with a desire to uncover, and then promulgate, rules whereby Muslims might become more observant servants of God. These rules of personal life are found in both Sunnī and Shīʿī collections and demonstrate that the example of the Prophet Muḥammad is, for most Muslims, not merely a legal source of the *sharīʿa*. The Prophet Muḥammad also provided an exemplary and recommended way of living (one of the meanings of the Arabic term

[1] Muḥammad Bāqir al-Majlisī, *Biḥār al-anwār* (Beirut: Dār iḥyāʾ al-turāth al-ʿArabī, 1403/1983), 73:113,115–16.

sunna). For the more pious and devotional Muslim, the prosaic acts of the Prophet can provide a social order by which his or her life is regulated. Through their imitation of the Prophet, Muslims can be improved personally and spiritually.

Following the Prophet's actions can have material and spiritual benefits, but it can also have profound theological implications. For example, various hair-care procedures are among the ten practices of personal hygiene that the Prophet mentions as signs of a good, natural disposition (or *fiṭra*, first attributed to the prophet Abraham in Muslim tradition):

> The Prophet said, "There are ten things which are signs of *fiṭra*: shaving one's mustache, not trimming the beard, using a toothpick, washing one's nostrils with water, cutting one's nails, washing the knuckles, removing armpit hair, shaving one's pubic hair and washing one's genitals and anus [after urination or defecation]." Musʿab, who transmitted this [report], said, "I forgot the tenth – it may have been rinsing one's mouth."[2]

The common Muslim view is that human beings have been endowed, by God, with a natural disposition (*fiṭra*). By giving human beings this *fiṭra*, God has implanted in them a natural tendency toward correct living in submission (i.e., *islām*) to Him. The Prophet is reported, then, as saying that these elements of personal hygiene are signs of this *fiṭra* – by performing them, the individual is expressing his or her inbuilt human tendency toward correct living.

If the notion of *fiṭra* seems to move the Muslim into a particularly pure physical and spiritual state, other actions, such as cutting one's nails on Friday, result in more mundane blessings:

> The Prophet said, "God removes any disease from the fingertips of he who cuts his nails on Friday, and replaces it with blessings." It is also related that [the Prophet added that], "and no madness, or leprosy or skin ailment will afflict him."[3]

Even if one does not cut one's nails on Friday, they should be cut every forty days:

> The Prophet said, "Every forty nights [the believers] should cut their nails, shave their mustaches and shave their pubic hair."[4]

[2] Muslim b. al-Hajjāj, *Ṣaḥīḥ Muslim* (Beirut: Dār Ibn Ḥazm, 1995), 1:153: There are many different versions of these lists of characteristics of *fiṭra*. In some lists (normally shorter than this one), circumcision (male and female) is also included.

[3] Ibn Bābūya, *al-Khiṣāl* (Qumm: Manshūrāt jamāʿat al-mudarrisīn, 1403), 2:30.

[4] Muḥammad b. ʿĪsā al-Tirmidhī, *al-Jāmiʿ al-ṣaḥīḥ* (Beirut: Dār al-fikr, 1983), 4:185.

Shortening one's nails should clearly be done with a blade, as biting one's nails is clearly disapproved of and could even be thought to bring the individual under the influence of evil forces. In his final words of advice to his close companion, cousin, and son-in-law, ʿAlī, the Prophet says:

> Oh ʿAlī! There are three things which are from the Whispering One [i.e., Satan]: eating dirt, biting one's nails and chewing on one's beard.[5]

These rules may seem superstitious, and we moderns often pride ourselves on distinguishing superstitious from rational behavior. Yet for those who believe that God and Satan have an active presence in the world, and that Muḥammad is God's chosen Prophet, following Muḥammad's every advice is a very rational response.

These reports are only a small sampling of the huge literature devoted to recalling the Prophet's everyday words and actions, and not all of these have obvious theological implications. For example, this literature also informs us that the Prophet's favorite perfume was musk, that he liked to eat pieces of gourd, and that the Prophet said, "The best of all condiments is vinegar."[6] If one disagrees and dislikes vinegar, is one guilty of refusing to recognize the authority of the Prophet? Are Muslims really commanded to have all the subjective likes and dislikes of the Prophet? The treatment of this and related questions by Muslims through the centuries demonstrates that these were serious issues that vexed theologians, jurists, and others.

First, most Muslim thinkers said the duty to imitate the Prophet does not extend to adopting his personal preferences; Muslims are not required to develop a preference for musk and wear it when the appropriate occasion arises. But one might reasonably ask how one can come to know that the Prophet's love of musk is irrelevant to the valid completion of religious duties and is merely a personal preference. What is it about the report of the Prophet's sayings or actions that enables the individual Muslim to make this distinction? And even if Muslims do not need to like musk, would it be better if they did? It is reported, for example, that the Prophet's companion, Anas b. Mālik (d. ca. 91/710), made a special effort to like gourd after seeing the Prophet's enjoyment of a gourd, barley, and meat soup.[7] The legal scholars would put the question this way: how does one know whether a particular action of

[5] Ibn Bābūya, *al-Khiṣāl*, 2:62.

[6] Muslim, *Ṣaḥīḥ*, 6:125.

[7] Muḥammad b. Ismāʿīl al-Bukhārī, *al-Ṣaḥīḥ* (Beirut: Dār al-fikr, 1983), 6:197.

the Prophet is merely a piece of personal advice (*masnūn*) or a ritual or religious requirement (*farḍ*)? If it is a religious requirement, then failing to perform it is a transgression of God's law, the *sharīʿa*, and any transgression of the *sharīʿa* will be punished (in this life or the next). If it is merely a piece of personal advice, then ignoring it is not a transgression of God's law but instead is a missed opportunity. The believer had a chance to make his or her imitation of the Prophet more perfect but did not take it.

For example, these hygienic practices are not to be confused with rituals that achieve the ritual purity (*ṭahāra*) required to complete a valid prayer. If, for example, the Muslim has urinated or defecated since the last prayer, he or she must perform a formulaic set of washing rituals (*wuḍūʾ*) to regain purity status. So what of him washing his knuckles, one of the ten characteristics of *fiṭra* in the previously mentioned report? Al-Bayhaqī (d. 458/1066) tells us that "'washing the knuckles' means cleaning the places [on the fingers] that are dirty, and where filth gathers."[8] In his commentary on this report, the eleventh-century-AH (seventeenth-century-CE) commentator al-Munāwī clarifies that this is not related to the ritual washing of the hands in preparation for prayer. Instead, it is a separate act that Muslims should perform, not forming part of the ritual wash (*wuḍūʾ*).[9] Washing one's knuckles, therefore, is not a ritual or religious requirement but Prophetic advice. It is, in the language of medieval Muslim religious thought, a *sunna*.[10] It is good to do it, but God's law is not broken if it is ignored.

THEORETICAL QUESTIONS

A number of issues arise when considering the many reports of what the Prophet did and their implications for the behavior of the individual

8 Bayhaqī, *Maʿrifat al-sunan wa'l-āthār* (Beirut: Dār al-kutub al-ʿilmiyya, 1991), 1:248.

9 ʿAbd al-Raʾūf al-Munāwī (d.1031/1621), *Fayḍ al-qadīr* (Beirut: Dār al-kutub al-ʿilmiyya, 1994), 4:417.

10 The term *sunna* has many meanings in Islamic discourse. The *sunna* can refer to the example of the Prophet Muḥammad in all its elements (be it obligatory, recommended, or permitted); it can mean the way of doing things in a particular locality (as in "this is our *sunna*" – meaning, "our tradition"); and it can, as I am using it here, mean an action that it is good to do and that will bring spiritual benefit to the agent but is not obligatory within the *sharīʿa*. Under this usage, if one neglects a *sunna*, one is not committing a sinful act. Though the terminology is not used in an identical fashion by all authors, a *sunna* in this usage refers to a practice that brings a spiritual benefit (by enabling the individual to more closely imitate the Prophet), whereas a recommended action (*mustaḥabb*) brings a specific reward in the next life.

Muslim believer. These were discussed extensively in the premodern sources and are still debated today. I will address three of the most important ones:

1. The fraught area of the authenticity of such reports (how can one trust that the events have been reported correctly?)
2. The Prophet's intention in performing these actions (was he prescribing for the believers how they should act, or did he simply perform an act in a way that was comfortable for him?)
3. The Prophet's potential to make (major or minor) mistakes (if he can commit minor, unintentional errors, as some theologians thought, then can we be certain that these acts, or indeed any of his acts, are a guide?)[11]

The first of these is a question of sources and the reliability of oral and written reports. The second is a hermeneutical problem: determining which evidence is applicable to a given situation and then determining the meaning of that evidence. The last is a theological question that extends well into the theory of Islamic prophetology. Together, they represent the intellectual debate over the authority of the Prophet's example.

THE AUTHENTICITY OF PROPHETIC REPORTS

As we have seen, reports describe in great detail how, for example, the Prophet trimmed his body hair, cleaned his teeth, and cut his nails. But can it be known whether the Prophet actually did any of these things? The importance of the issue of reliability and authenticity for Muslim jurists and thinkers cannot be underestimated. The science of distinguishing reliable from unreliable, authentic from inauthentic prophetic reports was sophisticated and extremely well developed. It was a central element of Muslim religious discussions in law, theology, and Qur'ānic exegesis, and it was not immune from sectarian gloss and influence. Premodern Muslim writers debated this topic at length, but generally speaking, they reached the following conclusions:

- The reliability of a report is usually assessed through the individuals who have transmitted it through time and up to the point when it was written down.

[11] There are other important theoretical issues that could be addressed here, including the relationship of the Prophet's deeds to the rest of revelation.

- Even if all these transmitters were reliable and trustworthy, a single chain of these transmitters (an *isnād*) is not enough to prove for certain that the report is authentic.
- For a report to be proved beyond any doubt to be authentic, and therefore useful as a source of knowledge, more than one chain of transmitters is necessary (i.e., many people need to have heard the Prophet say or do something, and they need to have passed this on to many other people, and so on).
- The scholars differed over the exact number of chains necessary to bring certainty as to a report's authenticity, but they all agreed it was enough to mean that not many reports fulfilled this criterion (known as *tawātur*).
- This does not mean that the vast majority of reports that do not fulfill this criterion are useless; it merely means that absolute certainty of these reports' authenticity cannot, on most occasions, be obtained.

The result of all this is that when a scholar is trying to describe the *sharīʿa* in books of law, morality, and personal etiquette, he has to make an assessment as to which reports are most likely to be authentic and accurate and derive his rules or conclusions for conduct from them.

Hence, although one does not know (i.e., with absolute certainty) that a report is true, one does know that using a report as a guide for personal conduct can be justified. No scholar can claim to know the law of God as revealed by the Prophet Muḥammad, but he can claim to have assessed the reports and come up with his own conception of the law, which represents his best efforts. The authenticity question applies to all Prophetic reports, whether they describe momentous decisions of diplomacy and statecraft or mundane advice on personal hygiene. But assessing the authenticity of a report is only the first step; now begins the process of interpreting the meaning of that report.

UNDERSTANDING THE PROPHET'S INTENTIONS

The issue of whether the Muslims are commanded to treat both the Prophet's everyday and his more portentous acts as model behavior is discussed in some detail in works of Muslim legal theory (*uṣūl al-fiqh*).

Muslim thinkers who pondered these questions normally made a distinction between explicit statements spoken by the Prophet and the Prophet's actions. These thinkers felt that when the Prophet said something, he was certainly trying to convey information to us. However, when he did something, he may have been trying to convey this information, but he may have equally just been doing it in the way he liked. Speaking always reveals a desire to communicate information; actions may also be inspired by this desire, but they may be unintentional (akin to the actions of a sleeping person). One cannot deduce very much from actions on their own, as the following anecdote shows:

> The Prophet of God prayed with us, and when he prayed, he took off his sandals, and put them to his left. So all the people took off their sandals as well. When he has finished his prayer he said, "Why did you take off your sandals?" They replied, "We saw you taking them off, so we took them off." The Prophet then said, "I didn't take them off as part of the ritual. Rather the Angel Gabriel informed me that there was some filth and dirt on them. Whenever one of you comes to the place of prayer, let him look at his sandals. If there is something on them, then wipe it [off and pray in them]."[12]

The Prophet took off his sandals not because praying barefoot is an obligation (or even a recommendation) but for another reason, one that was specific to this occasion (i.e., there was dirt on his sandals). He further makes clear that even when one's sandals are dirty, one need not remove them – one can wipe them clean and then pray.

This story is interesting for several reasons. First, it seems to suggest that the Prophet was well aware that his community was already following his every move and that he needed to intervene to clarify personal whim from exemplary action. But premodern Muslim thinkers saw much more in this tale. For example, Ibn Ḥazm, the controversial fifth-century-AH (eleventh-century-CE) Andalusian writer, cites this *ḥadīth* and goes on to say that it demonstrates that "the Prophet denied that imitating his actions was necessarily obligatory." Instead, it shows that "the only things that create obligations are his orders."[13] It is not that the Prophet's actions are never proofs for Ibn Ḥazm. His view is that on their own (i.e., without any Prophetic statement to confirm them), the Prophet's actions cannot create an obligation. They could, though, create a recommendation.[14]

[12] Aḥmad b. Ḥanbal, *Musnad Aḥmad* (Beirut: Dār al-ṣādir, n.d.), 3:97.

[13] ʿAlī b. Aḥmād Ibn Ḥazm (456/1064), *al-Iḥkām fī uṣūl al-aḥkām* (Beirut: Dār al-kutub al-ʿilmiyya, n.d.), 4:466.

[14] English-language accounts that discuss this issue are not numerous. One can find brief summaries in Bernard Weiss, *The Search for God's Law: Islamic Jurisprudence in the Writings of Sayf al-Dīn al-Āmidī* (Salt Lake City: University of Utah Press, 1992), 69–178; and in Mohammed Hashim Kamali, *Principles of Islamic Jurisprudence* (Cambridge, U.K.: Islamic Texts Society, 1991), 48–57.

Regarding statements, the most common position was that a Prophetic statement that is merely a personal preference (with no moral or legal relevance) can be identified as such by additional evidence (*qarā'in*). This evidence can be the question to which the Prophet's statement is a reply, or it can be found within the context in which the Prophet made the statement. From these scraps of evidence, the Muslim jurists argued, one can usually make a judgment as to whether a statement of the Prophet has legal or ethical relevance. Even when this trail runs cold, most agreed that both God and the Prophet may use the grammatical form of the imperative (*ṣīghat al-amr*), but this does not necessarily mean that an obligation is created. For example, in Q 5:02, God says, "After [you have performed your pilgrimage] and you have left the sacred area, go hunting." He does not mean you must go hunting. He means that hunting is forbidden while on pilgrimage, but once this is over and you have left the area of Mecca (and perhaps Medina also), you can, if you wish, hunt again. So, when the Prophet gives an order, he could be expressing a divine law; but he could equally be expressing a recommendation or even a permission. Into which category a Prophetic statement might fall all depends on external evidence.

The situation is slightly different with the Prophet's actions. Often these lack extraneous evidence to help one make a decision, and even when they do have external evidence, it is not always clear what that might mean. Also, there is, theoretically, a greater potential that the report simply describes the way in which the Prophet did an ordinary everyday action, and he would have had no objection to someone performing the same action in a different way. The report that the Prophet used to put his right shoe on before his left shoe is a good example of this, because he is supposed to have had a general preference for "starting actions with the right" (*tayammun*): "The Prophet used to begin things with the right – whether it was the acts of ritual purification, putting on shoes or putting on sandals."[15] This report of the Prophet's actions is ambiguous, but it could suggest that beginning with the right shoe is not an exemplary action but simply part of the Prophet's general tendency to begin things with the right. However, there is also a saying of the Prophet:

> The Prophet said, "Whenever you put on your shoes, put on the right one first. When you take them off, take the left one first."[16]

[15] Bukhārī, *Ṣaḥīḥ*, 1:110.
[16] Muslim, *Ṣaḥīḥ*, 6:103.

This statement, in contrast, is not at all ambiguous and serves as convincing evidence that this action is a *sunna*. Examples such as this indicate that the words of the Prophet take precedence over his actions because orders made manifest in statements are explicit (or at least potentially explicit), whereas orders expressed through actions will always remain implicit.

Painstaking as it is, this distinction is only the beginning of the long process of determining how to follow the Prophet's example. One extensive taxonomy of the Prophet's actions was put together by the fifth-century-AH (twelfth-century-CE) theologian, Imām al-Ḥaramayn al-Juwaynī.[17] His schema can be set out as follows:

> Actions of the Prophet can be divided into:
>
> (1) Actions which the Prophet explicitly said were exemplary and
> (2) Actions which the Prophet did not say were exemplary

The first type, Juwaynī says, is not really relevant here. If the Prophet says, "Pray just as you see me praying [*ṣallū kamā ra'aytumūnī uṣallī*],"[18] then, in reality, the Prophet's words are the guide and the actions are just a demonstration of what the believer should do. It is the second section that is more problematic, where the Prophet's actions are, in themselves, potential sources of guidance. Here is Juwaynī's description of how this second category of action can be divided:

> [Actions] which [are described in reports] and are not related to a saying which bears witness [to it being exemplary] are divided into:
>
> (2.1) Natural actions [*al-af'āl al-jibilliyya*]. These [are actions] which any living being cannot avoid doing – such as resting, moving, standing, sitting and things like this – which people perform in different ways....
> (2.2) Actions for which there is nothing which indicates that it might be an action which occurs out of habit [i.e., the natural actions of 2.1]. This [type of action] is further subdivided into [actions] which function as an explanation [*bayān* – of something the Prophet or God said elsewhere] and those that do not appear to act as [an explanation]:

[17] 'Abd al-Malik al-Juwaynī (d. 478/1085), *al-Burhān fī uṣūl al-fiqh* (Beirut: Dār al-kutub al-'ilmiyya, 1997), 182–8.

[18] This is a very well-known saying of the Prophet. In Bukhārī's *Ṣaḥīḥ* alone there are at least three (variant) versions: 1:155; 7:77; 8:133.

(2.2.1) [Actions] which function as an explanation are those which embellish something that was said in a general manner in the Qur'ān....
(2.2.2) [Actions] that do not apparently act as [an explanation], are yet further subdivided into
  (2.2.2a) Those which occurred in the context of a pious act, and that it is clear that the Prophet intended by [performing the act] to achieve piety, and
  (2.2.2b) Those which did not occur in this context.[19]

Juwaynī's schema was adopted by many, but not all, who wanted to address these questions.[20] First of all, one has natural actions (i.e., 2.1) that everyone does but that are done in different ways by different people. Not everyone's gait is the same; not everyone sits in exactly the same manner. Once one has determined that an action falls into this category, Juwaynī states that it ceases to be a potential *sunna*.[21] One is not commanded to stand, walk, or sit in the manner the Prophet did, unless standing, walking, and sitting were part of a ritual act. Actions that are not natural actions can be divided into those that are clearly a means of acting out something indicated elsewhere in God's revelation (i.e., 2.2.1) and those that are not (i.e., 2.2.2). When God says, "Perform the pilgrimage" in the Qur'ān (as He does in many places; e.g., Q 2:196 and Q 22:27), and there are reports of how the Prophet performed the rituals while on pilgrimage, then the Prophet's actions explain how one is to obey God's general command (i.e., 2.2.1). If an action does not appear to be linked to a command found elsewhere in revelation, then it could be something that the Prophet did in the context of a pious act (i.e., 2.2.2a). For example, when the Prophet arrived to perform his prayers, he used to clean his teeth with a toothpick (*miswāk*). However, when he described the ritual preparations for prayer, he did not mention the toothpick. Using a *miswāk* was done in the context of a pious act, but it does not appear to be part of that pious act (see 2.2.2a). Finally, there are actions that the Prophet did but that are unconnected with pious acts

[19] Juwaynī, *Burhān*, 183. The numbering is mine.

[20] In particular there were those who disagreed with the notion that one need not imitate habitual actions (category 2.1). Juwaynī sees no need to imitate them and excludes them from the discussion. But some jurists said this was unproved. See, e.g., Āl Taymiyya, *al-Musawwada fī uṣūl al-fiqh* (Cairo: Maṭbaʿat al-Madanī, 1964), 67–8, discussed later in this chapter.

[21] He says, "When it is clear that [the action in question] is of this [type], then the action of the Prophet is unconnected with the [issue under] investigation here." Juwaynī, *Burhān*, 183.

(e.g., putting on his right shoe first; see 2.2.2b). As one moves through Juwaynī's category 2.2 (nonhabitual actions) and its subcategories, the actions appear as less and less binding. An action that clearly acts as an explanation (*bayān*) would appear to have the strongest evidence of being demanded of the believers (e.g., pilgrimage rites). Actions that do not act as explanations but occur within the context of pious acts are less likely to be required, but there is still a strong case for them (e.g., using a toothpick before prayer). Actions that do not appear to have any connection with pious intent (e.g., putting on one's right show first) seem quite close to habitual actions, though perhaps their evidence for being *sunna* is slightly stronger than habitual actions.

The interplay of these categories becomes clearer when one considers an example. The Prophet said many times that using the toothpick (*siwāk* or *miswāk*) was good, and he recommended its use to Muslims. Most Muslim writers have accordingly seen it as recommended (*mustaḥabb*) to use the toothpick but not obligatory. It has been a popular, though not universally observed, practice among Muslim communities through history. The many reports of the Prophet using a toothpick (before ritual ablutions and before prayer) are confirmed by his statements in which he explicitly recommends the practice to the Muslims. On the basis of this evidence, most thinkers considered this action that "occurred in the context of a pious act" clearly aimed at achieving piety (i.e., 2.2.2a) and hence recommended. Both Sunnī and Shīʿī thinkers have agreed on this. So, for example, the Shīʿī theologian Muḥammad b. al-Ḥasan al-Ṭūsī (d. 460/1067) not only defended the use of the toothpick but also defended it being recommended and not obligatory for Muslims. He argued:

> [1] [Using] the *siwāk* is recommended, not obligatory (*masnūn ghayr wājib*). This is what all the jurists say.
> [2] Dāwūd [al-Ẓāhirī] says it is obligatory.
> [3a] Our proof [against him] is that the *firqa* agree upon this position.[22] [3b] Furthermore, there is the principle of freedom from obligation [*bara'at al-dhimma*].[23] [For using the toothpick

[22] *Firqa* is sometimes translated as "sect" or "grouping," and Ṭūsī here refers to his own "saved sect," the Twelver Shīʿīs.

[23] This principle is commonly used by Shīʿī jurists (and Sunni *uṣūlīs*) to solve an ambiguity in the revelatory material. If the source seems unclear, or if two sources seem to recommend two mutually exclusive courses of action, the least onerous path is the one that the individual should choose. *Barā'at al-dhimma* refers to the most economic fulfillment of the law. In this case, it may be unclear whether the use of the *siwāk* is obligatory or recommended. Treating it as recommended is the least onerous action, and therefore under *barā'at al-dhimma*, it should be selected.

> to be obligatory,] it would need a proof [and there is none].
> [3d] The Prophet said, "If it had not been so difficult for my community, I would have made them use the *siwāk* [before] every prayer." If it had been obligatory, then he would have ordered them to use it, whether it was difficult or not....
> [3e] Abū Jaʿfar [the Shīʿī Imām al-Bāqir] said, "The Prophet used to use the *siwāk* a lot, but not because it was obligatory. Not doing it every now and again does not harm you."[24]

A lone voice considers using the *siwāk* obligatory: Dāwūd al-Ẓāhirī (d. 270/884). His school, the Ẓāhiriyya, advocated taking the apparent meaning of any statement by God or the Prophet and forbade seeking the possible motivation behind God's or the Prophet's words and actions. For them, every imperative (or order) from God or the Prophet creates an obligation because the apparent meaning of an order is that it is obligatory. They argued that when the Prophet gives the order, "Use the *siwāk*," this creates an obligation on all Muslims to use the *siwāk*.

For the other schools, however, no order necessarily creates an obligation. There are many orders that clearly did not (e.g., the earlier example about hunting), and even an imperative that does create an obligation does so only if there is evidence to show this. For al-Ṭūsī there are additional reasons not only for rejecting Dāwūd's position but also for adopting the view that using the *siwāk* is *sunna*. These are the fact that the Prophet expressly states that he did not make it obligatory before every prayer because it would be too great a burden on the Muslims (i.e., 3d). This means that *siwāk* use is a good thing and that the Prophet approved of it, but it is not obligatory. Second (and this will be a convincing argument only for Shīʿīs), the Imām al-Bāqir (d. 114/732) says that the Prophet used the *siwāk* not out of obligation but because it was recommended (i.e., 3e).

If the Prophet performed an action out of obligation (i.e., because God had ordered him to do it), then the community must perform it, too, because an order to the Prophet is an order for the Muslims. This principle holds in all cases except when there is evidence that God is revealing an obligation for the Prophet that is exclusive to him (*makhṣūṣ bihi*). When there is evidence that an order was *makhṣūṣ bihi*, then the rest of us can ignore it (the famous example of this is the permission granted to the Prophet to have more than four wives – a license that is not available to other males in the Muslim community). The use of

[24] Al-Ṭūsī, *al-Khilāf* (Qumm: Mu'assasat al-nashr al-islāmī, 1407), 1:71.

the *siwāk* was, for the vast majority of Muslim scholars, an action in which "the Prophet clearly intended by [performing the act] to achieve piety" – that is, 2.2.2a in Juwaynī's foregoing schema, and therefore it is only recommended (good to do but not essential). Dāwūd and his school were isolated in thinking it obligatory.

An issue emerges with the use of the toothpick in Ramaḍān. It could be argued that, when using the toothpick, a morsel of food may become dislodged and the fasting person may swallow it. Logic would seem to indicate that the use of the *siwāk* either breaks the fast or runs a high risk of breaking the fast (and should be avoided). However, "ʿĀmir b. Rabīʿa says, 'I saw the Prophet using the toothpick [*siwāk*] while he was fasting more times than I can count.'"[25]

So, one might think, Ramaḍān does not affect the categorization of the Prophet's use of the *siwāk*. It remains an action "which occurred in the context of a pious act, and that it is clear that the Prophet intended by [performing the act] to achieve piety" (i.e., the foregoing category 2.2.2a).

But does this report prove this? Someone who, despite this report, continued to be concerned about toothpick use during the day in Ramaḍān might consider the following argument. The toothpick is used to clean teeth and freshen breath (breath can become fetid while fasting). But the Prophet also said: "The foul breath of the one fasting is more pleasing to God than the smell of musk."[26]

It would appear, then, that God has a preference for us having bad breath while fasting. However, the fact that the Prophet used the toothpick during the day in Ramaḍān means that its use must be a dispensation or an allowance (*rukhṣa*). God, magnanimously, has allowed us to use the *siwāk* during the day in Ramaḍān (to prevent the antisocial situation of everyone having bad breath during Ramaḍān). It was, then, this dispensation that the Prophet was following in the report of ʿĀmir. The use of the *siwāk* is recommended or *sunna* throughout the year (and hence the individual received benefit from it) but permitted (and benefit neutral) only during Ramaḍān. Hence, some premodern jurists argued that using the toothpick during the day in Ramaḍān was an action that "did not occur in the context of a pious act and that it was not "clear that the Prophet intended by [performing the act] to achieve piety." That is, it falls into category 2.2.2b in Juwaynī's schema. Outside of Ramaḍān, toothpick use was a good thing (and classified in 2.2.2a). Hence, the Prophet's actions in using a *siwāk* during Ramaḍān prove that it is

[25] Bukhārī, *Ṣaḥīḥ*, 3:225.
[26] Abū Dāwūd al-Sijistānī, *Sunan Abī Dāwūd* (Beirut: Dār al-fikr, 1990), 1:317.

permitted to use one but do not show that it is recommended to use one. Indeed, the preceding report would indicate that it is better not to use a *siwāk* so that God can appreciate the bad breath of the one performing the fast. No jurists actually went this far, but the Shāfiʿīs did argue that using the *siwāk* was discouraged (*makrūh*) after midday and into the evening in Ramaḍān, presumably so God could appreciate the bad breath of those fasting during the Ramaḍān evening ceremonies.

The debate around using a toothpick (and the subsidiary debate about using it during Ramaḍān) highlights a problem with Juwaynī's categorization schema. With regard to any individual action of the Prophet, there are debates about whether or not it is habitual (i.e., 2.1). Even if this is solved, there are subsequent debates about whether it is part of a pious act (2.2.2a) or not (2.2.2b). Even if there is agreement over the category into which an action should be placed, there is a debate about whether being in a particular category necessarily leads to the action being assessed as permitted, recommended, or obligatory. Ibn Taymiyya (d. 728/1328), a jurist much revered by contemporary Salafī Muslims, is associated with the view that the default position when encountering a report concerning an action of the Prophet is that the action is "recommended."[27] This "includes actions [such as] eating and drinking, getting dressed and what to wear, mounting [a beast] and riding [it], marital relations, how to live, and where to live, sleeping and lying down, walking and talking."[28] He went further than this, arguing that it is quite possible that even when an action was not obligatory for the Prophet, it could be obligatory for everyone else. The duty to imitate the Prophet meant that an action that was not obligatory for him became obligatory for the community:

> It is obligatory for the subjects of a leader to follow that leader, even though the [things he orders] are not actually obligatory for him individually; and it is obligatory for an army to follow the general, even though the things he orders are not obligatory for him personally.[29]

In battle, a general is not obligated to attack with the left flank or the right (he makes a choice, depending on which course of action he considers tactically better). However, the soldiers in the left flank are obligated to attack when he orders them. Similarly, an action of pure, indifferent

[27] The terms used are *mustaḥabb*, *mandūb*, and *sunna*, and some jurists argued for subtle differences among these subcategories of "recommended."

[28] Āl Taymiyya, *Musawwada*, 67.

[29] Āl Taymiyya, *Musawwada*, 68.

choice for the Prophet (e.g., putting on the right shoe before the left) can become a recommended (or even an obligatory) act for the Muslims because they are his servants. Ibn Taymiyya does not, it seems, differentiate between so-called habitual acts (*jibilliyya*) and the rest (between 2.1 and 2.2 in Juwaynī's schema). His reason appears to be that, in the absence of evidence, one cannot determine the Prophet's motives for performing this or that action. Therefore, the default position is that such actions are highly recommended to all Muslims (and with minimal evidence in their favor, they can become obligatory). Although Ibn Taymiyya's apparent rejection of the distinction between habitual and nonhabitual actions was not unanimously held, his idea that the default position was recommendation chimed with the views of a number of jurists. Although most jurists, along with al-Juwaynī, believed it possible to determine whether an action was habitual (*al-afʿāl al-jāriyya fī'l-ʿādāt*, or *al-afʿāl al-jibilliyya*), many also believed that the Prophet's nonhabitual actions, once known, were to be initially assessed as creating recommendations for the believers.

CAN THE PROPHET MAKE MISTAKES?

For Ibn Taymiyya, there are spiritual, moral, and legal benefits to imitating every recorded action of the Prophet. To argue for this position, one must, at the same time, believe that it is impossible for the Prophet to sin (or even to make mistakes). If the Prophet did commit sins or make mistakes, then it becomes irrational and irresponsible to follow his every action. Without additional evidence that confirms that an action of the Prophet was a valid enactment of the law of God, the individual risks committing a sin by imitating the Prophet. Hence, for Ibn Taymiyya, the Prophet could never have transgressed the *sharīʿa* without informing the Muslims immediately that he had.

The premodern jurists and theologians debated the sinlessness of prophets at length. Here is Fakhr al-Dīn al-Rāzī's (d. 606/1209) description of the various positions:

> The community has divided into two views concerning the sinlessness of the Prophets:
>
> (1) First, there are those who argue that it is not [logically] permitted for them to commit a sin, be it great or small, be it intentionally or inadvertently or through a [mis]understanding. This is opinion of the Shīʿa.

(2) Then there are those who argue that they can [commit sins], and then they differ over what is permitted with regard to [the Prophets] and what is not permitted.... The community is here divided into four positions:

(2.1) [T]he first are those who say it is permitted for prophets to commit major sins intentionally, and one group – the Ḥashwiyya – say this has actually happened. Abū Bakr [al-Bāqillānī] says that it is possible rationally speaking, but there is revelation which demonstrates that it never happened.

(2.2) There are those who say it is not permitted for them to commit any sin, major or minor intentionally. However, they could do it on the basis of a misunderstanding [of what God had ordered]. This was [the Muʿtazilī Abū ʿAlī] al-Jubbāʾī's (d. 303/915) opinion.

(2.3) There are those who say it is not possible, either intentionally, or on the basis of a misunderstanding, but it is possible as a mistake....

(2.4) There are those who say that it is not permitted for the prophets to commit major sins, but they could commit minor sins either intentionally, or by mistake, or because of a misunderstanding. Excluded from this are [those sins] which drive [the people] away, such as lying or meanness.[30]

Let us deal with the various Sunnī positions (2.1–2.4) first. The Sunnīs all agree that the Prophet did, at times, perform acts at variance with the *sharīʿa*. They differ among themselves along two axes. First, they differ with regard to the seriousness of the transgression (major sin–minor sin). Second, they differ with regard to intentionality between intentionally transgressing the *sharīʿa* and unintentionally doing so. Unintentionality is further subdivided into not intending to transgress but doing it by mistake and mistakenly thinking an act is not a transgression when it actually is. The various Sunnī positions described by al-Rāzī can be mapped on this categorization of actions and intention. One might argue that if all the Sunnīs agree that the Prophet transgressed the *sharīʿa* on occasions – even if he did it by mistake and unintentionally – then the whole enterprise of imitating him is called into question. Fakhr al-Dīn al-Rāzī does not believe this is a necessary conclusion to draw. He

30 Fakhr al-Dīn al- Rāzī, *al-Maḥṣūl fi ʿilm al-uṣūl* (Beirut: Dār al-kutub al-ʿilmiyya, 1408/1988), 1:501–2.

argues that it is rationally possible that the prophets might commit a transgression by mistake.[31] However, it is not possible that a prophet, having committed that transgression, would leave that action unremarked and uncorrected (*bi-sharṭ an yatadhakkarṭūhu fī'l-ḥāl*). Hence, if there is a report of the Prophet's action and there is no indication either in the report or elsewhere that the Prophet corrected himself, then we are justified in treating that action as at least permitted within the *sharīʿa*. For al-Rāzī, the Prophet's actions on their own, without any indicator, should be treated as recommended because, even if they are not recommended, there is no harm in imitating the Prophet in every possible manner.

In opposition to these positions, there are the Shīʿīs, who argue that the Prophet never committed a major or minor sin either through ignorance, forgetfulness, or misunderstanding, and he never made a mistake. They argue this because they wish to make the same claim for their Imāms – the descendants of the Prophet Muḥammad who should have led the community after Muḥammad's death in 632. The key doctrine in Shīʿī Islam is the idea of unquestioning obedience and devotion to the Imām. Because they cannot claim that the Imāms are superior to the Prophet, if the Imām is sinless, the Prophet must also be sinless. However, even though they maintain the highest notion of the Prophet's sinlessness, their attitude toward the Prophet's actions in isolation is not that they establish an obligation. In fact, Shīʿī authors such as Sayyid Murtaḍā ʿAlam al-Hudā (d. 436/1044) and al-Ṭūsī have argued that an action on its own cannot be assessed. Murtaḍā argues that because the Prophet is sinless and never made mistakes, his actions have the same status as his statements. When the Prophet gives an imperative, we do not know whether he is saying the action is obligatory, recommended, or permitted. Similarly, when he performs an action, we do not know which category it falls into. Hence, for Shīʿī thinkers, one cannot decide what category a Prophetic action falls into on the basis of the action alone. In such cases, one must suspend judgment (*tawaqquf*) until additional evidence comes to light.[32] However, as the Shīʿī writers argue, it is extremely rare that an action of the Prophet is recorded without any evidence to help the individual assess it. On such occasions, one knows that the action is at least permitted. Hence, one cannot disallow others from performing it, and one cannot recommend or compel

[31] He was criticized in this by Tāj al-Dīn al-Subkī (see his *Rafʿ al-ḥājib ʿan mukhtaṣar Ibn al-Ḥājib* [Beirut: ʿĀlam al-kutub, 1999], 2:100–2).

[32] Sayyid al-Murtaḍā, *al-Dharīʿa ilā uṣūl al-sharīʿa* (Tehran: University of Tehran, 1376 AH) 2:578. See also, al-Ṭūsī, *ʿUddat al-uṣūl* (Qumm: Sitāra, 1417 AH), 2:575–80.

its performance either. Ultimately, the Prophet's actions on their own are, for Shīʿī thinkers, certainly not sins or errors, but beyond this, one cannot assess them according to the moral and legal categories of the *sharīʿa*.

CONCLUSIONS

There was, then, a difference of opinion (*ikhtilāf*) among medieval Muslim thinkers on how to initially assess the actions of the Prophet in themselves (i.e., before the assessment is affected by extraneous evidence). It was these everyday, humdrum actions of the Prophet that some Muslims used, and continue to use, as guides for personal etiquette (*adab*). The *ikthilāf* was summarized by Nāṣir al-Dīn al-Bayḍāwī (d.685/1286) in his highly abbreviated summary of jurisprudence *Minhāj al-wuṣūl*:

[A] Those who argue [that the Prophet's actions indicate] permission say that the [Prophet's] action cannot be disapproved, or forbidden [because he was sinless], and the principle is that one [assumes an action] is not obligatory or recommended. [After this] only permitted remains [as a possible category]....

[B] Those who argue for recommendation say that God said, "There is for you a good example in the Prophet of God." This proves that [his actions] are preferred, and since the principle is that one [assumes an action] is not obligatory [it must be recommended].

[C] Those who argue for obligation [say] that God says [in the Qur'ān], "Obey him!" (Q 7.158 [meaning the Prophet]), and "Say! If you love God, obey me!" (Q 3.31), and "Whatever the Prophet brings you, adopt it" (Q 59.7), and the fact that all the Companions [of the Prophet] agreed that it is obligatory to wash the male and female private parts [before prayer] on the basis of a saying by ʿĀʾisha [the Prophet's wife] "Both the Prophet and myself did this, and we washed ourselves [in this way]."[33]

[D] [There are those who] suspend judgment. This view is the best because [the action's inherent] ambiguity [i.e., it could be classified in any of the above three categories]. Also, it could have been an action particular to him [and not permitted to everybody].[34]

33 Muḥammad b. Yazīd Ibn Mājah, *Sunan Ibn Mājah* (Beirut: Dār al-fikr, n.d) 1:199.

34 Nāṣir al-Dīn al-Bayḍāwī, *Minhāj al-wusul fī maʿrifat ʿilm al-uṣūl* (Cairo: Muḥammad ʿAlī Ṣubayḥ, 1969), 42; the section D actually comes before the others – but for comprehension, it is best read after sections A, B, and C.

It is not easy to determine which of the four options outlined by al-Bayḍāwī was the most popular. Suspending judgment (position D, which al-Bayḍāwī advocates) appears to have been dominant, particularly among the Shāfiʿīs and was the Shīʿī position also. Many jurists did not dare to make a distinction between habitual and nonhabitual actions, as they did not feel that anyone could look into the mind of the Prophet and determine his motive. Hence, they suspended judgment on the issue. If they did distinguish between habitual and nonhabitual actions, they reduced the importance of the distinction. Tāj al-Dīn al-Subkī (d. 771/1370), the influential Shāfiʿī writer, expresses this nicely:

> Following [the Prophet's] habitual actions is not the law. This is because they may have been performed without any intention. If you do them, that's fine. If you don't do them, that is also fine, as long as you do not refrain from doing them because you are intentionally refraining from following the Prophet.... However, I think that to model oneself [*al-taʾassī*; on the Prophet] is an approved action... but this approval does not mean that the action should be described as recommended [*mustaḥabb*]. Rather it can be classed as modelling oneself on the [Prophet] and [thereby] making oneself blessed....
>
> It is always possible that [an action] is not habitual, but actually makes a rule. In such circumstances, [the action] should be enacted in the particular way [of the Prophet].... This would make the action a little below [actions] for which there is a clear indication of piety, but a little above those which are clearly habitual.... The Companions have different opinions on this matter – should one interpret such actions as habitual, and therefore not recommended, or should they be seen as making rules – and therefore recommended? It is God who grants us prosperity.[35]

Subkī's answer neatly sums up the common Muslim view concerning the Prophet's everyday practices. It is quite possible (and in some cases, it may be quite likely) that his prosaic actions have no power to place moral, legal, or ritual demands (*tashrīʿ*) on the community. Nonetheless, imitating the Prophet in all his actions brings benefits. It cultivates an attitude of piety and blessedness within the individual. If this is so, the legal assessment of the action (permitted, recommended, or obligatory) becomes less important. The individual spiritual dividend accrued from

[35] Tāj al-Dīn al-Subkī, *Rafʿ al-ḥājib*, 2:105, 123–4.

living one's life in imitation of the Prophet renders the complexities of juristic argumentation irrelevant.

Further reading

Berg, Herbert. *Development of Exegesis in Early Islam*. Richmond, VA: Routledge and Curzon, 2000.

al-Ghazālī, Muḥammad. *Remembrance and Prayer: The Way of the Prophet Muḥammad*. Translated by Yusuf Talal De Lorenzo. Leicester, U.K.: Islamic Foundation, 1986.

Hallaq, Wael. "The Authenticity of Prophetic Ḥadîth: A Pseudo-Problem." *Studia Islamica* 89 (1999): 75–90.

Kister, M. J. "Pare Your Nails: A Study of an Early Tradition." In *Ḥadīth: Origins and Developments*, edited by Harald Motzki, 279–86. Aldershot, U.K.: Ashgate, 2004.

Rubin, Uri, ed. *The Life of Muhammad*. Aldershot, U.K.: Ashgate, 1998.

Schimmel, Annemarie. *And Muhammad Is His Messenger: The Veneration of the Prophet in Islamic Piety*. Chapel Hill: University of North Carolina Press, 1985.

al-Shahrazūrī, Taqī ʿl-Dīn b. al-Ṣalāh. *An Introduction to the Science of the Ḥadīth: Kitāb Maʿrifat anwāʿ ʿilm al-ḥadīth*. Translated by Eerik Dickinson. Reading, MA: Garnet, 2005.

Weiss, Bernard. *The Search for God's Law: Islamic Jurisprudence in the Writings of Sayf al-Dīn al-Āmidī*. Salt Lake City: University of Utah Press, 1992.

6 Muḥammad as the pole of existence

CARL W. ERNST

The peculiar concerns of modern society tend to furnish the lenses through which figures like Muḥammad are viewed today. That is, modern biographies of the Prophet tend to see him chiefly as a leader responsible for establishing a movement, the significance of which is to be gauged mainly in terms of its social and political impact. His prophetic role is often understood primarily in terms of the establishment of ritual and legal norms that, in principle, governed the habits of an emerging Islamic civilization. The modern European concept of multiple religions carries with it assumptions about a contest between major religions for establishing a dominant position in the world today. Thus, a prophet who is viewed as the founder of one of the world's major religions is inevitably seen, in retrospect, mostly as a key player in this historic struggle. This observation holds both for non-Muslim Euro-Americans alarmed about the very existence of Islam, and for Muslim triumphalists who take refuge in Islam as an anticolonial identity. Modern reformist Muslims tend to downplay suggestions that the Prophet could have had any extraordinary status beyond ordinary human beings, and the Protestant inclinations that characterize much of the contemporary climate of opinion on religion (for Christians and non-Christians alike) reinforce the notion that Islam is a faith that lacks the supernatural baggage to be found, for instance, in Catholic Christianity. The legacy of anti-Islamic polemics among Christians since medieval times has also helped focus attention (mostly negative) on Muḥammad as a political and military leader.

From such a sociopolitical perspective, it therefore might seem surprising that Muḥammad has also been seen for centuries in a quite different light, as the prophet whose spiritual and cosmic role is the most important aspect of his career. Far from being viewed as a mere postman who delivered a message that happened to be of divine origin, Muḥammad, for a considerable portion of premodern Muslims, was the primordial light through which God created the world, viewed in semiphilosophical terms as the Muḥammadan reality. The ascension of Muḥammad into the heavens and the divine presence, possibly alluded to in a couple of passages in the Qur'ān, became a major theme defining his spiritual supremacy as the seal of the prophets. Muḥammad was described as a human being of perfect beauty, immune from sin, whose life was marked by miracles testifying to his extraordinary status. He became the focus of a speculative prophetology, which, particularly in the hands of mystical thinkers of the Ṣūfī tradition, drew on the metaphysical concepts of philosophers like Ibn Sīnā to formulate a cosmic understanding of Muḥammad's role in relation to the emerging notion of sainthood (*walāya*). Concomitantly, the Prophet became increasingly invested with the power of intercession for the souls of the faithful on Judgment Day, a concept that would have wide repercussions in popular religious practice. This salvific power of Muḥammad became tangible in the form of devotional performances of literary texts in different languages, as well as in the dreams and visions through which both elite mystics and ordinary believers could have direct access to the spirit of the Prophet. For these mystical understandings of the Prophet Muḥammad, we are particularly indebted to the research of Annemarie Schimmel, whose work is the standard reference on this subject.[1]

MUḤAMMAD AS LIGHT

Because the literature on the Prophet's mystical qualities is vast, it is convenient to begin with a short text that illustrates a number of important themes occurring in later Muslim piety. This is one of the short essays in rhyming Arabic prose composed by the early Ṣūfī and martyr al-Ḥallāj (d. 309/922), titled *Ṭā-Sīn of the Lamp*. Without dwelling on the esoteric letter symbolism alluded to in the first words of the title, one can quickly recognize the powerful imagery of light that occurs throughout this passage, presenting Muḥammad as the vessel through which the light of God is communicated to humanity. Moreover, Ḥallāj makes it clear that Muḥammad not only is foremost among humanity's elite, the prophets, but also has a transcendental status beyond the confines of space and time. Although Ḥallāj securely anchors the career of Muḥammad to the sanctuary of Mecca and the historical context of his Companions such as Abū Bakr, he nevertheless identifies the actions of

1 Annemarie Schimmel, *And Muhammad Is His Messenger: The Veneration of the Prophet in Islamic Piety* (Chapel Hill: University of North Carolina Press, 1985).

the Prophet as transparent reflections of the will of God and even as an indication of his unity with God:

> A lamp appeared from the light of the hidden realm; it returned, and surpassed the other lamps, and prevailed. A moon manifested itself among the other moons, a star whose constellation is in the heaven of secrets. God called Muḥammad "illiterate" [Q 7:157] to concentrate his inspiration, "man of the Sanctuary" to increase of his fortune, and "Meccan" to reinforce his nearness to Him. God "opened his breast" [Q 6:125], raised his rank, enforced his command, and revealed his full moon. His full moon arose from the cloud of Yamāma, his sun dawned in the environs of Tahama, and his lamp radiated a mine of generosity. He only taught from his own insight, and he only commanded his example by the beauty of his life. He was present before God and made God present, he saw and informed, he cautioned and warned.
>
> No one has seen him in reality except his companion, [Abū Bakr] the Confirmer. For he was in agreement with him, and then he was his companion, so that no division would occur between them. No one really knew him, for all were ignorant of his true description. "Those to whom We gave the Book know Muḥammad as they know their own sons, but there is a division among them, who conceal the truth although they know it" [Q 2:146]. The lights of prophecy emerged from his light, and his lights appeared from the light of the Hidden. None of their lights is brighter, more splendid, or takes greater precedence in eternity, than the light of the Master of the Sanctuary.
>
> His aspiration preceded all other aspirations, his existence preceded nothingness, and his name preceded the Pen, because he existed before all peoples. There is not in the horizons, beyond the horizons, or below the horizons, anyone more elegant, more noble, more knowing, more just, more fearsome, or more compassionate, than the subject of this tale. He is the leader of created beings, the one "whose name is glorious [Aḥmad]" [Q 61:6]. His nature is unique, his command is most certain, his essence is most excellent, his attribute is most illustrious, and his aspiration is most distinctive. How wonderful! How splendid, clear and pure, how magnificent and famous, how illuminated, capable, and patient he is! His fame was unceasing, before all created

beings existed, and his renown was unceasing before there was any "before" and after any "after," when no substance or colors existed. His substance is pure, his word is prophetic, his knowledge is lofty, his expression is Arabic, his direction of prayer is "neither of the East nor the West" (Q 24:35), his descent is paternal, his peer [Gabriel] is lordly, and his companion [Abū Bakr] is of his people.

Eyes have insight by his guidance, and inner minds and hearts attain their knowledge through him. God made him speak, the proof confirmed him, and God dispatched him. He is the proof and he is the proven. He is the one who polished the rust from the mirror of the suffering breast. He is the one who brought an eternal Word, timeless, unspoken, and uncreated, which is united with God without separation, and which passes beyond the understanding. He is the one who told of the ends, and the end of the end. He lifted the clouds and pointed to "the house of the Sanctuary" [Q 5:97]. He is the perfect one, he is the magnanimous one, he is the one who ordered the idols to be smashed, he is the one who tore away the clouds, he is the one sent to all humanity, and he is the one who distinguishes between favor and prohibition.

Above him, a cloud flashed lightning, and beneath him, lightning flashed and sparkled. It rained and brought forth fruit. All sciences are but a drop from his ocean, all wisdom but a spoonful from his sea, and all times are but an hour from his duration. Truth exists through him, and through him reality exists; sincerity exists through him, and companionship exists through him. Chaos exists through him, and order exists through him [cf. Q 21:30]. He is "the first" in attaining union and "the last" in prophecy, "the outward" in knowledge "and the inward" in reality [Q 57:3]. No learned man has attained to his knowledge, and no sage is aware of his understanding. God did not give him up to His creation, for he is He, as I am He, and "He is He."

Never has anyone departed from the M of Muḥammad, and no one has entered the Ḥ. [As for] his Ḥ, the second M, the D, and the M at the beginning: the D is his permanence [*dawām*], the M is his rank [*maḥall*], the Ḥ is his spiritual state [*ḥāl*], and the second M is his speech [*maqāl*]. [God] revealed his proclamation,

> He displayed his proof, "He caused the Criterion [the Qur'ān] to descend" [Q 3:4], He made his tongue speak, He illuminated his paradises, He reduced his opponents to impotence, He confirmed his explanation, He raised his dignity. If you fled from his field, then where would be the path when there is no guide, you suffering one? For the wisdom of the sages, next to his wisdom, is "shifting sand" [Q 73:14].[2]

The density of the Qur'ānic allusions that Ḥallāj summons to evoke his mystical portrait points to what was already in his time a tradition of deep interiorization of scripture combined with speculation about the text's relationship with the messenger who delivered it.

The theme of Muḥammad as light seems to be anticipated in the Qur'ān, where the Prophet is called "a shining lamp" (*sirāj munīr*; Q 33:46), a phrase to which Ḥallāj clearly refers by the title of his treatise. Several other Qur'ānic texts dealing with light have also been frequently understood as symbols for the Prophet Muḥammad, particularly the famous light verse (24:35), where the eighth-century interpreter Muqātil understood the lamp (*miṣbāḥ*) mentioned there to be once again a symbol for the Prophet as the vessel of the divine light. Likewise, Sūra 93, "The Morning Light" (*al-ḍuḥā*), was convincingly interpreted as an address to the Prophet.

The stage had been set for the interpretation of Muḥammad as the light of the world by Ḥallāj's teacher and predecessor, Sahl al-Tustarī (d. 283/896), who explicitly states that Adam was created from the light of Muḥammad:

> When God willed to create Muḥammad, he displayed from his own light a light that he spread through the entire kingdom. And when it came before [God's] Majesty it prostrated itself, and God created from its prostration a column of dense light like a vessel of glass, the inside being visible from the outside and the outside being visible from the inside. In this column of light Muḥammad worshiped before the Lord of the Worlds a thousand thousand years with the primordial faith, being in the revealed presence

[2] This translation of Ḥallāj's *Ṭā-Sīn al-sirāj* has been modified from an earlier version, *Teachings of Sufism*, trans. Carl W. Ernst (Boston: Shambhala Publications, 1999), 15–20, by comparison with the new edition by Stéphane Ruspoli, *Le Livre Tâwasîn de Hallâj* (Beirut: Dar Albouraq, 2007), 319–23, along with Rūzbihān al-Baqlī, *Manṭiq al-asrār* (Ms. catalogued anonymously as *Tafsīr al-shaṭḥiyyat bi-lisān al-ṣūfiyya*, Tashkent State Institute of Oriental Studies, no. 3198), fols. 132–6.

> of the invisible within the invisible realm a thousand thousand years before the beginning of creation. And God created Adam from the light of Muḥammad, and then Muḥammad from the clay of Adam; and the clay is created from the column in which Muḥammad worshiped.[3]

The key to this striking image of the light of Muḥammad is clearly his emanation from the divine light and his priority over Adam as the beginning of the sequence of prophecy.

As Schimmel has observed, the subsequent elaboration of the symbolism of the light of Muḥammad owes a great deal to the Andalusian Ṣūfī master Ibn ʿArabī (d. 638/1240) and his interpreter ʿAbd al-Karīm al-Jīlī (d. ca. 810/1408), and there are numerous reflections of this doctrine in poetry composed in Arabic, Persian, and other languages.[4] On a more abstract level, this light symbolism merges into the notion of the Muḥammadan reality (*al-ḥaqīqa al-Muḥammadiyya*), which in turn is interpreted in terms of the perfect human being (*al-insān al-kāmil*), combining both a cosmic and a revelatory function that is inherited by the prophets and, eventually, the Ṣūfī saints.

In dramatic terms, the most striking aspect of the spiritual itinerary of the Prophet is undoubtedly his ascension (*miʿrāj*) into the heavens, and that voyage is commonly merged into the account of his Night Journey (*isrāʿ*) from Mecca to Jerusalem, which becomes the point of departure for the heavenly journey. Muslim interpreters have typically seen two Qur'ānic texts (17:1–2 and 53:1–18) as the locations for these events. A large narrative tradition has emerged on this topic, beginning with stories found in the standard Ḥadīth collections but expanding beyond that to encompass a broad range of texts in various languages, which may be fruitfully compared with the heavenly journeys found in other religious traditions of the Near East. Some of these texts are accompanied by extraordinary miniature paintings depicting the story's celestial landscapes and encounters with angels and prophets.[5] The complicated

[3] Abū 'l-Ḥasan ʿAlī b. Muḥammad al-Daylamī, *A Treatise on Mystical Love*, trans. Joseph Norment Bell and Hassan Mahmood Abdul Latif Al Shafie, in *Journal of Arabic and Islamic Studies Monograph Series 1* (Edinburgh: Edinburgh University Press, 2005), 54.

[4] Schimmel, *And Muhammad*, 123–43.

[5] Marie Rose Séguy, *The Miraculous Journey of Mahomet: Mirâj nâmeh* (New York: G. Braziller, 1977); Frederick Colby and Christiane Gruber, eds., *The Prophet's Ascension: Cross-Cultural Encounters with the Islamic Mi'raj Tales* (Bloomington: Indiana University Press, 2010).

history of these ascension narratives has recently been traced by Frederick Colby.[6]

As an example of this literature, one may take the important Arabic collection of Ṣūfī sayings on the topic of the ascension, which was compiled by the noted Ṣūfī scholar al-Sulamī (d. 412/1021) under the title *The Subtleties of the Ascension*. As Colby points out, there are several separate emphases to be found in this text: first, the Night Journey and ascension "as proof for the unique status and favor that Muḥammad enjoyed"; second, the notion that Muḥammad was "clothed with the lights of the divine attributes," which links up with the theme of the light of Muḥammad; third, Muḥammad's direct vision of God, something that is not typically found in the standard Ḥadīth collections; and fourth, the stipulation that this experience of ascension was an esoteric one that could not be fully revealed to the public.[7] In this distinctively Ṣūfī approach to the ascension of the Prophet, one may see an increasing refinement in the notion of his distinctive status and unique proximity to God.

HIS PHYSICAL AND SPIRITUAL PERFECTION

The special ontological status of the Prophet Muḥammad found more direct expression in the widespread literature devoted to Muḥammad as the physical and spiritual model of beauty.[8] This emphasis on his beauty goes beyond formal obedience to the Prophet, which is enjoined in several passages from the Qur'ān: "Whoever obeys the messenger obeys God" (4:80), and "Those who swear allegiance to you swear allegiance to God" (48:10). Although texts like those might have established a model of his legal and political authority, the Qur'ān also conveys a much loftier and more attractive status for him by calling Muḥammad "a mercy for creation" (21:107), "of noble character" (68:4), and "a beautiful model" (33:21). This combination of obedience and admiration as attitudes toward Muḥammad helps to explain the profound emotional attachment that many Muslims have had for the Prophet. Although this

6 Frederick Colby, *Narrating Muhammad's Night Journey: Tracing the Development of the Ibn 'Abbas Ascension Discourse* (Albany: State University of New York Press, 2008).

7 Abū 'Abd al-Raḥmān Sulamī, *The Subtleties of the Ascension: Early Mystical Sayings on Muhammad's Heavenly Journey*, ed. and trans. Frederick Colby (Louisville, KY: Fons Vitae, 2006), 16–19.

8 Schimmel, *And Muhammad*, 24–55.

personal connection to the Prophet is by no means restricted to Ṣūfī adepts, devotion directed toward him is an exceptionally strong characteristic of Ṣūfī practice. An example of this kind of devotion is found in the description of the physical appearance of the Prophet by a woman named Umm Maʿbad, who entertained the Prophet and his companion Abū Bakr on their way from Mecca to Medina:

> I saw a man, pure and clean, with a handsome face and a fine figure. He was not marred by a skinny body, nor was he overly small in the head and neck. He was graceful and elegant, with intensely black eyes and thick eyelashes. There was a huskiness in his voice, and his neck was long. His beard was thick, and his eyebrows were finely arched and joined together. When silent, he was grave and dignified, and when he spoke, glory rose up and overcame him. He was from afar the most beautiful of men and the most glorious, and close up he was the sweetest and the loveliest. He was sweet of speech and articulate, but not petty or trifling. His speech was a string of cascading pearls, measured so that none despaired of its length, and no eye challenged him because of brevity. In company he is like a branch between two other branches, but he is the most flourishing of the three in appearance, and the loveliest in power. He has friends surrounding him, who listen to his words. If he commands, they obey implicitly, with eagerness and haste, without frown or complaint.[9]

This description, with its laconic Bedouin eloquence, found its way into artistic representation in the calligraphic pieces known as the adornment of the Prophet (*ḥilyat al-nabī*; see cover), an art form that was highly developed in the Ottoman realms. Surrounded by medallions bearing the names of the four "rightly-guided" caliphs, and prominent quotations of the Qurʾānic passages on the cosmic and ethical centrality of the Prophet, these descriptions of Muḥammad's physical beauty, whether by Umm Maʿbad or ʿAlī, formed a kind of verbal icon to create the imaginative picture of the Prophet in one's mind while avoiding the idolatry of visual representation.[10] Short texts like this were complemented by extensive works on the virtues of the Prophet, such as the extraordinarily popular

[9] From a calligraphic *ḥilya* composed by Rasheed Butt, depicted in Carl W. Ernst, *Following Muhammad: Rethinking Islam in the Contemporary World* (Chapel Hill: University of North Carolina Press, 2003), 77.

[10] Ernst, *Following Muhammad*, 76–9.

Guides to Blessings (*Dalā'il al-khayrāt*) of al-Jazūlī (d. 869/1465), a collection of prayers for the Prophet that included descriptions of his tomb in Medina and commonly featured facing pages of illustrations of that shrine or showed both Medina and Mecca.[11]

The admiration for the Prophet that is evident in the examples just mentioned found further devotional expressions that increasingly stressed his perfection, his charisma, and his ability to intercede with God for the forgiveness of others. All of these tendencies admittedly move away from those passages of the Qur'ān that repeatedly remind Muḥammad he is only a human being.[12] Scholars began to enunciate the doctrine of his immunity from sin, a stipulation that included all other prophets as well.[13] Despite the well-known doctrine that the Prophet's only miracle was the Qur'ān, it was not long before the story of this life was embroidered with tales of miracles.[14] Some of these stories could take the form of exegetical elaborations of enigmatic passages in the Qur'ān. Thus, a modern dictionary of the Qur'ān takes the opening lines of Sūra 94 literally, "Did We not open your breast?" as a figure of speech meaning, "Did We not prepare you to receive something spiritual?"[15] Traditional commentators took it in a different direction, providing a detailed narrative of an initiatory experience, in which angelic visitors removed from Muḥammad's heart the black spot of sin deposited in all other humans by Satan. Likewise, the eschatological sign mentioned in Sūra 54, where the moon was split, was understood as a miracle by which the Prophet split the moon into halves to demonstrate his authority to the pagans of Mecca.[16] The growth of these miraculous accounts of Muḥammad in literature was considerable. Alongside these tendencies was an increasing focus on Muḥammad as the intercessor who could act to obtain God's forgiveness for the sins of others. On this important question of intercession, the Qur'ān has a number of ambiguous passages, sometimes rejecting the possibility, yet at other times conceding,

[11] Muḥmmad ibn Sulaymān Jazūlī, *Guide to Goodness (Dala'il al-khayrāt)*, trans. Hassan Rosowsky (Chicago: Great Books of the Islamic World, n.d. [2001?]); Jan Just Witkam, "The Battle of the Images: Mekka vs. Medina in the Iconography of the Manuscripts of al-Jazūlī's *Dalā'il al-Khayrāt*," in *Theoretical Approaches to the Transmission and Edition of Oriental Manuscripts: Proceedings of a Symposium Held in Istanbul March 28–30, 2001*, ed. Judith Pfeiffer and Manfred Kropp (Beirut: Ergon Verlag Würzburg, 2007), 67–84.

[12] Schimmel, *And Muhammad*, 25.

[13] Ibid., 53–66. See also Chapter 5 of this volume.

[14] Ibid., 67–80.

[15] Arne A. Ambros, with Stephan Procházka, *A Concise Dictionary of Koranic Arabic* (Wiesbaden: Reichert Verlag, 2004), 146.

[16] See the discussion in Chapter 2 of this volume.

that God may permit others to intercede with Him at the resurrection.[17] This theme is enlarged in Ḥadīth, where the standard collections of the Sunnis emphasize Muḥammad's ability to obtain God's forgiveness for his community and indeed for humanity at large.

The classic expression of devotional piety toward the Prophet, in terms of these themes of sinlessness, miraculous deeds, and intercession, is unquestionably the Arabic "Poem of the Cloak" ("Qaṣīdat al-Burda") of the Egyptian poet al-Būṣīrī (d. 696/1298).[18] Written to celebrate the author's miraculous recovery from illness, which he attributed to the intervention of the Prophet, the "Burda" encapsulates all these key features of popular Islamic prophetology. One passage will suffice as an example of this text's insistence on Muḥammad's preeminence:

> Leave aside what Christians claim about their prophet,
> But award to him [Muḥammad] whatever you want in terms of praise, and stand by it,
> And ascribe to his person whatever you want in terms of nobility
> And ascribe to his power every greatness you want,
> For the excellence of the Messenger of God has no limit
> So that anyone who speaks with his mouth could express it completely.[19]

It is especially noteworthy that this Arabic poem was itself credited with miraculous and healing abilities, something that doubtless contributed to its widespread popularity in different regions from North Africa to Indonesia.

MUḤAMMAD AS EXEMPLAR

At this point, we may pause for a moment to consider a fundamental problem that Henry Corbin has summarized under the phrase "the paradox of monotheism." Although his exposition of this issue is complex, it can be simplified as follows: if the God of Revelation is indeed beyond intellect and explanation, the need of humanity decrees that there must be an intermediary to provide a connection to that transcendent source. In the case of a human prophet, after his demise there is a crisis, when

[17] Schimmel, *And Muhammad*, 80–104; A. J. Wensinck and Annemarie Schimmel, "Shafāʿa," in *Encyclopedia of Islam*, 2nd ed., ed. Hamilton A. R. Gibb et al. (Leiden: E. J. Brill, 1960–2004), 9:177–9.

[18] Schimmel, *And Muhammad*, 183–9.

[19] Ibid., 187.

Figure 4. The Prophet Muḥammad, covered from head to toe in white cloth and surrounded in a halo of gold; he and a series of figures surround the beloved Saint Ahmadu Bamba (d. 1927). Reverse glass painting by the Senegalese artist Mor Gueye, from the collection of Dr. Anna Bigelow.

the community of believers must decide how to proceed in his absence. Although one formulation historically has moved toward scriptural codification of legal and authoritarian systems as ways to preserve the legacy of a prophet, there has always been a constituency that demands continuous access to the sources of inspiration. In the case of Shīʿism, the Imāms step in to provide that continuing access to divine authority, at least for a few generations, and thereafter the religious class as a whole stands as the intermediary. In the broader stream of spirituality called Ṣūfism, it is through the Ṣūfī saints that God continues to manifest on an ongoing basis.

In either instance, there is an insistence on the notion of proximity to God, inadequately translated in English as "sainthood" and summarized in the Arabic term *walāya*.[20] It is especially noteworthy that the insistence on the intermediate authority of the Prophet Muḥammad

[20] Vincent Cornell, *Realm of the Saint: Power and Authority in Moroccan Sufism* (Austin: University of Texas Press, 1998); Carl W. Ernst, "Introduction," in *Manifestations of Sainthood in Islam*, ed. Grace Martin Smith (Istanbul: Isis Press, 1993), xi–xxviii.

also entails working out the roles of later saintly figures who continue to relay the divine message to humanity but whose own authority is closely linked to and dependent on that of the Prophet.

Speculative understanding of prophecy and sainthood therefore went hand in hand, and in some respects, it was difficult to disentangle the two concepts. As the Persian Ṣūfī Rūzbihān Baqlī (d. 605/1209) put it, "The oceans of sainthood and prophethood interpenetrate each other."[21] Although the devotional approach to the Prophet elevated his status to a cosmic principle comparable to the Christian Logos doctrine, the mystical knowledge of the Ṣūfī saint who could announce such a discovery also, in effect, came close to claiming an authority equivalent to that of prophecy. This tension between sainthood and prophecy is prefigured in the Qur'ānic account (in Sūra 18) of the encounter of Moses with the "servant of God," identified as the immortal prophet Khiḍr, who has a divine knowledge that is not available to the prophet, and the same theme recurs regularly in the history of Ṣūfism. One famous example is the first encounter between the great Persian Ṣūfī Jalāl al-Dīn Rūmī (d. 672/1273) and his master Shams-i Tabrīz; according to one account, Shams announced that the Prophet Muḥammad had said he could not praise God adequately, whereas the Ṣūfī saint Bāyazīd Bisṭāmī had proclaimed, "Glory be to me! How great is my majesty!" – so which had the higher state? This question was so shocking that it reportedly caused Rūmī to faint.[22] Although most Ṣūfī theorists insisted on the supremacy of the Prophet Muḥammad, the issue of the relationship between prophecy and sainthood remained volatile, as the mystical knowledge of sainthood was, in effect, necessary for the validation of prophecy.

The most extensive formulation of mystical prophetology in Ṣūfism is found in the works of Ibn ʿArabī and his successors.[23] Building on the theories of al-Ḥakīm al-Tirmidhī (d. ca. 318/936), he developed the concept of the seal of the saints (*khatm al-awliyā'*) as an esoteric and eschatological parallel to the status of Muḥammad as "the seal of the

[21] Ruzbihan Baqli, *The Unveiling of Secrets: Diary of a Sufi Master*, trans. Carl W. Ernst (Chapel Hill, NC: Parvardigar Press, 1997), 7.

[22] Annemarie Schimmel, *The Triumphal Sun: A Study of the Works of Jalāloddin Rumi* (Albany: State University of New York Press, 1993), xvii–xviii.

[23] Michel Chodkiewicz, *Seal of the Saints: Prophethood and Sainthood in the Doctrine of Ibn ʿArabi*, trans. Liadain Sherrard (Oxford: Islamic Texts Society, 1993); Naṣr Ḥāmid Abū Zayd, *Hakādhā takallama Ibn ʿArabī* (Cairo: al-Hay'ah al-Miṣriyya al-ʿĀmma lil-Kitāb, 2002; 2nd ed., Casablanca: al-Markaz al-Thiqāfī al-ʿArabī, 2004), 62–72.

prophets."[24] Ibn ʿArabī was scrupulous in stating the supremacy of the Prophet, yet it cannot be denied that his claims about his own status were spectacular, though the boldest of his declarations were circumspectly concealed in books that were esoteric to the point of creating secret alphabets.[25] In any case, the cosmic role of the Prophet was accompanied by an impressively detailed portrait of the invisible hierarchy of the saints, who form an extensive retinue, as it were, for the supreme spiritual figure of Muḥammad. From a historical and ritual perspective, the centrality of the Prophet for the mystical tradition was evident in the formulation of the spiritual genealogies of the Ṣūfī orders, which in every case were traced back to the Prophet as the source of spiritual knowledge. The oath of allegiance (*bayʿa*) that the Arabs gave to the Prophet, sealed by a handshake, became the rite of initiation that was transmitted through the chain (*silsila*) of Ṣūfī masters and disciples, constituting the authentic path of knowledge because of its prophetic source.

Yet there is certainly an overlap between the spiritual and cosmic status of the Prophet and the saint. An illustration is provided by the following poem addressed to the Prophet by al-Jīlī, known as a theorist of the doctrine of the perfect human:

> O Center of the compass! O inmost ground of the truth!
> O pivot of necessity and contingency!
> O eye of the entire circle of existence! O point of the Koran and the Furqan!
> O perfect one, and perfecter of the most perfect, who has been beautified by the majesty of God the Merciful!
> Thou art the Pole [*quṭb*] of the most wondrous things. The sphere of perfection in its solitude turns on thee.
> Thou art transcendent, nay thou art immanent, nay thine is all that is known and unknown, everlasting and imperishable.
> Thine in reality is Being and not-being; nadir and zenith are thy two garments.
> Thou art both the light and its opposite, nay but thou art only darkness to a gnostic who is dazed.[26]

[24] Bernd Radtke and John O'Kane, trans., *The Concept of Sainthood in Early Islamic Mysticism: Two Works by Al-Ḥakīm Al-Tirmidhī* (London: Routledge, 1996).

[25] Gerald Elmore, *Islamic Sainthood in the Fullness of Time: Ibn Al-ʿArabī's Book of the Fabulous Gryphon* (Leiden: E. J. Brill, 1999).

[26] Translated by R. A. Nicholson, in *Studies in Islamic Mysticism*, 86–7, qtd. in Schimmel, *And Muhammad*, 137–8.

The key term here is the pole or axis (*quṭb*), a symbol invoking the centrality of the polestar as the pivot around which the cosmos turns. Although al-Jīlī applies this epithet to the Prophet Muḥammad, it is most commonly addressed to eminent mystics considered to perform the central role of sustaining the universe in their own day. And though from an ordinary geometric view it might seem superfluous or contradictory to have more than one center, the mystical imagination has no problem with multiple centers of the world, so that the phrase "pole of poles" (*quṭb al-aqṭāb*) frequently occurs as a hyperbolic expression for the spiritual supremacy of a particularly favored saint. It is, moreover, on the basis of the applicability of that term, pole (*quṭb*), both to the Prophet and to the saints that it can be used in the title for this chapter.

The horizontal transmission of prophetic blessing through the Ṣūfī lineages was certainly an important manifestation of the ongoing role of the Prophet Muḥammad in Muslim religious life, but this institutional framework far from exhausted the possibility of connecting to his spiritual essence. From an early date, it was recognized that dreams were a less intense version of the divine communication of prophecy, and dreams of the Prophet were accorded a special status; it was, after all, recorded in a *ḥadīth* that Satan could never insinuate himself into a dream in the Prophet's form, so dreams featuring Muḥammad had the distinction of being true.[27] Thus, even for ordinary people, it was possible to have direct vertical contact with the Prophet through a dream without being dependent on a Ṣūfī initiation. But for elite mystics, waking visions also offered direct access to encounters with prophets and angels, sometimes on a daily basis.[28] A number of Ṣūfīs are reported to have made regular visits to the tomb of the Prophet in Medina, by miraculous means, where they received *ḥadīth*s directly from his spirit without any intermediary. There were even some Ṣūfīs who specialized in the talent of producing dreams of the Prophet for others, in this way democratizing access to the source of spirituality.[29]

[27] Nile Green, "The Religious and Cultural Roles of Dreams and Visions in Islam," *Journal of the Royal Asiatic Society* 13 (2003): 287–313; Jonathan G. Katz, *Dreams, Sufism and Sainthood: The Visionary Career of Muhammad al-Zawâwî* (Leiden: E. J. Brill, 1996); Pierre Lory, *Le rêve et ses interprétations en Islam* (Paris: Albin Michel, 2003); Annemarie Schimmel *Die Träume des Kalifen: Träume und ihre Deutung in der islamischen Kultur* (Munich: C. H. Beck, 1998).

[28] Carl W. Ernst, *Ruzbihan Baqli: Mystical Experience and the Rhetoric of Sainthood in Persian Sufism* (London: Curzon Press, 1996); Ruzbihan Baqli, *The Unveiling of Secrets: Diary of a Sufi Master*, trans. Carl W. Ernst (Chapel Hill, NC: Parvardigar Press, 1997).

[29] Meenakshi Khanna, "Dreams, and Visions in North Indian Sufic Traditions ca. (1500–1800) A.D.," Ph.D. diss., Jawaharlal Nehru University, New Delhi, 2001.

CONCLUSION

If anything, it may be said that the focus on the Prophet Muḥammad in Ṣūfī circles has continued to increase, regardless of whether the means of transmission was extraordinary, as in dreams or visions, or through the normal course of the study of Ḥadīth. Scholars have sometimes observed that the seventeenth and eighteenth centuries were a time of considerable activity, focused in Arabia, in the study of Ḥadīth, and that the principal networks fostering this scholarship were articulated through Ṣūfī orders, prior to the rise of the Wahhābī movement with its strongly anti-Ṣūfī attitude.[30] It was a highly mystical form of devotion to the Prophet Muḥammad that sustained the work of eminent Ṣūfī scholars such as ʿAlī al-Muttaqī, ʿAbd al-Ḥaqq Muḥaddith Dihlawī, Ibrāhīm Kūrānī, and others. Indeed, it may be said that the forms of devotion sometimes referred to as the Muḥammadan path (*ṭarīqa Muḥammadiyya*) were not any kind of new ideology or institutional structure of Ṣūfism but simply a marked emphasis on the centrality of the Prophet.[31] In modern Egypt, for example, classical Ṣūfī concepts such as the annihilation (*fanāʾ*) of the self have been redefined, in effect, as intense devotional absorption in the Prophet and his family.[32]

The major changes in Islamic thought signaled by the emergence of the Wahhābī movement in the late eighteenth century are still being felt today, but this is particularly the case with respect to its radical critique of the entire worldview associated with the notion of spiritual intercession. Recalling the view of Ibn Taymiyya that an intention to visit the tomb of the Prophet invalidates the performance of the *ḥajj* to Mecca, his successors in Wahhābī and Salafī circles have rejected many pious practices involving the visitation of the tombs of saints, imams, and indeed the Prophet himself, where police officials today severely discourage any undue expression of emotion that might be construed as an idolatrous reverence of the Prophet as more than human. Thus, celebrating the Prophet's birthday is unlawful in Saudi Arabia today, and it is striking to see how many historical sites associated with the Prophet Muḥammad and his family (particularly the Jannat

[30] John O. Voll, "Hadith Scholars and Tariqahs: An Ulama Group in the 18th-Century Haramayn and Their Impact in the Islamic World," *Journal of Asian and African Studies* 15, nos. 3–4 (1980): 264–72.

[31] Schimmel, *And Muhammed*, 216–38, where the political unity of this tendency is perhaps overstated.

[32] Valerie Hoffman, *Sufism, Mystics, and Saints in Modern Egypt* (Columbia: University of South Carolina Press, 1995).

al-Baqīʿ cemetery in Medina) have been demolished or, more recently, removed in the name of urban development. This debate is not confined to Arab circles, either. Nineteenth-century reformist thinkers in India engaged in intense debates over questions such as standing or making other gestures of respect when the Prophet's name was mentioned. The controversies between the two major schools of the Barelwis and the Deobandis in South Asia swirl around the practices of intercessory piety, which the former defend and the latter reject, and the same issue applies regardless of whether it is the Prophet or the Ṣūfī saints whose status is under discussion.[33] Examples of this debate among contemporary Muslims over the Prophet's status could be multiplied indefinitely. But the strength of the emotional and spiritual attachments to the Prophet Muḥammad among a significant proportion of Muslims today must be considered to demonstrate the ongoing importance of this tradition that reveres his central place in the cosmos. It can still be summarized in the memorable Arabic verses of the poet Saʿdī (d. 691/1292):

> He reached the acme [peak] of grandeur by his perfections,
> He dispersed the tenebrous clouds of darkness through his beauty.
> Excellent were all his character traits;
> Then shower your blessings upon him and his family![34]

Further reading

Colby, Frederick. *Narrating Muhammad's Night Journey: Tracing the Development of the Ibn 'Abbas Ascension Discourse.* Albany: State University of New York Press, 2008.

Ernst, Carl W. *Ruzbihan Baqli: Mystical Experience and the Rhetoric of Sainthood in Persian Sufism.* London: Curzon Press, 1996.

Ernst, Carl W. *Teachings of Sufism.* Boston: Shambhala Publications, 1999.

Hoffman, Valerie. *Sufism, Mystics, and Saints in Modern Egypt.* Columbia: University of South Carolina Press, 1995.

Schimmel, Annemarie. *And Muhammad Is His Messenger: The Veneration of the Prophet in Islamic Piety.* Chapel Hill: University of North Carolina Press, 1985.

Schimmel, Annemarie. *The Triumphal Sun: A Study of the Works of Jalāloddin Rumi.* Albany: State University of New York Press, 1993.

33 Usha Sanyal, *Devotional Islam and Politics in British India: Ahmad Riza Khan Barelwi and His Movement, 1870–1920* (New Delhi: Oxford University Press, 1999).

34 Gholamreza Aavani, "Glorification of the Prophet Muhammad in the Poems of Sa'adi," http://www.irip.ir/userfiles/Archive/Papers/English/R&M/Glorification%20of%20the%20Prophet%20Muhammad%20in%20the%20Poems%20of%20Sa'adi.pdf.

7 The Prophet Muḥammad in ritual

MARION HOLMES KATZ

That the Prophet Muḥammad plays a central role in establishing Islamic teachings is well known; all subsequent generations of Muslims have studied the history of his life, mastering and transmitting his reported words and actions. It is less obvious, however, how he might come to be an immediate and emotionally vital presence to individual believers. In Christianity, images of Jesus play a central role in evoking intimate emotional responses to the life and passion of Christ, but physical representations of the Prophet Muḥammad hold a marginal and disputed place in Muslim piety. No Islamic rite plays a role analogous to that of the Christian Eucharist, which places the figure of Jesus firmly at the center of the ritual life of the community. The three most central ritual acts in Islam – the five daily prayers, Ramaḍān fasting, and the pilgrimage to Mecca – emphasize the individual believer's immediate encounter with God over any vivid evocation of the Prophet himself. Nevertheless, believing Muslims throughout the centuries have not merely acknowledged Muḥammad's prophethood and followed his teachings; they also have experienced him as an intimately known and intensely beloved presence in their lives. Indeed, in well-authenticated reports, the Prophet is said to have declared that no one is truly a believer unless he loves the Prophet more than his own parent or child.[1] This sense of deep love and personal connection to the Prophet has been generated in many ways, including a rich tradition of devotional poetry describing the Prophet's physical beauty, moral perfection, and abundant miracles. It has also been evoked and sustained by many ritual activities.

The most obvious way in which the Prophet Muḥammad figures in Islamic ritual is as a model for emulation. In a *ḥadīth* presented in the *Ṣaḥīḥ* of al-Bukhārī, the collection most revered by Sunnī Muslims, the Prophet instructs a group of young men who are about to leave him

1 Muḥammad ibn Ismāʿīl al-Bukhārī, *Ṣaḥīḥ al-Bukhārī* ([Beirut]: Dār al-fikr, 1411/1991), 1:11.

and return to their families outside of Medina, "Pray as you have seen me pray."[2] He is also reported to have declared, "Take your rites of pilgrimage [*manāsik*] from me."[3] All Muslim authorities agree that the more closely an act of worship such as prayer or pilgrimage adheres to the example set by the Prophet, the more perfect and meritorious it is. However, they have not always agreed on how to determine the precise nature of the Prophet's precedent, because over time, conflicting reports about various details of ritual multiplied and the customs of various parts of the Muslim community diverged. Desiring to specify the precise bodily postures, verbal utterances, and other qualities of the Prophet's prayer, believers resorted to different means of recovering his example. For adherents of the school of thought pioneered by the early scholar Mālik ibn Anas (d. 179/795), the best indicator of the Prophet's example was the continuous practice of the early community in Medina, where the revelation of the Qurʾān was completed and where the Prophet modeled proper behavior until his death in 11/632. Early Medinan practice was reported to have involved standing in prayer with one's hands hanging down by one's sides (*sadl*), and the Mālikīs held that this represented the authentic practice of the Prophet (the Sunna). Other scholars, such as al-Shāfiʿī, held that the best way to determine the Prophet's practice (in ritual as in other areas) was to collect verbal reports about his practice, examine their chains of transmission ("So-and-so told me that so-and-so told him that the Prophet said/did . . . "), and follow the practices contained in the most reliable reports. Basing themselves on these reports (*ḥadīth*s), these scholars held that the Prophet had stood in prayer not with his hands at his sides but rather clasped over his belly button, right hand over left. So already in the early centuries of Islam, Muslims prayed in somewhat different ways, based on different methods of determining exactly how the Prophet had performed his ritual duties.[4] Nevertheless, all were in agreement that rituals ought to be faithfully based on the Prophet's example, and the effort to determine and adhere to the precise details of the Prophet's practices shaped pious people's ritual lives.

Although the principle of emulating the Prophet underlay scholars' efforts to define how rituals should be performed, and ordinary Muslims

[2] Bukhārī, *Ṣaḥīḥ*, 1:175–6.

[3] This statement is transmitted in a number of classical *ḥadīth* compilations, though not in Bukhārī or Muslim; see Muḥammad al-Saʿīd ibn Basyūnī Zaghlūl, *Mawsūʿat Aṭrāf al-Ḥadīth al-Nabawī al-Sharīf* (Beirut: Dār al-kutub al-ʿilmīya, n.d.), 4:605.

[4] Yasin Dutton, "ʿAmal v. Ḥadīth in Islamic Law: The Case of Sadl al-Yadayn (Holding One's Hands by One's Sides) When Doing the Prayer," *Islamic Law and Society* 3 (1996): 13–40.

surely valued the fact that their ritual activities mirrored those of the Prophet himself, the principle of emulation did not necessarily make the Prophet vividly present to believers. The primary objective was correct performance of ritual duties in fulfillment of one's obligations to God. However, Muslim ritual life includes festivals, prayers, and actions not encompassed by these duties, and many of these activities evoke the symbolic or literal presence of the Prophet, allowing the individual believer to build a personal relationship of love and reverence with him.

CELEBRATING THE PROPHET: THE PROPHET'S BIRTHDAY

Although the Prophet Muḥammad is not known to have celebrated his own birthday, or to have instructed others to do so, Sunnī Muslims began to hold celebrations commemorating his birth (known in Arabic as the *mawlid*) beginning in the sixth century AH (twelfth century CE).[5] State-sponsored commemorations of the Prophet's birth were held even earlier by the Shīʿī Fāṭimid dynasty of Egypt and Syria, whose claims to religious and political legitimacy rested on lineal descent from the Prophet Muḥammad. There is little evidence, however, that the Sunnī celebration was based on this Fāṭimid precedent. Instead, it had deep roots in a tradition of pious storytelling particularly cultivated by Imāmī Shīʿīs (who followed a different line of descent than the Fāṭimids). Although often associated with Shīʿīs, this tradition transcended sectarian boundaries in its appeal to believers' love for the Prophet and his family. These devotional narratives surrounded the birth of the Prophet (and, in the Shīʿī case, of other figures such as Fāṭima) with a wealth of miraculous events. They often depicted the Prophet's nativity not merely as the birth of the historical figure Muḥammad ibn ʿAbd Allāh in Mecca in around 570 CE but also as the earthly manifestation of a cosmic principle, the light of Muḥammad, which had been created by God before the earth itself.[6] The concept of the light of Muḥammad may be rooted in both mystical Ṣūfī and esoteric Shīʿī ideas; both strands of Islamic piety posited a kind of illumination that invested certain figures (whether Shīʿī Imāms or Ṣūfī saints) with holiness and gnosis.[7] Narratives about the

5 For a discussion of the historical origins of the *mawlid* ceremony, see N. J. Kaptein, *Muḥammad's Birthday Festival* (Leiden: E. J. Brill, 1993).

6 See Marion Holmes Katz, *The Birth of the Prophet Muḥammad: Devotional Piety in Sunni Islam* (London: Routledge, 2007), 1–7, 38–9.

7 See Annemarie Schimmel, *And Muḥammad Is His Messenger: The Veneration of the Prophet in Islamic Piety* (Chapel Hill: University of North Carolina Press, 1985), 123–43; Uri Rubin, "Pre-existence and Light: Aspects of the Concept of Nūr Muḥammad," *Israel Oriental Studies* 5 (1975): 62–115.

light of Muḥammad recounted how it was implanted in Adam and then transferred to the womb of Eve; it passed through generations of prophets to the forefathers of Muḥammad, beaming from his father's brow until it passed to his mother, Āmina, at the Prophet's conception. Such narratives long predated the rise of the Prophet's birthday celebration.[8]

Although these stories' mythic richness contrasted with the spare Qur'ānic account of creation and with the more sober narratives produced by early Muslim historians, they appear to have been widely circulated and accepted by many Muslims. They were well known by the rise of the *mawlid* celebration, and they shaped it deeply. Recitation of the story of the Prophet's birth – often beginning with the story of the light of Muḥammad – became an integral part of *mawlid* piety. The content of these stories reflects the piety of ordinary people as well as of scholars and displays an unusual sensitivity to the concerns of women. Countless versions of the *mawlid* story described how Āmina went into labor frightened and alone, only to be comforted and aided by four mysterious women who passed through the walls of her room. These women revealed themselves to be visitors from Paradise, including Sarah, the wife of Abraham, and Maryam, the mother of Jesus. Although this story has no basis in the scholarly disciplines of history and Ḥadīth, it has been cherished by many Muslims (including untold women and some elite scholars) for more than a millennium.[9]

As depicted in the most widely circulated *mawlid* texts, the infant Prophet was a luminous figure whose radiance lighted his mother's room and whose holiness blessed all who approached him. Traditional *mawlid* narratives (on this point, paralleling the historical tradition) recount that it was customary for the women of Mecca to entrust their infants to wet nurses from the surrounding tribes, offering the children healthful exposure to fresh air and (later) early exposure to the pure Arabic of the tribes. Both early histories and *mawlid* texts recount that a woman named Ḥalīma, whose family was starving in a year of drought, rode slowly toward Mecca on an emaciated donkey, tormented by the wails of her own hungry infant. Arriving long after her less unfortunate fellow tribeswomen, she found only the orphaned Muḥammad ibn ʿAbd Allāh

[8] The Qur'ān commentary of Muqātil ibn Sulaymān (d. 150/767), one of the earliest preserved works of Qur'ānic exegesis, briefly evokes the narrative of the light of Muḥammad in the interpretation of verse 24:34. It refers to "the Light of Muḥamamd [sws] when it was deposited in the loins of his father, ʿAbd Allāh ibn ʿAbd al-Muṭṭalib." Muqātil ibn Sulaymān, *Tafsīr Muqātil ibn Sulaymān* (Beirut: Dār al-Kutub al-ʿIlmīya, 1424/2003), 2:419.

[9] See Katz, *Birth*, 32–9.

(whose father had died during Āmina's pregnancy) left to suckle. Taking him, she found that her breasts instantly overflowed with milk, and her mount was miraculously restored to health and vigor. She and her family enjoyed fertility and plenty as long as the infant Prophet remained in their care.

Neither Āmina nor Ḥalīma is a major figure in the mainstream historical tradition dealing with the Prophet's life.[10] Āmina, who died during Muḥammad's childhood, did not live to hear his prophecies or to accept his faith. Muslim historians debate how long Ḥalīma survived and whether she embraced Islam. Neither woman played a part in Muḥammad's career as a prophet and leader, the phase of his life that necessarily has loomed largest in scholarly Islamic thought. Nevertheless, they are the main figures (aside from the Prophet himself) in some of the most widely circulated *mawlid* narratives. Their prominence is based not on their role as the Prophet's religious followers but on their emotional closeness to the infant Muḥammad and their experience of the blessings of his intimate presence.

Mawlid texts, which often end in the Prophet's childhood or only briefly sketch his adult career, present a very different view of the Prophet and his relationship with the individual believer than does most of the scholarly Islamic tradition. These texts seem to suggest that the most important relationships with the Prophet are ones not of obedience and emulation but of intimacy and nurture. In their contact with the Prophet, Āmina and Ḥalīma both give and receive life and nourishment. These women's powers of fertility and sustenance are mirrored on a vaster scale by those of the Prophet, who brings life, growth, and fruitfulness to the world around him.

The celebration of the Prophet's birthday itself, like the narratives whose recitation was often their centerpiece, focused on the cultivation of relationships of reciprocity and love. Well-authenticated *ḥadīth* texts affirm that a true believer loves the Prophet above all else; love of the Prophet is considered an integral component of faith. According to many scholars who supported the celebration, celebration of the *mawlid* was one of the ritual means by which feelings of love for the Prophet could be evoked. Especially for children, women, and unlearned Muslims, the enjoyment of good foods, pleasant scents, and beautiful accounts of the Prophet's birth and life helped to nurture religiously

[10] As noted previously, however, the narrative about Ḥalīma seems to be extremely old; see the Sīra of Ibn Isḥāq (d. 150/767), *The Life of Muhammad: A Translation of Ibn Ishaq's Sirat Rasul Allah*, trans. A. Guillaume (Karachi: Oxford University Press, 1967), 70–2.

meritorious sentiments.[11] Eventually, statements promising bounteous spiritual rewards for those who expended resources on the celebration of the *mawlid* were attributed to the Prophet himself and circulated widely.[12] In a sense, such expenditures represented gifts offered to the Prophet himself; the authors of *mawlid* texts affirmed that the Prophet never failed to be gracious to those who expended their wealth to express their love for him and their joy at his birth. Although the duty to rejoice in the Prophet was not as textually well established as the obligation to love him, the authors of *mawlid* texts (and legal scholars who supported the celebration) also emphasized that it was religiously meritorious to rejoice at the Prophet's birth. Indeed, it was believed that such rejoicing could effect the salvation of even the most sinful believer. In an anecdote that was tirelessly recounted in works about the Prophet's birthday, the Prophet's uncle Abū Lahab – a stubborn unbeliever who virulently opposed Muḥammad's religious mission – was informed of his nephew's birth by a female slave and manumitted her in his delight at the news. Appearing in a dream vision after his death, he explained that his sufferings in hell were mitigated once a week on Monday (the day on which the Prophet was born) as a reward for his rejoicing at the Prophet's birth. For devotees of the *mawlid* celebration, this anecdote proved without doubt that their rejoicing would be rewarded by God, given that even the rankest unbeliever had enjoyed some surcease by virtue of his joy.[13] A Ṣūfī-flavored anecdote from the seventh century AH (thirteenth century CE) recounts that a man was criticized for holding yearly *mawlid* celebrations but saw the Prophet in a dream declaring, "Whoever rejoices in me, I will rejoice in him."[14]

Whether on the vast scale possible for rulers and prominent Ṣūfīs or on the modest level accessible to private households, the celebration of the *mawlid* often featured the feeding of guests. Such feeding served both as a way of earning religious merit (because it represented a pious expenditure of one's resources in honor of the Prophet) and as a form of fellowship that brought together family members, neighbors, or followers around shared nourishment and rejoicing. Fragrant perfumes created an atmosphere of pleasure and joy and suggested the sweet scent that is said to have wafted from the Prophet. Illumination of mosques, or of the domestic spaces where ordinary individuals held *mawlid* ceremonies, added to the atmosphere of rejoicing and probably suggested the

[11] See Katz, *Birth*, 117–25.
[12] Ibid., 83–7.
[13] See ibid., 106–9.
[14] Ibid., 105.

radiance that the infant Prophet shed on the world. Participants often contributed money or items such as candles to their friends' and neighbors' *mawlid* celebrations, tying themselves into a network of giving that also included such occasions as weddings.[15]

The merit accruing to the sponsor of a *mawlid* ceremony could be donated to the deceased, thereby improving his or her lot in the afterlife; thus, in some societies, *mawlids* became associated with funerals and the commemoration of the dead.[16] By bequeathing money for the yearly celebration of the *mawlid*, a pious individual could reap the fruits of pious action even beyond the grave.[17] In the ninth century AH (fifteenth century CE) Shams al-Dīn al-Asyūṭī produced a manual providing fill-in-the-blank forms for various transactions performed by Muslim judges and notaries. It included a standard form for a bequest of productive property to support the yearly recitation of the story of the Prophet's birth. The overseer of the trust was obligated to maintain the property and to spend a set amount of the proceeds to hire a scholar to read the *mawlid* story on the Prophet's birthday. He was also to hire a specialist to chant poems in praise of the Prophet, his miracles, and his moral virtues, as well as several groups of Qur'ān reciters who would collectively complete an entire recitation of the Qur'ān. The rest of the money was to be expended on lamb, bread, honey, sugar, rice, and other foodstuffs, as well as on oil and candles for illumination. With these materials, he would serve a banquet to the gathered guests. Funds were also devoted to rose water and incense, as well as to firewood for cooking. The Qur'ān reciters and the praise chanter were to complete their performances with the invocation of blessings on the Prophet and with prayers for the deceased and for all Muslims.[18]

The creation of pious foundations (*awqāf*) to support the celebration of the *mawlid* was a long-lived practice; the nineteenth-century Ottoman historian ʿAṭā' reported that in areas he visited in Anatolia and the Balkans, wealthy families sometimes established such foundations

[15] For instance, the fifteenth-century Syrian diarist Ibn Ṭawq brought a large gilt candle to a *mawlid* held by one of his neighbors. Shihāb al-Dīn Aḥmad ibn Ṭawq, *al-Taʿlīq: Yawmīyāt Shihāb al-Dīn Aḥmad Ibn Ṭawq, 834–915/1430–1059*, ed. al-Shaykh Jaʿfar al-Muhājir (Damascus: al-Maʿhad al-Faransī liʾl-Sharq al-Awsaṭ, 2000–), 1:243.

[16] For modern Turkey, see Nancy Tapper and Richard Tapper, "The Birth of the Prophet: Ritual and Gender in Turkish Islam," *Man*, n.s. 22 (1987): 69–92.

[17] This practice was opposed by some scholars who considered the *mawlid* celebration religiously unfounded; for two *fatwās* to this effect by two Mālikī scholars of the eighth century AH (fourteenth century CE), see Kaptein, *Muḥammad's Birthday Festival*, 135–7.

[18] Shams al-Dīn Muḥammad ibn Aḥmad al-Manhājī al-Asyūṭī, *Jawāhir al-ʿuqūd wa-muʿīn al-quḍāt waʾl-muwaqqiʿīn waʾl-shuhūd*, 2nd printing (n.p.: n.d.), 1:368–9.

for the glorification of the Prophet and the benefit of the souls of the deceased.[19] The celebration of the *mawlid* placed participants in a network of relationships in which blessings, food, and shared emotions of love and joy tied individuals to one another, to the deceased, and to the Prophet himself.

Like the anniversary of the Prophet's miraculous ascension to heaven (the *miʿrāj*), the *mawlid* became an important date in the Muslim calendar. The two popular festivals lent a commemorative dimension to the ritual year, gathering masses of people in mosques and other public places to revive and glorify the memory of religiously vital events in the Prophet's life.[20] Particularly in a domestic setting, however, celebration of the *mawlid* was not limited to the anniversary of the Prophet's birth. A fifteenth-century diarist records that at a wedding feast in June of 1481 CE (Rabīʿ al-Awwal 886 AH), the prominent Ḥadīth scholar Ibrāhīm al-Nājī recited the story of the Prophet's birth. Sugar water and sweets were distributed, and rose water and incense were used, before the guests settled down to a sumptuous meal.[21] This particular event occurred in the month of the Prophet's birthday, but over time, *mawlid*s were not limited to any specific time of year. They were performed in honor of other auspicious occasions, including the birth of a baby, the circumcision of a son, the completion of a new home, or a safe return from the *ḥajj*. The celebration of the Prophet's birth became an integral part of the celebration of the most significant moments in many people's lives.

Because the celebration of the Prophet's birthday had not been modeled or commanded by the Prophet himself, it was vulnerable to the accusation that it constituted a religious innovation (*bidʿa*). Many authoritative voices nevertheless spoke in support of the new celebration, which was seen as expressing and reinforcing pious sentiments in ordinary Muslims. Some of the most prominent scholars from the fourteenth to the nineteenth centuries either composed devotional texts for recitation at *mawlid* ceremonies or composed legal opinions in its defense. However, others denounced it as a religious ritual with no basis in the Prophet's normative practice, the Sunna. Most prominent among its detractors was Ibn Taymīya (d. 728/1328), a brilliant and influential

[19] N. Çağatay, "The Tradition of Mavlid Recitations in Islam Particularly in Turkey," *Studia Islamica* 28 (1968): 131. I thank Leslie Peirce for confirming this reference in the original source.

[20] For examples of the observance of the night of the *miʿrāj*, see Jan Knappert, "Miʿrādj literature in East and West Africa," and "Miʿrādj literature in Indonesia," in "Miʿrādj," in *Encyclopedia of Islam*, 2nd ed., ed. Hamilton A. R. Gibb et al. (Leiden: E. J. Brill, 1960–2004), 7:103–4.

[21] Ibn Ṭawq, *al-Taʿlīq*, 1:60.

but – at least in his own time – dissident and somewhat isolated scholar who championed a return to the basic sources of Qur'ān and Ḥadīth and criticized the living traditions of piety predominant in his day. Ibn Taymīya held that, because the *mawlid* celebration lacked a precedent from the Prophet, it was an illicit innovation. The Prophet's companions loved him more than later Muslims could hope to do, yet they did not celebrate his birthday. Unlike the devotees of the *mawlid*, Ibn Taymīya thought of the believer's relationship to the Prophet in terms of obedience and emulation, not of mutuality and emotion. Nevertheless, Ibn Taymīya acknowledged that a person who celebrated the *mawlid* as an expression of love for the Prophet might be rewarded by God for his pious intent and his effort. He also warned potential zealots that it was unwise to interdict misguided acts of devotion such as the *mawlid* unless the person in question was likely to turn to better founded forms of piety.[22] Ibn Taymīya was certainly not the only religious scholar who opposed *mawlid* celebrations in the premodern period, but most mainstream scholars condoned the celebration until the modern period. More common than outright rejection was the attempt to appropriate and channel *mawlid* piety, drawing on the depth of the religious sentiments expressed in the celebration and the power of the salvific relationship with the Prophet that it promised while striving to tame its excesses. Religious authorities often composed *mawlid* narratives that drew on the scholarly historical tradition around the Prophet's biography, deemphasizing or excising motifs from the stock of folk narratives about his birth. Nevertheless, their involvement in the *mawlid* tradition demonstrates that premodern Islamic piety was not imposed from the top down. Scholars were themselves powerfully moved by forms of piety that were deeply rooted in the religious practices of ordinary people and strove to influence them even as they failed to dictate them.

THE LOCATION AND RESPONSIVENESS OF THE PROPHET

For most Muslims of the medieval period (and for many still today), the Prophet Muḥammad was not a historical figure who lay dead and unresponsive in his grave. It is possible that the earliest generations of Muslims considered the separation occasioned by the Prophet's death to be decisive until the Day of Resurrection; early Islamic grave inscriptions describe the Prophet's death as "the greatest misfortune," a bereavement

[22] See Raquel Margalit Ukeles, "Innovation or Deviation: Exploring the Boundaries of Islamic Devotional Law," Ph.D. diss., Harvard University, 2006, 227–35.

that overshadowed the loss of one's own buried kin.[23] Some *ḥadīth* texts that circulated in the early centuries of the Islamic era at least suggest the Prophet's continued life and/or accessibility, although they did not fully resolve the question of his location or the nature of his existence before the Day of Judgment.[24] At least by the sixth century AH (eleventh century CE), however, the Prophet was understood as a conscious being who (according to many scholars, as well as widespread folk beliefs) is aware of the pious invocations, the personal greetings, and the hopes and fears of individual believers.[25] A *ḥadīth* declared that "the prophets are alive in their graves, and perform their prayers," and the Prophet Muḥammad was thus understood as accepting, acknowledging, and even reciprocating the efforts of those who loved him.

One form of pious interaction with the Prophet involved the invocation of blessings on him. The Qur'ān (33:56) declares, "God and His angels send blessings on the Prophet; O believers, invoke blessings upon him, and greet him with the best of greetings."[26] According to *ḥadīth* reports, one's blessings and greetings would be relayed to the Prophet by an angel, no matter how distant one might be from his final resting place in Medina.[27] For every blessing one invoked on him (usually using

[23] See Fritz Meier, "A Resurrection of Muḥammad in Suyūṭī," in *Essays on Islamic Piety and Mysticism*, trans. John O'Kane (Leiden: Brill, 1999), 511 (and 511n21); Leor Halevi, *Muhammad's Grave: Death Rites and the Making of Islamic Society* (New York: Columbia University Press, 2007), 20–1. Halevi discusses the grave inscription of ʿAbbāsa bint Jurayj, which dates from the year 71 AH (691 CE) and thus numbers among the earliest Islamic inscriptions. The inscription begins, "In the name of God, the Merciful, the Compassionate, the greatest of misfortunes for the people of Islam [*ahl al-Islām*] is their loss [*muṣība*] of the prophet Muḥammad." Halevi notes, "The lament over the death of Muḥammad as a calamity [*muṣība*] has a distinctive elegiac quality," and that ʿAbbāsa's kin "mourned at her graveside the death of the prophet Muḥammad as if it had happened yesterday, although two generations had passed."

[24] Fritz Meier provides a thorough discussion of this issue in "A Resurrection," 505–47.

[25] See Meier, "A Resurrection," 519, who states that ʿAbd al-Qāhir al-Baghdādī (d. 429/1037) and Aḥmad ibn al-Ḥusayn al-Bayhaqī (d. 458/1066) "say more or less the same thing: Muḥammad came back to life again after his death. He continues to participate in his community, takes pleasure in their acts of obedience and is saddened by their sins." Meier sees this development in Muslim piety as occurring largely in dialogue and in competition with Christians (see 505–9); this is not a necessary assumption, however, as both the implications of *ḥadīth* texts and the independent spiritual needs of Muslims would suffice to explain the growing conviction that the Prophet was alive, aware, and responsive to the tributes and appeals of individual believers.

[26] In this verse, the same verb (*ṣallā ʿalā*, "to pray over," "to invoke blessings on") is predicated of God, the angels, and the believers. Commentators observed that God could not "pray" in the same sense as human beings and identified God's *ṣalāt* with His compassion or His glorification. See Constance Padwick, *Muslim Devotions: A Study of Prayer-Manuals in Common Use* (Oxford: Oneworld, 1996), 156–7.

[27] See Muḥammad ibn ʿAbd al-Raḥmān al-Sakhāwī, *al-Qawl al-badīʿ fī al-ṣalāt ʿalā al-ḥabīb al-shafīʿ* (Medina: al-Maktaba al-ʿIlmīya, 1977), 153–4.

the set formula "May God bless and greet our master Muḥammad"), one would be recompensed tenfold.[28] According to another set of *ḥadīth* texts, a prayer of supplication accompanied by the invocation of blessings on the Prophet will never be rejected by God; without blessings on the Prophet, the prayer will linger between heaven and earth, denied access to heaven.[29] Frequent blessings and greetings on the Prophet were a simple form of piety that reinforced the individual's personal connection with the Prophet.[30] Such blessings are incorporated into many rituals, including the five daily obligatory prayers. The invocation of blessings on the Prophet is also the main form of participation by guests at *mawlid* ceremonies, punctuating the recitation of the story of the Prophet's birth. *Mawlid* texts were composed with this practice in mind; the blessing often took the form of a rhyming couplet appearing as a repetitive refrain throughout the text. The enormously popular prose *mawlid* of Jaʿfar al-Barzanjī (d. 1187/1764) is punctuated by the couplet "O God, perfume [the Prophet's] noble tomb / with an aromatic fragrance of prayers and greetings."[31] Here the pious utterances of *mawlid* participants are likened to the scent of incense offered up at his tomb. Because of the immense popularity of Barzanjī's work, the rhymed blessing on the Prophet that separated individual passages of a *mawlid* came to be known as a *taʿṭīra* ("perfuming").

Invocation of blessings and greetings on the Prophet could also be an independent ritual activity. The power and efficacy of blessings on the Prophet were such that they were specially deployed in times of peril. The repetition of special blessings on the Prophet was particularly cultivated as a means of protection against the black plague in the middle of the fourteenth century CE.[32] A century later, the Moroccan

[28] For references to the many *ḥadīth* compilations that contain versions of this report, see Zaghlūl, *Mawsūʿa*, 9:366–7.

[29] Fritz Meier, "Invoking Blessings on Muḥammad in Prayers of Supplication and When Making Requests," in *Essays*, 552–5.

[30] See Padwick, *Muslim Devotions*, 152–66; Schimmel, *And Muhammad*, 92–6.

[31] See the text of Barzanjī's *mawlid* in Muḥammad ibn ʿAlawī al-Mālikī al-Ḥasanī, *Bāqa ʿaṭira min ṣiyagh al-mawālid wa'l-madā'iḥ al-nabawīya al-karīma* (n.p., 1983), 103–19.

[32] Meier, "Invoking Blessings," 565–8. Poetry describing and praising the Prophet could also have important ritual uses in protection and healing. Among the most beloved poems in praise of the Prophet was the "Burdah" of al-Buṣīrī (d. 694–6/1294–1297), which was believed by many later Muslims to have talismanic and miraculous qualities; Suzanne Pinckney Stetkevych has pointed out, "The liturgical uses of al-Buṣīrī's Burdah are... extensive and varied. They range from personal acts of piety and devotion to the Prophet, to Sufi (particularly the Shādhiliyyah order) in chanted or sung form with decidedly mystical intent (especially to see the Prophet in one's dreams), to its widespread public recitation, especially, in many areas, on the Prophet's birthday (*mawlid al-nabī*), at funerals, or weekly recitations associated with the Friday

Ṣūfī Muḥammad al-Jazūlī produced the prayer book *Dalā'il al-khayrāt*, which is primarily a compilation of different forms for the invocation of blessings on the Prophet (along with a list of his ninety-nine names and a description of his tomb). This work became one of the most popular pieces of devotional literature in many parts of the Islamic world and a part of the daily piety of multitudes of pious believers.[33]

Among the most cherished desires of many Muslims (following, and in some cases emotionally eclipsing, the desire to perform the pilgrimage to Mecca) was and is to visit the Prophet personally at his tomb in Medina. Because the Prophet was understood to be alive and aware, visitation of his tomb was understood by many scholars as involving much of the etiquette involved in visiting a living dignitary. The Prophet is supposed to have declared, "Whoever visits my grave after my death, it is the same as if he had visited me during my life."[34] Although the matter was debated, some scholars affirmed that the Prophet had unmediated awareness of greetings uttered by his grave (unlike those uttered elsewhere in the world, which were relayed to him by an angel).[35] Suitable comportment in the presence of the entombed Prophet was similar to that appropriate when he was alive. Thus, it was improper to approach too closely or to turn one's back on the tomb.[36] Just as the Qur'ān forbade believers from raising their voices over that of the Prophet or from speaking to him loudly (Q 49:2), it was appropriate to speak in hushed tones in the vicinity of his grave. In an anecdote transmitted by later Mālikīs, Mālik ibn Anas is said to have reproved the caliph for debating him vociferously in the Prophet's mosque, citing verse 49:2 and declaring that "[the Prophet's] sanctity when he is dead is the same as it was when he was alive." The caliph is then supposed to have asked Mālik whether it was better to utter invocations facing the Mecca (and thus turning his back on the Prophet) or facing the Prophet; Mālik reportedly instructed him to face the Prophet and ask for his intercession.[37]

prayer – the uses vary from location to location and no doubt have varied over time." Suzanne Pinckney Stetkevych, "From Text to Talisman: al-Buṣīrī's *Qaṣīdat al-Burdah* (*Mantle Ode*) and the Supplicatory Ode," *Journal of Arabic Literature* 37 (2006): 145–89.

33 See Padwick, *Muslim Devotions*, 163; Schimmel, *And Muhammad*, 94–6.

34 See Zaghlūl, *Mawsū'a*, 9:287; Christopher Schurman Taylor, *In the Vicinity of the Righteous:* Ziyāra *and the Veneration of Muslim Saints in Late Medieval Egypt* (Leiden: Brill, 1999), 196 (from the *Shifā' al-siqām* of Taqī al-Dīn al-Subkī, d. 1355).

35 Ibid., 197.

36 Ibid., 213. Although the level of deference owed to the Prophet surpassed that for any ordinary deceased person, the same general principle applied to all grave visitation; the visitor "should see himself or herself as a visitor in precisely the same way as when visiting the homes of living friends and relatives" (ibid., 73).

37 Cited in Ibn Taymīya, *Majmū' fatāwā Ibn Taymīya*, ed. Muṣṭafā 'Abd al-Qādir 'Aṭā (Beirut: Dār al-Kutub al-'Ilmīya, 1421/2000), 1:192.

The sense of the Prophet's presence at his tomb was often powerful. The seventeenth-century Moroccan traveler ʿAbd Allāh al-ʿAyyāshī describes the lifestyle of the corps of eunuchs who at that time served as guardians of the Prophet's mosque and tomb. After the supererogatory devotions following the last prayer of the evening, they ushered all of the worshipers out of the mosque: "After the doors were closed, their voices became quiet, and they were overcome with humility; you would scarcely hear a word from any one of them." When necessary, they communicated in hushed voices; they even muffled their sneezes. None of this was merely a matter of custom, al-ʿAyyāshī insisted; rather, they were moved by feelings of awe. When other people were present in the mosque, the eunuchs ensured that everyone behaved with appropriate reverence toward the Prophet; they allowed no one to raise his voice, to take a nap, or to stretch out his feet in the direction of the tomb.[38] Particularly for natives of Medina, however, there was also a sense of joyful intimacy attaching to the Prophet's grave. At the end of the seventeenth century, the Syrian traveler and mystic ʿAbd al-Ghanī al-Nābulusī described a yearly Medinan ritual involving the removal and cleaning of the carpets of the Prophet's Mosque and the cleaning of its roof. As tomb guardians and dignitaries swept the roof with specially produced gilt brooms, they tossed cakes, candy, nuts, and dried fruit down to the assembled children of Medina, who shouted joyfully as they gathered up the sweets. ʿAbd al-Ghanī himself declined to participate in sweeping the roof, as he found it unmannerly to place his own feet above the level of the Prophet's tomb.[39]

The view that the Prophet was alive and conscious, receiving devotees as personal guests and listening responsively to their supplications, was not one that went uncontested among premodern scholars. In Ibn Taymīya's view, there was no analogy between the accessibility of the Prophet to his contemporaries during his lifetime and his accessibility to latter-day Muslims after his death. Thus, although he acknowledged that the Prophet's companions had requested his supplications to God during his lifetime, Ibn Taymīya held that such requests were no longer licit after his death.[40] In response to the *ḥadīth* "Whoever visits me after my death, it is as if he had visited me during my life," Ibn Taymīya retorted

[38] ʿAbd Allāh ibn Muḥammad al-ʿAyyāshī, *Muqtaṭafāt min Riḥlat al-ʿAyyāshī (Māʾ al-mawāʾid)*, ed. Ḥamd al-Jāsir (Riyadh: Dār al-Rifāʿī, 1404/1984), 178–9. For a history of the corps of eunuchs who attended the Prophet's Mosque, see Shawn Marmon, *Eunuchs and Sacred Boundaries in Islamic Society* (New York: Oxford University Press, 1995).

[39] ʿAbd al-Ghanī al-Nābulusī, *al-Ḥaqīqa wa'l-majāz fī al-riḥla ilā bilād al-shām wa-miṣr wa'l-ḥijāz* (Cairo: al-Hayʾa al-Miṣrīya al-ʿĀmma li'l-Kitāb, 1986), 430.

[40] Taylor, *Vicinity*, 180.

that it was "a manifest lie in violation of the religion of the Muslims." Anyone who visited the Prophet during his lifetime as a believer, Ibn Taymīya reasoned, was counted as one of his Companions; and it was well established by Ḥadīth that later Muslims could never achieve the status of the Prophet's Companions no matter what they did, let alone by virtue of an illegitimate act of devotion like visiting his grave.[41] In any case, although one should face the Prophet's grave while uttering one's greeting to him, one should turn toward Mecca to utter invocations.[42] Whereas Ibn Taymīya's opponent, the more mainstream scholar Taqī al-Dīn al-Subkī, interpreted visitation of the Prophet's grave as a personal visit to the Prophet, Ibn Taymīya argued that the only religiously legitimate motive for visiting his tomb was a pilgrimage to the mosque that contains it – perhaps a technical distinction but a religiously and emotionally central one for the faithful pilgrim. In terms of the behavior of the individual believer, Ibn Taymīya denied that there were any ritual means (pilgrimage, invocation, celebration) by which one could enjoy a personal relationship with the Prophet.

Ibn Taymīya's criticisms, although they found numerous adherents in later centuries, did not end the many devotional practices based on people's belief in the awareness and accessibility of the Prophet. The Moroccan scholar Muḥammad al-Nāṣirī, who wrote an account of his lengthy journey to make the pilgrimage to Mecca at the end of the seventeenth century CE, describes how he was consulted in Sijilmasa about the custom of sending letters to the Prophet with pilgrims on their way to Arabia. The letters, which would contain greetings to the Prophet and the personal wishes and grievances of their authors, would be cast into the chamber that held the Prophet's tomb. In his reply, al-Nāṣirī acknowledges that this has long been customary, but he expresses reservations about the matter. He notes that latter-day believers are often poor Arabic stylists, incapable of expressing themselves with appropriate felicity and deference. People are too prone to ask the Prophet's help in their worldly affairs, rather than focusing on the afterlife, he writes. Furthermore, he has seen the caretakers of the Prophet's Mosque sweeping out the letters accumulated there; he does not know what becomes of them, but if they are burned it would be better not to write them at all. (Of course, he observes, if no one disposed of them, the chamber would

41 Ibn Taymīya, *Majmūʿ fatāwā*, 1:195–6.

42 Ibid., 1:193. Ibn Taymīya does seem to have accepted the idea, firmly based on *ḥadīth*, that greetings to the Prophet were relayed to him by angels; he did not, however, believe that there was any difference between greeting him at his grave and in any other location. See Taylor, *Vicinity*, 196.

not be big enough to contain them all.) Al-Nāṣirī prefers that those who are unable to visit the Prophet themselves entrust an appropriate person with an oral greeting.[43]

Even for those who were unable to visit the Prophet at his grave site, some believed that there were even more immediate ways of experiencing his presence. Both Ṣūfīs and ordinary Muslims often believed that the Prophet was personally present (literally, though in the spirit rather than in the body) at the culmination of the *mawlid* ceremony, when the chanter recounted Muḥammad's birth and all present rose to greet the infant Prophet amid clouds of incense. A question addressed to the great Yemeni scholar Muḥammad al-Shawkānī (d. 1250/1834) mentions with disapproval that this hope was cherished by ordinary *mawlid* participants in Sanaa.[44] The Ṣūfī master al-Mirghanī relates that the Prophet, who personally instructed him to compose a *mawlid* narrative, promised to be present when it was recited. A manual from a nineteenth-century reformist Ṣūfī order, the Tijānīya, instructs the inductee, "You shall not read Jawharat al-Kamāl [the order's most important prayer] except in a state of ritual cleanliness, because the Prophet will come at the seventh reading."[45]

The Prophet Muḥammad also appeared to people, both Ṣūfī adepts and ordinary believers, in dreams and in waking visions. In a widely circulated *ḥadīth* appearing in the best-authenticated Sunnī compilations, the Prophet declared that "whoever sees me in a dream, will see me when awake."[46] Some scholars argued that this statement referred to meeting on the Day of Resurrection or inferred that it was addressed to individuals who embraced Islam without meeting the Prophet during his lifetime. Other authorities (both Ṣūfīs and those scholars who, like the majority of premodern Muslims, were deeply influenced by Ṣūfī thought) affirmed that it was valid even after the Prophet's death, although they differed with respect to the physical or spiritual nature of the vision.[47] Seeing the Prophet, whether in sleep or awake, was a highlight of the spiritual lives of mystical masters and occasionally of ordinary individuals. In his diary for the year 889/1484, Ibn Ṭawq notes laconically of a

43 Muḥammad al-Nāṣirī, *al-Riḥla al-ḥijāzīya al-kubrā*, ms. Rabat, al-Khizāna al-ʿĀmma, microfilm no. 77, 39–40.

44 Muḥammad ibn ʿAlī al-Shawkānī, *Kitāb al-Fatḥ al-rabbānī min fatāwā al-imām al-Shawkānī* (Sanaa: Maktabat al-Jīl al-Jadīd, 1423/2002), 2:1083.

45 J. Spencer Trimingham, *The Sufi Orders in Islam* (Oxford: Oxford University Press, 1998), 191.

46 See Bukhārī, *Ṣaḥīḥ*, 8:91–2. The report ends, "And Satan cannot assume my form."

47 See Taqī al-Dīn al-Subkī, *Tanwīr al-ḥalak*, in *al-Ḥāwī li'l-fatāwī* (Beirut: Dār al-Kutub al-ʿIlmīya, 1975), 2:25–6.

Friday in the month of the Prophet's birth, "That evening we were at the house of Sayyidī ʿAlī ibn Qabbās; he held a banquet for the *mawlid* and his wife's vision/dream [*ruʾyā*] of the Prophet, may God bless and greet him."[48] Although Ibn Ṭawq does not provide any details, it seems likely that the host's wife had a dream in which the Prophet instructed her to hold a banquet in celebration of his birth, a widespread motif in the *mawlid* tradition.[49] In this case, ritualized feasting and rejoicing in the season of the Prophet's birthday were responses to a personal encounter with the Prophet.

Not only might the Prophet appear in a dream to command the performance of a ritual such as the *mawlid*; some believers hoped to induce visions of the Prophet through ritual means. This seems to have been a phenomenon of limited orthodox legitimacy, though of deep popular appeal. A spurious *ḥadīth* appearing in several medieval collections of forged reports (a genre whose function was to alert people to the inauthenticity of some statements attributed to the Prophet) provides a detailed description of a special prayer intended to produce such a vision. On the eve of the Friday day of congregational prayer, one was to perform a prayer of two prostration cycles, in each cycle of which one recited the first chapter of the Qurʾān once and chapter 112 twenty-five times. After this, one was to say, "May God bless and greet Muḥammad, the unlettered prophet" one thousand times. According to this report, the Prophet promised that anyone who performed this prayer would see him in a dream and that God would forgive his sins.[50] The enduring appeal of such rituals is suggested by an account by Emine Foat Tugay, a member of the Ottoman Turkish royal family. She describes an experience that her mother, Princess Nimetullah, had at the age of twelve, which would have been in approximately 1887. As the season of the Prophet's birthday approached, the women of the family began to discuss the belief that "the pure of heart may be granted a vision of the Prophet." Because they were convinced that "absolute innocence [was] essential," they chose the young Nimetullah as a likely candidate. She fasted during the daylight hours for forty days before the Prophet's birthday, performing her

[48] Ibn Ṭawq, *Taʿlīq*, 1:353.

[49] One of the most widely disseminated *mawlid* texts, an anonymous work known as *Sharaf al-anām*, recounts the story of a Jewish man and wife who convert (and begin to celebrate the Prophet's birthday) as a result of dreams of the Prophet Muḥammad. See Katz, *Birth*, 74.

[50] Muḥammad ʿAbd al-Salām Khiḍr al-Shuqayrī, *al-Sunan al-mubtadiʿāt al-mutaʿalliqa bi'l-adhkār wa'l-ṣalawāt* (Cairo: Maktabat al-Jumhūrīya al-ʿArabīya, n.d.), 132–3. The report appears in several collections of forged *ḥadīths*; see Muḥammad Zaghlūl, *Mawsūʿat aṭrāf al-ḥadīth al-nabawī al-sharīf*, 8:282.

five daily prayers punctiliously. On the final evening of her fast, which was the eve of the Prophet's birthday, Nimetullah was finishing her last prayer of the evening

> when she suddenly saw the familiar surroundings melt away. She seemed to be standing before a green door, which opened of its own accord. Entering a large circular hall, surmounted by a dome, she saw in its centre a column of light. As she approached it dissolved and revealed the Prophet Mohamed. Clad in a green robe and wearing a white turban, he smiled at her.[51]

Although efforts to induce visions by ordinary laypeople did not receive much support from religious experts, within Ṣūfī orders, mystical aspirants were sometimes encouraged to engage in practices of visualization and meditation that brought them into intimate contact with the Prophet. Although it is unknown whether such practices became widespread at the time, it has been demonstrated that they were expounded in some detail by ʿAbd al-Karīm Jīlī (d. 811/1408), a leading interpreter of the arcane and controversial (though also deeply influential) thought of the mystical master Ibn ʿArabī (d. 638/1240). Basing himself on Ibn ʿArabī's thought, al-Jīlī regards the Prophet Muḥammad, created directly from the light of God's essence, as the perfect manifestation of all of the attributes expressed by the Ninety-Nine Most Beautiful Names of God. Every human being, unlike any other created thing, is a microcosm potentially reflecting all of the different aspects of God's being; however, only in the Prophet Muḥammad are all of the divine attributes brought to full expression. Al-Jīlī provides mystical adepts with a detailed description of the Prophet's physical appearance,[52] and he encourages them to visualize the Prophet mentally until they have "reached the rank of those who witness him, may God bless him and grant him peace." (Al-Jīlī affirms that the mystic will then join the ranks of the Prophet's companions, those who knew him as believers in his lifetime – a possibility that, as we have seen, Ibn Taymīya indignantly denied.[53]) If the individual has seen the Prophet in a dream, he can visualize that image. Otherwise, if he has visited the Prophet's tomb, he

[51] Emine Foat Tugay, *Three Centuries: Family Chronicles of Turkey and Egypt* (London: Oxford University Press, 1963), 198–9, at 199.

[52] Early sources such as al-Tirmidhī's (d. 279/892) *Shamāʾil* contain detailed verbal descriptions of the Prophet's physical appearance; for a translation of one of the most widespread descriptions, see Annemarie Schimmel, *And Muhammad*, 34.

[53] Valerie J. Hoffman, "Annihilation in the Messenger of God: The Development of a Sufi Practice," *International Journal of Middle East Studies* 31 (1999): 356.

can envision that instead. He should imagine himself with the Prophet in his lifetime and invoke blessings on him; al-Jīlī affirms, "He hears you and sees you whenever you mention him, for he is described the by attributes of God, and God sits with those who remember him."[54] Two centuries later, the Ṣūfī master Aḥmad al-Zawāwī (d. 1230/1815) described his mystical companions' practice of invoking blessings on the Prophet "over and over again until he sits with us while we are in a waking state. Thus we may become his disciples, just as his Companions were, and we may ask him about all sorts of difficulties in the ḥadīth."[55]

Although most of the texts and practices discussed herein remain current among many communities of Muslims today, the modern era has seen shifts in emphasis in attitudes toward the Prophet Muḥammad and toward the ritual means that the believer may use to cultivate a proper relationship with him. The rise of the first Saudi state in the eighteenth century, under the religious leadership of Muḥammad ibn ʿAbd al-Wahhāb (d. 1792), brought new life to the religious attitudes pioneered by Ibn Taymīya in the fourteenth century CE. As did Ibn Taymīya, Ibn ʿAbd al-Wahhāb opposed the view that the Prophet was mobile and aware (although he accepted some limited form of subsistence within the grave).[56] The restrictive attitudes toward religious innovations associated with Ibn Taymīya and other opponents of the *mawlid* celebration also enjoyed new currency. Particularly after oil wealth offered Saudi authorities unprecedented opportunities for the dissemination of their views in the last quarter of the twentieth century, many people either became personally persuaded of the illegitimate nature of practices such as the *mawlid* celebration or were pressured to discontinue them. Saudi control of the Prophet's Mosque in Medina also allowed them to suppress devotional practices associated with his grave. Increasingly, emulation and obedience have been promoted as the exclusive forms of ritual relationship to the Prophet, reflecting both the conscientious convictions of growing numbers of Muslims and the power relationships within the contemporary global community. Such critiques have been less influential in places such as Indonesia, where a revival of *mawlid* performances flourished in the 1990s.[57] Ritual practices based on the expression and reinforcement of love and reciprocity with the Prophet Muḥammad have played an enormous role in Islamic piety and continue to do so in many communities today.

54 Ibid., 357.

55 Qtd. in Fritz Meier, "A Resurrection," 539 (from *Jawāhir al-maʿānī*).

56 Ibid., 532, 545–6.

57 Anna Gade, *Perfection Makes Practice: Learning, Emotion, and the Recited Qur'ān in Indonesia* (Honolulu: University of Hawaii Press, 2004), 13–14.

Further reading

Kaptein, N. J. *Muḥammad's Birthday Festival*. Leiden: E. J. Brill, 1993.
Katz, Marion Holmes. *The Birth of the Prophet Muḥammad: Devotional Piety in Sunni Islam*. London: Routledge, 2007.
Katz, Marion Holmes. "Women's Mawlid Performances in Sanaa and the Construction of 'Popular Islam.'" *International Journal of Middle East Studies* 40 (2008): 467–84.
Meier, Fritz. *Essays on Islamic Piety and Mysticism*. Translated by John O'Kane. Leiden: E. J. Brill, 1999.
Schimmel, Annemarie. *And Muḥammad Is His Messenger: The Veneration of the Prophet in Islamic Piety*. Chapel Hill: University of North Carolina Press, 1985.
Sorabji, Cornelia. "Mixed Motives: Islam, Nationalism and Mevluds in an Unstable Yugoslavia." In *Muslim Women's Choices: Religious Belief and Social Reality*, edited by Camillia Fawzi El-Solh and Judy Mabro, 108–27. Oxford: Berg, 1994.
Tapper, Nancy, and Richard Tapper. "The Birth of the Prophet: Ritual and Gender in Turkish Islam." *Man*, n.s., 22 (1987): 69–92.

8 Muslim philosophers' rationalist explanation of Muḥammad's prophecy

FRANK GRIFFEL

The tradition of philosophy in Islam is a direct result of the translation movement of Greek scientific literature into Arabic. About five generations after the death of the Prophet, at the middle of the second century AH (eighth century CE), the early ʿAbbāsid caliphs began to patronize and support the translation of Greek texts into Arabic. Another hundred years later, there was in Baghdad and other cities a thriving movement of Arabic philosophy in which Muslims, Christians, and even members of traditional Mesopotamian religions like the so-called Sabians took part. The Arabic philosophers – the *falāsifa* – continued the late-antique tradition of commenting on and developing the teachings of Aristotle and Plato. On the basis of Aristotle's teachings about the human soul and on the Neoplatonic commentaries thereon, the *falāsifa* developed distinct ideas about prophecy that went far beyond what had existed in Greek philosophy. Particularly the Muslim members of the movement created a fast-expanding body of teachings on prophecy and the role of the prophet in society that were geared to give philosophical – one might also say scientific – explanations for Muḥammad's prophecy and for the revelation that he brought. These theories adapted earlier ideas about prophecy and divination to the particular circumstances of Muḥammad's prophethood and his achievements as a statesman.

The Muslim *falāsifa* provided a detailed account of how divine revelation reaches the soul of the Prophet and why it manifests itself as a text that bears the distinct features of the Qurʾān. The *falāsifa* also explained why prophethood includes a political office and why the prophet is the best ruler of a society. These explanations were a distinctly Muslim manifestation of philosophical ideas. They understood prophecy as a natural phenomenon and regarded Muḥammad as the most perfect of all prophets. These theories culminated at the beginning of the fifth century AH (eleventh century CE) in the prophetology of Ibn Sīnā, who developed a comprehensive and systematic explanation of most phenomena connected to Muḥammad's prophethood as part of his teachings on the human soul. Ibn Sīnā provided a rationalist foundation for the belief that Muḥammad was the most perfect of all humans, endowed both with exceptional theoretical insight as well as the ability to communicate that insight to all the different kinds of humans. Soon after, at the turn of the sixth century AH (twelfth century CE), these teachings were appropriated by the influential theologian al-Ghazālī to become part of Muslim theology and of Ṣūfism. From that moment on, the rationalist explanation of prophecy, as it was developed by the *falāsifa*, had a lasting influence on what Muslim theologians and Ṣūfīs thought about Muḥammad and the quasi-prophetical faculties of Ṣūfī saints (*awliyāʾ*).

ARISTOTLE ON PROPHECY

Aristotle (384–322 BCE) lived and worked in a society where prophecy and divination were generally acknowledged and were part of common religious belief and practice, yet prophecy and revelation were not the foundation of the existing religions. Aristotle taught that there is a single God in the sense that there is a being that is the ultimate cause of all movements in this world – including the "movements" of souls (i.e., ideas and thoughts) – and that this being is also the final end point of all movements, meaning that all other beings strive to resemble this being as closely as possible. Aristotle did not write on whether this ultimate supreme and transcendent being sends revelations to humankind. In the short text *On Prophecy in Sleep*, he denies that dreams have a supernatural origin and that a dreamer can foresee events in the future. Dreams do not come from a god but are natural events in the human faculty of imagination.[1] In a second short work, *On Dreams*, Aristotle clarifies how dreams can reflect certain physiological processes that happen while a human sleeps. Other dreams are the residue of earlier perceptions in our sense organs, and they are too subtle to be noticed except when we are asleep. They are like the spots we see after we look into a bright light.[2] Aristotle did not believe in divination or clairvoyance and regarded people who pretended to have knowledge about the future as charlatans. Yet in his two short texts on divination and dreams, he

1 Aristotle, *On Prophecy in Sleep/Peri tēs kath' hypnon mantikēs*, in *On the Soul, Parva Naturalia, On Breath*, trans. W. S. Hett (Cambridge, MA: Harvard University Press: 1936), 374–85.

2 Aristotle, *On Dreams/Peri enypníōn*, in *On the Soul, Parva Naturalia, On Breath*, trans. W. S. Hett (Cambridge, MA: Harvard University Press: 1936), 348–74. The two works *On Prophecy in Sleep* and *On Dreams* are part of a larger work known as *Parva Naturalia*, or *Fī l-ḥiss wa-l-maḥsūs* in Arabic.

lays much of the groundwork for later theories by Muslim philosophers who aimed to establish prophecy and revelation. We will see that their theories regard prophecy as a natural faculty within the soul of certain human beings. This position is based on an Aristotelian psychology for which his book *On the Soul* is the base text.[3] In book 3, chapter 5 of that work, Aristotle explains how thinking arises in the mind of every human being. Drawing an analogy to other natural processes, he points out that there is an active component, which is the cause of thinking, and a passive component, which he describes as something that potentially becomes or receives the thought. In this short passage, Aristotle compares the process of acquiring thought to perceiving colors with the eye. Only light turns the colors, which are there even without the light, into objects of perception: "for in a sense light makes potential into actual colors."[4] Accordingly, there must be something that, like light, turns potential thinking or potential knowledge into actual thinking and actual knowledge.

EARLY DEVELOPMENTS OF PHILOSOPHICAL THEORIES ON PROPHECY

Already the Greek commentators on Aristotle's works focus on this same chapter in *On the Soul* and develop epistemological theories that assume the existence of various intellects that take over the different functions described in this passage. The Greek commentary literature develops within a Neoplatonic frame, where the light metaphor of that chapter is eagerly picked up. The source of this light becomes a celestial intellect (i.e., one of those beings that reside in heaven and govern the movements down on the earth). For example, Alexander of Aphrodisias and Themistius, who worked in Alexandria in the late second and the fourth century CE, respectively, came to agree that the active component in the process of thinking and acquiring knowledge is taken over by an "active intellect," which is one of those celestial intellects that transcend the earthly sphere.[5] Like light, the active intellect shines

3 "Psychology" here means teachings on the soul and has no relation to the contemporary Freudian understanding of the word.

4 Aristotle, *On the Soul/Peri psyché*, 430a 10–25, in *On the Soul, Parva Naturalia, On Breath*, trans. W. S. Hett (Cambridge, MA: Harvard University Press: 1936), 171. See the modern commentary on that passage by Ronald Polansky, *Aristotle's De anima* (Cambridge: Cambridge University Press, 2007), 458–72.

5 For English translations of Alexander of Aphrodisias's and Themistius's Greek commentaries, see *The De Anima of Alexander of Aphrodisias: A Translation and Commentary*, trans. A. P. Fotinis (Washington, D.C.: University Press of America, 1979); Themistius, *On Aristotle: On the Soul*, trans. R. B. Todd (London: Duckworth, 1996).

on the individual objects of knowledge that we perceive with our senses and allows our own personal intellect to abstract universal qualities from those perceived objects. For these philosophers, only universal qualities count as knowledge. We do not know what we perceive with our senses until we are able to describe it, such as a box or a dog. Box and dog are universal concepts that cannot come from the objects of perceptions themselves. They come from the celestial active intellect outside of the human soul in a process of abstraction that is similar to light enabling us to perceive colors. The universal knowledge from the active intellect is gathered in the human intellect, which is the passive component in the process of thinking and acquiring knowledge. For the Greek commentators, there was thus an active intellect (*noūs poētikós*), which reigned in the sky and shone with its universal concepts on the individual objects of human perception, and a human passive intellect or material intellect (*noūs hylikós*) – *material* because matter represents the principle of passivity – that abstracts the universal concepts from the individual objects of knowledge that we perceive with our senses. Acquiring knowledge is seen as a process in which the individual human material intellect receives the universal concepts from the celestial active intellect by abstracting them from the objects that we perceive with our senses.

In the early Islamic period, the Nestorian Christian Isḥāq ibn Ḥunayn (d. 298/910–911) translated Aristotle's *On the Soul* into Arabic together with works and commentaries of Alexander of Aphrodisias and Themistius.[6] These works form the nucleus of the psychological theories that emerge in the movement of the *falāsifa*. Prophecy is regarded as a part of those psychological theories. It must be stressed again that the Arabic philosophers did not "find an Aristotle pure and undiluted, but an Aristotle commented upon, re-interpreted and rewritten by a millennium of philosophical tradition."[7]

A generation before the Arabic translations of Aristotle's *On the Soul* and its commentaries became available, al-Kindī (d. after 256/870) had already written what is probably the first philosophical treatment

[6] Alexander of Aphrodisias's commentary on *On the Soul* was not fully available in Arabic, yet there was his epistle on the intellect; see James Finnegan, "Texte arabe du Peri Noū d'Alexandre d'Aphrodise," *Mélanges de l'Université Saint-Joseph* 33 (1956): 159–202. The commentary of Themistius was translated: *An Arabic Translation of Themistius' Commentary on Aristoteles' De anima*, ed. M. C. Lyons (Columbia: University of South Carolina Press, 1973).

[7] Gerhard Endress, "Alexander Arabus on the First Cause," in *Aristotele e Alessandro di Afrodisia nella tradizione araba*, ed. Christina D'Ancona and Giuseppe Serra (Padua: Il Poligrafo, 2002), 20.

of prophetical dreams in Arabic. Al-Kindī was a Muslim, and with him began the tradition of adopting concepts and ideas that were developed in Greek philosophy to explain processes of prophecy and revelation. The Greek tradition had stressed the fundamental difference between perceiving sensible data and universal concepts or intelligibles. Al-Kindī accepts this premise and teaches that perceiving sensible data is done by the human senses, whose information is gathered to form a picture or a form (*ṣūra*) in the faculty of imagination (*takhayyul*). Intelligibles, on the other hand, are actualized in the human intellect (*ʿaql*) and come from a source that transcends the human. In his work *On Sleep and Dream Visions*, which seems to have been written right after Aristotle's two shorter works on that subject became available in Arabic, al-Kindī teaches that some humans do have the capacity to perceive future events in their dreams.[8] This theory is based on Aristotle's position that, in sleep, the soul is still active and awake, whereas many other activities that usually distract the soul – most important, sense perception – are not taking place. The soul thus can come to itself and find in itself a kind of knowledge that also exists while awake but is usually perceived only while asleep. For Aristotle, this kind of knowledge was largely irrelevant and was only an insignificant residue of knowledge we perceive while awake. Al-Kindī sees this differently; for him, the soul may tell of future events while we are asleep. The human soul "knows all that is in the worlds, and everything manifest and hidden," and in the time of slumber, when it abandons the use of the senses, finds this knowledge within itself.[9] These dreams may be of varying accuracies depending on, it seems, how receptive one's organs are. In a less-than-optimal receptive state, a human may see future events not as they will be but merely as a symbol (*ramz*). A dream of flying could, for instance, symbolize a journey.[10] Already in al-Kindī there is an aspect that will later become very important. In addition to having organs able to receive the dreams, the souls of those people who receive divination and prophecy must have "attained a certain degree of purity" (*balaghat... al-nafs mablaghahā fī l-ṭahhāra*).[11]

[8] Al-Kindī, *Fī māhiyyat al-nawm wa-l-ruʾyā*, in *Rasāʾil al-Kindī al-falsafiyya*, ed. M. ʿA. Abū Rīda (Cairo: Dār al-fikr al-ʿarabī, 1950–1953), 1:293–311. On al-Kindī's teachings on prophecy and divination, see Peter Adamson, *al-Kindī* (New York: Oxford University Press, 2007), 135–43.

[9] Al-Kindī, *al-Qawl fī l-nafs*, in *Rasāʾil al-Kindī al-falsafiyya*, ed. M. ʿA. Abū Rīda (Cairo: Dār al-fikr al-ʿarabī, 1950–1953), 1:276–7.

[10] Al-Kindī, *Fī māhiyyat al-nawm wa-l-ruʾyā*, 304.

[11] Al-Kindī, *al-Qawl fī l-nafs*, 277; see also *Fī māhiyyat al-nawm wa-l-ruʾyā*, 301.

AL-FĀRĀBĪ EXPLAINS PROPHECY AND DETERMINES ITS ROLE IN SOCIETY

Al-Kindī does not explain why the human soul is able to foretell the future, nor does he in any way tackle the much more complex phenomenon of a revelation that produces texts such as the Qurʾān or the earlier revelations that Moses or Abraham had received. This next step is undertaken by al-Fārābī, who was born around 256/870, and received at least part of his education in Baghdad, where he also taught students in philosophy. After 330/942 he found patrons in Damascus and Aleppo and traveled to Egypt. He died in 339/950–951 in Damascus. Whereas al-Kindī only had a translation of an anonymous late-antique paraphrase of Aristotle's *On the Soul*,[12] al-Fārābī had Aristotle's text itself together with its major commentaries. His theories of prophecy are rooted in the epistemological tradition of the distinction between the active intellect (*al-ʿaql al-faʿʿāl*) that causes all thought and the passive intellect (*al-ʿaql al-munfaʿil*) of the individual human that receives universal concepts from the celestial active intellect.

Relying on Ptolemy's (d. ca.165 CE) geocentric model of the planetary system, al-Fārābī taught that the whole universe consists of ten spheres. The sphere of the earth is a true globe at the center of the universe. It is surrounded in the heavens by nine other spheres, wrapped around one another like layers of an onion. At the upper end of the universe, above the spheres of the sun, the moon, the five planets, and the fixed stars, sits the first sphere, which contains no visible object. The spheres are thought of as organisms that have a body, which is the rotating sphere itself, and a soul, which is governed by an intellect. At the upper end of the universe, the intellect that governs the first sphere is the highest created being. Beyond it is only the First Principle, of which al-Fārābī says, "One should believe this is God."[13]

[12] Rüdiger Arnzen, *Aristoteles' De anima. Eine verlorene spätantike Paraphrase in arabischer und persischer Überlieferung. Arabischer Text nebst Kommentar, quellengeschichtlichen Studien und Glossaren* (Leiden: E. J. Brill, 1998).

[13] Al-Fārābī, *al-Siyāsa al-madaniyya*, ed. F. M. Najjār (Beirut: al-Maṭbaʿa al-Kāthūlīkiyya, 1964), 31; Richard Walzer, trans., *On the Perfect State: Abū Naṣr al-Fārābī's Mabādiʾ ārāʾ ahl al-madīna al-fāḍila* (Oxford: Clarendon Press, 1985), 38–9. For an overview of al-Fārābī's cosmology, see Herbert A. Davidson, *Alfarabi, Avicenna, and Averroes, on Intellect: Their Cosmologies, Theories of the Active Intellect, and of Human Intellect* (New York: Oxford University Press, 1992), 44–8; Thérèse-Anne Druart, "Al-Fārābī's Causation of the Heavenly Bodies," in *Islamic Philosophy and Mysticism*, ed. P. Morewedge (Delmar, NY: Caravan Books, 1981), 35–45; David C. Reisman, "Al-Fārābī and the Philosophical Curriculum," in *The Cambridge Companion to Arabic Philosophy*, ed. P. Adamson and R. C. Taylor (Cambridge: Cambridge University Press, 2005), 52–71.

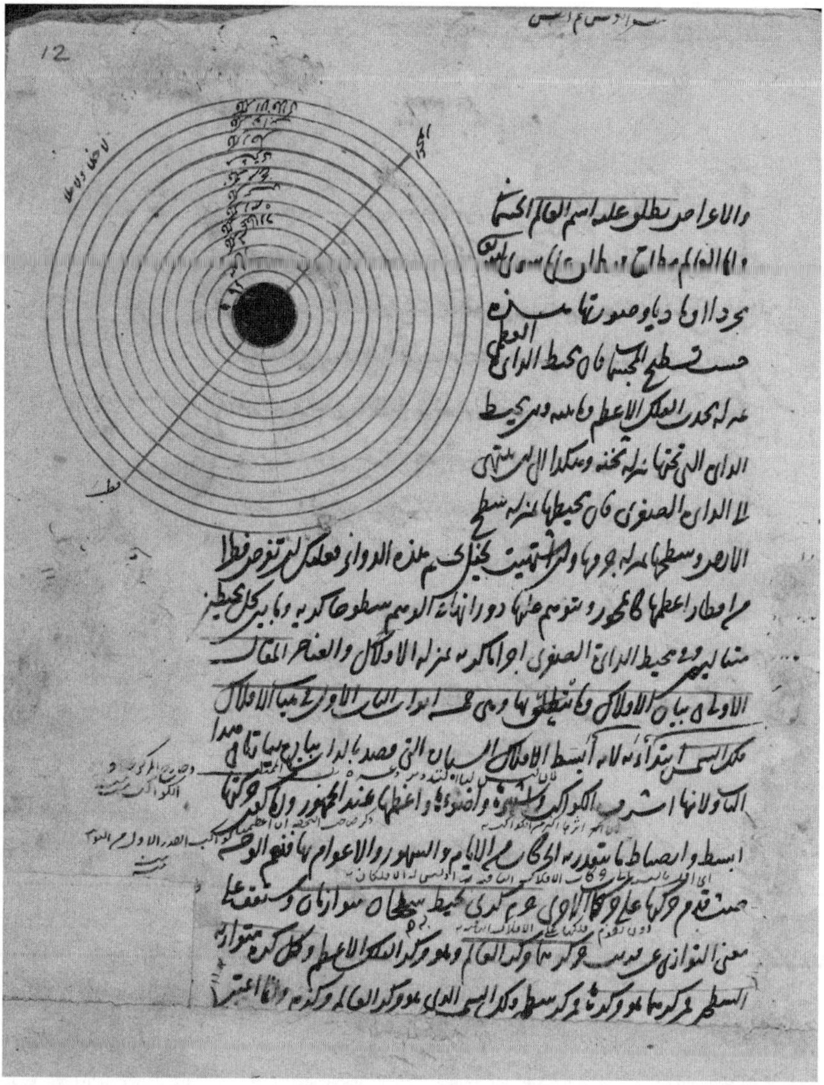

Figure 5. A diagram of al-Fārābī's model of the universe. Arabic MSS 436 fol. 12r. Beinecke Rare Book and Manuscript Library, Yale University.

God creates events in the world by directly acting on only one being, the intellect of the uppermost sphere. God's acting is described as emanation (*fayḍ*), meaning that His acts flow out of Him like rays flow out of the sun in a continuous process that never begins and never ends. The intellect that receives this emanation functions as an intermediary of God; it acts on the intellect of the second sphere in like manner, meaning that it emanates its actions on it. Every divine action passes as emanation through the intermediacy of the celestial intellects until it arrives at the intellect that governs over the lowest sphere, the so-called sublunar sphere of the earth. The numerous Qurʾānic allusions to the angels in heaven were understood by the philosophers as references to the intellects of the heavenly spheres. For example, "The Lord reveals [*yūḥī*] to the angels: 'I am with you'" (Q 8:12) was viewed as a figurative expression of the downward procession of God's creative activity from the higher spheres to the lower ones. The angels (i.e., the intellects of the heavenly spheres) act on behalf of God as intermediaries in His creation.

Al-Fārābī identifies the active intellect with the tenth intellect that governs the sublunar sphere.[14] In al-Fārābī, the active intellect has a triple function: (1) being one of the celestial intermediaries for God's actions (al-Fārābī calls them "secondary causes," or *al-asbāb al-thawānī*)[15]; (2) governing and ordering the sublunar sphere; and (3) giving universal concepts to humans, thus enabling them to think and acquire knowledge. The active intellect takes on functions toward this sphere similar to those that God has toward the whole universe. It is an efficient cause of everything that happens in the sublunar sphere, and it is the final cause for all the beings therein. This means that all creatures in the sublunar sphere, particularly humans, strive to resemble the active intellect as perfectly as possible. This Aristotelian concept that the development and functioning of every organism are driven by entelechy (i.e., a striving toward the full realization of one's potential) had a firm hold on the philosophical tradition of the *falāsifa*. For humans, entelechy means endeavoring to perfect that faculty that distinguishes them from all other animals: their ability to come to rational judgments. Not only is this the noblest of all human activities; it is also acting toward the realization of the full human potential.

Given that the active intellect contains all universal concepts and ideas and can be understood as pure thought, humans strive to acquire as much of those universal ideas as possible, to the extent that their individual passive intellects begin to resemble the active intellect. Doing so, the individual human intellect advances through different stages until it reaches a level that al-Fārābī calls the acquired intellect (*al-ʿaql al-mustafād*).[16] This is the highest stage of human perfections, at which the human intellect becomes almost identical to the content of the active intellect. It is reached when the human being masters "all or most" (*kulluhā . . . aw julluhā*) intelligible thought.[17] Al-Fārābī calls

[14] Al-Fārābī, *On the Perfect State*, 104–5, 202–3; al-Fārābī, *al-Siyāsa al-madaniyya*, 32.
[15] Al-Fārābī, *al-Siyāsa al-madaniyya*, 31–2.
[16] Al-Fārābī, *On the Perfect State*, 242–5.
[17] Al-Fārābī, *Risāla fī l-ʿaql*, 2nd ed., ed. M. Bouyges (Beirut: Dār al-mashriq, 1983), 21–2, with English translation in *Philosophy of the Middle Ages: The Christian, Islamic and*

this stage the conjunction with the active intellect (*ittiṣāl bi-l-ʿaql al-faʿʿāl*), when the active intellect enters into (*ḥalla fī*) the human. Only very few human beings can reach this stage, and these are the best of the philosophers. After describing this stage, al-Fārābī continues:

> When this occurs in both parts of his rational faculty, namely the theoretical and the practical rational faculties, and also in his imaginative faculty, then it is this man who is granted divine revelation [*yūḥī ilayhi*]. God Almighty grants him revelation through the mediation of the active intellect, so that the emanation from God Exalted to the active intellect is passed on to his passive intellect through the mediation of the acquired intellect, and then to his imaginative faculty.[18]

The perfect human, who has reached the stage of conjunction with the active intellect, receives divine revelation from the active intellect via the mediation of his acquired intellect. That revelation (*waḥy*), however, is immediately passed on to the imaginative faculty (*quwwa mutakhayyila*), where it produces the kind of prophecy that we know from the text of the Qurʾān. The imaginative faculty is part of the human soul and is located in the heart. It is located immediately below the rational faculty, yet it also contains sense perceptions and impressions even at times when the objects of a perception are no longer present. The imaginative faculty is particularly active while the body is asleep and not occupied with the actual perception of objects; therefore, it is responsible for our dreams. Likewise, the imaginative faculty receives revelation while the body is asleep, but in rare cases; when the imaginative faculty is powerful and developed to perfection and when it is not overpowered by sense perception or attending to the rational faculty, "then its state in waking life . . . is like its state during sleep when it is relieved of these two activities." It then represents the emanations received from the active intellect "as visible objects of sense perception that imitate [*yuḥākī*] that which comes from the active intellect."[19] The imaginative faculty of the prophet thus transforms the rational and universal knowledge received from the active intellect into representations that express the purely rational intelligibles by means of examples,

Jewish Traditions, ed. A. Hyman and J. J. Walsh (New York: Harper & Row, 1967), 217. See also Davidson, *Alfarabi, Avicenna, and Averroes on Intellect*, 69.

18 Al-Fārābī, *On the Perfect State*, 244–5 (I altered Walzer's English translation). See also *al-Siyāsa al-madaniyya*, 79–80; Davidson, *Alfarabi, Avicenna, and Averroes on Intellect*, 54, 58–9.

19 Al-Fārābī, *On the Perfect State*, 222–3.

parables, or metaphors. The imaginative faculty cannot help but recast what it receives into figurative images.[20]

Although this is the highest level of prophecy, lower levels may affect people who have a less-than-perfect imaginative faculty and who may not have reached the level of the acquired intellect. These people receive revelation only in sleep and in ways that the imaginative faculty represents distance or future events as if they were happening here and now. Still, even the lower level includes the figurative representation of theoretical truths. Al-Fārābī calls this not revelation (*waḥy*) but merely prophecy (*nubuwwa*), and the higher of these two levels is incomparably more superior to the lower.[21]

It is clear that, although the lower level of prophecy largely follows along the lines of what al-Kindī had already established on this subject, the higher level accounts for precisely the kind of prophecy that the earliest generation of Muslims had witnessed in the actions of the Prophet Muḥammad. Muḥammad and earlier messengers such as Moses and Abraham had reached a level of prophecy that far outstretched the mere foretelling and warning of future events or the production of insights about past events. When the Qur'ān (2:97) says that the archangel Gabriel brings down (*nazzala*) revelation to Muḥammad's heart, the philosophers understood it as a reference to the most important of the heavenly angels (i.e., the active intellect), which is the immediate cause of the revelation in the Prophet's soul. In addition, it was well established that Muḥammad received his revelations not only while asleep but also in his waking hours. Finally, al-Fārābī's theory of prophecy explains characteristics of the Muslim text of revelation. The Qur'ān is not cast as a theoretical epistle that employs rational arguments, but it is full of figurative language, parables, metaphors, and visual descriptions of past or future events. Al-Fārābī's theory explains how a divine message, which, according to the philosophers, can come only in the form of purely universal intelligibles, is expressed in a book that appeals more to the common folk than to the philosopher. It is clear that, in al-Fārābī, we find a distinctly Muslim development of earlier philosophical theories about prophecy that aims to answer questions and solve philosophical problems that were posed by the historical circumstances of Muḥammad's prophecy and the revelation he brought.

[20] Davidson, *Alfarabi, Avicenna, and Averroes on Intellect*, 58–63.

[21] Al-Fārābī, *Fuṣūl al-madānī/Aphorisms of the Statesman*, ed. and trans. D. M. Dunlop (Cambridge: Cambridge University Press, 1961), 75, 167; Davidson, *Alfarabi, Avicenna, and Averroes on Intellect*, 61.

For al-Fārābī, reaching the highest level of prophecy requires the development of an acquired intellect and the conjunction with the active intellect. Muḥammad, Moses, and Abraham were, according to al-Farabī, not only messengers of God but also philosophers who had mastered all the theoretical sciences. They were also founders of political communities, and each of them had brought a religious law that formed the legal foundation of the state he had created. The prophets' most important achievement is, according to al-Fārābī, their ability to cast theoretical knowledge in a figurative and metaphorical language that most people can understand. The only person fully qualified to govern a virtuous state is such a philosopher-prophet.[22] Only he is able to hold authority over the ordinary people and the elite alike and to pass just legislation.

This latter aspect of al-Fārābī's teaching on prophecy forms his political philosophy,[23] and it can be understood as an Islamization of Plato's concept of a philosopher-king from his *Republic*.[24] The perfect ruler appears in al-Fārābī as a lawgiving prophet-philosopher-king whose prime interest is to increase the knowledge and the virtue of his subjects. Revealed religion plays an important part in that project. Although the intellectual elite of the perfect state need no instruction in theoretical or practical matters, all others rely on revealed religion to achieve some kind of training in metaphysics and ethics: "Because it is difficult for the multitude (*al-jumhūr*) to comprehend these things themselves as they are, the attempt was made to teach them these things in other ways, which are the ways of imitation (*wujūh al-muḥākāt*)."[25] Revealed religion is the most effective of those imitations. It is an imitation of philosophy, which also means there is no conflict between philosophy and religion.[26] Still, although the true prophet is also a philosopher, not every philosopher has the talent and ability to be an astute statesman and to direct the multitude by means of persuasive figurative speech and

[22] Al-Fārābī, *On the Perfect State*, 244–7.

[23] On al-Fārābī's political philosophy, see Michael E. Marmura, "The Philosopher and Society: Some Medieval Arabic Discussions," *Arab Studies Quarterly* 1 (1979): 312–15; Charles E. Butterworth, "Ethical and Political Philosophy," in *The Cambridge Companion to Arabic Philosophy*, ed. P. Adamson and R. C. Taylor (Cambridge: Cambridge University Press, 2005), 275–80.

[24] The translation movement from Greek rendered only few works by Plato into Arabic. We know that passages from Plato's *Republic* were available in Arabic (see David C. Reisman, "Plato's Republic in Arabic: A Newly Discovered Passage," *Arabic Science and Philosophy* 14 [2004]: 263–300). More important, however, was a Greek synopsis of the book by Galen (second century CE) that was translated into Arabic.

[25] Al-Fārābī, *al-Siyāsa al-madaniyya*, 86, with English translation in *Medieval Political Philosophy: A Sourcebook*, 3rd ed., ed. R. Lerner and M. Mahdi (Ithaca, NY: Cornell University Press, 1983), 41.

[26] Marmura, "Philosopher in Society," 313.

exemplary deeds. Al-Fārābī believed, for instance, that Socrates, who, for him, was a master of theoretical investigation, lacked the abilities to address the masses and brought his condemnation by the Athenians on himself when he began teaching philosophy to those who were not properly initiated.[27]

In all this, al-Fārābī never mentions the name of the Prophet Muḥammad, the religion of Islam, or the Islamic caliphate created by Muḥammad's companions. Still, it is clear that al-Fārābī's theory of prophecy aims to give a scientific explanation for Muḥammad's prophecy, and his political philosophy legitimizes Muḥammad's activities as statesman and lawgiver. Although al-Fārābī's political theory may be meant to describe the situation among the first generation of Muslims, there is a utopian aspect in it that makes it all but impossible to apply it to the Islamic state in which he lived. The political situation in the ʿAbbāsid caliphate of the fourth century AH (tenth century CE) is described as a state in which the theoretical opinions of the people are defective, yet their actions are virtuous. Once the prophet-philosopher – that is, Muḥammad – has revealed the law and established the virtuous state, he has been succeeded by rulers who are neither prophets nor philosophers but who follow his example, adhere to the law, and, by the use of analogical reasoning, adapt it to new circumstances: "The ruler in this kind of leadership is called 'a leader and king who follows the example (*raʾīs al-sunna wa-malik al-sunna*),' and his leadership is one that follows the example (*riʾāsat al-sunna*)."[28]

IBN SĪNĀ'S SYSTEMATIZATION OF PROPHETOLOGY

Arabic philosophers after al-Fārābī accepted his distinction between prophecy (*nubuwwa*) and revelation (*waḥy*). Miskawayh (d. 421/1030), who worked in Baghdad and Iran, calls *nubuwwa* the capacity to see a "truthful dream" (*manām ṣādiq*) that presents events happening at a distant place or in the future. The higher of the two capacities is an emanation on the prophet's soul, whose extraordinarily powerful faculties

[27] Al-Fārābī, *Alfarabius De Platonis Philosophia*, ed. F. Rosenthal and R. Walzer (London: Warburg Institute, 1943), 21–2, with English translation by Muhsin Mahdi in *Alfarabi's Philosophy of Plato and Aristotle* (Glencoe, IL: Free Press of Glencoe, 1962), 66–7.

[28] Al-Fārābī, *Kitāb al-Milla*, 2nd ed., ed. M. Mahdi (Beirut: Dār al-Mashriq, 1986), 56; cf. idem, *Fuṣūl muntazaʿa*, 2nd ed., ed. F. M. Najjār (Beirut: Dār al-Mashriq, 1991), 66–7; Marmura, "Philosopher and Society," 314. This should not be viewed as a commitment to Sunnism but rather a mere description of the political constitution in the ʿAbbāsid caliphate. Al-Fārābī says that a more perfect situation would be reached in a constitution that he calls "imamic" (*al-sīra al-imāmiyya*) (i.e., in a Shīʿī state, where both the actions and the theoretical opinions would be virtuous and true). See Patricia Crone, "What Was al-Fārābī's 'Imamic' Constitution," *Arabica* 50 (2003): 306–21.

transform it into revelation.[29] This view of two distinct capacities of prophecy – one that may roughly be described as clairvoyance and divination, and another as higher capacity, where the prophet represents a universal truth received from a celestial intellect in figurative language – is also put forward in the *Epistles of the Brethren of Purity*, a collective work of encyclopedic character authored by a group of Shīʿī scholars in Basra in the second half of the fourth century AH (tenth century CE).[30]

At the beginning of the fifth century AH (eleventh century CE), Ibn Sīnā (Avicenna) significantly expands al-Fārābī's explanation of prophecy and creates what will become the most elaborate theory on this subject that influenced many Muslim theologians and Ṣūfīs. Ibn Sīnā was born around 369/980 in Bukhara. He served as vizier and physician at the courts of the Būyid dynasty in western Iran and died in 428/1037 in Isfahan. Because of the systematic and comprehensive character of his works, he became the most important and influential figure in the intellectual movement of the *falāsifa*. In the psychological part of his philosophical encyclopedia *The Healing* (*al-Shifāʾ*), he tries to give an explanation of all phenomena known to be connected to the human soul.[31] Like al-Fārābī, he aims to explain the kind of prophecy that brought about Islam as well as all other types of divination like clairvoyance or even the experience of what we would call déjà vu. Ibn Sīnā also addresses the question of the miracles performed by prophets and holy men, a subject that al-Fārābī and Miskawayh, for instance, have not touched on.

Ibn Sīnā attaches the term "prophecy" to a much broader range of phenomena than al-Fārābī does. As does his predecessor, he sees two different processes at work that may affect different people or also affect a single person all at once. Al-Fārābī's two different capacities of prophecy and revelation, however, both fall into the category of imaginative revelation.[32] As does al-Fārābī, Ibn Sīnā recognizes knowledge

[29] Miskawayh, *Kitāb al-Fawz al-aṣghar*, ed. S. ʿUḍayma, trans. R. Arnaldez (in French) (Tunis: Dār al-ʿArabiyya li-l-Kitāb, 1987), 133–44. See Peter Adamson, "Miskawayh's Psychology," in *Classical Arabic Philosophy: Sources and Reception*, ed. P. Adamson, (London and Turin: Warburg Institute and Nino Aragno Editore, 2007), 39–54.

[30] Yves Marquet, "Révélation et vision véridique chez les Ikhwān al-ṣafā," *Revue des Études Islamiques* 32 (1964): 27–44.

[31] Ibn Sīnā, *Avicenna's De Anima (Arabic Text) Being the Psychological Part of Kitāb al-Shifāʾ*, ed. F. Rahman (London: Oxford University Press, 1959). Unfortunately, there exists no translation in English. The corresponding part in Ibn Sīnā's philosophical handbook *al-Najāt*, however, is translated into English: *Avicenna's Psychology: An English Translation of Kitāb al-Najāt, Book II, Chapter VI*, trans. F. Rahman (London: Oxford University Press, 1952).

[32] *Imaginative revelation* is a term used by Fazlur Rahman in his *Prophecy in Islam: Philosophy and Orthodoxy* (London: Allen and Unwin, 1958), 36. It is maintained here to distinguish this way of revelation from intellectual revelation mentioned later.

that results when an emanation from one of the celestial beings – for Ibn Sīnā, it needs to be a celestial soul – acts on the human faculty of imagination. Such an emanation produces prophecy in the sense of knowledge of future or distant events. The celestial souls contain such knowledge and can reveal it to the imaginative faculty (*quwwa mutakhayyila*) of the human being. In both al-Fārābī's and Ibn Sīnā's theories of prophecy, the celestial beings – understood as angels – have foreknowledge of events that happen in the sublunar world. The disposition for these events passes from the cosmologically higher being to the lower until it finally reaches the earth. In the process of imaginative revelation, prophets get a glimpse of the foreknowledge contained in the celestial souls. The imaginative faculty of the human being enters conjunction with the world of sovereignty (*ittiṣāl bi-l-malakūt*), referring to the souls of the celestial spheres. Such imaginative revelation is, for Ibn Sīnā, a natural phenomenon that differs in strength depending on the power of the human faculty of imagination. In most people, it manifests itself as an occasional vision of a future event in a dream that might later cause déjà vu. Only extraordinarily strong souls are able to cut out the distracting influence of their external senses and experience imaginative revelation in their waking state as clairvoyance or divination. Prophets lack the impeding forces that suppress visions and therefore receive in their waking hours visions that less gifted people sometimes receive in their sleep.[33] At the top of the spectrum stands a phenomenon that Ibn Sīnā calls the holy spirit (*al-rūḥ al-qudsī*), where a high degree of imaginative revelation is combined with an optimal disposition for the second channel of prophecy in Ibn Sīnā: intellectual revelation.

Unlike al-Fārābī, Ibn Sīnā recognizes the possibility of attaining instantaneous scientific knowledge without following procedures for the acquisition of this knowledge, which some have called the human capacity of "intellectual revelation."[34] This, according to Ibn Sīnā, is the capacity to find the link that combines two independent propositions into a compelling rational argument. These propositions then become premises in a correct argument, a so-called syllogism. Intellectual insight is thus the capacity to hit on the middle term of a syllogism. Ibn Sīnā calls this capacity *ḥads*, which may be translated as "quick wit," "intuition," or "acumen." The moment we exercise this capacity and hit on the middle term of a syllogism, we have the flash of a connection with the active intellect. We more or less receive the middle term from the active intellect. Some people have a talent to find that middle term,

33 Ibn Sīnā, *De anima*, 173.

34 *Intellectual revelation* is also a term coined by Fazlur Rahman in *Prophecy in Islam*, 30.

whereas others are slow at doing so. Philosophers usually have a higher degree of *ḥads* than ordinary people. As in the case of imaginative revelation, every human has a share in this capacity – and many have only a very small one – yet at the higher end of the spectrum, it becomes part of prophecy. Ibn Sīnā argues that, because there are people who have next to no ability to find such middle terms – meaning that, because there are people who are very, very slow at learning – there must be people at the upper range who are "burning with insights, that is, with the reception from the active intellect."[35] These are the most brilliant of the philosophers. The universal ideas in the active intellect regarding every subject are imprinted on these persons "instantaneously or almost so." Again, reaching such stage requires purity and training: "It is possible that there is a person amongst human beings whose soul has been rendered so powerful through extreme purity and intense contact with intellectual principles that he blazes with *ḥads*."[36] This person receives instantaneous scientific knowledge without having to expend any effort in learning or formulating arguments. People at this stage experience a conjunction with the active intellect; they possess a "holy faculty" or "holy intellect."[37]

If such a strong intuitive capacity (*quwwat al-ḥads*) is combined with an equally strong imaginative faculty (*quwwa mutakhayyila*), then the effects of the holy spirit (*al-rūḥ al-qudsī*) emanate onto the person's imaginative faculty. These effects are depicted in images that can be perceived by the senses. In other words, the person who combines imaginative with intellectual revelation is able to recast theoretical knowledge that he or she has received through conjunction with the active intellect as figurative images. These people are the philosopher-prophets who receive revelation (*waḥy*).

In addition to receiving knowledge from the heavenly realm through the two channels of intellect and imagination there is a third property (*khāṣṣa*) of prophets: their ability to perform miracles by virtue of an

[35] Ibn Sīnā, *De anima*, 248–50; and idem, *al-Najāt*, ed. M. Ṣabrī al-Kurdī (Cairo, 1357/1938) 166–7. English translation of the passage in *al-Najāt* in *Avicenna's Psychology*, 35–7.

[36] Ibid. On Ibn Sīnā's argument see Michael E. Marmura, "Avicenna's Psychological Proof of Prophecy," *Journal of Near Eastern Studies*, 22 (1963): 49–56, and Dimitri Gutas, *Avicenna and the Aristotelian Tradition* (Leiden: Brill, 1988), 159–76. On the influence of Avicenna's prophetology in Latin European literature see, Dag Nikolaus Hasse, "Arabic Philosophy and Averroism," in *Cambridge Companion to Renaissance Philosophy*, ed. J. Hankins (Cambridge: University Press, 2007), 113–36, esp. 121–5.

[37] Ibn Sīnā, *De anima*, 250; Ibn Sīnā, *al-Najāt*, 167, with English translation in *Avicenna's Psychology*, 36.

exceptionally powerful "practical faculty of the soul (*quwwa nafsiyya ʿamaliyya*)."[38] All souls have the capacity to effect physical changes in our own bodies, but prophets' souls have the capacity to bring about changes in natural objects outside of their own bodies. Prophets have the capacity to cause storms, let rain fall, cause earthquakes, or cause people to sink into the ground, but they are not capable of changing a piece of wood into an animal or of splitting the moon.[39]

Prophecy in Ibn Sīnā thus consists of three elements: strong imaginative revelation, intellectual revelation, and a powerful practical faculty of the soul. These properties are not unique to prophets; indeed, all people share in them to some degree. Through purity and training humans can increase the strength of these faculties in their souls. Revelation of the kind received by Muḥammad, however, requires the utmost degree of all these three properties. The true prophet, for Ibn Sīnā, is a philosopher. He may not have devoted as much time to learning, but his power of intuition puts his theoretical insight at par with the most advanced among the philosophers. Both of them achieve conjunction with the active intellect. Yet where the philosopher may teach his insights only to those who practice philosophy, the prophet can convey them in a figurative language and thus make them accessible to all people.

His ability to convey theoretical insights to the mass of the people makes the prophet the best of all rulers, and in his political philosophy, Ibn Sīnā follows al-Fārābī closely. If we compare the prophet's law with that of the laws passed by monarchic or even democratic states, we find that people have the strongest motivation to follow the prophet's law, because they aim at reward in the afterlife; they avoid transgression because they fear punishment both in this world and in the next.

In his chapters about the political actions of the prophets, Ibn Sīnā is most outspoken about the qualities, merits, and virtues of Muḥammad. Unlike al-Fārābī, who never explicitly refers to the prophet of Islam, Ibn Sīnā leaves no doubt that Muḥammad has fulfilled all requirements of

[38] Ibn Sīnā, *De anima*, 199.

[39] Ibid., 199–201. The turning of a staff into a serpent is the prophetical miracle confirming Moses prophecy (Q 7:107, 20:69, 26:32, 26:45). Some Muslim scholars held that the splitting of the moon mentioned at the beginning of Sūra 54 (see Chapter 2 in this volume) was one of the prophetic miracles performed by Muḥammad. Ibn Sīnā implicitly denied that these events happened in the way they were understood by most Muslim theologians and jurists. He explains the turning of a staff into a serpent, for instance, as the mere impression of such a turning on the observers, similar to how people who witness sorcery are given certain impressions about events that do not happen in this way.

what a prophet should do as a lawgiver and what he should convey in his revelation to create the most benefit for God's creation.[40] In his psychology and his prophetology, Ibn Sīnā gives a distinctly Islamic expression to a theory that has its earliest roots in the works of Aristotle. For Ibn Sīnā, Islam is "the true religion which was brought to us by our Prophet, our lord, and our master, Muḥammad – God's prayer be on him and his family."[41]

AL-GHAZĀLĪ'S APPROPRIATION OF IBN SĪNĀ'S PROPHETOLOGY

Although Ibn Sīnā regarded himself as a distinctly Muslim thinker and his philosophy as a scientific expression of Islamic beliefs, his contemporaries among theologians and jurists saw things differently. They accused him of introducing a doctrine of prophecy that contradicts the Qur'ān (*mu'āraḍat al-Qur'ān*).[42] A systematic assessment, however, of the *falāsifa*'s teachings on prophecy was done only three generations after Ibn Sīnā by the eminent theologian and Ṣūfī al-Ghazālī. Al-Ghazālī was born around 488/1056 in Ṭūs in northeastern Iran and rose to fame in Baghdad, where he held the most distinguished teaching post in Islamic theology of his time. At age forty, however, he quit that position and taught at a small school and Ṣūfī convent in his hometown, where he died in 505/1111. Al-Ghazālī's theology formed during a period in which he critically investigated the teachings of the *falāsifa* – chief among them al-Fārābī and Ibn Sīnā – and tried to assess which elements posed a threat to Islam, which were false but harmless, and which offered valuable explanations that Muslim theologians could benefit from and should therefore apply.[43] Although he never commented on it, al-Ghazālī adopted many of Ibn Sīnā's teachings on prophecy as his own, implicitly saying that they fall into the last category of teachings that Muslim theologians should accept as true.

Rather than being an adaptation, al-Ghazālī's strategy toward Ibn Sīnā's teachings on prophecy is better viewed as an appropriation that

[40] Ibn Sīnā, *The Metaphysics of The Healing*, trans. M. E. Marmura (Provo, UT: Brigham Young University Press, 2005), 365–78.

[41] Ibid., 347–8.

[42] Ibn Sīnā, *al-Intifā' 'ammā nusiba ilayhi min mu'āraḍat al-Qur'ān*, ms. Berlin, Staatsbibliothek, Preussischer Kulturbesitz, Petermann II 466, fols. 57a–58a (Ahlwardt 2072).

[43] Al-Ghazālī, *al-Munqidh min al-ḍalāl*, ed. F. Jabre (Beirut: Commission Libanaise, 1968), 26–7; English translation: *Deliverance from Error: Five Key Texts Including His Spiritual Autobiography, al-Munqidh min al-Dalal*, trans. R. J. McCarthy (Louisville, KY: Fons Vitae: 2000), 67–70.

rejects some elements and transforms others to better serve the requirements of the Muslim theological discourse. First, al-Ghazālī severely criticizes the *falāsifa*'s position that prophets teach only the masses and that philosophers are not in need of divine revelation. Although al-Ghazālī implicitly accepts the position that prophets convey their message in figurative terms, he also insists that this message goes far beyond what humans can acquire through other sources of knowledge. No rational argument, for instance, can tell us anything about what will happen in the afterlife. In fact, rational arguments cannot even tell us which of our actions will be punished and which will be rewarded in the world to come. The prophets' revelations are full of original information that humans cannot acquire through the practice of their reason. All humans, including the philosophers, must heed the prophets' revelations and study them closely. Al-Ghazālī alters the philosophical theories about prophecy in such a way that prophecy now entails knowledge that goes beyond the rational faculties of the human intellect. Equally, he rejects the view that the benefits of prophecy are limited to their political activities of creating states and bringing laws. Although these are important elements of the prophets' actions, they are only a tiny part of the numerous benefits prophets bring to humanity.

Explicitly al-Ghazālī says that, as long as the *falāsifa* do not teach that the prophets lie or misrepresent the truth in an effort to create benefits (*maṣlaḥa*) for the ordinary people and for society, their views on prophecy do no harm.[44] Implicitly, he goes much further and applies many of their teachings. Ibn Sīnā's three properties of prophecy appear in many passages of al-Ghazālī's theological works.[45] Never, however, does al-Ghazālī mention his sources for these ideas. When he expresses these teachings, al-Ghazālī uses not the technical terminology of the *falāsifa* but rather words and concepts that are familiar to Muslim theologians and Ṣūfīs. One such passage is the brief chapter "The True Nature of Prophecy" (*ḥaqīqat al-nubuwwa*) in his popular autobiography *Deliverer from Error* (*al-Munqidh min al-ḍalāl*). After giving a rough sketch of how human beings acquire knowledge – one that closely follows Ibn Sīnā's

[44] Al-Ghazālī, *Fayṣal al-tafriqa bayna l-Islām wa-l-zandaqa*, ed. S. Dunyā (Cairo: ʿĪsā al-Bābī al-Ḥalabī, 1381/1961), 192; English translation in *Deliverance from Error*, 138; see also *Faḍāʾiḥ al-Bāṭiniyya wa-faḍāʾil al-Mustaẓhiriyya*, ed. A. Badawī (Cairo: Dār al-Qawmiyya, 1383/1964), 153–4; abbreviated English trans. in *Deliverance from Error*, 267.

[45] M. Afifi al-Akiti. "The Three Properties of Prophethood in Certain Works of Avicenna and al-Ġazālī," in *Interpreting Avicenna: Science and Philosophy in Medieval Islam*, ed. Jon McGinnis (Leiden: Brill, 2004), 189–212; Davidson, *Alfarabi, Avicenna, and Averroes on Intellect*, 116–23; Rahman, *Prophecy in Islam*, 129–44.

psychology – al-Ghazālī presents an explanation of how prophets receive imaginative revelation (in Ibn Sīnā's sense) from the celestial souls. He avoids the terminology of Ibn Sīnā and casts his theory in a language that introduces some philosophical terms into the accepted parlance of Muslim theology and Ṣūfism. In this passage, al-Ghazālī also stresses that prophecy reaches insights otherwise unattainable for the human intellect:

> Beyond the intellect there is another stage, where another eye is opened that looks into what is unknown and what will happen in the future and other things from which the intellect is far removed.... God most high has made this understandable to humankind by giving them a sample of the prophetic property: sleep. For the sleeper perceives what will happen in the (otherwise) unknown future either clearly or in the guise of an example whose meaning is disclosed by dream-interpretation.... Just as the intellect is one of the stages in which the human being acquires an eye that is able to see various kinds of intelligibles..., so is prophecy an expression signifying a stage in which the prophet acquires an eye that has a light wherein the unknown and other phenomena, which the intellect cannot perceive, become visible.[46]

Shortly after this, al-Ghazālī introduces Ibn Sīnā's intellectual revelation in a language that makes next to no references to the philosopher's original teachings and does not mention technical details such as the active intellect as its source. Al-Ghazālī calls this property of the prophets "divine inspiration" (*ilhām ilāhī*).[47] It is a way to acquire theoretical knowledge without the help of a teacher and without pursuing empirical experiments (*tajriba*). Inspiration (*ilhām*) is described similarly to Ibn Sīnā's *ḥads*, yet in the work of al-Ghazālī, it is a way to perceive theoretical knowledge that cannot be acquired by any other means, not even by the rational faculties of the intellect. For al-Ghazālī, the inspiration of prophets – meaning their intellectual revelation through their strong *ḥads* – accounts for much of the theoretical knowledge that is current among humans. Medical knowledge, such as which medicine cures which disease, or astronomical knowledge about the size of the planets, for instance, cannot be achieved by means of the intellect or through

[46] Al-Ghazālī, *al-Munqidh min al-ḍalāl*, 41–2, English translation in *Deliverance from Error*, 84.

[47] Al-Ghazālī, *al-Munqidh min al-ḍalāl*, 42–3; English translation in *Deliverance from Error*, 85.

experiments. Rather, it had once been revealed to earlier prophets, from which physicians and astronomers adopted it. For al-Ghazālī, prophecy is responsible for the human acquisition of a whole body of theoretical knowledge that the intellect alone cannot arrive at.

Among the many features that attracted al-Ghazālī to Ibn Sīnā's psychology was the comprehensive way it approaches phenomena like clairvoyance, divination, and prophecy. All these are different degrees of strength of a single human faculty, namely the faculty of imagination (*quwwa mutakhayyila*). For al-Ghazālī, this opened up a way to explain the extraordinary insight achieved by those who have purified their soul and cleansed their heart from the stains of bodily desires, immorality, and vice. If Ibn Sīnā teaches that purity and training can lead to a strengthening of the imaginative faculty, then he has also explained why an ascetic Ṣūfī may have a deeper insight into the secrets of religion than one of the most learned among the rationalist theologians (*mutakallimūn*). The conviction that piety and asceticism prepare the soul for the reception of theoretical and practical knowledge not acquired by any other means is at the foundation of al-Ghazālī's Ṣūfism and it is expressed on many pages of his main work *The Revival of the Religious Sciences* (*Iḥyāʾ ʿulūm al-dīn*). Yet this is also what alienated many theologians from the teachings of al-Ghazālī, as they rejected a connection between the pious deeds of a Muslim and his or her knowledge in matters of religion.[48]

THE INFLUENCE OF IBN SĪNĀ'S PROPHETOLOGY AMONG OTHER MUSLIM THEOLOGIANS AND ṢŪFĪS

Ibn Sīnā's prophetology provided a congruent explanation of prophecy that satisfied the requirements of the scientific discourse of the day. It regarded prophecy not as a supernatural phenomenon but as one that is rooted in the way God created the human soul. Al-Ghazālī shows how these teachings could be adopted to explain the superior insights of ascetics and "friends of God" (*awliyāʾ*), or Ṣūfī saints. These were often said to be able to predict the future and have other kinds of clairvoyance (*kahāna*). They were also said to perform wondrous deeds (*karāmāt*) that bordered on miracles. According to Ibn Sīnā, the human soul's practical faculty (*quwwa ʿamaliyya*) and the soul's readiness to receive insights increase with its purity. The practical faculty can become so strong that it might affect organisms and natural processes outside of its own body

[48] Delfina Serrano Ruano, "Why Did the Scholars of al-Andalus Distrust al-Ghazālī? Ibn Rushd al-Jadd's *Fatwā* on *Awliyāʾ Allāh*," *Der Islam* 83 (2006): 137–56.

but still within its vicinity. Thus, Ibn Sīnā offered a welcome explanation of convictions held by many Ṣūfī Muslims.

In the period after al-Ghazālī, many Ṣūfī authors and many rational theologians were attracted to Ibn Sīnā's psychology and applied it in their works. Not always were they aware that the ideas they found in al-Ghazālī and or in such prominent Ṣūfīs like Ibn ʿArabī (d. 638/1240) had their roots in the writings of the *falāsifa*. Once they had found a way into Muslim religious discourse, these ideas often shed their philosophical context and began a life on their own. This is particularly true in Ṣūfism, where the initial connection to Ibn Sīnā is almost immediately lost. Key doctrines such as the widespread assumption of a state of dissolution (*fanāʾ*) of the individual Ṣūfī and his or her ascent or union with the transcendent realm, Ibn ʿArabī's teachings on the perfect man (*al-insān al-kāmil*), and Jalāl al-Dīn Rūmī's (d. 672/1273) conviction that the distinguished Ṣūfī (*walīy*) can receive revelation (*waḥy*) and produce poetry that is on par with the Qurʾān are unthinkable without the earlier philosophical concept of a conjunction with the active intellect.[49] By proposing that prophecy is the result of the extraordinarily strong presence of faculties that exist in every human being, the philosophical concept of prophecy reduced epistemological barriers between the prophet and his most pious followers. In Ṣūfism, this led to the construction of ever-closer affinities between the Ṣūfī saint (*walīy* or *pīr*) and the Prophet.

A philosophical perspective on prophecy implies that Muḥammad's personality and his extraordinary faculties played a far greater role in the formation of Islam and the Qurʾān than the traditional accounts of Muslim historians acknowledge. The revelation of the Qurʾān, for example, is still caused by God and fully under His control but also is dependent on Muḥammad's faculty of imagination. This implication challenges the traditionally held view that God is the author of the Qurʾān. Al-Ghazālī, for instance, had no problem accepting the implication that Muḥammad formed the wording of the Qurʾān, albeit he never expressed that openly.[50] Whereas traditional accounts stress that Muḥammad was an ordinary human with no supernatural abilities, thinkers who are influenced by the philosophical teachings on prophecy tend to stress the

[49] John T. Little, "Al-Insān al-Kāmil: The Perfect Man According to Ibn al-ʿArabi," *Muslim World* 77 (1987): 43–54; Jalāl al-Dīn Rūmī, *The Mathnawí of Jaláluʾddín Rúmí*, ed. and trans. R. A. Nicholson (London and Leiden: Luzac and Brill, 1925–1940) 3:244–5 (text); 4:239–40 (translation, of part 3, lines 4273–91).

[50] Griffel, "Al-Ġazālī's Concept of Prophecy," 140.

uniqueness of Muḥammad and the extraordinary talents and capacities that have come together in his personality.

The appropriation of Ibn Sīnā's psychology therefore had the dual effect of helping to explain the epistemological superiority of the Ṣūfī master (*ʿārif*) over his followers and defining the unique position of the Prophet Muḥammad. This latter effect is particularly visible within the discipline of rationalist theology (*kalām*), where al-Ghazālī's works led to a widespread reception of Ibn Sīnā's psychology among the Ashʿarī school. From here it spread to other schools of thought, particularly to Twelver Shīʿism, where it helped to explain the superior insights of the Imāms. The rationalist theologians (*mutakallimūn*) – unlike the Ṣūfīs – soon discovered the origins of these ideas in the works of Ibn Sīnā and al-Fārābī, and they began to study them directly. Generations of Muslim theologians thereby received training in the psychology of Ibn Sīnā, which thus had an influence on Muslim theological discourse that continues to our own day.

Further reading

Butterworth, Charles E., ed. *The Political Aspects of Islamic Philosophy*. Cambridge, MA: Harvard University Press, 1992.

Davidson, Herbert A. *Alfarabi, Avicenna, and Averroes, on Intellect: Their Cosmologies, Theories of the Active Intellect, and Theories of Human Intellect*. New York: Oxford University Press, 1992.

Elamrani-Jamal, Abdelali. "De la multiplicité des modes de la prophetie chez Ibn Sīnā." In *Etudes sur Avicenne*, edited by J. Jolivet and R. Rashed, 125–42. Paris: Belles Lettres, 1984.

Gätje, Helmut. "Philosophische Traumlehren im Islam." *Zeitschrift der deutschen morgenländischen Gesellschaft* 109 (1959): 258–85.

Griffel, Frank. "Al-Ġazālī's Concept of Prophecy: The Introduction of Avicennan Psychology into Ašʿarite Theology." *Arabic Sciences and Philosophy* 14 (2004): 101–44.

Griffel, Frank. *Al-Ghazālī's Philosophical Theology*. New York: Oxford University Press, 2009.

Hasse, Dag N. *Avicenna's De Anima in the West: The Formation of a Peripatetic Philosophy of the Soul 1160–1300*. London and Turin: Warburg Institute and Nino Aragno Editore, 2000.

Rahman, Fazlur. *Prophecy in Islam: Philosophy and Orthodoxy*. London: Allen and Unwin, 1958.

Streetman, W. Craig. "If It Were God Who Sent Them . . . ": Aristotle and al-Fārābī on Prophetic Vision." *Arabic Sciences and Philosophy* 18 (2008): 211–46.

9 Where earth and heaven meet: remembering Muḥammad as head of state

ASMA AFSARUDDIN

> God has elevated the dignity of His prophet and granted him virtues, beautiful qualities and special prerogatives. He has praised his high dignity so overwhelmingly that neither tongue nor pen are sufficient [to describe him]. In His book, He has clearly and openly demonstrated his high rank and praised him for his qualities of character and his noble habits. He asks His servants to attach themselves to him and to follow him obediently.[1]

The foregoing quote, taken from a well-known work composed in praise of the Prophet Muḥammad by Qāḍī ʿIyāḍ b. Mūsā (d. 545/1150), underscores for Muslims the importance of emulating their prophet in many facets of their lives. This imperative is established by the Qurʾān itself, which declares Muḥammad to be "a beautiful example" (*uswa ḥasana*; Q 33:21). According to a report, when ʿĀʾisha, the Prophet's wife, was asked to describe her husband's character, she replied succinctly that his character was the Qurʾān.[2] The notion of *imitatio muhammadi* is thus a central one for believing Muslims, allowing for a remarkable consistency in their ethical, cultural, and social outlook and practices, regardless of the diversity of their lives and circumstances.

It was only natural, therefore, that when Muḥammad died in 11/632, his followers, unprepared for his death, would turn to the Qurʾān and the Prophet's *sunna* (customs, practices) for guidance on the fraught issue of leadership of the polity. According to the majority of Muslims, Muḥammad had not named a successor to himself or stipulated how Muslims should govern themselves. But general Qurʾānic principles and prophetic precedent could be mined to construct a paradigm (or paradigms) of righteous, legitimate leadership; both Sunnī and Shīʿī sources record to a considerable extent this hermeneutic enterprise. This

[1] Quoted by Annemarie Schimmel, *And Muhammad Is His Messenger* (Chapel Hill: University of North Carolina Press, 1985), 46.

[2] Ibn Saʿd, *al-Ṭabaqāt al-kubrā*, ed. Muḥammad ʿAbd al-Qādir ʿAṭā (Beirut: Dār sādir, 1997), 1:364.

chapter first delineates the Qur'ānic and sunnaic foundations of these competing discourses during the earliest period as recorded in relevant sources. It then proceeds to describe changing conceptions of leadership during the Umayyad and ʿAbbāsid periods, reflecting to a large measure increasing concessions to realpolitik while attempting to maintain a connection, however tenuous, with the prophetic era and custom.

DEFINING LEGITIMATE LEADERSHIP

Qur'ānic warrants in early proto-Sunnī discourses

The Qur'ān does not speak directly to the nature of political authority, nor does it mandate any specific form or system of government. However, it advocates two broad principles that, according to particularly Sunnī sources, were broadly understood to be constitutive of moral, administrative, and ultimately political authority. These two principles are *sābiqa*, which may be translated as "precedence" or "priority," particularly in conversion to Islam, and *faḍl* or *faḍīla*, which may be translated as "virtue" or "moral excellence."[3] Qur'ānic verses that point to the greater moral prominence of the earliest and most committed believers indicate a divinely ordained vision of a hierarchy of moral excellence, both in this world and the next. For example, Q 57:10 states, "Those among you who spent and fought before the victory are not of the same rank [as others], but greater in rank than those who spent and fought afterwards," and Q 9:100 runs, "God is pleased with the foremost in precedence (*al-sābiqūna al-awwalūna*) from among the Emigrants and the Helpers and those who follow them in good works, and they are pleased with Him" (see also Q 56:10–12; 9:20).

The Qur'ān further makes a causal link between the political dominance of a nation and its moral excellence (as well as the converse – the collapse of a nation on account of its moral degeneration). For example, Q 10:13–14 proclaims:

> We have destroyed generations before you when they committed wrong while their messengers had come with clear proofs, and they did not believe. This is how we recompense the nation of evildoers. Then we made you the successors (*khalāʾif*) on earth after them in order to see how you behave.

[3] For a fuller discussion of these concepts and their deployment in early Muslim discourses on leadership, see my book *Excellence and Precedence: Medieval Islamic Discourse on Legitimate Leadership* (Leiden: E. J. Brill, 2002).

Another group of verses (Q 7:128–9) states:

> Moses said to his people, "Ask help of God and be patient, for the earth belongs to God. He causes whomever He wishes from among His servants to inherit (*yūrithuhā*) and the end belongs to the righteous." They said, "We were oppressed before you came to us and after you came to us." He said, "Perhaps God will destroy your enemies and set you as vicegerents on earth, in order to see how you behave."

Q 24:55 further points to divine "obligation" to reward the righteous with stewardship on earth, which may be (but is not *a priori*) political in nature. The verse states:

> God has promised those among you who believe and perform righteous deeds to cause you to succeed (*li-yastakhlifannahum*) on earth just as He made those before you succeed (*istakhlafa*), so as to strengthen their religion for them which He has chosen for them and so that He may replace them after that, and they are evil-doers.

Other verses that make this equation between righteous action and "inheriting" the earth, explicitly or implicitly, are Q 7:69, 74, 128–9,169; 17:38; 57:7; 6:133; 4:133; 14:19; 28:5–6; and 35:16.[4] Qur'ānic coupling of moral excellence and stewardship on the earth in this manner, both at the individual level and at the group level, appears to have made a strong impression on the early Muslims. This message is, after all, at the root of ʿUmar's official promulgation of a merit-based moral and social order, most conspicuously embodied in the *dīwān* that controlled the disbursement of stipends on the basis of *sābiqa* and *faḍl/faḍīla*."[5] This preferential system of awarding stipends had already been established by the Prophet, according to a number of sources.[6] The establishment of the *dīwān* itself reflects the recognition of the centrality of these principles for the organization of the early Muslim community.

However, our sources indicate that there were competing definitions of these principles and thus of their attendant implications for

[4] See Wadad al-Qadi, "The Term 'Khalīfa' in Early Exegetical Literature," *Die Welt des Islams* 28 (1988): 392–411.

[5] Al-Balādhūrī, *Futūḥ al-buldān*, ed. M. J. de Goeje (Leiden: E. J. Brill, 1866), 448ff.; Abū Yūsuf, *Kitāb al-kharāj*, ed. Iḥsān ʿAbbās (Beirut, 1405/1985), 140–4.

[6] Al-Bukhārī, *Ṣaḥīḥ* (Cairo: Maṭbaʿat Ḥassān, 1973), 6:389, no. 3692; Muslim, *Ṣaḥīḥ* (Beirut: Dār Ibn Ḥazm, 1995), 3:1109, no. 57. See also Ibn Taymiyya, *Minhāj al-sunna* (Riyadh: Idarat al-thaqafa wa-l-nashr bi-l-jāmiʿa, 1986), 6:101ff., where he asserts that this was a prophetic precedent adopted by ʿUmar.

leadership, both moral and political, of the Muslim polity. Kinship to Muḥammad, primarily through marriage, was also a point of consideration in the allotment of stipends by the *dīwān* but in conjunction with *sābiqa*. Thus, the Prophet's widows, among the earliest converts to Islam and closest to Muḥammad, were awarded more generous pensions than anyone else.[7] Reports that suggest that blood kinship in itself was a priority in the setting up of the *dīwān*, however, are certainly politically motivated and spurious. Of this ilk are the pro-ʿAbbāsid reports that state that heading the register of pensions was the Prophet's uncle al-ʿAbbās (d. ca. 32/653), who had converted disgracefully late to Islam compared to the most prominent *ṣaḥāba* and who would thus not have satisfied the essential criteria of precedence and excellence.[8]

The well-known Sunnī exegete and historian al-Ṭabarī (d. 310/923) in the ʿAbbāsid period emphasizes *sābiqa* as a key determinant in the early debates concerning the office of the caliph. In his universal history, al-Ṭabarī refers to the Saqīfa episode when Abū Bakr rose to address the Anṣār, who at first had opposed his nomination as the caliph. In his address, he reminded them that God had bestowed special distinction on the early Muhājirūn (*fa-khaṣṣa allāh al-muhājirīn al-awwalīn*) on account of the fact that they had believed in the Prophet before others, placed their faith in him, and offered him consolation while patiently bearing the afflictions that had been visited on them. Furthermore,

> They are the first to worship God on earth and to place their faith in Him and His messenger. They are his [the Messenger's] closest associates (*awliyāʾ*) and his kinfolk (*ʿashīratuhu*) and are the most entitled to this matter [sc. the caliphate] after him. Only the wrong-doer (*ẓālim*) opposes them in that. O gathering of the Anṣār, [you are] those whose excellence (*faḍluhum*) in religion cannot be denied or whose great precedence (*sābiqatuhum al-ʿaẓīma*) in Islam cannot be denied. It pleased God to make you helpers of His religion and His Messenger. He made his [the Messenger's] emigration to you, and from among you are the majority of his wives and his Companions. After the first Emigrants, there is no one else of your status in our estimation. Thus we are the rulers (*al-umarāʾ*) and you are the assistants

[7] Ibn Saʿd, *Ṭabaqāt*, 3:225, 228; also cf. Ibn Ḥazm, *al-Fiṣal fī 'l-milal wa-'l-ahwāʾ wa-'l-niḥal* (Baghdad: Muʾassasat al-Khanjī, 1903), 4:91, 94.

[8] For such reports, see Ibn Saʿd, *Ṭabaqāt*, 3:224-25.; *contra* Wilferd Madelung, *The Succession to Muhammad* (Cambridge, U.K.: Cambridge University Press, 1997).

> (*al-wuzarāʾ*). We do not fail to consult you (*la tuftatūna bi-mashwara*) and we do not adjudicate (*la naqḍī*) matters without you.[9]

In this report, moral excellence is made contingent primarily on priority in conversion to Islam. Although the Anṣār are certainly among the most excellent of Muslims, on the basis of their record of service to Islam, this speech affirms that they can never aspire to outstrip the Muhājirūn, who, equally pious, enjoy the added advantage of having accepted Islam prior to them and thus are to be regarded as more deserving of leadership positions.

An earlier source, the *Risālat al-ʿuthmāniyya* of the celebrated belle-lettrist al-Jāḥiẓ (d. 255/868–869), preserves a variant account of this key address, in which Abū Bakr is quoted as counseling the people gathered before him:

> You must be Godfearing, for piety is the most intelligent practice and immorality is the most foolish. Indeed I am a follower, not an innovator; if I perform well, then help me, and if I should deviate, correct me.... O gathering of the Anṣār, if the caliphate [lit. "this matter"] is deserved on account of *ḥasab* and attained on account of kinship (*bi-'l-qarāba*), then Quraysh is more noble than you on account of *ḥasab* and more closely related than you [to the Prophet]. However, since it is deserved on account of moral excellence (*bi-'l-faḍl*) in religion, then those who are foremost in precedence (*al-sābiqun al-awwalūn*) from among the Muhajirūn are placed ahead of you in the entire Qur'ān[10] as being more worthy of it compared to you.[11]

The assembly of people, remarks al-Jāḥiẓ, was swayed by the cogency of Abū Bakr's arguments and proceeded to express their loyalty to him.[12] Al-Jāḥiẓ finds confirmation in this episode of the widespread recognition in the earliest period of Islam of the importance of the principles of "religiosity (*al-dīn*), precedence (*al-sābiqa*), and indispensable service to Muslims" as constitutive of political leadership.[13]

[9] Al-Ṭabarī, *Taʾrīkh al-umam wa-'l-mulūk* (Beirut: Dār al-kutub al-ʿilmiyya, 1997), 2:242–3.

[10] Al-Jāḥiẓ thus understands the Qur'ānic collocation "al-Muhājirūn wa-'l-Anṣār" to indicate the former's precedence in Islam in general because they were placed before the Anṣār ("wa-innamā quddimu fī 'l-qurʾān li-taqaddumihim fī 'l-islām"); see his *Risālat al-ʿUthmāniyya*, ed. ʿAbd al-Salām Hārūn (Cairo, 1955), 203.

[11] Al-Jāḥiẓ, *ʿUthmāniyya*, 202.

[12] Ibid.

[13] Ibid., 216.

The principle of *sābiqa* and the hierarchy of moral excellence it generated acquired strong political implications in particularly Sunnī–Shīʿī debates about righteous and legitimate leadership of the Muslim community, as is described later here. Such implications sometimes tended to be read back into the Qurʾān. Thus, al-Ṭabarī in his exegetical work understands Q 10:13–14, for example, to be a reference to the righteous reigns of Abū Bakr and ʿUmar after the Prophet.[14]

Shīʿī views

It is generally assumed that the Shīʿa have always subscribed to a legitimist view of religio-political leadership and insisted that the ruler of the Muslim polity be a blood relative of the Prophet Muḥammad. However, early Shīʿī sources sometimes offer a different perspective and suggest that we must be wary of retrojecting later entrenched assumptions back into the very early period.

For example, when comparing early and later Shīʿī sources, we notice a certain evolution in Shīʿī interpretation of the Qurʾānic term *sābiqūn*. Early Shīʿī views appear to be similar to the general Sunnī understanding of this term, whereas later views (roughly after the fourth century AH [tenth century CE]) on the *sābiqūn* diverged markedly from the Sunnī perspective. The typical (and expected) Shīʿī view is that *sābiqūn* refers only to the Prophet and his legatee (*waṣiyyihi*) (i.e., ʿAlī) and, ipso facto, excludes all the other Companions. However, in his commentary on Q 46:10, the early-fourth-century-AH (tenth-century-CE) Shīʿī exegete ʿAlī b. Ibrāhīm al-Qummī (d. after 307/919) says that, according to the Companion Hudhayfa b. al-Yaman, the Prophet referred only to himself as "one of those who preceded and who was the best among them," with no mention of ʿAlī as one who closely follows him.[15] The fourth-century-AH (tenth-century-CE) Shīʿī scholar al-Kulaynī (d. 329/941) says in exegesis of Q 9:100 that the verse assigns the highest rank to the earliest Muhājirūn, second place to the Anṣār (*thannā bi-'l-anṣār*), and third place to the Successors (*thallatha bi-'l-tābiʿīn*), a view that is in complete accordance with the general Sunnī conception of *sābiqa*.[16] A well-known report, attributed to the sixth Shīʿī Imām Jaʿfar al-Ṣādiq (d. 148/765) and frequently cited in Sunnī sources, quotes the Prophet as saying, "The best of people (*khayr al-nās*) are from my generation (*qarnī*), then from

[14] See al-Ṭabarī, *Jāmiʿ al-bayān fī tafsīr al-Qurʾān* (Beirut: Dār al-kutub al-ʿilmiyya, 1997), 15:37–8.

[15] Al-Qummī, *Tafsīr*, ed. Ṭayyib al-Mūsawī al-Jarāʾirī (Najaf, 1966), 2:347.

[16] See al-Kulaynī, *Uṣūl al-kāfī*, ed. Muḥammad Jaʿfar Shams al-Dīn (Beirut: Dār al-taʿāruf li-l-maṭbūʿāt, 1990), 2:48.

the second [generation], then from the third; then will come a group of people in whom there will be no good."[17] The people from the Prophet's generation would, undoubtedly, include all his Companions.[18] Another fourth-century-AH (tenth-century-CE) Shīʿī author, Abū l-Qāsim ʿAlī b. Aḥmad al-Kūfī (d. 352/963), comments that it is possible to interpret *al-sābiqūn* in Q 9:100 as a reference to the ʿAqabiyyun, the seventy people who came to Mecca one night and pledged their allegiance to the Prophet in the house of ʿAbd al-Muttalib in ʿAqaba.[19] This view is also in accordance with that of the majority of Sunnī scholars.[20]

This early trend in Shīʿī political thought concerning the *sābiqūn* has several significant ramifications. The fact that a number of early Shīʿī exegetical works state that the *sābiqūn* referred to the pious Muslims of the first generation signifies that the proto-Shīʿa (sc. the precursors of the later fully formed Shīʿa) of the early period apparently made no distinction between those Companions who were blood relatives of the Prophet (notably ʿAlī) and those who were not. This perception is further bolstered by the fact that a number of Shīʿī authors relate that some of the earliest supporters of ʿAlī (pro-ʿAlid) were vigorous participants in the debates regarding the qualifications of Abū Bakr and ʿAlī for the caliphate-imamate. According to the pro-ʿAlid Muʿtazilī scholar Ibn Abī 'l-Ḥadīd (d. 655/1257), immediately after the death of the Prophet, these partisans of ʿAlī were the first to put into circulation reports that praised their preferred candidate's unique virtues. In response, Abū Bakr's partisans, the Bakriyya,[21] are said to have come forth with traditions of their

[17] Al-Ṭabarānī, *al-Muʿjam al-awsaṭ*, ed. Ṭāriq b. ʿIwad Allāh b. Muḥammad and ʿAbd al-Muḥsin b. Ibrāhīm al-Ḥusaynī (Cairo: Dār al-Ḥaramayn, 1995), 3:339, no. 3336; for variants, see ibid., 2:27, no. 1122; 8:358, no. 8868.

[18] Cf. Joseph van Ess, *Anfänge muslimischer Theologie: Studien zum Entstehen prädestinatianischer Überlieferung* (Beirut: Orient Institute, 1977), 4, where he points to an early Shīʿī positive attitude toward Abū Bakr and ʿUmar.

[19] Al-Kūfī, *al-Istighātha* (N.p.: n.d.), 69.

[20] Ibn Saʿd, *Ṭabaqāt*, 3:452–70; Ibn Hishām, *al-Sīra al-nabawiyya*, ed. Suhayl Zakkār (Beirut: Dār al-fikr, 1992), 1:299–300.

[21] For references to the principal groups to which the appellation Bakriyya was applied, see al-Ashʿarī, *Maqalāt al-islāmiyyin*, ed. H. Ritter (Istanbul: Devlet matbaasi, 1929–1933), 273–4; al-Baghdādī, *Kitāb al-milal wa-'l-niḥal*, ed. Albīr Naṣrī Nādir (Beirut: Dār al-mashriq, 1970), 146; al-Masʿūdī, *Kitāb al-tanbīh wa-'l-ishrāf*, ed. M. J. de Goeje (Leiden: E. J. Brill, 1893), 337; Montgomery Watt, *The Formative Period of Islamic Thought* (Edinburgh: Edinburgh University Press, 1973), 362n19; Josef van Ess, *Theologie und Gesellschaft im 2. und 3. Jahrhundert Hidschra: eine Geschichte des religiösen Denkens im frühen Islam* (Berlin: de Gruyter, 1991–1997), 2:108–18. See also my article, "In Praise of the Caliphs: Recreating History from the *Manāqib* Literature," *International Journal of Middle East Studies* 31 (1999): 329–50.

own that espoused the merits of their candidate, thus creating this distinctive *manāqib* or *faḍā'il* genre within the evolving *ḥadīth* corpus.[22] Other, mainly Shī'ī, sources mention that when Abū Bakr entered the mosque at Medina after having been appointed the first caliph, twelve men from among the Muhājirūn rose up one after the other to recite the excellences of 'Alī and proclaim his right to the imamate.[23] Ibn Abī 'l-Ḥadīd notably commented that, because a debate centered around the key concepts of "precedences, excellences, and relationship [to the Prophet]" did ensue regarding a leader after the death of Muḥammad and because there was no mention of *naṣṣ* ("explicit designation") in this debate, one must logically conclude that there was no explicit designation by the Prophet of either Abū Bakr or 'Alī as his successor.[24]

Sunnī-Shī'ī debates on the basis of the Qur'ān, *Ḥadīth*, and *Sīra* literature

Reflecting these intra-Muslim debates concerning legitimate leadership, Sunnī and Shī'ī *faḍā'il* works emphasize the following specific traits as having been best displayed or exercised by Abū Bakr and 'Alī, respectively, as attested to by the Qur'ān, *ḥadīth*, and biographical (*sīra*) literature. They are veracity/honesty, generosity, courage, and possession of knowledge. These were, after all, characteristic traits of Muḥammad himself, creating a mimetic precedent for his followers, particularly for those who would assume the mantle of leadership of the Muslim polity after him.[25] Closeness or kinship (*qurb* or *qarāba*) to the Prophet was also an important – and highly contested – factor.[26]

[22] Cited by G. H. A. Juynboll, *Muslim Tradition: Studies in Chronology, Provenance and Authorship of Early Ḥadīth* (Cambridge: Cambridge University Press, 1983), 12–13, and n. 10.

[23] See 'Abd al-Jalīl Rāzī, *Kitāb al-naqḍ*, ed. S. Jalāl al-Dīn Muḥaddith (Tehran, 1331/1952), 656–64, as cited by Muḥammad Dja'far Mahdjoub, "The Evolution of Popular Eulogy of the Imams among the Shi'a," in *Authority and Political Culture in Shi'ism*, ed. Said Amir Arjomand (Albany: State University of New York Press, 1988), 54; Aḥmad b. Abī Tālib al-Ṭabarsī, *Kitāb al-iḥtijāj*, ed. Muḥammad Bāqir al-Khurāsān (Najaf: Dār al-nu'mān, 1386/1966), 1:97; "Ya'qūbī," in his *Ta'rīkh*, ed. M. T. Houtsma (Leiden: E. J. Brill, 1883), 2:137.

[24] Ibn Abī 'l-Ḥadīd, *Sharḥ nahj al-balāgha*, ed. Ḥasan Tamīm (Beirut: Dār maktabat al-ḥayah, 1963), 2:267.

[25] For example, Ibn Sa'd, *Ṭabaqāt*, 1:364–73; see particularly ibid., 1:373, where Muḥammad is described by Anas b. Malik as "the most courageous, the kindest, and the most generous of people."

[26] For a fuller discussion of these attributes and their relevance to conceptions of leadership, see Afsaruddin, *Excellence and Precedence*, 80–188.

For example, Sunnī exegetes interpret the Qur'ānic verses (92:5–8) that begin, "So he who gives [in charity] and fears [God],"[27] and 57:10, which assigns a higher rank (*a'ẓamu darajatan*) to those who gave of their money and fought before the conquest of Mecca in 9/630 as scriptural testimony to Abū Bakr's exemplary generosity.[28] Sunnī *ḥadīth* works record many reports that attest to Abū Bakr's generosity. One well-known *ḥadīth* from Abū Sa'īd al-Khudrī recorded by Muslim relates that the Prophet said, "The most gracious of people towards me with regard to his wealth and his companionship is Abū Bakr."[29] In the *manāqib* and historical literature in general, generosity as a hallmark of greater moral excellence points to a greater aptitude for leadership. One account that describes the preparations of the Muslims for the Tabūk expedition makes this equation quite clear. The report states that when the Prophet urged his followers to contribute to the outfitting of the army, Abū Bakr was the first to contribute all his wealth, which was four thousand dirhams at that point. 'Umar contributed half his wealth, whereas 'Uthmān gave a third. On learning of this, 'Umar is said to have remarked to Abū Bakr, "Whenever we vie with one another in goodness, you always outstrip me with regard to it!"[30] It is highly significant that the level of generosity of each of these companions corresponds to his respective position in the hierarchy of moral excellence and becomes a trope for his qualifications to assume the caliphate.

Similarly, Shī'ī scholars find Qur'ānic and *ḥadīth* warrants to establish 'Alī's greater generosity vis-à-vis other companions. Qur'ān 76:7–22, which begins, "They fulfill the vow and fear a day whose evil is widespread and they feed for the love of God, the indigent, the orphan, and the captive," is understood to be a specific reference to 'Alī. As ancillary traits, 'Alī's *zuhd* and *taqashshuf* ("abstemiousness") find frequent mention in the *manāqib* and biographical literature on him, of both Sunnī and Shī'ī provenance. Ibn 'Abd al-Barr (d. 463/1071)[31] and 'Alī b. 'Īsā al-Irbilī (d. 692/1296), for example, record reports that point to 'Alī's contempt for fine clothes and rich food as a marker of his abstemiousness. Aḥmad b. Hanbal (d. 240/855) records reports that relate that, after

[27] Ibn Hishām, *Sīra*, 1:212.

[28] See, e.g., al-Bayḍāwī, *Anwār*, 2:468; Abū Nu'aym al-Iṣbahānī, *Ḥilyat al-awliyā' wa-ṭabaqāt al-aṣfiyā'* (Cairo: Maktabat al-Khanjī, 1351–/1932–), 1:28.

[29] For example, Muslim, *Ṣaḥīḥ*, 7:108.

[30] Cf. Ibn 'Asākir, *al-Ta'rīkh al-kabīr* (Damascus: Maṭba'at rawḍat al-Shām, 1911), 1:110.

[31] Ibn 'Abd al-Barr, *al-Istī'āb fī ma'rifat al-aṣḥāb*, ed. 'Alī Muḥammad al-Bajjāwī, 4 vols. (Cairo: Maktabat nahḍat Miṣr wa-maṭba'atuhā, n.d.), 3:1112; al-Irbili, *Kashf al-ghumma fī ma'rifat al-a'imma*, ed. Hāshim al-Rasūlī (Tabriz: Maktabat banī Hāshim, 1961), 1:217.

having distributed all the funds from the treasury, ʿAlī would clean the premises with water (*naḍaḥahu*) or sweep them, and then pray two cycles of prayer there.[32] All these reports highlight ʿAlī's exceptional generosity in almsgiving and his Spartan lifestyle, thereby establishing his superior qualifications for leadership of the *umma*.

Caliphal (or in the case of Shīʿism, Imāmic) authority was mainly conceived of as epistemic; greater possession of and access to both religious and mundane knowledge, as recognized and eulogized by the Prophet himself, conferred greater authority on a Companion. Mastery of the Qurʾānic text followed by superior knowledge of the *sunna* was deemed to be a primary index of leadership potential. A well-known *ḥadīth* is related by the Companion Abū Masʿūd al-Anṣarī in which Muḥammad says, "The best reciter of them [sc. the people] of the Book of God will lead the people. If they should be equal with regard to [proficiency in] reciting, then the most knowledgeable of them with regard to the *sunna*."[33] It is not surprising that both Sunnī and Shīʿī authors cite this report as evidence in favor of the superior qualifications of Abū Bakr and ʿAlī, respectively, for the caliphate or imamate on account of each being the best reciter of the Qurʾān. The Andalusian jurist Ibn Ḥazm (d. 456/1064) maintained that the Prophet's appointment of Abū Bakr as the prayer leader during his final illness proves that Abū Bakr was so appointed on account of his superior knowledge of the prayer rituals. Similarly, the Prophet appointed Abū Bakr to collect alms and to lead the *ḥajj* and several military expeditions, all of which testify to his greater knowledge regarding prayer, almsgiving, the pilgrimage, and *jihād*, and "these," asserts Ibn Ḥazm, "are the support (*ʿumda*) of religion.[34]

Shīʿī scholars similarly emphasize ʿAlī's greater knowledge of religious and mundane matters, which rose nearly to the level of prophets, falling short only because it did not encompass prophecy nor "the knowledge of the unknown/unseen" (*ʿilm al-ghayb*).[35] But Ibn Shahrāshūb (d. 558/1192) maintained that ʿAlī was privy to such knowledge and could prophesy future events.[36] Many branches of learning derive directly from ʿAlī's wide-ranging knowledge, according to a number of Shīʿī scholars.

32 Ibn Ḥanbal, *Faḍāʾil al-ṣaḥāba*, ed. Waṣī Allāh b. Muḥammad ʿAbbās (Mecca: Jāmiʿat Umm al-Qurā, 1983), 1:541, nos. 905, 914.

33 Al-Fasawī, *Kitāb al-maʿrifa wa-ʾl-taʾrīkh*, ed. Akram al-ḍiyāʾ al-ʿAsmarī (Baghdad: Riʾāsat dīwān al-awqāf, 1976),1:449–50; al-Rāzī, *Faḍāʾil al-Qurʾān wa-tilāwatuh*, ed. Amīr Ḥasan Ṣabrī (Beirut: Dār al-bashāʾir al-Islāmiyya, 1994), 97.

34 Ibn Ḥazm, *Fiṣal*, 4:108.

35 Al-Qandūzī, *Yanābīʿ al-mawadda* (Qum: Maktabat al-Muḥammadī, 1966), 66.

36 Ibn Shahrāshūb, *Manāqib āl Abī tṬālib*, ed. Yūsuf al-Biqāʿī (Qum: Dhawī al-qurba, 1980), 2:304; cf. Muḥammad b. al-Ḥasan al-Qummī, *Baṣāʾir al-darajat fi faḍāʾil āl*

Thus, al-ʿAllāma al-Ḥillī (d. 726/1325) maintained that *kalām* originated with ʿAlī as did Ṣūfism, eloquent speech (*faṣāḥa*), grammar, *tafsīr*, and *fiqh*.[37]

Sometime after the third century AH (ninth century CE), Shīʿī exegetical and doctrinal works became more consistent in foregrounding blood kinship to the Prophet as the most important criterion for establishing ʿAlī's superior qualifications for the caliphate. In contrast to those reports that reference proto-Shīʿī discourses within the paradigm of *sābiqa* and *faḍīla* as previously indicated, later Shīʿī understanding of certain relevant Qurʾānic verses became markedly particularist. The sixth-century-AH (twelfth-century-CE) Shīʿī commentator Aḥmad b. ʿAlī al-Ṭabarsī (d. 548/1154) reports that Muḥammad himself, in exegesis of Q 9:100 and 56:10, had commented that these verses referred to the prophets and their legatees. He added, "And I am the most excellent of the prophets and messengers of God and ʿAlī b. Abī Ṭālib, upon whom be peace, my legatee, is the most excellent of legatees."[38] One report maintains that only the three greatest monotheistic prophets had legatees, and each of these had only one. This report, quoted in later Shīʿī and Sunnī *manāqib* works on ʿAlī, is attributed to Ibn ʿAbbās, who states in exegesis of Q 56:10 that the *sābiqūn* were Yūshaʿa b. Nūn who was the first to reach (*sabaqa ilā*) Moses; the companion (*ṣāḥib*) mentioned in Yā Sīn who was the first to reach Jesus, and ʿAlī who was the first to reach Muḥammad.[39] This kind of preelection of ʿAlī as Muḥammad's successor, which these reports convey, foregrounded both their blood relationship and their spiritual kinship and established in classic Shīʿī political thought ʿAlī's claim nonpareil to the imamate.

In response to this heightened emphasis on kinship to the Prophet, Sunnī scholars emphasized Abū Bakr's emotional, spiritual, and physical propinquity (*ṣuḥba*; also sometimes *qurb or qarāba*) to Muḥammad. Thus, they stressed, for instance, the importance of his residing in the cave with the Prophet for three days and nights to avoid detection by the pagan Meccans on their way to Medina, an event understood to

Muḥammad, ed. Mīrzā Muḥsin Kūja Bāghī al-Tabrīzī (Qum: Maktabat āyat Allāh al-ʿuẓma al-marʿachī, 1404 AH), 2:109.

37 Al-ʿAllāma al-Ḥillī, *Minhāj al-karāma*, in Ibn Taymiyya, *Minhāj al-sunna al-nabawiyya*, ed. Muḥammad Rashād Sālim (Riyadh: Jāmiʿat al-imām Muḥammad ibn Saʿūd al-ilāmiyya, 1986), 1:177–80.

38 See his *Kitāb al-iḥtijāj*, 1:213. For Shīʿī invocation of these verses in support of the notion of *sābiqa*, see al-Kulaynī, *Usūl al-kāfī*, 2:45–7.

39 For example, Ibn al-Maghāzilī, *Manāqib ʿAlī b. Abī Ṭālib* (Tehran: al-Maktaba al-Islāmiyya, 1974), 320.

be alluded to in Q 9:40 and thus providing divine affirmation of his exceptional courage. The historian Ibn al-Athīr (d. 630/1233) reports that some scholars had eulogized Abū Bakr's role in this episode thus:

> If someone were to say that all the Companions except Abū Bakr did not have companionship [with the Prophet], he would not be guilty of unbelief. But if someone were to say that Abū Bakr was not the Companion of the Messenger of God, peace and blessings be upon him, he would be guilty of unbelief for the Glorious Qur'ān has mentioned that he was his Companion.[40]

Moreover, Muḥammad is widely reported to have expressed a preference for Abū Bakr as his "bosom friend" (*khalīl*) if he were to choose one,[41] and he affirmed the latter's special status by appointing him the prayer leader during his last illness.[42] This last fact is particularly emphasized by Sunnī scholars as encoding Muḥammad's tacit selection of Abū Bakr as his successor. Thus, the historian al-Balādhurī (d. 279/892–893) records a version of the prayer tradition, as related by Anas b. Mālik from ʿAlī b. Abī Ṭālib, who said:

> The Messenger of God, peace and blessings be upon him, fell ill and ordered Abū Bakr to lead the prayer while he was aware of my presence. When he died, the Muslims chose for their world one whom the Prophet had chosen for their Religion. So they appointed Abū Bakr their leader and by God, he was qualified for it. What is then to delay him from a position in which the Messenger of God, peace and blessings be upon him, had installed him?[43]

It should be pointed out that the Shīʿa in turn adduce the *mabīt bi 'l-firāsh* episode (during which ʿAlī served as the Prophet's decoy when

[40] Ibn al-Athīr, *Usd al-ghāba fī maʿrifat al-saḥāba*, ed. Shihāb al-Dīn al-Najafī (Tehrann.p.: n.d.), 3:209; cf. al-Munāwī, *Fayḍ al-qadīr*, ed. Aḥmad ʿAbd al-Salām (Beirut: Dār al-kutub al-ʿilmiyya, 1994), 1:120.

[41] See the numerous *ḥadīth*s affirming this as recorded by, among others, Ibn Abī Shayba, *al-Kitāb al-muṣannaf fī 'l-aḥādīth wa-'l-athār*, ed. Kamāl Yūsuf al-Ḥūt (Beirut: Dār al-tāj, 1989), 6:348; al-Bukhārī, *Ṣaḥīḥ*, 6:78–9, no. 3266; 6:80, no. 3267; Muslim, *Ṣaḥīḥ*, 4:1478–9; Ibn Saʿd, *Ṭabaqāt*, 3:131, and so on.

[42] See, e.g., al-Fasawī, *Maʿrifa*, 1:454; Ibn Saʿd, *Ṭabaqāt*, 3:133; Ibn Ḥanbal, *Faḍā'il al-ṣaḥāba*, 1:182, no. 190.

[43] Al-Balādhūrī, *Ansāb al-ashrāf*, ed. Muḥammad Ḥamīd Allāh (Cairo: Dār al-maʿārif, n.d. [project incomplete?]) 1:560–1.

the latter slipped out under the cover of darkness for Medina) as a counter prooftext to the cave event to similarly attest to ʿAlī's closeness to Muḥammad and his exceptional courage.[44] They also deny that the prayer tradition cited by Sunnī sources indicates any kind of prophetic endorsement of Abū Bakr's succession.[45]

UMAYYAD AND ʿABBĀSID PERIODS

It is in the Umayyad period that we must seek the impetus for increasing Shīʿī emphasis on kinship as a primary criterion for assuming the leadership of the polity. Remarkably lacking in the requisite criteria of *sābiqa* and *faḍīla*, the Umayyads chose to emphasize instead their shared genealogy with Muḥammad to establish their claim to the caliphate. It is not difficult to imagine how the proto-Shīʿa would be tempted to respond by highlighting ʿAlī's much closer blood relationship to the Prophet and thus trump the early Umayyad claim to kinship with the Prophet.[46] It is, however, not easy to reconstruct the details of this process on the basis of the few extant Umayyad sources and more numerous ʿAbbāsid works that are largely hostile in tenor toward the Umayyads. Extratextual sources – coins, inscriptions, and so on – establish for us, however, that the Umayyads adopted the regnal title *khalīfat allāh* ("the deputy of God") and attempted to acquire legitimacy through conspicuous displays of religiosity.[47] This is in contrast to the Rāshidūn caliphs, who are said to have eschewed this title as self-aggrandizing and presumptuous. Both Abū Bakr and ʿUmar are on record as having repudiated the honorific of *khalīfat allāh*.[48]

At the height of the ʿAbbāsid period, we begin to discern a growing emphasis on more pragmatic and utilitarian considerations in assessing legitimate leadership, mostly in deference to the political realism of the time. *Sābiqa* understood primarily as pointing to early conversion to Islam and participation in the key events of the community during

44 This was the view of al-ʿAllāma al-Ḥillī; see his *Minhāj al-karāma*, 153–4.

45 See the discussion in Afsaruddin, *Excellence and Precedence*, 180–1.

46 Moshe Sharon, "The Development of the Debate around the Legitimacy of Authority in Early Islam," *Jerusalem Studies in Arabic and Islam* 5 (1984): 121–41.

47 Cf. Patricia Crone and Martin Hinds, *God's Caliph: Religious Authority in the First Centuries of Islam* (Cambridge: Cambridge University Press, 1986), which establishes the usage of this title for the Umayyads in general, but this practice cannot be retroprojected to the Rāshidūn period in the absence of firm evidence by simply asserting that this must have been so, as the authors do.

48 For Abū Bakr, see al-Balādhurī, *Ansāb al-ashrāf*, 1:529; for ʿUmar, see al-Ṭabarī, *Taʾrīkh*, 2:569.

the Prophet's time understandably began to lose its relevance after the second generation of Muslims, although moral probity and excellence continued to be invoked as desiderata in the rightful leader. But tumultuous times predisposed many of the scholars of the middle ʿAbbāsid period to focus primarily on the ability of the leader to maintain law and order at all times by curbing internal political rebellion and warding off external threats.

Not that the concept of pragmatism or the public good was lacking in the early period. The term *istiṣlāḥ* rather than *maṣlaḥa* appears to have been more common then, particularly as a juridical term.[49] *Istiṣlāḥ* referred to the heavy reliance on reasoning and discretionary opinion (*raʾy*) by the Medinan jurists, including Mālik b. Anas and the Iraqi Ḥanafīs of the second century AH (eighth century CE).[50] In the political realm, as already discussed, most of the historical sources inform us that during the *ridda* wars, Abū Bakr's practical knowledge of tribal genealogies was deemed critical to maintaining the unity and, therefore, the welfare of the polity, even though the word *istiṣlāḥ/maṣlaḥa* may not have been specifically used in this context.

The view that the caliphate was a religious requirement appears not to have been formally articulated until al-Ashʿarī (d. ca. 324/935).[51] In the following century the well-known Shāfiʿī jurist and political theorist al-Māwardī (d. 450/1058) would emphasize this point in his influential work *al-Aḥkām al-Sulṭāniyya*. In this work, al-Māwardī describes the caliphate as necessary both for the "protection of religion" (*ḥirāsat al-dīn*) and for "the proper administration of the world" (*siyāsat al-dunyā*).[52] Al-Māwardī points to the existence of two camps in his day on the question of the caliphate (which he frequently refers to as the imamate), one of which believed that the office was mandated rationally, whereas the other subscribed to the position that the office was decreed by the revelation (*al-sharʿ*). According to the rationalist camp, all intelligent people conceded the importance of submitting to a leader who would prevent them from oppressing one another and keep them from

[49] For example, see Ibn al-Muqaffaʿ (d. ca. 139/757) in his "Risāla fī al-ṣaḥāba," in *Āthār Ibn al-Muqaffaʿ*, ed. ʿUmar Abū al-Naṣr (Beirut: Dār maktabat al-ḥayāh, 1966), 360.

[50] Muḥammad b. Aḥmad al-Khwārazmī (d. after 387/997) lists *istiṣlāḥ* as one of the sources of law for the Mālikī school; see his *Mafātiḥ al-ʿulūm*, ed. G. van Vloten (Leiden: E. J. Brill, 1895), 9; cf. Wael Hallaq, *The Origins and Evolution of Islamic Law* (Cambridge: Cambridge University Press, 2005), 145.

[51] ʿAbd al-Qāhir b. Ṭāhir al-Baghdādī, *Uṣūl al-dīn* (Istanbul: Maṭbaʿat al-dawlā, 1928), 271.

[52] Al-Māwardī, *Al-Aḥkām al-sulṭāniyya wa ʾl-wilāyat al-dīniyya*, ed. ʿIṣām Fāris al-Harastānī and Muḥammad Ibrāhīm al-Zaghlī (Beirut: al-Maktab al-Islāmī, 1996), 13.

disputing with one another. In the absence of rulers (*al-wulāh*), there would be disorder and general pandemonium. The second camp consisted of people who insisted that the imamate was ordained by revelation alone because the imam undertook matters decreed by the religious law. However, even this camp conceded a major role to reason in matters that had to be decided by the imam. Thus, according to al-Māwardī, this second group, as did the first group, maintained that human intelligence prevented individuals from wronging one another and helped to enforce the criterion of justice in social relations. Once installed, the caliph is deserving of the obedience of his people, in support of which belief he adduces as prooftext Q 4:59, which states, "O those who believe, obey God and obey the messenger, and those possessing authority among you."[53] It is significant that this verse, which was understood to refer mainly to "people of intelligence and discernment" (*ahl al-ʿilm wa'l-fiqh*),[54] or to the military commanders during the Prophet's time only by early exegetes,[55] acquires an overt political meaning by the fifth century AH (eleventh century CE). As the ʿAbbāsid caliph's power in fact waned during the Buwayhid period when al-Māwardī was writing this work, mandating obedience to the legitimate leader and thereby preventing further fragmentation of the polity came to be of overriding importance, creating the imperative to deploy Q 4:59 as a scriptural warrant to this end.[56]

A diversity of views on the necessity of the caliphate, however, continued to exist beyond al-Māwardī's time, especially among the Muʿtazila. This is indicated by the Muʿtazilī theologian ʿAbd al-Jabbār (d. 415/1025), who identifies three broad trends of thought in his time on the issue of the caliphate. The first, a minority, held that the caliphate was not necessary; the second believed that it was required on the basis of reason; and the third maintained that it was necessary according to the religious law.[57] In the eighth century AH (fourteenth century CE), the Ashʿarı ʿAḍud al-Dīn al-Ījī (d. 756/1355) continued to maintain that popular consensus from the time of Abū Bakr onward and social utility, rather than religious doctrine, had established the necessity of this

53 Ibid.

54 Mujāhid b. Jabr, *Tafsīr Mujāhid*, ed. ʿAbd al-Raḥmān al-Surtī (Beirut: al-Manshūrāt al-ʿilmiyyah, n.d.), 1:162–3.

55 Muqātil b. Sulaymān, *Tafsīr Muqātil b. Sulaymān*, ed. ʿAbd Allāh Maḥmūd Shiḥāta (Cairo: al-Hay'a al-miṣriyya al-ʿāmma li-'l-kitāb, 1979–1989), 1:246.

56 Al-Māwardī, *Aḥkām*, 13.

57 See his *al-Mughnī fi abwāb al-tawḥīd wa'l-ʿadl*, ed. ʿAbd al-Ḥalīm Maḥmūd and Sulaymān Dunyā (Cairo: n.p., n.d.), 20:16.

institution.[58] These alternative voices remind us that there was always a range of scholarly thought on issues of sound governance and sociopolitical administration in the premodern period, despite the axiomatic status eventually accorded to al-Ashʿarī's opinion. It also affirms that the more utilitarian concept of the public good rather than *imitatio muhammadi*, as exemplified in the *sābiqa-faḍīla* paradigm, often determined political behavior and administrative policies in reality.

It is in the works of the Ḥanbalī theologian Taqī al-Dīn Ibn Taymiyya (d. 728/1328) that we meet with one of the clearest articulations of *maṣlaḥa* as the primary criterion for the appointment of public officials in general and of military commanders in particular. Ibn Taymiyya grounds the validity of this criterion by locating precedents for it in prophetic and caliphal praxis. It is for pragmatic reasons, Ibn Taymiyya affirms, that Muḥammad appointed Khālid b. al-Walīd as a military commander after his acceptance of Islam, even though the latter was guilty of a number of misdeeds, of which the Prophet clearly disapproved. In spite of this, the Prophet made use of Khālid's martial skills, because, Ibn Taymiyya comments, "he was more qualified (*aṣlaḥ*) than others in this regard."[59] Muḥammad did not appoint Abū Dharr al-Ghifārī, who was more trustworthy and truthful than Khālid, to any position of leadership because he perceived him as physically weak. Out of similar considerations for the greater public good (*li-maṣlaḥa rājiḥa*), Ibn Taymiyya affirms, Muḥammad appointed ʿAmr b. al-ʿĀṣ and Usāma b. Zayd as military commanders, even though there were others who were more knowledgeable in religious matters and more pious than them.[60]

After the Prophet, both Abū Bakr and ʿUmar b. al-Khaṭṭāb made political and military appointments on the basis of public interest as they perceived it in their own time, continues Ibn Taymiyya. Thus, although Abū Bakr deemed it wise to retain Khālid in his leadership position, ʿUmar did not and had him removed and replaced him with Abū ʿUbayda b. al-Jarrāḥ. One of the reasons for this was that the formidable Khālid was an appropriate counterfoil to the gentle Abū Bakr, whereas the stern ʿUmar was better counterbalanced by the more lenient Abū ʿUbayda.[61]

When the objectives of good governance in certain matters were better served through the selection of someone who was trustworthy and

58 See his *al-Mawāqif fī ʿilm al-kalām* ("Postulates Regarding Theology") (Cairo: Maktabat al-Mutanabbī, 1983), 396–7.

59 Ibn Taymiyya, *al-Siyāsa al-sharʿiyya fī iṣlāḥ al-rāʿī wa ʾl-rāʿiyya* (Beirut, n.d.), 23.

60 Ibid., 25; see also Ibn Taymiyya's *Fiqh al-jihād*, ed. Zuhayr Shafīq al-Kibbī (Beirut: Dār al-fikr al-ʿarabī, 1992), 31–3.

61 Ibn Taymiyya, *Siyāsa*, 26.

honest, such as in financial matters, then a person endowed with such qualities was to be preferred, maintains Ibn Taymiyya.[62] But, in general, he maintains that pragmatic, mundane considerations of public benefit and communal welfare take priority over idealized notions of moral-political leadership. Thus, one should appoint the individual who is most suitable (*al-aṣlaḥ*) for a particular position, but such qualifications have to be assessed in view of who would best serve the public interest. Thus, for the position of a military commander, the strongest and the most courageous man should be picked, even though he may have moral failings (*wa-in kāna fīhi fujūr*), over the weaker and less capable man, even though he may be more trustworthy. Given the crisis-ridden world that he inhabited – with the memory of the Crusades still very strong and the Mongol invasion underway – it is perfectly understandable that Ibn Taymiyya would emphasize courage and physical strength over moral probity as the required desiderata in the most qualified leaders of his time.

Ibn Taymiyya's conception of leadership thus represents a clear concession to hardheaded realism and a significant modification of the *sābiqa-faḍīla* paradigm. *Aṣlaḥ* ("the most suitable") replaces *afḍal* ("the most excellent") in Ibn Taymiyya's thought, and an individual's greater precedence in some activity (*asbaq*) is established not on the basis of any a priori generalized standard of moral excellence but through his fit for that particular activity according to relevant criteria, which maximizes the public benefit to be derived from his appointment.

CONCLUSION

Our survey here establishes that influential Muslim authorities in the formative period remembered the early debates about legitimate leadership of the polity after the death of Muḥammad as having crystallized around the two key concepts of excellence and precedence based on Qurʾānic discourse. Both concepts were fleshed out in reference to the Prophet – his normative practices, personal traits, and his degree of closeness with various Companions. Because the Prophet, as described by early biographers and historians, was the most generous, courageous, and most knowledgeable of humankind, his successor, too, in emulation of him, was expected to possess these traits in abundance. He was also required to have enjoyed an especially close relationship with Muḥammad – going beyond the *ṣuḥba* of all Companions to achieve *qurb* or *qarāba* (or to *khulla* attained only by Abū Bakr) reserved for

[62] Ibid.

a select few. However, the key concepts of moral excellence and precedence, predicated particularly on early conversion to Islam, progressively receded in sociopolitical importance with distance from the first and second generations of Muslims. Although moral excellence as a central trait of the most qualified leader continued to be idealized, more pragmatic considerations of effective leadership began to gain ground, particularly in the ʿAbbāsid period, as becomes evident in al-Māwardī's writings in the fifth century AH (eleventh century CE) and receiving greater emphasis in Ibn Taymiyya's works by the seventh century AH (fourteenth century CE) in the Mamlūk period. The latter author, in particular, synthesizes in his oeuvre the two principal modes of leadership – one based on individual merit and the other on conceptions of the common good – and presents this synthesis as reflective of the Prophet's own predilections and praxis.

As for the Shīʿa, there is strong documentary evidence that they, too, subscribed to the *sābiqa-faḍīla* paradigm as a scripturally mandated formula for legitimate leadership in the early period. It appears that in the Umayyad period, the proto-Shīʿa would progressively come to advocate a kinship-based paradigm of leadership in response to similar Umayyad claims. Kinship, in the case of the Umayyads, compensated after all for their lack of requisite precedence and moral excellence. It is precisely for this reason that the majoritarian proto-Sunnī community never embraced the Umayyads as legitimate rulers and therefore rejected the possibility of kinship trumping precedence and moral excellence as hallmarks of righteous leadership. The Shīʿa, however, would foreground ʿAlī's close blood relationship with Muḥammad as establishing his greater claim to the caliphate. Sunnī and Shīʿī views would continue to diverge from this point on, resulting in distinctive conceptions of legitimate leadership that have persisted to this day. The variegated models of leadership developed by Muslim scholars as described herein encode in themselves competing images of the Prophet and his styles of governance as preserved in the collective memory of the polity.

Further reading

Ibn Hishām, ʿAbd al-Mālik. *The Life of Muḥammad*. Translated by Alfred Guillaume. Karachi: Oxford University Press, 2001.

Hodgson, Marshall G. S. *The Venture of Islam: Conscience and History in a World Civilization*. Vols. 1–2. Chicago: University of Chicago Press, 1974.

Muranyi, Miklos. *Die Prophetengenossen in der fruhislamischen Geschichte*. Bonn: Friedrich-Wilhelms-Universität, 1973.

Rosenthal, Erwin Isak Jacob. *Political Thought in Medieval Islam: An Introductory Outline*. Westport, CT: Greenwood Press, 1985. Originally published 1958.

Al-Ṭabarī. *The Crisis of the Early Caliphate*. Translated and annotated by R. Stephen Humphreys. Albany: State University of New York Press, 1990.

Al-Ṭabarī. *The Foundation of the Community*. Translated and annotated by W. Montgomery Watt and M. V. McDonald. Albany: State University of New York Press, 1987.

Part III

Muḥammad in memory

10 Muḥammad in Ṣūfī eyes: prophetic legitimacy in medieval Iran and Central Asia

SHAHZAD BASHIR

To understand Muḥammad's active presence in Muslim societies over the centuries is, in considerable part, a matter of trying to interpret narratives of miracles, dreams, trances, and other such phenomena that reside outside the purview of ordinary perception. Materials of this nature are available in great abundance in works penned by Ṣūfī Muslims because of their investment in the idea of an esoteric counterpart to the physical universe that is accessible to the spiritual elect. This is evident most prominently in Ṣūfī hagiography, a genre that began with the establishment of the first Ṣūfī communities in early Islamic centuries and continued to expand throughout the Middle Ages as Ṣūfī ideas gained greater currency across various Muslim societies. Saintly figures encountering Muḥammad in the esoteric world (*bāṭin*) is a familiar trope in this vast literature, usually aimed to establish a protagonist as an heir to the Prophet. Although this is a pattern relevant for the beliefs of many different Muslim groups, for medieval Ṣūfīs, encountering the Prophet in dreams and visions was an especially significant component in putting forth their claims of religious authority.[1]

In this chapter, I aim to use Ṣūfī authors' descriptions of miraculous events and visionary encounters with Muḥammad for historiographical purposes. From the start, this approach to the material raises a number of significant methodological questions: How do we evaluate reports of miraculous encounters as historical data? On what basis can we extrapolate general social patterns from descriptions of particular individuals' psychological experiences? Is it legitimate to try to interpret fantastical episodes from venues long forgotten with reference to our modern understandings? And, what is one to do with the gap between a purported experience and its narration in words? Instead of being roadblocks,

[1] For a partial survey of Ṣūfī (and other) views on Muslims' ability to interact with Muḥammad after his death, see Fritz Meier, "A Resurrection of Muḥammad in Suyūṭī," in *Essays on Islamic Piety and Mysticism*, trans. John O'Kane, with editorial assistance of Bernd Radtke (Leiden: Brill, 1999), 505–47.

questions such as these can frame a meaningful historical exploration of this data because they identify what the narratives can and cannot reveal. Although events that take place within the psyches of individual Ṣūfīs are by definition beyond our grasp, the words of those who wrote about them appear solidly before us and deserve analysis as reflections of sociocultural preoccupations in particular settings. However, in attempting to extract historical meaning out of these narratives, we must remain consistently cognizant of the historical and literary contexts in which they occur. Our greatest security lies in trying to establish patterns through which we can generalize regarding larger intellectual and social concerns. Approached in this way, Ṣūfī stories containing miracles, dreams, visions, and auditions of Muḥammad can become invaluable sources for our understanding of Islamic religious history.[2]

My specific quarry in this essay is Ṣūfī literature produced in the Persianate Islamic world in Tīmūrid times, which brims with Muḥammad's presence. By the Persianate world I mean the geographical area that today encompasses the modern states of Iran, Afghanistan, and the Central Asian republics of the former Soviet Union. The Tīmūrid period in the history of this region corresponds roughly to the fifteenth century of the Common Era. This was an age characterized by political fragmentation caused by internecine struggles between different princes of the family of the conqueror Tīmūr-i Lang (d. 807/1405) known to Europe as Tamerlane.[3] Interestingly, the intensely contested political climate of this historical setting was complemented by efflorescence in the spheres of art, architecture, and belles lettres as well as religious literature. Ṣūfī ideas and practices constituted the common denominator among these various arenas of cultural production and consumption. Furthermore, social life in this context was dominated by Ṣūfī networks held together through common liturgical practices and affiliation with prominent masters and their disciples or lineal descendants, who very often presided over well-endowed shrines. Looking closely at the lives

[2] The issue of understanding Ṣūfī materials in this context is related to the problem of finding appropriate ways to read mystical texts in general. My perspective can be correlated to the approach taken by authors such as Michael Sells, who writes that his study of Muslim and Christian mystical writings is concerned not with judgments about purported experiences but with identifying "the distinctive semantic content" of aphophatic statements (*Mystical Languages of Unsaying* [Chicago: University of Chicago Press, 1994], 9). Although Sells's main concern is philosophical and literary analysis, I am interested in following a similar path for the sake of writing cultural and socioreligious history.

[3] For a general political history of the period, see H. R. Roemer, "The Successors of Tīmūr," in *The Cambridge History of Iran*, ed. Peter Jackson and Laurence Lockhart (Cambridge: Cambridge University Press, 1986), 6:98–146.

and work of some Ṣūfīs therefore amounts to examining this period's societal mainstream.[4]

Of the vast amount of Ṣūfī literature produced in the Tīmūrid period, I will concentrate here on only three works to be able to describe things in some detail. Quite different in terms of their genres as well as in the preoccupations of their authors, these works reflect different facets of the period's socioreligious environment. Notwithstanding the differences, Muḥammad is a central character in all three works, both as a historical exemplar and as a transhistorical guide available to true seekers directly through the medium of dreams, visions, and extraordinary auditions. In the context of the present volume, the material I cover can help us understand Muḥammad's place in Muslims' religious imagination over time. Further, concentrating on the use to which the Prophet's image is put can enable us to specify distinctive aspects of the period's religious environment. Retaining simultaneous cognizance of these two complementary arenas in Islamic religious history will allow us to mine the relevant sources in the most fruitful way.

MIRACLES AS RELIGIOUS ARGUMENT

The first of the three works I treat in this essay is ʿAbd al-Raḥmān Jāmī's (d. 1492) *Witnesses to Prophecy* (*Shavāhid al-nubuvvat*), likely the most widely authoritative Persian treatise on Muḥammad written in medieval times. Jāmī was a grand man of letters of the Tīmūrid period, equally renowned for his poetry, religious and philosophical works, and an extensive compendium of notices on the lives of earlier Ṣūfīs entitled *Breaths of Intimacy* (*Nafaḥāt al-uns*).[5] As he explains in his preface, Jāmī considered his treatise on the Prophet to be a companion to his earlier *Breaths*, as both works were concerned with proofs for the exalted religious status that Jāmī accorded certain men and women. Jāmī saw Ṣūfīs devoted to ideals of a chivalrous code called *futuvvat* as the main audience for his work on the Prophet, as his full title for the work reads *Witnesses to Prophecy for Strengthening the Certitude of the*

4 For the most recent panoramic treatments of the period's cultural environment, with particular emphasis on assessing elite patronage, see Beatrice Manz, *Power, Politics, and Religion in Timurid Iran* (Cambridge: Cambridge University Press, 2007); Maria Subtelny, *Timurids in Transition* (Leiden: E. J. Brill, 2007). For an assessment of the Ṣūfī social world in particular, see my forthcoming book *Bodies of God's Friends: Sufis in Persianate Islamic Societies* (New York: Columbia University Press).

5 For a recent survey of Jāmī's life and overall influence, see Ertuğrul Ökten, "Jāmī (817–898/1414–1492): His Biography and Intellectual Influence in Herat," Ph.D. diss., University of Chicago, 2007.

Chivalrous (*Shavāhid al-nubuvvat li-taqviyyat yaqīn ahl al-futuvvat*).[6] He states that he had read numerous earlier works on Muḥammad's miracles in Arabic, and by composing *Witnesses*, he intended to make this material available to Persian readers for the first time. Seen without reference to the time of its composition, *Witnesses* reads like a chronologically arranged catalogue of reports in which hundreds of witnesses relate miraculous or other extraordinary experiences that affirm Muḥammad's prophetic role. The cast of characters ranges from biblical figures active centuries before Muḥammad to people who lived up to two centuries after the Prophet. The later "witnesses," who never met Muḥammad, reflect on the Prophet solely through the idea that the simple adherence to Islam of such extraordinary men and women was a posthumous ratification of his status.

On one level, Jāmī's work is the culmination of long-standing traditions of literary piety in Arabic and Persian, also forming a bridge between them.[7] But on another level, his work is very much a product of his time; Jāmī's arguments about the validity and significance of miracles as witnesses to Muḥammad's extraordinary religious status were proxies for exemplifying the charisma of Ṣūfīs active in the later middle period. Jāmī was himself part of this religious scene through his active affiliation with the Naqshbandī Ṣūfī chain of authority, and his plan and execution of the work make it clear that he considered the work's topic relevant to questions that exercised his contemporaries. Considering some of the details of *Witnesses* is therefore a window onto both Muḥammad's image and the Tīmūrid religious world.

The work is divided into a preface, an introduction, seven chapters that progress chronologically from before Muḥammad's own time to the second and third generations of Muslims after the Prophet's death, and

[6] ʿAbd al-Raḥmān Jāmī, *Shavāhid al-nubuvvat*, ed. Ḥasan Amīn (Tehran: Mīr Kasrā, 2000), 80. In writing this article, I have also consulted a second edition of the work that contains no academic apparatus (Istanbul: İhlas Vakfı, 1995). For a review of the history and different connotations associated with *futuvvat*,see Claude Cahen, "Futuwwa," in *Encyclopaedia of Islam*, 2nd ed., ed. Hamilton A. R. Gibb et al. (Leiden: E. J. Brill, 1960–2004), 2:961–5. In keeping with the historical context that concerns me, names and technical terms mentioned in this essay are transliterated in their Persian versions (e.g., *futuvvat* rather than the Arabic *futuwwa*, which denotes the same phenomenon).

[7] For a survey of the origins and evolution of narratives of Muḥammad's miracles, see M. J. Kister, "The Sirah Literature," in *Cambridge History of Arabic Literature*, ed. A. F. L. Beeston et al. (Cambridge: Cambridge University Press, 1983), 352–67. Gabriel Said Reynolds's *A Muslim Theologian in the Sectarian Milieu: ʿAbd al-Jabbār and the Critique of Christian Origins* (Leiden: E. J. Brill, 2004) treats one such work and its context in detail.

a final critical comment on Islam's opponents. The work's overarching argument can be seen most clearly in the beginning and the end, as much of the material in the middle reflects Jāmī's attempt to present his encyclopedic knowledge of major texts already written on the topic.[8] The preface identifies belief in Muḥammad as the cornerstone of salvation, as it is required by the profession of faith (*shahāda*), the first pillar of Islam. As Jāmī puts it, this is more central to being Muslim than is profession in God's oneness (the first part of *shahāda*), because that can also be professed by monotheistic philosophers, though it does not provide them a pathway to salvation.[9]

In the wake of this imperative, Jāmī's expansive work is driven by one central question: how can one arrive at certain knowledge that Muḥammad was indeed a divinely designated prophet? His answer, which forms the essential framework for *Witnesses*, is that such surety can be arrived at either through an extraordinary heartfelt intuition or by becoming a witness to miracles. This leads him to divide all of humanity into four groups that have different reactions to Muḥammad's prophetic career. First are people who were alive in Muḥammad's time and professed belief in him through certitude in their hearts, without requiring any external testimony. These individuals – a small group – felt assured about his mission on, quite literally, "seeing" him in the flesh. The second category of people are those who felt a positive inclination toward Muḥammad but were too bound by existing conventional thinking to embrace him outright. This group, who in Muḥammad's time comprised the majority of those who became Muslims, needed to see the Prophet's miracles to make the transition to Islam.

Critically for Jāmī's overall argument, what he implies about these two groups contemporary to the Prophet's lifetime is extendable to those who encounter reports about Muḥammad's exemplary conduct and miracles in the time since his death. Hearing a narration of the Prophet's works has efficacy equal to direct observation, indicating the value and, indeed, necessity of writing compilations such as the one composed by Jāmī. The potential of Muḥammad's miracles to affect people extends far beyond his own period; although Jāmī does not proclaim this directly at

[8] For Jāmī's sources, cited as well as unacknowledged, see the editor's introduction in Jāmī, *Shavāhid*. Jāmī seems to have relied particularly heavily on Jaʿfar b. Muʿtazz al-Mustaghfirī's (d. 431/1040) *Kitāb dalāʾil al-nubuwwa*, which remains unedited. For a summary description, see Georges Vajda, "Un manuscrit du Kitab dalaʾil al-nubuwwah de Gaʿfar al-Mustaghfiri," in *Studi orientalistici in onore di Georgio Levi della Vida* (Rome: Instituto per l'Oriente, 1956), 2:567–72.

[9] Jāmī, *Shavāhid*, 75–6.

this juncture in his work, his overall formulation makes the writing of narratives about miracles a necessary activity for the sake of maintaining and expanding the Islamic community.

The remaining two groups in Jāmī's taxonomy of humanity get a negative valuation. First among these are those who saw or heard about the miracles but refused to believe them as signs of divinely bestowed distinction. The most prominent examples of this group were Muḥammad's fellow Quraysh tribespeople of Mecca who dismissed the extraordinary occurrences as trickery or sorcery. Although Jāmī's condemnation of this group is easy to anticipate, the second group in the negative column is of greater interest. This group consists of those who affirm the miracles in public but, in their actual beliefs, explain them away as allegories meant for the simpleminded. The miracles must, in Jāmī's view, be seen as actual occurrences marking the rending of ordinary observable reality. The objects of his critique here are philosophically inclined Muslims, from his own period and earlier, for whom conventional religious beliefs and actions correspond with an underlying philosophical truth that is available directly to the intellectual elite capable of comprehending abstractions. A majority of human beings, in this view, cannot reach such understandings and must be aided by the myths and metaphors revealed through prophetic figures.[10] For Jāmī, to treat miracles as symbolic stories is a grave error worthy of the severest condemnation. As in the case of those evaluated positively, Jāmī's understanding of the two wrongful groups is not limited to those who may have come into contact with Muḥammad – it extends to those who react in the described way to reports about the miracles.[11]

Jāmī's preface makes clear that, to be a genuine believer in Islam, one must accept Muḥammad as a true subject of events that defy explanation in ordinary terms. This, however, leads to the question of whether all such events must be seen as divine gifts. And the problem is redoubled when we expand to the necessity of believing in reports about miracles, without direct observation, as Jāmī indicates should be the case. Clearly, it cannot be the case that one must believe every miraculous story one encounters, which begs the provision of other criteria to adjudicate the matter. Jāmī's solution to these difficulties lies in his classification of

[10] See Griffel's discussion in Chapter 8 of this volume. A vivid example of this differentiation can be found in the famous philosophical allegory of Ḥayy b. Yaqẓān (cf. Lenn Goodman, trans., *Ibn Tufayl's* Hayy ibn Yaqzan [New York: Twayne Publishers, 1972]). For the historical context that may have compelled Jāmī to condemn the philosophical perspective with particular severity, see Ökten, "Jāmī (817–898/1414–1492)," 181–99.

[11] Jāmī, *Shavāhid*, 76–9.

miraculous events into three different categories: prophetic miracles (*muʿjizāt*), miracles associated with saints or friends of God (*karāmāt*), and deception (*istidrāj*) of false pretenders. This scheme removes the evaluation of miracles from the purported events themselves to the status of those who perform them as it may be evaluated from non-miraculous aspects of their behavior. The first two categories are distinguished on the basis of nomenclature: a *muʿjiza* is the miracle performed by someone appointed a prophet, the last of such persons being Muḥammad, and a *karāma* is the work of a saint, who must be recognized as such not merely on the basis of miracles but on all other properties associated with saints, such as adherence to the *sharīʿa* and extraordinary ethics and piety. The third category of *istidrāj* then affirms the possibility that persons may come to possess extraordinary powers to manipulate reality, without this indicating an exalted religious status.[12]

Jāmī's formulations as I have summarized them here seem to lead to a tautology: one believes in Muḥammad as a prophet on the basis of his miracles, but the reason these miracles are true divine gifts, and not fraudulent magic, is that he is a prophet. To escape the circle, one must conclude that the miracles are enhancing affirmations of Muḥammad's status rather than the beginning points for recognizing him as a prophet. The true significance of miracles lies in the fact that they solidify a preexisting positive inclination or belief in the truth of Muḥammad's mission. The power of miracle stories derives not from their logical position in the acceptance of true religion but in providing memorable narratives that bear witness to a truth that one has already acknowledged or toward which one is inclined. In this sense, the more stories of miracles that can be recounted, the better, as these work to solidify and enrich the rhetorical construction of Muḥammad's character.

Querying Jāmī's stated aims in *Witnesses* as I have attempted here can help us understand the repeated composition of quite similar texts describing Muḥammad's miracles over the course of Islamic history. The vast majority of the content of Jāmī's work is straightforward repetition from works by earlier authors. Jāmī's individual contribution in *Witnesses* includes the translation of miracle stories from Arabic into Persian and a framework for their proper appreciation. Between the first and the sixth chapters, he progresses chronologically from biblical times

[12] Ibid., 81–2. Jāmī's descriptions here parallel the discussion of the same topic in his *Nafaḥāt*, where he cites a long passage from Fakhr al-Dīn Rāzī's *Tafsīr al-kabīr* (ʿAbd al-Raḥmān Jāmī, *Nafaḥāt al-uns min ḥażarāt al-quds*, ed. Maḥmūd ʿĀbidī [Tehran: Intishārāt-i Iṭṭilāʿāt, 1997], 16–17).

to immediately prior to Muḥammad's birth, to the Prophet's own times and of those who came into physical contact with him. The sixth chapter also includes a section on the twelve Shīʿī Imams, from ʿAlī b. Abī Ṭālib to the Mahdī in occultation, who are given special mention because of their status as the Prophet's preeminent descendants. Jāmī's choice to honor the Imāms despite his otherwise stridently Sunnī views reflects the general mixing of Ṣūfī and Shīʿī ideas in the Tīmūrid period.[13]

The seventh chapter in *Witnesses* is particularly interesting because it reports on the seemingly incongruous cases of witnesses for Muḥammad's miracles who never came into direct contact with the Prophet. The title of this chapter, "On Recollecting the Testimonies and Proofs That Have Appeared from the Followers and the Followers' Followers until the Generation of the Ṣūfīs," makes an explicit connection to Jāmī's earlier work on biographies of eminent Ṣūfīs.[14] Here the paradigmatic (and hence most useful) notice from the viewpoint of the history of Ṣūfism is that on Uvays Qaranī, a man famous for converting to Islam while Muḥammad was alive but without ever meeting him. Jāmī's entry on Uvays begins by citing the second caliph ʿUmar, who certifies that Muḥammad said that Uvays would intercede with God on behalf of other Muslims to allow them to enter paradise. Jāmī reports that, on hearing this in ʿUmar's company, a Companion of the Prophet named Haram b. Ḥayyān decided to go to Kūfa with the sole aim of locating Uvays and remaining with him. He found him doing ablutions by the banks of the Euphrates and was able to recognize him on the basis of a description he had heard. He greeted him and got a response, but Uvays refused to shake his hand. After this, Haram felt overcome by his emotion of love for Uvays and began weeping. Uvays joined him in this and, once they had stopped, greeted Haram by his full name. When he asked him how he knew the name given that they had never met before, Uvays replied with a Qurʾānic quotation: "The Knowing, the Aware informed me" (66:3). He then told Haram that ʿUmar had died since Haram's departure from Medina. He prayed for him and then said that they would now part company and would never see each other again. This is exactly what

[13] For the details and historical consequences of this overlap, see the second section of this chapter as well as Shahzad Bashir, *Messianic Hopes and Mystical Visions: The Nūrbakhshīya between Medieval and Modern Islam* (Columbia: University of South Carolina Press, 2003), 31–41; Kathryn Babayan, *Mystics, Monarchs, and Messiahs: Cultural Landscapes of Early Modern Iran* (Cambridge, MA: Center for Middle Eastern Studies of Harvard University, 2002).

[14] Jāmī, *Shavāhid*, 429. *Followers* (*tābiʿūn*) and *followers' followers* (*tabʿa tabiʿūn*) are technical terms indicating the generations of Muslims who came immediately after the Companions (*ṣaḥāba*) who had had direct contact with Muḥammad.

happened, as Haram never encountered him again physically. However, Uvays continued to appear in his dreams at least once or twice every week for some time.[15]

This story – reminiscent of the meeting between Moses and an unnamed "divine servant" in Qur'ān 18:59–81 – contains perspectives on the construction of religious authority that were critical to Ṣūfī communities in Jāmī's context.[16] The qualities attributed to Uvays – ratification from Muḥammad, intercession, knowledge communicated directly from God, and the ability to guide a disciple in person and through dreams – were central to the role of Ṣūfī masters who dominated the socioreligious scene in Tīmūrid times. Similarly, Haram's role as a seeker who traveled to find a master on hearing about him and was overcome by love for him were stock qualities for Ṣūfī disciples in the later middle period. The principal miracle in the story pertains to Uvays's knowledge of Haram's name and condition and the fact that he was aware that 'Umar had died in the time it took for Haram to travel from Medina to Kūfa. Haram's appreciation for Uvays's capacity for special knowledge begins with what he hears about Uvays from 'Umar, and his impression is ratified when he meets the man in person and becomes witness to what he receives from God. From a wider perspective, the interaction between Haram and Uvays ratifies not just the credentials of the latter but also the process through which witnessing miraculous knowledge can have an initiatory effect. The story reinforces the overall rhetorical purpose of Jāmī's work by showing that, in conjunction with other religious merits, miracles ratify the status of prophets and saints, with stories pertaining to Muḥammad in particular acting as models for later Muslims. This is also precisely the formula that formed the basis for extended Ṣūfī hagiography, a literary genre that underwent a boom in the Tīmūrid period. Jāmī's *Witnesses* is therefore simultaneously one more in a continuous tradition of literature on Muḥammad's biography

[15] Ibid., 437–8. Jāmī's account of Uvays's story as it appears in the two published editions of *Witnesses* available to me reads like a truncated version of accounts given in earlier Ṣūfī sources. I do not have access to manuscripts of the work to be able to determine whether this represents Jāmī's active manipulation of the narrative or is a case of editions prepared on the basis of poor manuscripts. For an earlier version of the story, translated from the first comprehensive work on Ṣūfīs composed in Persian, see 'Ali b. 'Usman Hujwiri, *Revelation of the Mystery*, trans. R. A. Nicholson (New York: Pir Press, 1999), 83–5. For a review of early Arabic narratives regarding Uvays, see Katia Zakharia, "Uvays al-Qaranī, Visages d'une légende," *Arabica* 46, no. 2 (1999): 230–58.

[16] For the Qur'ānic story and its interpretations that identify the unnamed servant as the long-lived prophet Khiżr, see John Renard, "Khaḍir/Khiḍr," in *Encyclopaedia of the Qur'ān*, ed. Jane Dammen McAuliffe (Leiden: Brill, 2001–2006), 3: 81–4.

and a creative, new work that is deeply connected to the social and literary currents of his own time.[17]

Jāmī's portrayal of the relationship between Uvays and Haram forms an example of what he expects from his readers regarding a proper understanding of Muḥammad's miracles. His reports are meant to beckon them to a deeper faith in the Prophet by placing themselves in the position of those who witnessed the miracles with their own eyes. However, to be fully effective, this process requires the presence of living agents who can be said to have powers and responsibilities akin to those of the Prophet. Muḥammad's presence is made tangible through initiation in the hands of other guides, such as Uvays, who are empowered intercessors between ordinary Muslims on one side and Muḥammad and God on the other. In Jāmī's times, Ṣūfī masters great and small who dotted the landscape all across Persianate Islamic societies legitimized themselves through the claim of channeling the Prophet's charisma. Their power derived fundamentally from being acknowledged publicly as recipients of the ability to perform miracles. As Jāmī explains in the *Breaths of Intimacy*, his extensive dictionary of great Ṣūfī masters that preceded his work on the Prophet: "When God . . . renders one of His friends the exhibitor of His complete power, he is enabled to act in the created world in whatever way he wishes. In reality, this is an effect and expenditure of effort on the part of the True Himself . . . that appears in him without his own self being present in the middle."[18] Jāmī's work on Muḥammad's miracles therefore served as much to affirm the status of Ṣūfī masters contemporary to him as it did to glorify the Prophet. Far from being a mere repetition of earlier sources, it was a text thoroughly engaged in the process of affirming structures of religious and societal authority prevalent in his day.

GENEALOGY, PROJECTION, AND RELIGIOUS EXCELLENCE

Although Jāmī's work exalts Muḥammad and places the continuation of his charismatic power in a class of human beings capable of performing miracles, his near contemporary Sayyid Muḥammad Nūrbakhsh (d. 869/1464) argued that he himself was a new physical manifestation of the spiritual entity that constituted the Prophet's essence. A man with a reputation very different from that of Jāmī, Nūrbakhsh came

[17] Persianate hagiography as a genre is treated in detail in my forthcoming work *Bodies of God's Friends*.

[18] Jāmī, *Nafaḥāt al-uns*, 22.

from a Twelver Shīʿī background and became a Ṣūfī through affiliation with the Kubravī lineage that was a major rival to Jāmī's Naqshbandiyya. The title *sayyid* in his name points to his family's claim of descent from Muḥammad through the marriage between his daughter Fāṭima and ʿAlī, the first Shīʿī Imām. Nūrbakhsh's historical notoriety rests on the fact that in 826/1423, at the age of thirty-one, he proclaimed himself the Mahdī, the messianic figure most Muslims expect to appear just before the end of time. Nūrbakhsh's *Treatise on Guidance* (*Risālat al-hudā*), written in Arabic rather than in his native Persian, contains an extended justification for this claim.[19] Following the general Islamic messianic paradigm, Nūrbakhsh's self-portrait as the Mahdī is tied closely to Muḥammad's purported statements. The work reads much like Jāmī's *Witnesses*, except, of course, that the arguments and stories he presents aim to prove his own status rather than that of the Prophet. Nūrbakhsh's exercise in self-legitimation is rooted in his contention that, on the basis of his genealogy and religious accomplishments, he is a new Muḥammad, appointed by God to call Muslims to the pristine Islam that had existed in the Prophet's time. In addition to being a verbal self-portrait, Nūrbakhsh's work is also a novel way to interpret Muḥammad's own life.

Nūrbakhsh's *Treatise on Guidance* is an unusual work in the annals of Islamic religious literature, as most Muslims who have put forth messianic claims over time have concentrated on proving themselves by worldly actions rather than by writing apologetic treatises. It is also an odd text from a Ṣūfī perspective because great Ṣūfī masters are universally extolled as such in the works of their devotees and successors rather than in their own works.[20] Although atypical on these scores, Nūrbakhsh fits well as a charismatic character in the religious history of his times who was able to gather a significant following. His claim was a part of the general rise in messianic activity during the Tīmūrid period, and considering his work provides us access to a larger socioreligious current.[21]

The *Treatise on Guidance* is a tapestry of apologetic arguments that weave multiple connections between Nūrbakhsh and Muḥammad. The

[19] Cf. Shahzad Bashir, "The *Risālat al-hudā* of Muḥammad Nūrbak̲š: Critical Edition with Introduction," *Rivista degli Studi Orientali* 75, nos. 1–4 (2001): 87–137.

[20] I am disregarding poetry containing hyperbolic self-aggrandizement in making this statement because that would not have been taken literally in the context. My comment reflects the way the hagiographic process works in Islamic history.

[21] For a review of this aspect of the period's history, see Bashir, *Messianic Hopes and Mystical Visions*.

author presents the evidence for his claims in a somewhat unstructured way, requiring one to impose a critical taxonomy onto the text to appreciate the implications of his arguments. To this end, I divide my discussion of the material into textual, genealogical, experiential, ontological, and historical sections that all seek to ratify the connection between Nūrbakhsh and Muḥammad.

Nūrbakhsh's first line of argument in the work is to cite copious amounts of *ḥadīth* regarding the Mahdī, with his contention naturally being that all that is indicated here about the identity and the activities of this messianic figure has come true for himself. The material he cites ranges from a general affirmation of the notion of an end-time savior to the report about the Mahdī's physical appearance that states that he would have "an aquiline nose, clear brow, thin hair, sensitive nose, the complexion of an Arab, the body of a Jew [*Isrāʾīlī*], and a mole on his right cheek."[22] The well-known reports he cites provide him with prophetic ratification through textual proofs, a form used by many Muslims to justify their positions throughout Islamic history. His extensive reliance on *ḥadīth* as his main textual source for the idea of the messiah is dictated by the fact that the Qurʾān makes no mention of such a figure and the various sectarian understandings on the subject were all constructed on the basis of statements attributed to the Prophet.[23] Although significant in terms of the space they occupy in the *Treatise on Guidance*, *ḥadīth* citations are the least emphatic points within Nūrbakhsh's overall argument.

Nūrbakhsh indicates that, far from being an ordinary Muslim citing Muḥammad's purported words, he should be seen as the Prophet's definitive genealogical heir, decreed by God to appear in the world at a particular time in history. Here he appeals not just to the authority of the Prophet but also to that of his cousin and son-in-law ʿAlī b. Abī Ṭālib, the first Shīʿī Imām, whose children through Muḥammad's daughter Fāṭima and their later descendants formed Shīʿism's core. Nūrbakhsh cites a purported conversation between the Prophet and ʿAlī where the latter asks whether the Mahdī would be from their progeny. Muḥammad replies:

> He will certainly be from us. God will seal religion with him just as he opened it with us. They will be rescued from dissension (*fitna*) through us just as they were rescued from polytheism (*shirk*). God will join their hearts together as brothers through

[22] Bashir, "*Risālat al-hudā* of Muḥammad Nūrbakš," 105.
[23] Cf. Bashir, *Messianic Hopes and Mystical Visions*, 3–28.

> us following the animosity of dissension, just as he joined their hearts after the animosity of polytheism. And through us they will become brothers after the animosity of dissension just as they became brothers in religion after the animosity of polytheism.[24]

In the normative Twelver Shīʿī context, this report is used to legitimize the idea that the Mahdī is the Twelfth Imām who went into occultation in 260/874 and is expected to make a miraculous return shortly before the end of time. But Nūrbakhsh argues that the Twelfth Imām lived a normal human lifespan and died a natural death. According to him, the idea that the Imām had gone into occultation was invented by those who wished to deprive Shīʿī Muslims of capable living leaders among Muḥammad's descendants.[25] With this argument, Nūrbakhsh runs contrary to the Shīʿī belief he inherited from his family, claiming that he, as a sayyid with exemplary religious accomplishments, could claim to be the Imām.

In addition to *ḥadīth* and a sayyid genealogy, Nūrbakhsh states that the Prophet had made direct appearances in the dreams and visions of Nūrbakhsh's followers to confirm his claim. One of his close companions saw Muḥammad saying to people while pointing to Nūrbakhsh, "Come and take the oath with this son of mine . . . and be certain that he is the Mahdī I promised." Another companion said that he saw Muḥammad and asked him about a problem having to do with the knowledge of ultimate realities (*ḥaqāʾiq*). In reply, the Prophet pointed toward Nūrbakhsh and said that no one knows the truth of all things except the Mahdī.[26] Nūrbakhsh also relates some of his own visions in support of his claim, although none of these involve the Prophet. The most intimate among them mention ʿAlī, who made an appearance at a time when Nūrbakhsh was very sad because of the relentless way in which he was being persecuted for his claim. He relates that as ʿAlī approached him, "I stood up and welcomed him, and he embraced me and sat opposite me such that there was about two arm lengths of distance between us. Then he said, 'Your affair will definitely progress.' I asked him, weeping, how will it progress, and when? He promised me a certain time, but without moving his lips, in metaphorical speech."[27] Experiences such as these worked to

[24] Bashir, "*Risālat al-hudā* of Muḥammad Nūrbak̲š," 106.
[25] Ibid., 120.
[26] Ibid., 111.
[27] Ibid., 114.

make great figures of the past such as Muḥammad, ʿAlī, and famous Ṣūfī masters active participants in the lives of Nūrbakhsh and his followers.

The fact that Nūrbakhsh describes no visionary interactions between himself and the Prophet can be traced to his biggest claim in the *Treatise on Guidance*, namely that he was substantially the same being as Muḥammad. His explanation for this claim rests ultimately on the idea that the bodies of the spiritually adept can become hosts to the spirits of the great from the past through a process he terms spiritual projection (*burūz*). He is quick to point out that he is not endorsing the idea of transmigration of souls (*tanāsukh*), a hallmark of heresy in classical Islamic thought. He explains that transmigration is said to occur when a spirit leaves a dying body and enters a fetus that has just become capable of hosting a spirit. Projection, in contrast, happens when the spirits of perfected prophets and saints pour into the bodies of others who are fully grown human beings and have achieved a similarly high religious status. The implication for living human beings here is to raise themselves to spiritual levels where their bodies would become receptors for souls embodied in earlier times. This seems to have been thought of as a hierarchical process, with the projection of Muḥammad's soul reserved for designating the highest possible status.

Nūrbakhsh's grandest claim regarding projection implicates the spiritual entity Ṣūfīs term the "Muḥammadan reality" (*ḥaqīqa muḥammadiyya*). This is supposed to be the essence of Muḥammad's being, the very first entity to come into existence after God's decision to create the world. Nūrbakhsh states that the Muḥammadan reality has appeared in the corporeal world only twice: once in the form of Muḥammad at the beginning of Islam and again through the means of spiritual projection into his own body. This is the ultimate ontological distinction that affirms the idea that he is the Mahdī.[28] In addition to the connection to Muḥammad, he states that *ḥadīth* reports that indicate that the Mahdī was another name for Jesus in his Second Coming, and the belief that the Mahdī is the Twelfth Imām,who disappeared in 260/874, are true only in that the souls of these two have poured into his own body through the process of projection.[29] At a certain level, in Nūrbakhsh's cosmological understanding, all existing entities were derived ultimately from the Muḥammadan reality, so that the presence of various souls within his body was a case of mixing of beings with overlapping essences. However,

[28] Ibid., 107. Nūrbakhsh's understanding of Muḥammadan reality is based on the work of the great Ṣūfī author Ibn al-ʿArabī (d. 638/1240). For the details of this connection, see Bashir, *Messianic Hopes and Mystical Visions*, 97–102.

[29] Bashir, "*Risālat al-hudā* of Muḥammad Nūrbakš," 120.

his work does not provide a full logical explanation for whether the different souls present in his own body were melded into one another or retained a sense of mutual difference.

Nūrbakhsh's various citations and arguments lead eventually to his command to his readers that they should acknowledge him as the Mahdī here and now. He rejects the charge made by some that he seeks to be the Mahdī for worldly gain, comparing his situation to that of the Prophet:

> Some ignoramuses among the unjust allege regarding me that I have put forth the claim of being the Imām because of desire for status in the world or for amassing its treasures, just as the unbelievers would allege so about the Seal of the Prophets. This is not so, because I have not appropriated the Imāmate to myself by my own accord. The Pole of the Saints and the great among them have ordered me, indeed forced me, to it. They have taken my oath and stated it as their vow in the path of God, the Exalted. I am incapable of opposing their command, because this is not of their own volition but something from God, [revealed] by means of spiritual disclosure (*kashf*) and intuition (*ilhām*).[30]

By creating close parity between himself and Muḥammad, Nūrbakhsh's work dilutes the Prophet's religious authority, which resides both in the past and in the present through him. His Ṣūfī writing also recontextualizes Muḥammad's exclusiveness, as seen in a work that he dedicated to the Prophet's celebrated ascent to the heavens (*miʿrāj*). He argues that such apocalyptic journeys are part of the experience of all great prophets and saints and not something unique to Muḥammad. Moreover, he indicates that the traditional ascent narrative must be understood symbolically rather than literally. Its various elements – such as the journey from Mecca to Jerusalem, riding on the mythical creature the Burāq, and so on – represent the hierarchical stations through which the soul progresses on the path toward God.[31] If great religious figures other than Muḥammad experience different things in their heavenly journeys, this indicates variation in forms rather than placing Muḥammad in a category all his own.

Nūrbakhsh's work constitutes a comprehensive argument containing textual, genealogical, experiential, ontological, and historical elements. Although Jāmī's *Witnesses* celebrates Muḥammad's acts and

[30] Ibid., 122.

[31] Muḥammad Nūrbakhsh, "Risāla-yi miʿrājiyya," in *Taḥqīq dar aḥvāl va āsār-i Sayyid Muḥammad Nūrbakhsh Uvaysī Quhistānī*, ed. Jaʿfar Ṣadaqiyānlū (Tehran: n.p., 1972), 113–31.

words on most pages, Nūrbakhsh's *Treatise on Guidance* ultimately glorifies the author himself as a messiah come at the end of time. The work is, nevertheless, filled with references to *ḥadīth* reports and visionary encounters between Nūrbakhsh's contemporaries and people long dead, all of them put in the service of proving Nūrbakhsh's special historical function. Although the work has momentous dreams and trances as one of its most prevalent themes, it contains no direct encounter between Nūrbakhsh and the Prophet. This seeming omission is a key indicator of Nūrbakhsh's argument about himself, namely that he is a new Muḥammad sent to the world to rectify the corruptions that have entered Islam since the Prophet's days.

PROPHETIC INITIATION AND ISLAM ON THE MARGINS

The last of the three texts I treat here is a rare work that portrays an obscure Ṣūfī master from rural Central Asia named Shaykh Aḥmad Bashīrī, who neither was a scholar like Jāmī nor invested in a grand claim like Nūrbakhsh. His connection to Muḥammad seems to have been intensely personal, initiated through a visionary experience in his early youth and maintained throughout the rest of his long career. Our knowledge of this Ṣūfī master is limited to two sources: a hagiography composed in the middle of the fifteenth century by Nāṣir Farghāna'ī and an oral tradition in the region surrounding his shrine that has survived to modern times. The written hagiography – given the title *Eight Gardens* (*Hasht ḥadīqa*) or *The Gardens of Paradise-Dwellers* (*Ḥadā'iq al-jinān*) in the surviving manuscripts – is especially valuable because it was composed away from the urban literary circles that are the source of most of what survives for us from medieval Islamic societies.[32] It portrays Shaykh Bashīrī as having lived most of his life in the village of Bashīr near the city of Shahrisabz (in present-day Uzbekistan) and dying in 868/1463–4. His hagiographer represents him as an Uvaysī Ṣūfī, meaning someone who received his initiation into Ṣūfism through visionary experience rather than from the hand of a master alive in his own time. His master in the narrative is none other than the Prophet himself, and in

[32] The credit for bringing this unusual source to light belongs to Devin DeWeese in his *An "Uvaysī" Sufi in Tīmūrid Māwarānnahr: Notes on Hagiography and the Taxonomy of Sanctity in the Religious History of Central Asia* (Bloomington: Indiana University, Research Institute for Inner Asian Studies, 1993). I am grateful to Professor DeWeese and the Research Institute for Inner Asian Studies (RIFIAS) at Indiana University for providing me access to microfilms of the work's manuscripts.

the work, many significant moments in his life are shown to have close parallels with signature events in Muḥammad's legendary career. The work's depictions constitute a case of transporting themes pertaining to Islam's origins into the contested religious space of the rapidly Islamizing Central Asian hinterland where Shaykh Bashīrī resided. This work is remarkable for the details of Shaykh Bashīrī's personal experiences, providing a telling example of the significance of Muḥammad's story as a prototype for the way someone may construct a religious biography more than seven centuries after the Prophet's death.

The work cites relatively few literary sources and, instead, provides details about the lives of individuals of humble origins who formed Shaykh Bashīrī's following. It also mentions numerous female disciples, discussing them by name rather than talking about women in general terms and emphasizing that they had attained spiritual stations equal to the men in Shaykh Bashīrī's company.[33] In the midst of copious details regarding the immediate context, the author also makes a conscious effort to portray the shaykh's career as run in parallel with the traditional Islamic story of Muḥammad's life. These two remarkable aspects of the work – local color and connection to Muḥammad – are interlaced seamlessly in the narrative, suggesting an organic absorption of the prophetic legend rather than artifice on the part of the author or his subject.

As evident from Muḥammad Nūrbakhsh's arguments, descent from the Prophet is a significant source of legitimacy for religious and social leadership in Islamic societies. Shaykh Bashīrī's story provides an interesting twist on this in that his hagiographer states that he called himself a sayyid despite acknowledging fully that he had no genealogical connection to Muḥammad. He based his claim on the fact that he had been born after his father requested the famous Ṣūfī master Shāh Niʿmatallāh Vali (d. 835/1431), a well-known sayyid, to pray that he be granted a male child. The story goes that Shaykh Bashīrī's father met Niʿmatallāh when the latter was traveling through Kāsatarāshān, Bashīrī's ancestral village, after being forced to leave Central Asia on Tīmūr's orders. Niʿmatallāh fulfilled the request but added that he must name the child Aḥmad because he would be like the master's own son. Shaykh Bashīrī thus acquired a sayyid genealogy through spiritual designation before birth

[33] Nāṣir b. Qāsim b. Ḥājjī Muḥammad Turkistānī Farghāna'ī, *Hasht ḥadīqa*, Ms. 1477, Institute of Oriental Studies of the Academy of Sciences of Uzbekistan, Tashkent, 23a, 30b, 37a, and others. I plan to discuss this work's significance for understanding women's participation in medieval Ṣūfī communities in a separate article in the future.

rather than through his parents, and he even passed this on to his own children by including sayyid in their names.[34]

Niʿmatallāh Valī's indication that the child would distinguish himself spiritually came true as Shaykh Bashīrī grew older. He was inclined to solitude from an early age, often going out into the wilderness for extended periods. During one such episode, he had a great spiritual experience that involved his first personal encounter with the Prophet. The hagiographer reports that Bashīrī related to his companions that, one day as he was sitting under a tree by a stream, he went into a trance and saw himself go through seven levels of increasingly torturous hells where he experienced his body being burned intensely until all its negative qualities were incinerated one by one.

The journey eventually brought him to the source of the fire, where he realized that his whole body had become composed of nothing but fire. Here he saw many others with similar bodies and made his way to someone who appeared to be the leader. On being questioned, this person identified himself as the leader of hell and refused to help Shaykh Bashīrī escape the place. Shaykh Bashīrī was downcast over this, but then he saw an immensely beautiful person appear in the same place and was drawn to him. This turned out to be Muḥammad, and when Shaykh Bashīrī met him, he got the sensation of a drop falling into the ocean. The Prophet took charge of him and led him on an ascent to God's throne, which they circumambulated together. Shaykh Bashīrī then came out of his trance and realized that the experience he had just undergone had lasted sixteen days, during which his actual body had become covered with dust because of being exposed to the elements.[35]

The Prophet's guidance on this journey seems to have acted as an initiation for Shaykh Bashīrī, marking him as a Ṣūfī in the mold of Uvays Qaranī. The essential feature of this type of initiation – that Shaykh Bashīrī had no living master – caused him to become a target of criticism from more traditional Ṣūfīs in the region.[36] The hagiographer answers this criticism by recalling the well-known story of Uvays Qaranī, who is said to have become a follower of Muḥammad despite never meeting him. But he then goes on to say that the history of this type of

34 Farghāna'ī, *Hasht ḥadīqa*, 3a, 7a–b, 100a. For various hagiographic representations of the interaction between Niʿmatallāh Valī and Tīmūr, see Jean Aubin, ed., *Matériaux pour la biographie de Shâh Niʿmatullah Walí Kermânî* (Tehran: Département d'Iranologie de l'Institut Francoiranien 1956), 42–3, 164–7, 281–2.

35 Farghāna'ī, *Hasht ḥadīqa*, 3b–4a.

36 As DeWeese discusses, the strongest opposition seems to have come from Ṣūfīs affiliated with Yasavī lineages (*"Uvaysī" Sufi in Tīmūrid Māwarānnahr*, 20–5).

spiritual initiation goes back to earlier than the Prophet. In his understanding, this group originated with a certain Bābā Burkh, after whom they were called Burkhiyyān, and they derived benefit from the prophet of the age through esoteric means. The group's name changed to Uvaysīs rather than Burkhīs in the Islamic period simply because Uvays was their most prominent example in Muḥammad's time as a prophet.[37] As Devin DeWeese has suggested, the use of the name Burkh in *Eight Gardens* as well as another important Central Asian Ṣūfī source may reflect the historical process through which certain Buddhist modes of transmitting religious authority that had retained their vitality in the region well into the medieval period were absorbed into Muslim life. Burkh is both the name of a religious character popular in Central Asian Turkic folklore and a possible contraction of *Burkhān*, the Turkic name for the Buddha as it appears in some Islamic sources.[38]

Rooted in his identity as an Uvaysī, Shaykh Bashīrī's close affinity with the Prophet appears in a number of other ways as well in the *Eight Gardens*. Like Muḥammad, he is said to have been "unlettered" (*ummī*) so that his religious knowledge did not derive from written works.[39] His first fight with his opponents is likened to the Battle of Badr, in which Muḥammad's followers were able to overcome their Meccan enemies despite being vastly outnumbered.[40] As was Muḥammad, he is saved from bodily harm through the efforts of a young companion named ʿAlī.[41] His earliest and most steadfast disciple – a certain Ustād ʿUsmān Turkistānī – is referred to as the companion of the cave (*yār-i ghār*), an epithet usually applied to Muḥammad's friend and first male convert, the caliph Abū Bakr.[42] The reference to a cave here goes back to Shaykh Bashīrī's habit of retiring to the mountains in his youth to meditate. On one such occasion, he is said to have experienced extreme dejection that led him to try to commit suicide by jumping off from high ground. But his death wish is thwarted by angels and spiritual adepts who live esoterically and are known as Men of the Unseen (*rijāl al-ghayb*); they accost him and say that he could not carry through his wish because God needs him to do much good in the world. The hagiographer states that this story paralleled the story told in Rūmī's *Masnavī* where Gabriel saves Muḥammad from trying to destroy himself when the latter

[37] Farghāna'ī, *Hasht ḥadīqa*, 5a–b, 30a.

[38] DeWeese, *"Uvaysī" Sufi in Tīmūrid Māwarānnahr*, 27–32.

[39] Farghāna'ī, *Hasht ḥadīqa*, 27b.

[40] Ibid., 43b–44a.

[41] Ibid., 20a,

[42] Ibid., 106a.

is overcome by his state of separation from God during one of his retreats in the cave of Ḥirāʾ in the beginning of his career.[43] All these specific parallels between the lives of Muḥammad and Shaykh Bashīrī work to show the close connection between the two lives.

As in the traditional story of Muḥammad's life, Shaykh Bashīrī and his followers face persecution because of their beliefs. Recalling stories of the travails of Muḥammad's early Meccan followers, the most evocative story related in the *Eight Gardens* on this score involves a disciple named Mawlānā Khaṭāyī (a name that denotes origins in Chinese Turkestan) who was born into a family of so-called idol worshippers, likely indicating Buddhists. Right after birth, he developed a severe stomachache that would not yield to any medicine until he was fed some soup cooked by Muslim traders. Later, when his parents tried to feed him their own soup cooked according to the same recipe, his stomachache returned. In the end, his parents felt that they had no choice other than to have him be adopted by Muslims and he ended up being raised in their religion. This situation continued until he was seven, when his father died and his uncles told him that he must revert to the religion of his natal family. He refused, which led the uncles to torture him by bringing him in front of their idols and severing parts of his flesh to present to their deity. He remained steadfast in his faith despite this affliction and eventually fled to his Muslim foster father. But the uncles captured him again and tried to force him to prostrate in front of the idol. He refused and, instead, cursed the idols and those who worshipped them. The uncles then decided to put him to death, but just as they were about to go ahead, a woman who was this group's leader came on to the scene and declared that they had no right to try to convert him or kill him because he had been nothing but a Muslim from the very time of his birth. His oppressors then had no option but to let him go.

Mawlānā Khaṭāyī related that, just as he was about to be killed, he had seen appear before him a young man with a black beard, riding a white horse and wearing particular attire, who told him to have no fear because Muḥammad would save him. Then two other riders had appeared, with veiled faces and white turbans, who had come to stand above his head. As he became completely absorbed in observing their beauty and grandeur, the woman whose intervention saved him made her appearance and his captors let him go. He then decided to travel to Samarqand to try to find the man who had heralded Muḥammad's

[43] Ibid., 22b. For the original context of the verses cited here, see Jalāl al-Dīn Rūmī, *Masnavī-yi maʿnavī*, ed. R. A. Nicholson (Tehran: Nashr-i Muḥammad, 1995), 863 (vv. 3537–54).

arrival. After much searching among all the famous Ṣūfī masters of the realm, his savior turned out to be Shaykh Bashīrī. He then took an oath with him and became his lifelong disciple.[44] From a different part of the hagiography, we can surmise that this story implies that Bashīrī belonged to a class of saints known as Abdāls, whose total obedience to Muḥammad bestowed on them the powers to hide themselves from normal sight and to appear anywhere in the world at any time.[45]

Reflecting the kind of socio-intellectual currents at work in the case of Muḥammad Nūrbakhsh, the author of the *Eight Gardens* states that, at one point, some of Shaykh Bashīrī's followers started to spread the idea that he was the Mahdī who was keeping himself in hiding until the moment was right to make a proclamation. The master did not take well to this idea, denying any messianic pretensions and telling the followers to desist from their propaganda. However, this did not persuade the followers, and they tried to trick him into a proclamation. One day, they carried him away from his home under the ruse that someone had invited him to a meal. He became anxious about where they were taking him at one point in the journey, and when forced to divulge their plans, they acknowledged that they wanted to proclaim him as the king of the world. He once again quashed the idea and at a later date disavowed any such notion in front of Mīrzā Abū Saʿīd (d. 873/1469), the Tīmūrid ruler of Samarqand.[46]

Shaykh Bashīrī died in 868/1463–1464 at the ripe old age of ninety-seven. Although he was succeeded by children as well as disciples, this did not lead to the establishment of a significant Ṣūfī lineage or a powerful local family.[47] His main legacy was a circumscribed local cult centered on his shrine that continues today in the village of Hazreti Beshir situated about fifty kilometers from Shahrisabz in Uzbekistan.[48]

CONCLUSION: MUḤAMMAD'S MAGNETISM

The author of *Eight Gardens* writes that, during his lifetime, Shaykh Bashīrī's attractiveness was such that people in the surrounding areas could not help themselves flocking to him and becoming his devotees. To explain this, he cites an earlier Ṣūfī work that traces the attracting

44 Farghāna'ī, *Hasht ḥadīqa*, 40a–41a.

45 Ibid., 80a.

46 Ibid., 53b, 62a. Nūrbakhsh proclaimed himself the Mahdī in 826/1423 in Khuttalān (present-day Tajikistan), not very far from the venue of Shaykh Bashīrī's activity.

47 Ibid., 125b.

48 DeWeese, *"Uvaysī" Sufi in Tīmūrid Māwarānnahr*, 18.

powers of all great religious divines to charisma flowing through intergenerational chains originating in Muḥammad:

> The ancient love (*maḥabbat-i qadīm*) for being absorbed into the reality of the Refuge of Prophecy – Beloved of God, God's blessings and protection be upon him – is such that it turns [those in love with him] into "absorbed" (*majẕūb*) and "beloved" (*maḥbūb*). This is akin to the way a magnet turns the piece of iron [it attracts] into a magnet that is then capable of attracting more iron. Based on this analogy, the quality that attracts believers [to someone] is ultimately derived from the magnet of ancient love. It [first] exerted its pull on the spirits of a few thousand Companions from the environs [of Mecca], who themselves eventually acquired portions of it in the measures of their [different] capacities and later attracted the spirits of the Followers. From the Followers, the quality was transferred to the spirits of masters (*mashā'ikh*) and true scholars, century after century, from one interior reality (*bāṭin*) to another. This led to the arrangement of the chain that goes from a desiring person (*murīd*) to the one whom he desires (*murād*), the desirer himself eventually turning into one desired [by others]. The [whole] process issues from the effect of the blessing of obeying Muḥammad, the Pure, God's blessings and protection upon him and his family and Companions.[49]

Surrounded by legends of Ṣūfī masters and the types of authors and texts I have discussed in this chapter, most Ṣūfīs and non-Ṣūfīs in the Tīmūrid world would have agreed with this explanation. Although he had lived his earthly life centuries before them, Muḥammad was present in the lives of these Muslims because of their investment in citing and heeding his words and the fact that his charismatic presence could be made available to them through dreams and trances. The surest way for them to access this power was by attaching themselves to great living masters with the hope of one day becoming adepts in their own right. In this way, they could make Muḥammad's story their own story, becoming as intimate with the Prophet as had been his Companions.

[49] Farghāna'ī, *Hasht ḥadīqa*, 41b–42a. The author's source for this formulation is 'Izz al-Dīn Kāshānī's Persian adaptation of Shihāb al-Dīn Suhrawardī's famous Arabic Ṣūfī guidebook titled *'Awārif al-ma'ārif*. For the original text, which differs only slightly from Farghāna'ī's version, see 'Izz al-Dīn Kāshānī, *Miftāḥ al-hidāya va miftāḥ al-kifāya*, ed. 'Iffat Karbāsī and Muḥammad Riżā Barzgar Khāliqī (Tehran: Intishārāt-I Zavvār, 2003), 78–9.

Farghāna'ī's description of Muḥammad's magnetism offers a useful metaphor for visualizing the Prophet's legacy from a historiographical viewpoint as well. In this context, the conduction of power being talked about equates to the continuation of themes that originated in the time of the rise of Islam. More than simply affirming Muḥammad's special qualities, the visual image of pieces of metal becoming aligned through the application of a magnet recalls the power of some narratives to shape beliefs, behaviors, and, eventually, other narratives. The material I have discussed in this chapter provides some details for the working of this process in Islamic history.

Although Muḥammad's role in shaping Muslim ideas and practices can scarcely be overestimated, a historicizing view of religious sources provides ample evidence for the great diversity of ways in which Muslims may see the Prophet. Part of this difference can be attributed to the fact of various actors' different social locations in terms of class and prestige: the three authors considered herein saw Muuḥammad quite differently despite being contemporaries with a shared investment in Ṣūfī ideas. Jāmī belonged to the established scholarly class with close connections to the Tīmūrid court in Herat. He was a celebrated poet and prose author in his time, in touch with royal patrons such as the Ottoman Sultan Mehmet II (d. 886/1481), the Conqueror (Fatih), on whose request he composed his theological-philosophical work *The Precious Pearl* (*al-Durra al-Fākhira*).[50] His work on the Prophet has circulated widely ever since it was written, including through translation into Ottoman Turkish, Urdu, and Gujarati.[51] In contrast, Nūrbakhsh's fame rested on an audacious claim that caused him to spend most of his life in obscure places. During the last decade and a half of his life, he established himself in a village outside present-day Tehran and was regarded as an accomplished Ṣūfī master locally as well as by some rulers.[52] Still farther away from circles of prestige and power, Shaykh Aḥmad Bashīrī finds no mention in any source except the rare hagiography devoted to him.

[50] Cf. Nicholas Heer, trans., *The Precious Pearl: Al-Jāmī's Al-Durrah Al-Fākhirah* (Albany: State University of New York Press, 1979).

[51] The work was translated into Ottoman three times: first by the eminent scholar Maḥmūd b. Ilyās Lāmiʿī Chelebi (d. 1532 CE), whose devotion to Jāmī's work earned him the sobriquet the Jāmī of Anatolia (Jāmī-yi Rūm); then by Akhīzade ʿAbd al-Ḥalīm (d. 1604–1605 CE); and a third time by an author named Senā'ī (Günay Kut Alpay, "Lāmiʿī Chelebi˙ and His Works," *Journal of Near Eastern Studies* 35, no. 2 [1976]: 78). The Urdu and Gujarati translations exist in modern published versions: Bashīr Ḥusayn Nāẓim, trans., *Shavāhid al-nubuvvat* (Lahore: Maktaba Nabaviyya, 1974); Muḥammad Haphej Nabīpūrī, trans., *Shavahidunnabuwwat* (Ahmadabad: Bajhame Rukanuddina Nakasabandi Mujadidi, 1995).

[52] Cf. Bashir, *Messianic Hopes and Mystical Visions*, 64–8.

He thus represents the majority of the people in Tīmūrid times who, like in any period, lived their lives outside the very narrow social spectrum that usually finds representation in historical sources. In addition to their personal intellectual predilections, the three authors' perspectives index the different purviews of their circles of influence in their society.

The variety of meanings assigned to Muḥammad's life even in literature produced within a limited socio-intellectual milieu raises important issues regarding how we may approach the Prophet's figure as an object of academic study. It seems imperative that Muḥammad must be understood as a figure simultaneously transhistorical and local. In the context I have discussed here, the appeal to Muḥammad would have had little rhetorical force were it not for Muslims' investment in Islam's originary period as a source of authority. But equally significant, the impact of the historical figure would not be as widespread were it not for the fact that Persianate Ṣūfīs appropriated him for the way they constructed their models of religious authority in this period. Thus, the Prophet's image must be seen as having two faces in all contexts that must both be registered for effective analysis.

My focus on Ṣūfī texts in this chapter raises a further issue critical for interpreting Islamic religious materials in general. This is that Islamic discourses must be seen as a collection of dynamically interacting propositions rather than as stable intellectual systems with clear prescriptions and easily definable boundaries. All three authors I have examined self-identified as Ṣūfīs and lived quite close to one another in both time and space. And yet, leaving the matter at describing them as Ṣūfīs alone would be tantamount to eliding their very substantial mutual differences. The Muḥammads they imagine and interact with in their works are three substantially different figures, making it quite unfeasible to argue for a single Ṣūfī Muḥammad relevant for this period. To make note of this issue is not to advocate the interpretive position that religious thinking is merely personal and that there are as many Muḥammads as there are Muslims. Instead, it is to suggest that we must see the Prophet as a rhetorical figure forever under construction in keeping with the changing histories, ideas, and life circumstances of Muslims who think and write about him while being aware of contrasting or contradictory views. In studying Muḥammad, our true objects of analysis are not the different personalities attributable to Muḥammad but the intellectual and social processes that have constituted Muslims' dynamic investment in the Prophet over Islam's long history.

Further reading

Amir-Moezzi, Mohammad Ali, ed. *Le voyage initiatique en terre d'islam. Ascensions célestes et itinéraires spirituels.* Leuven: Peeters, 1996.

Bashir, Shahzad. *Messianic Hopes and Mystical Visions: The Nūrbkhshīya between Medieval and Modern Islam.* Columbia: University of South Carolina Press, 2003.

DeWeese, Devin. "The Legitimation of Bahā' ad-Dīn Naqshband." *Asiatische Studien/Études Asiatiques* 60, no. 2 (2006): 261–305.

DeWeese, Devin. *An "Uvaysī" Sufi in Tīmūrid Māwarānnahr: Notes on Hagiography and the Taxonomy of Sanctity in the Religious History of Central Asia.* Bloomington: Indiana University, Research Institute for Inner Asian Studies, 1993.

Green, Nile. "The Religious and Cultural Roles of Dreams and Visions in Islam." *Journal of the Royal Asiatic Society* 13, no. 3 (2003): 287–313.

Manz, Beatrice Forbes. *Power, Politics and Religion in Timurid Iran.* Cambridge: Cambridge University Press, 2007.

Meier, Fritz. "A Resurrection of Muḥammad in Suyūṭī." In *Essays on Islamic Piety and Mysticism,* translated by John O'Kane, with editorial assistance of Bernd Radtke, 505–47. Leiden: E. J. Brill, 1999.

Meister und Schüler im Orden der Naqsbandiyya. Heidelberg: Universitätsverlag C. Winter, 1995.

Ökten, Ertuğrul. "Jāmī (817–898/1414–1492): His Biography and Intellectual Influence in Herat." Ph.D. diss., University of Chicago, 2007.

Paul, Jürgen. *Doctrine and Organization: The Khwājagān/Naqshbandīya in the First Generation after Bahā'uddīn.* Berlin: Das Arabische Buch, 1998.

Renard, John. *Friends of God: Islamic Images of Piety, Commitment, and Servanthood.* Berkeley: University of California Press, 2008.

Scarcia-Amoretti, Biancamaria. "Religion in the Timurid and Safavid Periods." In *The Timurid and Safavid Periods.* Vol. 6 of *Cambridge History of Iran,* edited by Peter Jackson and Laurence Lockhart, 610–55.Cambridge: Cambridge University Press, 1986.

Schimmel, Annemarie. *And Muhammad Is His Messenger: The Veneration of the Prophet in Islamic Piety.* Chapel Hill: University of North Carolina Press, 1985.

11 European accounts of Muḥammad's life

JOHN V. TOLAN

For centuries, Muḥammad has been at the center of European discourse on Islam. For medieval Crusades chroniclers, he was either a golden idol that the so-called Saracens adored or a shrewd heresiarch who had worked false miracles to seduce the Arabs away from Christianity; both these descriptions made him the root of Saracen error and implicitly justified the Crusade to wrest the Holy Land from Saracen control. Such polemical images, forged in the Middle Ages, proved tenacious; in slightly modified forms, they provided the dominant European discourse on the Prophet through the seventeenth century. In the nineteenth and twentieth centuries, variants of the image of Muḥammad as an impostor have been used to justify European colonialism in Muslim lands and to encourage the work of Christian missionaries. Yet beginning in the eighteenth century, some European authors present the Prophet in a favorable light: as an inspired religious reformer and great legislator. These authors often have had polemical agendas, for example, lambasting Christian intolerance by contrasting it with the tolerance of Muḥammad and his followers. In the nineteenth and twentieth centuries, some scholars have tried to seek out the historical Muḥammad (just as contemporary scholars sought the historical Jesus) behind the hagiographical sources. In the late twentieth and twenty-first centuries, various European and American Christians have recognized that Muḥammad has played a positive role in spiritual history; some have called for their churches to recognize his status as a prophet. At the same time, the Prophet remains an object of polemical discourse, as the affair of the Danish caricatures has so clearly shown. Muḥammad occupies an important and ambivalent place in the European imagination: he figures as the embodiment of Islam, alternatively inspiring fear, loathing, fascination, and admiration but rarely indifference.

MAHOMET THE TRICKSTER IN TWELFTH-CENTURY LATIN LIVES

When northern Europeans first wrote about Muḥammad, they imagined him as an idol worshipped by pagan Saracens. The eleventh-century nun Hrotsvitha of Gandersheim, for example, portrays ʿAbd al-Raḥmān III, ʿUmayyad Caliph of Córdoba, as worshipping golden idols. In the *Chanson de Roland*, a French epic poem of the early twelfth century, Saracens worship a trio of idols: Apollin, Tervagant, and Mahomet. Many of the chroniclers of the First Crusade (1095–1099) imagine that their Saracen enemies are idolaters who have erected a statue of their god Mahomet in the "temple of the lord" (i.e., the Dome of the Rock).

Somewhat more accurate information about the Prophet of Islam was available in some European monastic libraries, notably in the ninth-century Latin translations of Theophanes' *Chronographia*, written in Constantinople around 815.[1] Theophanes claims that the Jews had first flocked to Muḥammad, thinking that he was their long-awaited Messiah; when they saw him eating camel (a forbidden food), they realized their error, yet some of them stayed with him out of fear "and taught him illicit things directed against us Christians."[2] Theophanes describes Muḥammad's marriage to Khadīja and his travels in Palestine, where he sought out the writings of Jews and Christians. Muḥammad had an epileptic seizure, and at this Khadīja became distressed; he soothed her by telling her: "I keep seeing a vision of a certain angel called Gabriel, and being unable to bear his sight, I faint and fall down." Khadīja sought the advice of "a certain monk living there, a friend of hers (who had been exiled for his depraved doctrine)"; this heretical monk seems to be based on the Christian figures Baḥīrā and Waraqa of Muslim tradition. The monk told Khadīja that Muḥammad was indeed a prophet to whom the angel Gabriel came in visions. Theophanes recounts that Muḥammad promised to all who fell fighting the enemy a paradise full of sensual delights: eating, drinking, and sex. He said "many other things full of profligacy and stupidity." Theophanes' *Chronographia*, which Anastasius the Librarian translated into Latin in the 870s, was to become one of

[1] Theophanes, *The Chronicle of Theophanes the Confessor*, trans. Cyril Mango and Roger Scott (Oxford: Clarendon Press, 1997), 464–5; Anne Proudfoot, "The Sources of Theophanes for the Heraclian Period," *Byzantion* 44 (1974): 386; John Tolan, *Saracens: Islam in the Medieval European Imagination* (New York: Columbia University Press, 2002), 64–6.

[2] Theophanes, *Chronicle*, 464.

the few widely available sources about Muḥammad in Western Europe before the twelfth century, supplying information, for example, in the monastic chronicles of Sigebert of Gembloux and Hugh of Fleury.[3]

Several twelfth-century Latin poets created more elaborate and more colorful portraits of Muḥammad as a wily pseudoprophet, founder of a heretical sect. Gautier de Compiègne composed his *Otia de Machometi*, a poem in 1,090 Latin verses, in the first half of the twelfth century; in 1258, Alexandre du Pont adapted Gautier's poem into French verse, as *Le roman de Mahomet*.[4] Gautier no doubt was familiar with Anastasius's text; it is also possible that he had read the brief biography of Muḥammad that Guibert of Nogent had inserted into his chronicle of the First Crusade.[5]

Gautier seeks to denigrate Islam for readers who have little chance of ever meeting a Muslim. This gives him great liberty to make Muḥammad conform to the stereotype of the scheming heresiarch and to paint him as a colorful scoundrel. Muḥammad (or Machomes, as he calls him) was a young man full of talent, expert in all the malefic arts. The servant of a rich widow, he longed to marry her to make himself rich. Here Gautier, like Theophanes, alludes to Muḥammad's marriage with Khadīja; their union is presented as scandalous because the couple is mismatched in age and in social standing. Machomes manipulated the widow, proffering dire predictions to dissuade her from marrying a young nobleman; he tried to convince her to marry him, speaking like "a second Cicero"; she feared lest their marriage become the butt of lewd jokes: people might say, "She who used to be on top is now lying underneath."[6] But Machomes succeeded in bribing local notables, who persuaded the widow to marry her servant.

Shortly after the wedding, the bride discovered that her new husband suffered from epileptic attacks: he fell at her feet, writhing and salivating. She fled into her bedroom, wept, and ripped her clothing. When Machomes came to, she heaped insults on him, expressing her shame at the marriage she had made. In Medieval Europe, epilepsy was often considered a symptom of demonic possession. Yet Machomes

[3] Benjamin Kedar, *Crusade and Mission: European Approaches toward the Muslims* (Princeton, NJ: Princeton University Press, 1984), 33–5, 86–9.

[4] Gautier de Compiègne, *Otia de Machomete*, ed. R. B. C. Huygens published by Y. G. Lepage along with Lepage's critical edition ofAlexandre du Pont's *Roman de Mahomet*, (Paris: Klincksieck, 1977). Reginald Hyatte, trans., *The Prophet of Islam in Old French: The Romance of Muhammad (1258) and The Book of Muhammad's Ladder (1264)* (Leiden: Brill, 1997). References are to line numbers of Gautier's Latin text.

[5] See Tolan, *Saracens*, chap. 6.

[6] Gautier, *Otia de Machomete*, ll. 170 and 246.

cleverly tricked his wife, claiming that he, in fact, had been visited by the archangel Gabriel, who had revealed a new law to him. Skeptical, she declares that she will go ask the advice of a holy hermit who lives nearby. Machomes gets to the hermit before his wife and threatens him with death if he does not comply with his orders. The terrified hermit thus proclaims that Machomes is a great prophet. Machomes' wife, thrilled, humbly begs her husband's pardon. She brags to her friends about her husband's prophetic gifts; in this way, Machomes gains unequaled fame.

To convert the people to his cause, a heresiarch must accomplish miracles – false ones of course but plausible enough to dupe the naive women and men of his entourage. Machomes hides milk and honey in holes that he had dug at the summit of a mountain. Then he bids the assembled people to climb the mountain with him, where he prays that God "[d]eign to give the world an unaccustomed sign."[7] He then "finds" the milk and honey, which all accept as true signs of divine favor. Emboldened by this miracle, Machomes again prays to God:

> We pray that, just as high on a mountain
> Christ gave laws to his disciples
> And as Moses received the Law on a mountain,
> Written by the finger of God,
> Just so may God deign to certify in writing
> The law by which he wishes humanity to live.[8]

Machomes compares himself to Moses, a lawgiver to his people. This provides him with the occasion for another trick miracle. He had raised a bull, training it to come kneel down before him as soon as he heard his master's voice. He wrote a book of laws and attached it to the horns of the bull, which he then hid in a cave at the summit of the mountain. When the young bull heard Machomes raise his voice in prayer, he emerged from his cave and kneeled before his master; the people, astonished at this new sign of divine favor, removed the book from the bull's horns and accepted it as their new, God-given law. This law abolished baptism, reinstated circumcision, and authorized each man to marry up to ten wives.

Gautier does not deny that Muḥammad produced miracles: on the contrary, his miracles are more numerous and more diverse than those attributed by the Ḥadīth (the Qur'ān, of course, attributes none to the Prophet). But for Gautier, they are false miracles, the result of tricks

[7] Ibid., l. 809.
[8] Ibid., ll. 831–6.

Figure 6. Muḥammad preaching with a dove on his shoulder, revealing the Qur'ān on the horns of a bull. From a French translation of Boccaccio, *De casibus*; manuscript from the early fifteenth century (Paris: Bibliothèque Nationale de France, ms. 226, fol. 243).

and magic; they explain how a vile heresiarch recruited numerous disciples. The fraud practiced by the founder of the so-called law of the Saracens shows readers the diabolical nature of this law and explains its formidable successes. The readers are omniscient: they clearly see that the miracles are false, yet they can see how they have duped a multitude of credulous Saracens.

Machomes was so admired by his followers that they considered him a God. But he eventually died and, Gautier affirms, received the punishment he deserved in hell. The false prophet was given an unusual funeral:

> And his people, believing that his spirit to the stars
> Had passed, dared not submit his body to the earth.
> They established therefore an ark of admirable workmanship:
> In this they placed him as best they could.
> For, as is told, [the ark] seems to hang
> With Machomes' members lying inside
> So that without any support it hangs in the air,
> And without any chains holding it from above.
> And if you ask them by what artifice it does not fall,
> They erroneously repute it to Machomes' powers.
> But in fact it is covered in iron,
> Placed in the center of a square building
> Made out of magnetic rock, on all four sides
> The measurements are the same inside and out.
> By nature it attracts the iron to itself equally
> So that it is unable to fall in any direction.[9]

Thanks to a final, posthumous, bogus miracle, Machomes causes the naive Saracens to venerate him. Gautier places his tomb in Mecha – an appropriately named place, because the false prophet was an adulterer (*mechus*); others, he says, place his tomb in Babel, an equally appropriate place, as his effrontery was matched only by those who built the tower of Babel.[10] This imaginary cultic center of the Saracen world – Muḥammad's floating coffin in Babel-Mecca – is a sort of deformed mirror image of Crusader Jerusalem, an anti-Jerusalem as it were: just as Christian pilgrims honor Christ's tomb in Jerusalem, Saracen pilgrims

[9] Ibid., ll. 1059–74.
[10] Ibid., ll. 1077–86.

flock to the floating coffin of their false god and prophet.[11] This helps explain to readers the force of attraction that Islam worked on the hoards of Saracens.

For Gautier, Machomes' aim was to moderate the law to permit sexual debauchery. Just like previous Christian authors, Gautier sees Islam as an illegitimate offshoot of Christianity, a heresy, rather than a distinct religion. The law of the Saracens is part of a panoply of errors inspired by the devil, which threaten the souls of Christians and the hierarchy of the church. Other twelfth-century authors wrote similar biographical sketches of the false prophet of the Saracen, a trickster and worker of bogus miracles: Adelphus, Embrico of Mainz, Guibert of Nogent.[12] Confronted by the threat represented by these Saracens (and also by Waldensians, Cathars, Jews, and others), many twelfth-century authors responded with hateful calumny, choosing not to refute their adversaries but to insult and denigrate them, so that their readers would not take their ideas seriously. There were, however, other European Christians in the twelfth century who tried to compose more serious refutations of Islamic doctrines.

THE LEARNED ASSAULT ON A FALSE PROPHET AND HERESIARCH (TWELFTH–FIFTEENTH CENTURIES)

Beginning in the twelfth century, a handful of Christian European theologians began to study and attack Islam. Instead of painting Muḥammad as a colorful scoundrel with trained animals, they sought to study and refute the fundamental texts of Islam, in particular the Qur'ān. These writers, too, were dependent on the earlier work of Oriental Christian polemicists. The most influential of these texts was no doubt the anonymous text known as the *Risālat al-Kindī* (*Letter of al-Kindī*), a purported exchange of letters between two friends in ninth-century Baghdad: a Muslim (not named in the text but whom later tradition identified as ʿAbd Allāh al-Hāshimī) writes to explain Islam to his Christian friend (traditionally known as ʿAbd al-Masīḥ al-Kindī) and invites him to convert. In response, al-Kindī presents a long and detailed refutation of Islam and invites his Muslim friend to convert to Christianity. In fact, both "letters" were probably written by an anonymous Iraqi Christian in the tenth century. The Christian's letter is both polemical and apologetical: it attacks Muslim doctrine and practice, and it presents a defense of the

[11] On the various versions of this legend, see John Tolan, *Sons of Ishmael: Muslims through European Eyes in the Middle Ages* (Gainesville: University Press of Florida, 2008), chap. 2.

[12] Tolan, *Saracens*, chap. 6.

fundamental Christian doctrines that offended Muslims (in particular, the Incarnation and the Trinity).[13]

A central part of his attack on Islam is an assault on the Prophet. He recounts Muḥammad's biography in an acerbic and derogatory fashion, showing all the while a good knowledge of the Qur'ān and early Muslim historiography. He notes that Muḥammad had first been an idolater and had enriched himself through trade and through his marriage with Khadīja. Wishing to rule over his tribe, he decided to pretend to be a prophet; his companions, gullible nomads who knew nothing of the signs of prophecy, believed him. He and his followers enriched themselves through war and pillaging. These acts, for the Christian writer, are enough to prove that Muḥammad was not a prophet, and the failures of some of the expeditions (especially the Battle of Uḥud) even more so: a true prophet would have foreseen (and avoided) defeat.

This Christian polemicist, who may well have been a monk, is particularly shocked by Muḥammad's sexual life, which he attacks with gusto. Muḥammad himself, he says, claimed to have the sexual powers of forty men. He presents a catalogue of the Prophet's fifteen wives, dwelling on the scandals surrounding Zaynab and ʿĀ'isha. Did not the apostle Paul proclaim that "he that is unmarried careth for the things that belong to the Lord, how he may please the Lord: But he that is married careth for the things that are of the world, how he may please his wife" (1 Corinthians 7:32–3)? Is this not even truer of a man with fifteen wives, a man, moreover, constantly involved in planning war? "How could he, with this continual and permanent preoccupation, find the time to fast, pray, worship God, meditate and contemplate eternal things and those things appropriate to prophets? I am certain that no prophet was as attached to the pleasures of this world as was your master."[14]

The Christian monk then explains "the signs of prophecy which oblige one to recognize the title of prophet and of apostle to him who shows them."[15] The two signs of prophecy are revelation of things unknown (past and future) and performance of miracles. Muḥammad

[13] There is no good modern edition and no English translation of this text. The text is available as *Risālat ʿAbd Allāh Ibn Ismāʿīl al-Hāshimī ilā ʿAbd al-Masīḥ Ibn Isḥāq al-Kindī wa-Risālat al-Kindī ilā al-Hāshimī (The Apology of El-Kindi: A Work of the Ninth Century, Written in Defence of Christianity by an Arab)*, ed. Anton Tien (London: Society for Promoting Christian Knowledge, 1885). A passable French translation, with a poor introduction, is Georges Tartar, trans., *Risālat al-Kindī (Dialogue islamo-chrétien sous le Calife al-Ma'mûn (813–834): Les épîtres d'al-Hashimī et d'al-Kindī* (Paris: Nouvelles Éditions Latines, 1985). On this text, see Tolan, *Saracens*, 60–4.

[14] Tartar, *Risālat al-Kindī*, 152–3.

[15] Ibid., 153.

foretold nothing, whereas the Hebrew prophets, Christ, and the apostles did. Muḥammad produced no miracles, as the Qur'ān expressly states; the miracles attributed to him are false. In much of this, the Christian author compares (explicitly or implicitly) Muḥammad with Jesus: Christ shunning sex and worldly power, Muḥammad eagerly pursuing both; Christ prophesying true things, Muḥammad failing to foresee his defeats in battle; Christ producing miracles, Muḥammad none. He carries this contrast into his description of the Prophet's death. Muḥammad, he says, ordered that his companions not bury him after his death, for angels would come within three days to carry his body up to heaven. At his death, his disciples did as he had ordered: "after they had waited for three days, his odor changed and their hopes of his being taken up to heaven disappeared. Disappointed by his illusory promises and realizing that he had lied, they buried him."[16]

The Arabic text of the *Risālat al-Kindī* circulated in Arab Christian milieus in Spain, and it was to have a significant impact on Latin European views of Islam through the work of two men, Petrus Alfonsi and Peter of Cluny. Petrus Alfonsi, an Andalusian Jew who converted to Christianity and traveled and taught in Aragon, England and France, in 1110 wrote his *Dialogi contra Iudeos* (*Dialogues against the Jews*), a polemic against his former religion in which he included a chapter against Islam, derived almost entirely from the *Risālat al-Kindī*. Thirty-two years later, Peter, the abbot of Cluny, commissioned Robert of Ketton to make the first Latin translation of the Qur'ān and had other Arabic texts about Islam translated – including the *Risālat al-Kindī*.[17]

In the thirteenth century, Dominican missionaries undertook the evangelization of Jews and Muslims in Christian Europe, in particular in the Crown of Aragon. They founded language schools where they learned Hebrew, Aramaic, and Arabic; some of them studied the Talmud, the Qur'ān, and the Ḥadīth to attack these texts from a Christian point of view.

One of the fundamental Dominican texts on Islam was Ramon Martí's *De seta machometi* (written before 1257), meant to be a practical guide for Christians in theological disputes.[18] *De seta* is a brief text in two parts: an attack on the life and deeds of Muḥammad followed by a

[16] Ibid., 166.

[17] F. González Muñoz, *Exposición y refutación del islam. La versión latina de las epístolas de Hasimi y al-Kindi* (La Coruña: Universidade da Coruña, 2005); Tolan, *Saracens*, 148–65.

[18] Ramón Martí, "*De seta machometi o De origine, progressu, et fine Machometi et quadruplici reprobatione prophetiae eius*," ed. and Spanish trans. Josep Hernando i Delgado, *Acta Historica et Archaeologica Medievalia* 4 (1983): 9–51. On this text, see Tolan, *Saracens*, 236–9.

defense of Christianity from the charge of falsification of the Scriptures. This sequence is calculated: the attack on Muḥammad must prove that Islam is false, whereas the defense of Christian scriptures – based on the Qur'ān – is meant to prove to the Muslim that Christianity is the true religion. Muḥammad is not a true prophet, Martí claims; rather, he is one of the false prophets that Jesus announced in Matthew 7:15–16: "Beware of false prophets, which come to you in sheep's clothing, but inwardly they are ravening wolves. Ye shall know them by their fruits." Martí organizes his tract around this central premise. The fruits mentioned in Matthew, Martí expounds, are the signs of prophethood, which are four: truthfulness, holiness, miracles, and a true law. Martí means to show that Muḥammad meets none of these four tests.

The brunt of Martí's attack is against the sexual foibles of Muḥammad and his followers; here he attacks Ḥadīth and especially the Qur'ān. Martí presents the Muslim paradise, full of the pleasures of eating and lovemaking, and contrasts it with the pure and austere heaven of Paul and the Gospels.[19] A recitation of the wives and concubines of Muḥammad is enough, for Martí, to prove that he did not lead a holy life; because holiness is the second "fruit of prophecy," this helps prove that Muḥammad was not a true prophet but a false one.[20] Martí's fourth fruit of prophecy is a good and holy law. He tries to show that the law brought by Muḥammad goes against both divine law (as mandated by Scripture) and natural law (as mandated by reason). Of the eleven Muslim laws that Martí here assails, seven involve sex and marriage: he derides polygamy as "manifestly against divine law, against natural law and against reason."[21] He similarly condemns what he presents as Muslim law regarding divorce, nonvaginal intercourse, concubinage, coitus interruptus, and homosexuality.[22] Acknowledging that homosexuality is, in fact, illegal in Islam, he nonetheless claims that, because four witnesses are needed to convict homosexuals, Muḥammad thus "gave cause and occasion to his followers to perpetrate this crime almost without shame and fear."[23] For Ramón Martí, a missionary friar under a vow of celibacy, the most false and shocking thing about Muḥammad and his followers is their sex life: polygamy, homosexuality, even sex in heaven! This obsession flavors Martí's description of Muḥammad's death. Martí, unlike other polemicists, eschews the horrendous tales of murder and dismemberment in favor of the Muslim story of his death, which shows the

[19] Martí, "*De seta*," 30.
[20] Ibid., 34–6.
[21] Ibid., 44.
[22] Ibid., 44–8.
[23] Ibid., 48.

Prophet surrounded by his loved ones, peacefully dying with his head in the lap of his beloved wife ʿĀʾisha. For Muslims, this touching scene emphasizes the Prophet's human frailty and the love that his family and followers held for him. Yet Martí is unable to see anything but filth in this scene: "When he died he had his head between ʿĀʾisha's breast and her chin, and she mixed her saliva with that of Muḥammad. In this way the death or end of Muḥammad was vile, unclean, and abominable. And such a death is in no way appropriate for a prophet or a messenger of God."[24] In a standard Christian deathbed scene, an attentive priest would hear confession and administer communion and extreme unction, and the dying man would prepare his soul to meet its Maker. Instead of the Body of Christ, Martí seems to be implying, that Muḥammad's last solace was the saliva of profane kisses; instead of the anointing hand of a priest, he is caressed by the breasts of a woman; instead of confessing and turning away from sin, he is clinging desperately to it.

Martí, unlike most earlier Latin polemicists, has sketched a biography of Muḥammad that Muslims would recognize as true in most of its details, gleaned as they are from Arab (and principally Muslim) sources. Yet the selection and presentation of these sources show an unshakable hostility: from the wide range of material in the Qurʾān and the works of Ibn Isḥāq, al-Bukhārī, and Muslim ibn al-Ḥajjāj, Martí focuses on what will shock a Christian clerical audience: the sex life of the Muslim prophet and Muslim laws regarding sex and marriage.

This vision of Muḥammad as a false prophet who forged a bogus revelation dominates European learned discourse on Islam well into the eighteenth century. We find it in learned polemics against the Qurʾān, such as Dominican Riccoldo da Montecroce's *Contra legem Saracenorum* or Nicholas of Cusa's *Cribratio Alcorani*.[25] Fifteenth-century Renaissance humanists echo traditional polemics: Andrea Biglia paints Muḥammad as "a horrible beast of hell"; Favio Biondo describes how the Arabs were "seduced by Muḥammad's tricks."[26] Many writers mixed elements from the poetic and the learned polemical traditions: this is the case, for example, of Vincent de Beauvais and Jacques de Voragine in the thirteenth century, Giovanni Villani in the fourteenth century, or Giovanni Mario Filelfo in the fifteenth century.

[24] Ibid., 52.

[25] Riccoldo da Montecroce, *Libellus contra legem Saracenorum*, ed. J. Merigoux, *Memorie Domenicane*, n.s., 17 (1986): 1–144; see Tolan, *Saracens*, 251–4. Nicholas of Cusa, *De pace fidei and Cribratio Alkorani*, trans. J. Hopkins (Minneapolis: Banning, 1990).

[26] Margaret Meserve, *Empires of Islam in Renaissance Historical Thought* (Cambridge, MA: Harvard University Press, 2008), 173, 187.

MAHOMET THE IMPOSTOR IN EARLY MODERN EUROPE

Indeed, in the sixteenth and seventeenth centuries, Europeans continued and renewed polemics against Islam and its prophet, motivated in part through fear of the expansionist Ottoman Empire – often simply referred to as the Turk. In 1543, Theodore Bibliander published, in Basel, Robert of Ketton's twelfth-century translation of the Qur'ān along with a collection of medieval polemics against Islam: the Latin translation of the *Risālat al-Kindī* and works by Riccoldo da Montecroce, Nicolas of Cusa, and others. There was even a preface by Martin Luther himself, who affirmed that there was no better way to combat the Turks than to expose the "lies and fables" of Muḥammad; Luther translated Riccoldo da Montecroce's *Contra legem Saracenorum* into German.[27]

In 1697, Humphrey Prideaux, an Anglican minister and Oxford-educated doctor of theology, published a work called *The True Nature of The Imposture Fully Display'd in the Life of Mahomet*.[28] Prideaux casts a critical eye on much of the legendary elements concerning the Prophet. He dismisses the stories of the bull bearing the Qur'ān on its horns and the pigeon passed off as the Holy Spirit as "idle fables not to be credited."[29] He similarly dispels what he identifies as other common misconceptions about the Prophet: that Muslims expected him to resurrect ("totally an error"[30]). When describing his burial beneath ʿĀ'isha's bed, he remarks, "There he lyeth to this day, without iron coffin or loadstones to hang him in the Air, as the Stories which commonly go about him among Christians fabulously relate."[31] Hostile stories that seem less improbable to him, however, such as Muḥammad's epilepsy, he includes without criticism. Prideaux claims to present, in lieu of fables, the "true nature" of Muḥammad's "imposture":

> The whole of this imposture was a thing of extraordinary craft, carried on with all the cunning and caution imaginable. The framing of the *Alcoran* (wherein lay the main of the cheat) was all contrived at home in as secret a manner as possible, and

[27] James Boyce and Sarah Henrich, "Martin Luther Translations of Two Prefaces on Islam: Preface to the *Libellus de ritu et moribus Turcorum* (1530) and Preface to Bibliander's Edition of the Qur'ān (1543)," *Word & World* 16 (1996): 250–66.

[28] Humphrey Prideaux, *The True Nature of the Imposture Fully Display'd in the Life of Mahomet with a Discourse Annex'd for the Vindication of Christianity from this Charge Offered to the Consideration of the Deists of the Present Age* (London: W. Rogers, 1697, and E. Curll, 1723). Page citations herein refer to the 1723 edition.

[29] Ibid., 38.

[30] Ibid., 102.

[31] Ibid., 103.

> nothing hazarded abroad, but the success of preaching it to the people. And in doing of this, no art or cunning was wanting to make it as effectual to the End design'd as possible: and therefore whatever stories are told of this matter, that are inconsistent with such a management, we may assure ourselves are nothing else but fables foolishly invented by some zealous Christians to blast the imposture, which needed no such means for its confutation.[32]

He uses a number of medieval polemical texts, citing by name Theophanes, Riccoldo da Montecroce, and others; he has consulted Robert of Ketton's twelfth-century Latin translation of the Qur'ān and the other works published by Bibliander. He also relies on more recent works, including Edward Pocock's 1650 edition and translation of Bar Hebraeus's *Specimen historiae arabum*. He presents Muḥammad as dominated by the twin passions of lust and ambition, which cause him to feign a religious vocation. Unable to produce miracles, Muḥammad gains adherents through threats of violence and promises of a carnal paradise, well adapted to the hot temperaments of the inhabitants of the "torrid zone."[33] Prideaux is moved less by the desire to attack Islam than to defend Christianity – not from Muslims but from Deists. In the opening passages of his tract, he lambastes Deists who affirm that Christianity is an imposture; his goal is to show them a true imposture, that of Muḥammad, and then to demonstrate (in a tract published in the same volume) that Christianity is no imposture but the true religion.

Prideaux was writing at the height of the Deist movement in England. Deists and atheists attacked the founders of the three great monotheisms, taking up many of the standard polemical tropes against Muḥammad and making similar attacks on Moses and Jesus. The most elaborate and most notorious such attack was made in *Le traité des trois imposteurs* (*The Treatise of the Three Impostors*), first published in 1719.[34] The anonymous author lambasts the priests and rulers of ancient Greece and Rome, who took advantage of the credulity of their people to

[32] Ibid., 38–9.

[33] Ibid., 21.

[34] The first edition was published in a book entitled *La vie et l'esprit de Mr. Benoit de Spinosa* (Amsterdam: Charles le Vier, 1719); it was subsequently printed under the title *Le traité des trois imposteurs* in 1721 and republished numerous times in the eighteenth century. For an English translation, based on the 1777 edition, see Abraham Anderson, *The Treatise of the Three Imposters and the Problem of the Enlightenment* (Lanham, MD: Rowman & Littlefield, 1997); the page numbers herein are to this translation. On this text, see S. Berti, F. Charles-Daubert, and R. Popkin, eds., *Heterodoxy, Spinozism, and Free Thought in Early-Eighteenth-Century Europe:*

give their power a sacred aura and to create a cadre of rich and compliant priests. But the greatest scoundrels, for this author, are the founders of the three monotheistic religions. Moses, a magician trained in Egypt, was an "absolute despot . . . a trickster and impostor."[35] Jesus Christ was no better; he "got himself followed by some imbeciles whom he persuaded that the Holy Spirit was his Father; & his Mother a Virgin."[36] He paints Muḥammad in similar colors:

> Mahomet was not a man who seemed fit to found an Empire, he excelled neither in politics nor in philosophy; he knew neither how to read nor how to write. He even had so little firmness that he would often have abandoned his enterprise if he had not been forced to stand by his wager by the skill of one of his Sectaries. As soon as he began to raise himself up & to become famous, Corais, a powerful Arab, jealous that a nobody had the audacity to deceive the people, declared himself his enemy & crossed his enterprise; but the People, persuaded that Mahomet had continual conferences with God & his Angels, brought it about that he defeated his enemy; the family of Corais had the worse of it, & Mahomet seeing himself followed by an imbecile crowd which believed him a divine man, judged he had no more need of his companion: but for fear that the latter would reveal his impostures, he wanted to prevent him, & in order to do it the more surely, he loaded him with promises, & swore to him that he only wanted to become great in order to share with him his power, to which he had contributed so much. "We are arriving," he said, "at the time of our elevation, we are sure of a great People which we have won over, we must now assure ourselves of it by the artifice which you have so happily imagined." At the same time he persuaded him to hide himself in the ditch of the Oracles.
>
> This was a well from which he spoke in order to make the People believe that the voice of God declared itself for Mahomet who was in the midst of his proselytes. Tricked by the caresses of this traitor, his associate went into the ditch to counterfeit the Oracle in his usual fashion; Mahomet passing by at the head of an infatuated multitude, a voice was heard which said: "I

Studies on the "Traité des trois imposteurs" (Dordrecht: Kluwer Academic Publishers, 1996).

[35] Anderson, *Treatise*, 22.

[36] Ibid., 23.

who am your God declare that I have established Mahomet to be the Prophet of all the nations; it will be from him that you will learn my true law which the Jews & the Christians have adulterated."

Muḥammad subsequently orders his people to fill in the ditch with stones, crushing his erstwhile rival Corais; the false prophet thus became the undisputed master of the Arabs. The anonymous author sketches a portrait of an impostor, similar to that of other European authors from the twelfth century on. Indeed, what is new is that he has applied to the lives of Moses and Jesus the same techniques of denigration and misrepresentation of religious traditions that Christian European authors had used against Muḥammad for centuries.

The portrait of Muḥammad the impostor remained the dominant image of the Prophet in European discourse, even in learned works such as Barthélemy d'Herbelot de Molainville's *Bibliothèque orientale* (1697), or in the *Encyclopédie*.[37] We find it in nineteenth-century apologists of empire and mission, such as William Muir (1819–1905), who wrote a massive, erudite four-volume study on Muḥammad: "Britain must not faint," he wrote, "until her millions in the East abandon both the false prophet and the idol shrines and rally around that eternal truth which has been brought to light in the Gospel."[38]

LAWGIVER AND SAGE

Yet in the eighteenth century, other Europeans began to see Muḥammad in another light, as a statesman and legislator. Henri, Count of Boulainvilliers (1658–1722), wrote the *Vie de Mahomed*, which was published posthumously in 1730. He presents the Prophet as a divinely inspired messenger whom God employed to confound the bickering Oriental Christians, to liberate the Orient from the despotic rule of the Romans and Persians, and to spread the knowledge of the unity of God from India to Spain: "Since if the fortune of this personage was not the effect of natural means, the success could be only from God; whom the impious will accuse of having led half the world into an error, and

[37] Barthélemy d'Herbelot de Molainville, *Bibliothèque orientale* (Paris: Compagnie des Libraires, 1697), 598–603; Denis Diderot and D'Alembert *Encyclopédie ou Dictionnaire raisonné des sciences, des arts et des métiers* 9 (Neufchâtel: Samuel Faulche, 1765), 864–88.

[38] William Muir, *The Mohammadan Controversy*, qtd. in Clinton Bennett, *Victorian Images of Islam* (London: Grey Seal Books, 1992), 111.

destroy'd violently his own revelation."[39] Arguing against Prideaux, he scoffs at the hostile Christian legends around the Prophet's supposed heretical Christian sidekick and denies that Muslim doctrine is irrational or that Muḥammad is a coarse impostor. On the contrary, the Prophet rejected all that was irrational and undesirable in Christianity as he found it: the cult of relics and icons, the grasping power of superstitious and avaricious monks and priests. Muḥammad "seems to have adopted and embraced all that is most marvelous in Christianity itself. So that what he retrenched, relates obviously to those abuses alone, which it was impossible he should not condemn."[40] Boulainvilliers's praise of Muḥammad is, of course, a ringing condemnation of the Catholic Church, an attack on the rites, privileges, possessions, and riches of the clergy. His works were banned in France and were published in Protestant Amsterdam and London. As often, when Europeans write about Muḥammad, they often do so to settle accounts with enemies closer to home.

Voltaire's instrumentalization of Muḥammad to attack the Catholic Church verges on the schizophrenic: he vilifies the Prophet as a symbol of fanaticism in his play *Le fanatisme, ou Mahomet le prophète* (first staged in 1741), yet in his later historical works, he came to regard him as a sage and tolerant legislator (to contrast with Catholic fanatics).[41] His play, as the title shows, presents Muḥammad as the paragon of fanaticism: an impostor desiring self-glorification and beautiful women who is willing to lie, to kill, and even to wage war against his homeland to get what he desires. In an essay published with the play in 1748, he calls Muḥammad "a sublime and hearty charlatan."[42] Yet in later years, Voltaire increasingly praised the religious tolerance preached by Islam and its founder, in sharp contrast with the intolerance that produced the wars of religion in Christian Europe. In his sweeping historical survey, the *Essai sur les mœurs*, he presents Muḥammad as a legislator and a

39 Henri de Boulainvilliers, *La vie de Mahomed* (Amsterdam: P. Humbert, 1730); Boulainvilliers, *The Life of Mahomet* (London: W. Hinchliffe, 1731), 179. The work, published posthumously, was left incomplete at the author's death; part 3, by another author, is of a quite different spirit: Muḥammad is described as an "impostor" and "false prophet" who "feigned a journey from Mecca to Jerusalem" (350).

40 Boulainvilliers, *Life of Mahomet*, 222.

41 Two books published in 1974 bear the same title – *Voltaire et l'Islam* – an analysis of Voltaire's play *Mahomet* by M. Badir, *Voltaire et l'Islam*, vol. 25, *Studies on Voltaire and the Eighteenth Century* (Oxford: Voltaire Foundation, 1974), and a much richer study of a number of Voltaire's works by Djavad Hadidi, *Voltaire et l'Islam* (Paris: Institut National des Langues et Civilisations Orientales, 1974).

42 Voltaire, "De l'Alcoran et de Mahomet," in *Les Œuvres complètes de Voltaire* (Oxford: Voltaire Foundation, 2002), 20B:333; the play is published in the same volume.

conqueror, not an impostor but an "enthusiast," so carried away that he believed himself inspired by God.[43]

Indeed, in Enlightenment France, Muḥammad is increasingly seen as a sage lawgiver and brilliant leader. Rousseau, in his *Social Contract* (1762), brushing aside hostile legends of Muḥammad as a trickster and impostor, presents him as a sage legislator who wisely fused religious and political powers.[44] Emmanuel Pastoret published in 1787 his *Zoroaster, Confucius and Muḥammad*, in which he presents the lives of these three "great men," "the greatest legislators of the universe," and compares their careers as religious reformers and lawgivers.[45] He defends the Prophet, too often calumniated as an impostor. In fact, the Qur'ān proffers "the most sublime truths of cult and morals"; it defines the unity of God with an "admirable concision."[46] The common accusations of the Prophet's immorality are unfounded: on the contrary, his law enjoins sobriety, generosity, and compassion on his followers: the "legislator of Arabia" was "a great man."[47]

In an age of empire, as Europeans subjected large swaths of the world to their dominion, Muḥammad is increasingly seen as a statesman and conqueror and, as such, is an object of admiration – frank or grudging. Edward Gibbon devotes a long chapter of his *Decline and Fall of the Roman Empire* to the life of the Prophet and the Islamic conquests. The impostor figure, indeed, has not disappeared: Muḥammad "consulted the spirit of fraud or enthusiasm, whose abode is not in the heavens, but in the mind of the prophet."[48] Yet he affirms that "the creed of Mohammed is free from suspicion or ambiguity; and the Koran is a glorious testimony to the unity of God."[49] He echoes Boulainvilliers (whom he cites frequently) in praising Muḥammad for instituting tithes (*zakat*) for the benefit of the poor. Even in his death, the Prophet showed himself worthy of emulation, a model of humility and penance. The violence of the Qur'ān, often the object of Christian polemicists, pales in comparison with that of the Torah. On the whole, Gibbon paints a portrait of a pious man and a brilliant leader who gave his people a

[43] Voltaire, *Essai sur les mœurs*, chap. 6.

[44] Jean-Jacques Rousseau, *Du contrat social* (Amsterdam: Marc Michel Rey, 1762), 303–4.

[45] Emmanuel Pastoret, *Zoroastre, Confucius et Mahomet, comparés comme sectaires, législateurs, et moralistes; avec le tableau de leurs dogmes, de leurs lois et de leur morale* (Paris: Buisson, 1787), 385, l. 1.

[46] Ibid., ll. 234 and 236.

[47] Ibid., l. 320.

[48] Edward Gibbon, *Decline and Fall of the Roman Empire* (New York: Modern Library, n.d.), 3:80.

[49] Ibid., 3:82.

unity and purpose that allowed them to subject half the world to their rule.

Napoléon Bonaparte, in a mixture of real admiration and calculated interest, made the Prophet into something of a role model, seeing himself as a new world conqueror and legislator walking in Muḥammad's footsteps. In May 1798, Napoléon set off to conquer Egypt at the head of a fleet of some fifty-five thousand men; in June, he captured Malta after a brief siege and continued toward Egypt. Hoping to gain the allegiance of the Egyptians and to convince them to throw off the yoke of their Ottoman masters, he addressed the following missive to the Egyptian people:

> In the name of God the Beneficent, the Merciful, there is no other God than God, he has neither son nor associate to his rule.
>
> On behalf of the French Republic founded on the basis of liberty and equality, the General Bonaparte, head of the French Army, proclaims to the people of Egypt that for too long the Beys who rule Egypt insult the French nation and heap abuse on its merchants; the hour of their chastisement has come.
>
> For too long, this rabble of slaves brought up in the Caucasus and in Georgia tyrannizes the finest region of the world; but God, Lord of the worlds, all-powerful, has proclaimed an end to their empire.
>
> Egyptians, some will say that I have come to destroy your religion; this is a lie, do not believe it! Tell them that I have come to restore your rights and to punish the usurpers; that I respect, more than do the Mamluks, God, his prophet Muḥammad and the glorious Qur'ān.... Qāḍī, shaykh, shorbagi, tell the people that we are true Muslims. Are we not the one who has destroyed the Pope who preached war against Muslims? Did we not destroy the Knights of Malta, because these fanatics believed that God wanted them to make war against the Muslims?[50]

It would be easy to dismiss such rhetoric as cynical and self-serving. Indeed, the following year (in autumn 1799), as he prepared to leave Egypt, he left instructions to French administrators in Egypt, explaining among other things that "one must take great care to persuade the

[50] Qtd. in Henri Laurens, *L'Expédition d'Egypte, 1798–1801* (Paris: Seuil, 1997), 108.

Muslims that we love the Qurʾān and that we venerate the prophet. One thoughtless word or action can destroy the work of many years."[51]

Years later, in exile on the British island of Saint Helena, Napoléon wrote his memoirs, including the description of his Egyptian campaign. It is here he develops his portrait of Muḥammad as a model lawmaker and conqueror:

> Arabia was idolatrous when Muḥammad, seven centuries after Jesus Christ, introduced the cult of the God of Abraham, Ishmael, Moses and Jesus Christ. The Arians and other sects that had troubled the tranquility of the Orient had raised questions concerning the nature of the Father, the Son and the Holy Spirit. Muḥammad declared that there was one unique God who had neither father nor son; that the trinity implied idolatry. He wrote on the frontispiece of the Qurʾān: "There is no other god than God."
>
> He addressed savage, poor peoples, who lacked everything and were very ignorant; had he spoken to their spirit, they would not have listened to him. In the midst of abundance in Greece, the spiritual pleasures of contemplation were a necessity; but in the midst of the deserts, where the Arab ceaselessly sighed for a spring of water, for the shade of a palm where he could take refuge from the rays of the burning tropical sun, it was necessary to promise to the chosen, as a reward, inexhaustible rivers of milk, sweet-smelling woods where they could relax in eternal shade, in the arms of divine houris with white skin and black eyes. The Bedouins were impassioned by the promise of such an enchanting abode; they exposed themselves to every danger to reach it; they became heroes.
>
> Muḥammad was a prince; he rallied his compatriots around him. In a few years, his Muslims conquered half the world. They plucked more souls from the false gods, knocked down more idols, razed more pagan temples in fifteen years, than the followers of Moses and Jesus Christ did in fifteen centuries. Muḥammad was a great man. He would indeed have been a god, if the revolution that he had performed had not been prepared by the circumstances.[52]

[51] Napoléon, *Campagnes d'Egypte et de Syrie* (Paris: Imprimerie Nationale, 1998), 275.
[52] Ibid., 140–1.

Bonaparte's Muḥammad is a model statesman and conqueror: he knows how to motivate his troops and, as a result, was a far more successful conqueror than was Napoléon, holed up on a windswept island in the South Atlantic. If he promised sensual delights to his faithful, it is because that is all they understood: this manipulation, far from being cause for scandal (as it had been for European writers since the twelfth century), provokes only the admiration of the former emperor.

Napoléon is ready to excuse, even to praise, parts of Muslim law that had been objects of countless polemics, including polygamy. Why did Muḥammad allow polygamy? First, explains Napoléon, it had always been a common practice in the Orient; Muḥammad actually reduced it by allowing each man a maximum of four wives. Moreover, polygamy has an important benefit:

> Asia and Africa are inhabited by men of many colors: polygamy is the only efficient means of mixing them so that whites do not persecute the blacks, or blacks the whites. Polygamy has them born from the same mother or the same father; the black and the white, since they are brothers, sit together at the same table and see each other. Hence in the Orient no color pretends to be superior to another. But, to accomplish this, Muḥammad thought that four wives were sufficient.... When we will wish, in our colonies, to give liberty to the blacks and to destroy color prejudice, the legislator will authorize polygamy.[53]

Adolph A. Weinman, a German-born American sculptor, gave visual expression to the image of Muḥammad as lawgiver in his 1935 frieze in the main chamber of the U.S. Supreme Court. The Prophet is one of eighteen great lawgivers commemorated in a series that ranges from Hammurabi to John Marshall and includes Moses, Confucius, and Napoléon. Muḥammad bears an open Qur'ān in his left hand and, in his right, a sword (as do many of the rulers in the frieze).[54]

This image of Muḥammad as a great man, a statesman, and conqueror was a common trope in nineteenth- and twentieth-century Europe. It allowed a relatively objective and irenic appreciation of the importance of the Prophet and of Islam on the stage of world history,

[53] Ibid., 153.

[54] Architectural notes provided by the Supreme Court (http://www.supremecourtus.gov/about/north&southwalls.pdf) qualify the image as "a well-intentioned attempt by the sculptor, Adolph Weinman, to honor Muhammad and it bears no resemblance to Muhammad. Muslims generally have a strong aversion to sculptured or pictured representations of their Prophet."

Figure 7. Muḥammad between Charlemagne and Justinian, from the eighteen lawgivers in Adolph A. Weinman's frieze in the U.S. Supreme Court.

avoiding the bitter religious polemics that had so often colored European discourse on Islam. Yet by presenting Muḥammad as first and foremost a political and military leader, his role as an envoy of God and a model for Muslims was willfully avoided.

MUḤAMMAD, PROPHET FOR THE SONS OF ABRAHAM

In the twentieth century, some Christian writers rethought the role of Muḥammad in the divine plan. Instead of seeing Islam as hostile to Christian truth, they stressed the common truths recognized by both religions. Most of these writers saw Muḥammad as a positive (if at times imperfect) witness to Christian truth: Islam is hence a sort of preparation for the realization of Christian truth, an intermediate step that Muslims will transcend when they ultimately convert to Christianity. Some twentieth-century Christian writers, such as Hans Küng and Montgomery Watt, have gone further. For them, the world's great religions are not inferior to Christianity but equal to it: the Prophet Muḥammad showed his followers a spiritual path to enlightenment and salvation that is neither inferior nor superior to that of the Christian Church.

A few Europeans had previously recognized Muḥammad as a prophet; the sixteenth-century French Orientalist Guillaume Postel had affirmed that Muḥammad was a bona fide prophet and should be recognized as such by Christians.[55] But it is in the twentieth century, in the context of interreligious dialogue, that a number of Christians have called for recognition of the Prophet's positive role in the divine plan.

Louis Massignon (1883–1962) was a brilliant and prolific scholar of Arabic and Islam and a fervent Catholic. Massignon's writings are a strange mix of remarkable erudition, profound appreciation of Muslim piety and mysticism, and a polemical vision of Islam as an imperfect expression of Christianity.[56] For Massignon, Muḥammad was a sincere, divinely inspired leader who preached truth and brought his people to the worship of the one supreme God. He was by no means a false prophet but a negative prophet, a witness to indisputable but partial truths.

Various disciples of Massignon carried on his work. The Franciscan Giulio Basetti-Sani is the author of numerous books on the relations between Islam and Christianity: he tells of how he first accepted the standard Christian view of Muḥammad as "a sad instrument of Satan," yet eventually (thanks in no small part to his meeting with Massignon) came to see him as "a valid instrument for bringing about the reign of God" and called on Christians to recognize him as a prophet.[57] Yet for him, as for Massignon, Islam is only a partial truth, as it fails to recognize the divine nature of Christ. Basseti-Sani's goal, as expressed in the title of one of his books is to find "Jesus Christ hidden in the Qur'ān."[58]

Various twentieth-century authors go further than Massignon and his followers: Muḥammad is a prophet and Christians should recognize this. Montgomery Watt, the author of a landmark biographical study of the Prophet, concluded that Christians in dialogue with Muslims

[55] Guillaume Postel, Πανθενωςία (Basel, 1547?), 111, qtd. in W. Bouwsma, *Concordia Mundi: The Career and Thought of Guillaume Postel* (Cambridge, MA: Harvard University Press, 1957), 204–5.

[56] Jacques Waardenburg, *Islam dans le miroir de l'Occident; comment quelques orientalistes occidentaux se sont penchés sur l'Islam et se sont formé une image de cette religion*, 3rd ed. (Paris: Mouton, 1969), 141–8; Edward Said, *Orientalism* (New York: Random House, 1978), 263–74;G. Harpigny, *Islam et Christianisme selon Louis Massignon* (Louvain la Neuve: Homo Religiosus, 1981).

[57] Basetti-Sani, *Il Corano nella luce di Cristo: saggio per una reinterpretazione cristiana del libro sacro dell'Islam* (Bologna: EMI, 1972), 17n; English translation is *The Koran in the Light of Christ: A Christian Interpretation of the Sacred Book of Islam* (Chicago: Franciscan Herald Press, 1977). Basetti-Sani, *Islam nel piano della salvezza* (Fiesole: Edizioni Cultura della Pace, 1992), 351, qtd. in C. Troll, "Changing Catholic Views," in Waardenburg, *Islam and Christianity*, 46–8.

[58] Basetti-Sani, *Gesù Cristo nascosto nel Corano* (San Pietro in Cariano: Il Segno, 1994).

"should reject the distortions of the medieval image of Islam and should develop a positive appreciation of its values. This involves accepting Muḥammad as a religious leader through whom God has worked, and that is tantamount to holding that he is in some sense a prophet."[59]

But it is no doubt the Swiss Catholic theologian, Hans Küng, who has developed in greatest detail a theological argument for such recognition. Küng begins by noting the evolution of the church's position concerning the salvation of those outside its fold. The Council of Florence in 1442 declared that no one outside the Catholic Church could be saved but was damned to the eternal flames of hell. In 1962, however, Vatican II proclaimed that "those who, through no fault of their own, do not know the Gospel of Christ or his Church, but who nevertheless seek God with a sincere heart and, moved by grace, try in their actions to do his will as they know it through the dictates of their conscience – they too may achieve eternal salvation."[60] Hence, those outside the church, including Muslims, may reach heaven. Indeed, the council expressed in particular its admiration for its two monotheistic sister religions, Judaism and Islam, praising Muslims for adoring the One God and for honoring Christ and Mary. Yet, as Küng notes, Vatican II did not mention the name of Muḥammad. What should Christians think of him? Should they recognize him as a prophet? Küng asks his reader to compare Muḥammad with the Hebrew prophets of the Old Testament: Muḥammad's authority, like that of the prophets, came not from any official capacity but from a special relationship with God; he saw himself as the verbal instrument of God, addressing God's message to his people; he proclaimed God's unity and justice and demanded submission to his will; and he did all this in the midst of a spiritual and political crisis among his people. In all these things, Muḥammad acted just like the Hebrew prophets. Küng concludes:

> In truth, Muhammad was and is for persons in the Arabian world, and for many others, *the* religious reformer, lawgiver, and leader; the prophet *per se*. Basically Muhammad, who never claimed to be anything more than a human being, is more to those who follow him than a prophet is to us: he is a model for the mode of life that Islam strives to be. If the Catholic Church, according to the Vatican II "Declaration on Non-Christian Religions," "regards with esteem the Muslims," then the same

[59] W. Montgomery Watt, *Muslim-Christian Encounters: Perceptions and Misperceptions* (London: Routledge, 1991), 148.

[60] Vatican Council II, Lumen Gentium, no. 16.

> church must also respect the one whose name is embarrassingly absent from the same declaration, although he and he alone led the Muslims to pray to this one God, for through him this God "has spoken to humanity": Muhammad the prophet.[61]

This brief survey has touched on only a few of the hundreds of European writers who have written about the Prophet of Islam. In the twenty-first century, European scholars, journalists, novelists, and cartoonists continue to be fascinated with the figure of Islam; their portraits show the same ambivalent mix of revulsion, attraction, curiosity, fascination, and admiration.

For centuries, Islam has been Christendom's *frère ennemi:* a rival, neighbor civilization whose roots tapped deep into a common heritage of Greco-Roman-Persian antiquity and of Jewish monotheism. When Christians have reflected on Islam as a religion, they have often focused on its prophet and founder, making him either the embodiment of error or a symbol of religious freedom and tolerance. European discourse concerning Muḥammad is often best understood as a deforming mirror: it often tells us more about the hopes and fears of the writer than of the elusive figure of seventh-century Arabia.

Further reading

Arkoun, Mohammed, ed. *L'Histoire de l'islam et des musulmans en France.* Paris: Albin Michel, 2006.

Bennett, Clinton. *Victorian Images of Islam.* London: Grey Seal Books, 1992.

Burman, Thomas. *Reading the Qur'ān in Latin Christendom, 1140–1560.* Philadelphia: University of Pennsylvania Press, 2007.

Carnoy-Torābī, Dominique. *Représentations de l'islam dans la France du XVIIe siècle: la ville des tentations.* Paris: l'Harmattan, 1998.

Gunny, Ahmad. "Protestant Reactions to Islam in Late Seventeenth-Century French Thought." *French Studies* 40 (1986): 129–40.

Kedar, Benjamin. *Crusade and Mission: European Approaches toward the Muslims.* Princeton, NJ: Princeton University Press, 1984.

Kerr, David. "'He Walked in the Path of the Prophets': Toward Christian Theological Recognition of the Prophethood of Muḥammad." In *Christian-Muslim*

[61] Hans Küng, "Christianity and World Religions: Dialogue with Islam," in *Muslims in Dialogue: The Evolution of A Dialogue,* ed. Leonard Swidler (Lewiston, NY: Edwin Mellen Press, 1992), 3:161–75. See also Küng, *Islam: Past, Present and Future* (Oxford: Oneworld, 2007). Troll, "Changing Catholic Views," 56–61; David Kerr, "'He Walked in the Path of the Prophets': Toward Christian Theological Recognition of the Prophethood of Muḥammad," in *Christian-Muslim Encounters,* ed. Yvonne Haddad and W. Haddad (Gainesville: University Press of Florida, 1995), 426–46.

Encounters, edited by Yvonne Haddad and Wadi Haddad, 426–46. Gainesville: University Press of Florida, 1995.

Said, Edward. *Orientalism*. New York: Random House, 1978.

Tolan, John. *Saracens: Islam in the Medieval European Imagination*. New York: Columbia University Press, 2002.

Tolan, John. *Sons of Ishmael: Muslims through European Eyes in the Middle Ages*. Gainesville: University Press of Florida, 2008.

Waardenburg, Jacques. *Islam dans le miroir de l'Occident; comment quelques orientalistes occidentaux se sont penchés sur l'Islam et se sont formé une image de cette religion*, 3rd ed. Paris: Mouton, 1969.

Waardenburg, Jacques, ed. *Islam and Christianity: Mutual Perceptions since the mid-20th Century*. Leuven: Peeters, 1998.

Watt, W. Montgomery. *Muslim-Christian Encounters: Perceptions and Misperceptions*. London: Routledge, 1991.

12 Religious biography of the Prophet Muḥammad in twenty-first-century Indonesia

ANNA M. GADE

Rasul Emang COOL (*The Prophet Is Totally COOL*) is an Indonesian book for children by an author named Bambang Q-Anees. It was published in 2006 by DAR! Mizan, a division of a well-known publisher, the Mizan Group. The book's title rhymes in spoken Indonesian, and the word *emang* is slang for the emphatic term *memang* ("truly," "certainly," "for real"). Without breaking the boundaries of its own print medium, *Rasul Emang COOL* references text messaging and electronic format in its diction, layout, and illustrations, such as a recurring visual theme of computer screens featuring the English words *Rasulullah Instant Messages.*

The opening chapter, "Chatting 1," is subtitled "A Letter from Muhammad." The first page begins, in Indonesian:

> One day, you get a special letter. This letter contains an unusual request. This is what it says . . . [1]

Turning the page, inset with an archaic-looking font and superimposed on a border image of crumpled paper, is the following paragraph:

> *Assalamu alaikum*! Hi. I am Muhammad Rasulullah! I miss you. Can I come over to your house sometime? I really want to *ngobrol bareng* ["hang out and chat"] with you. We can get up in the morning together, go to school, and of course get together with

[1] Bambang Q-Anees, *Rasul Emang COOL* (Bandung: DAR!Mizan, 2006), 23.

I am grateful for the support of the Faculty of the Humanities and Social Sciences, Victoria University, Wellington, New Zealand, in 2008. Many thanks for the assistance of Dr. Zainal Abidin Bagir, executive director, Centre for Religious and Cross-Cultural Studies, and Gajah Mada University, Yogyakarta, Indonesia; Dr. Moch. Nur Ichwan, Fakultas Dakwah, UIN Kalijaga, Yogyakarta, Indonesia; Dr. H. M. Shaleh Putuhena, former rector, UIN Alauddin, Makassar, Indonesia; and Ms. Nur Saktiningrum, M. Hum., Faculty of Cultural Sciences, Gajah Mada University. I am responsible for the content of this chapter. Translations are my own.

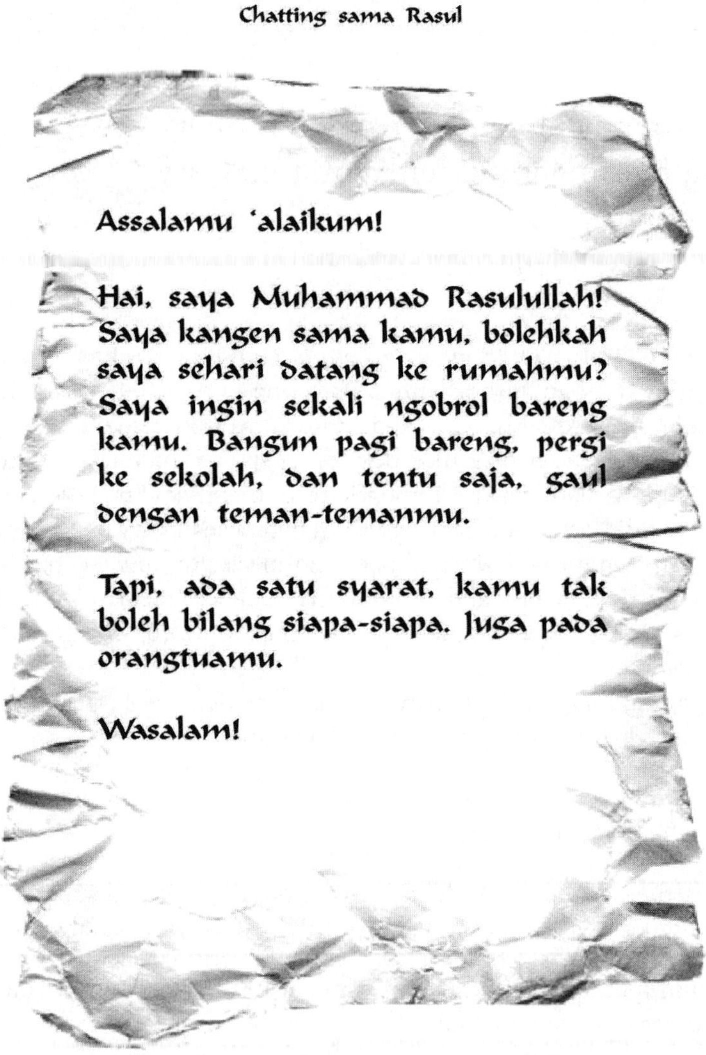

Chatting sama Rasul

Assalamu 'alaikum!

Hai, saya Muhammad Rasulullah! Saya kangen sama kamu, bolehkah saya sehari datang ke rumahmu? Saya ingin sekali ngobrol bareng kamu. Bangun pagi bareng, pergi ke sekolah, dan tentu saja, gaul dengan teman-temanmu.

Tapi, ada satu syarat, kamu tak boleh bilang siapa-siapa. Juga pada orangtuamu.

Wasalam!

Figure 8. Illustration from *Rasul Emang COOL*, by Bambang Q-Anees. Reproduced with permission from Mizan Publishing House.

> all your friends. But, there's one condition. You can't tell anyone. Not even your parents. *Wasalam*![2]

At first glance to the English-language reader, this may seem like some newer forms of global Christian piety or ministry, such as having a friend

[2] Ibid., 24.

in Jesus. However, the practice of generating a sense of personal closeness and engagement with the Prophet Muḥammad in contemporary Indonesia is based more, I think, on the past of Islam than on the present of other faiths. The message is consistent with some of the oldest Islamic traditions of piety and veneration of the Prophet that seek to render his presence intimate.

A presentation like this, common in Indonesia and aimed at youths in its tone and its content, is also direct extension of Muslim *dakwah* ("outreach") strategies from previous decades. During Ramaḍān, for example, it is now popular for preachers to hold sessions in which they chat and *ngobrol bareng* (a Javanese term) with local youths about religious issues and other concerns. In addition, prophetic piety specifically has been a focus of such programs of religious revitalization in Indonesia today.

Rasul Emang COOL teaches proper interaction with others while maintaining good morals (e.g., being kind and considerate). The final chapters of the book introduce *ḥadīth*s and other authoritative statements that draw on Islamic religious sciences. The book's conclusion, however, renders the figure of the Prophet Muḥammad with an added degree of proximity: not just as a friend to have but also an example to follow in personal conduct. The Prophet is a figure to try to resemble, especially in terms of becoming more *sahabat*, that is, in terms of how to have friends and to be one to others.

In *Rasul Emang COOL* and countless other Indonesian works, themes from *dakwah* and education have blended into new presentations of the life of the Prophet for the purpose of theory, practice, and piety. The book also represents some of the key trends in how the Prophet Muḥammad is imagined globally as an active religious model: as proximate, engaged, and educative. The modern concern with addressing pluralism and difference through totalized terms (e.g., Islam) has led to an emphasis on the Prophet as a religious model of interaction and dialogue in global Islam and in Indonesia.

The materials presented here draw on print media popularly available in Yogyakarta, Java, in 2008. Many of the books were published only recently, as turnover is rapid. The modern nonfiction accounts of the life of the Prophet Muḥammad have circulated across boundaries of language, region, and even religious tradition. Many of the translated materials relating to the Prophet's biography available in Indonesian in 2008 were originally published in Arabic. In Muslim Indonesia in the twenty-first century, translations of relatively recent biographies by the English-language authors Karen Armstrong, Tariq Ramadan, and Martin

Lings, as well as standards by W. Montgomery Watt and Muḥammad Haykal,[3] are found on the front table of shops alongside the new titles that are continually emerging and circulating regionally. Among Indonesian accounts, there is a tight loop between reception and production in new modes; when they are rendered in the language Bahasa Indonesia, I consider works available in Indonesia to be Indonesian expressions of global Islam.

GLOBAL ACCOUNTS IN CIRCULATION AND TRANSLATION

When Muḥammad Ḥusayn Haykal (d. 1956) first published his book, *Ḥayāt Muḥammad* (*The Life of Muḥammad*) in Arabic in 1935, it already anticipated several major trends of modern Muslim *Sīra*. For instance, Haykal's biography layered new expectations of methodological rigor onto the traditional presentation of *Sīra* through the author's own claim to have undertaken *ḥadīth* criticism. Although he writes that he viewed his own work as a response to Orientalists in the service of imperialism, Haykal's concern with the historical Muḥammad was also consistent with European trends in religious biography and the field of documentary history in the late-colonial era.

To varying degrees, modern Muslim religious biographies of the Prophet have tended either in the direction of historical accuracy and textual verification or toward an accessible and engaging narrative for the reader to enjoy. Although an engaging narrative sometimes means glossing over nuances in the complicated source texts, this is not always the case, especially when citations may be fewer, more selective, and possibly presented with more depth. Because of this, both tendencies (i.e., rigor and readability) may even be evident simultaneously in some accounts, such as Haykal's.

Haykal's nontraditional subject headings allow for easy summary and absorption of his relatively long text. Haykal also departed from

[3] English-language editions of these works are as follows: Karen Armstrong, *Muhammad: A Biography of the Prophet* (London: Phoenix, 2001); Armstrong, *Muhammad: A Prophet for Our Time* (New York: Atlas Books/HarperCollins, 2006); Tariq Ramadan, *In the Footsteps of the Prophet: Lessons from the Life of Muhammad* (Oxford: Oxford University Press, 2007); Ramadan, *The Messenger: The Meanings of the Life of Muhammad* (London: Allen Lane, 2007); Martin Lings, *Muhammad: His Life Based on the Earliest Sources* (London: Islamic Texts Society and Allen and Unwin, 1983); William Montgomery Watt, *Muhammad: Prophet and Statesman* (London: Oxford University Press, 1961); Muhammad Ḥusayn Haykal, *Life of Muhammad* [Arabic title: *Ḥayāt Muḥammad*], 8th ed., trans. Isma'il al-Faruqi (Plainfield, IN: American Trust Publications, 1997).

established formats of classical *Sīra* by including answers to questions he considered relevant to his modern readers. He also revised expected parts of the story, particularly episodes that he determined could not be verified historically. An example of this is Haykal's treatment of the episode of the Night Journey and ascent of the Prophet (*isrāʿ* and *miʿrāj*, respectively, reckoned to have occurred in 621 CE), about which Haykal concludes that Muḥammad's "experience may have been of the soul and not of the body." This allegorization is not the standard interpretation, although it is consistent with "modern science," as Haykal notes, as well as with traditions of Muslim mysticism and philosophy, which are the kind of sources he uses to support his own potentially controversial perspective in the text.[4]

In addition to qualities of accessibility and authenticity, Haykal's work prefigured two other trends of modern religious biography of the Prophet Muḥammad. First, it introduced nontraditional themes, such as gender, anticipating the shift to topicality in contemporary Muslim religious biography. Second, Haykal's biography was self-consciously a response to difference, showing an awareness of global others, seen starkly in the contrasts Haykal draws between Christian and Islamic civilizations.

Haykal's preface to the first edition of his work (there have been many editions published since) indicates an acute self-awareness with respect to the Orientalist tradition, both academic and political. As was his Egyptian near contemporary Muḥammad ʿAbduh (d. 1905), Haykal was a modernist concerned with the place of Islam and nation in a fast-approaching postcolonial order. Much of the discussion in his preface considers Christianity and Islam in this light. Haykal writes in the preface, "The objective of colonialism is to destroy in these [Muslim] countries the freedom of opinion, the freedom to seek truth." He then explains that resistance to this hegemony was the impetus for the present biographical project, focused on Islam and its Prophet:

> It was this consideration [colonialism and its effects on Islam] which led me at the end of the road of life to the study of the life of Muḥammad, the carrier of the message of Islām and the target of Christian attacks on the one side and of Muslim conservatives on the other. But I have resolved that this will be a scientific study, developed on the western modern method and written for the sake of truth alone.[5]

[4] Haykal, *Life of Muhammad*, 139–47.

[5] Haykal, *Life of Muhammad*, preface to 1st ed. (1976), trans. Faruqi, li.

Haykal next outlines how his method is to be viewed as a blend of the old and the new:

> I began to study the history of Muḥammad and to look more closely into the *Sīrah* of Ibn Hishām, the *Tabaqāt* of Ibn Saʿd, the *Maghāzi* of Wāqidī, and *the Spirit of Islam* [*sic*] of Sayyid Ameer Ali. Then I took care to study what some orientalists have written on the subject such as the work of... Washington Irving.... I was quite hesitant to publish my thoughts because I feared the storm which the conservatives and their followers who believe in superstitions might raise.... It was the encouragement of these friends [professors in the Islamic institutions of learning] that stirred me to search for the best means by which to analyze the biography of the Prophet.[6]

Haykal continues, presenting the guidelines he used for authenticating selected material; for example, he writes that he used the "occasions of revelation" of verses extensively to historicize Qurʾānic material. In the actual text, however, Haykal's explicit citations from the sources are almost entirely from the Qurʾān, and only occasionally does he cite a *ḥadīth* report.

Haykal's *Sīra* recounts the standard story of the life of Muḥammad but also has some lengthy digressions. An example of this is the book's introductory material on Near Eastern civilizations, materials much like those that probably would also have been found in biblical scholarship of the time. In addition, Haykal offers the occasional excursus on topics familiar to the colonial polemics of Orientalism and Occidentalism. An example of this is his treatment of the subject of gender, a highly charged symbolic sphere in the colonial era and after. Haykal interrupts the flow of the story, for instance, after the Battle of the Trench (5/627) to evaluate gender relations and apparently gendered expression among pre-Islamic, polytheistic Arabs. This is followed by a page and a half of material under the topic heading, "Women in Other Civilizations" (by which is meant, mostly, women in the so-called West). He writes, "[W]e do know that [at the rise of Islam] Europe was wallowing in such darkness that its family structure stood little higher than the most primitive levels of human organization."[7] Haykal then gives a quick historical survey, from Roman law to the European Christianity of his day, much along the same line of argument. Then, as suddenly as this discussion began, it ends, as the story of the life of the Prophet resumes with the narrative

6 Ibid.

7 Haykal, *Life of Muhammad*, 320.

leading up to the event of the Treaty of Ḥudaybiyya, including mention of the domestic relations in the house of the Prophet in that time period. Haykal's introduction of a nontraditional topical focus (here, gender) prefigures a new genre of topical *Sīra* that has been developed in Muslim Indonesia and elsewhere in more recent times.

Haykal's work circulated globally and was received in different ways in different Muslim settings. In his own context (Egypt and the Arab world in general), part of Haykal's immediate impact was to help inspire an Islamization of literature and social science. More widely, *Ḥayāt Muḥammad* was eagerly sought out in the 1940s and 1950s by Muslims and others as a reliable, authentic biography of the Prophet written by a professed Muslim. Publication of the English translation was delayed for some decades, but in the Muslim-majority world, its influence was direct and immediate.[8] For Muslim biographers and historians sympathetic to his approach and concerns, Haykal offered a model for a new Islamic genre of scholarship premised on historical authenticity and revitalized social concerns.

In Indonesia, Haykal's model and approach continue to be developed and enhanced, especially in the fields of teaching and learning. For example, in 2008, a work available in a book market known for academic textbooks was *Biografi Rasulullah: Sebuah Studi Analitis berdasarkan Sumber-Sumber yang Otentik* (*The Biography of the Prophet: An Analytic Study Based on the Authentic Sources*).[9] It is a translation of an Arabic work, and the Indonesian edition takes up more than a thousand printed pages. The front matter states that the book is intended for teachers and for students who want to study a trusted history. The introduction includes a survey of classical *Sīra* literature, which is natural, as the work actually is a compilation of material drawn from many standard sources. Its presentation evidences rigorous *ḥadīth* scholarship, providing explicit references to traditions, including occasions of revelation, which Haykal does not cite overtly in his text. The work would indeed be useful as a handbook for a modern Islamic university

8 An Indonesian author who replicated Haykal's work was H. M. H. Hamid al-Husaini. Husaini was born in 1910 and passed away in 2002. He ran a newspaper in the cosmopolitan Javanese city of Surabaya in the late 1930s. In the 1970s, Husaini published many books about Muḥammad and the early history of Islam under his name, such as the popular book *Riwayat Kehidupan Nabi Besar Muhammad SAW* (*The Biography of the Prophet Muḥammad*) and the later work *Rumah Tangga Nabi Muhammad SAW* (*The Household of the Prophet Muḥammad*).

9 Mahdi Rizqullah Ahmad, *Biografi Rasulullah: Sebuah Studi Analitis berdasarkan Sumber-Sumber yang Otentik* (Arabic title as transcribed in the book: *As-Sirah An-Nabawiyyah fi Dhau'i al-Mashadir al-Ashliyyah: Dirasah Tahliliyyah*), trans. Yessi H. M. Basyaruddin (Jakarta: Qisthi Press, 2005).

student, particularly one who was following the standard course curriculum in the formal subjects of Ḥadīth and *tafsīr* (Qur'ān interpretation) concurrently.

Evident across bookstores in Indonesia was another compatible model for the biography of the Prophet Muḥammad, one that abandons the claim to objectivity in the tradition of Haykal, yet is nevertheless consistent with his accessible "renarrativization." This voice is as old as that of the storyteller in Islam, but in the modern period, it also represents revitalizing trends toward access and engagement. It may also reflect the push of strengthening market forces.[10] For example, some Indonesian materials focusing on female companions of the Prophet, such as his first wife, Khadīja (some of them translations from Arabic-language popular literature), are prone to a subtle process of pious fictionalization. These accounts, which are only indirectly about the Prophet himself, afford a sentimentalized frame for presentation, although they still offer powerful biographical models from the original community of the Prophet Muḥammad.

The "biographical process" in Indonesia has also moved another step beyond Haykal in that religious readers do not just study the model of the Prophet Muḥammad through religious biography;[11] rather, they seek actively to internalize and to follow it. In Indonesian materials, the life of Muḥammad is embraced especially as a modern model for bridging difference. At least two developments have made this ongoing process of refocusing possible, at least in terms of formal features of the texts. One aspect of this shift has been thematic, that is, an awareness of diversity and its implied modern choice, whether among systems or even within a modern system (e.g., Islam). Another aspect of continuing biographical transformation is structural: the adaptive and creative use of the authoritative sources, that is, *ḥadīth* and narrative excerpted from classical *Sīra*.

"THE BIOGRAPHICAL PROCESS": ḤADĪTH AND SĪRA IN TWENTY-FIRST-CENTURY INDONESIA

Religious biography of the Prophet Muḥammad in Indonesia tends to follow typical structures as part of an ongoing, pious biographical

[10] One such account (promoted online as its portrayal being so vivid that "it makes you smell the frankincense"), widely available in Indonesian in 2008, was the translation of a work by Barnaby Rogerson, *The Prophet Muhammad: A Biography* (Mahwah, NJ: HiddenSpring, 2003). It is necessary in these notes to point out that what Gade is writing down is the Arabic transcription as it appears in the book, since it does not conform to standard Arabic transcription and occasionally also has mistakes as compared with the standard Arabic.

[11] The term was coined by Frank Reynolds and Donald Capps in *The Biographical Process: Studies in the History and Psychology of Religion* (The Hague: Mouton, 1976).

process. First, *ḥadīth* collections remain as common in Indonesia today as they have been in the past; offered with commentary, they present a particular facet of the character or life of the Prophet. Second, there are readable chronologies illustrated with episodes from *Sīra* and *ḥadīths*. Third, there are treatments of new or nontraditional themes, such as diversity and difference, which use *ḥadīth* material as support. In each of these types of modern religious biographies of the Prophet, *ḥadīth*s fulfill the expectation of narrative detail and authoritative accuracy on the one hand, and they may also provide a basis to present imaginative new topics and structures of religious biography on the other hand.

In the first category, there are Indonesian accounts of the life of the Prophet Muḥammad that are collections of *ḥadīths* compiled along the lines of exemplary features of the Prophet's conduct. These modern works typically offer a fresh mixture of *ḥadīth* citations and quotes from the Qur'ān, thus evidencing a relatively new and hybrid genre of *ḥadīth* compilation, even though they may still appear traditional. The topicality of arrangement and thematic selection from sources are what is modern about these works, not the familiar *ḥadīth*s they contain. For example, *Muhammad: Sang Agung Sepanjang Dunia: Sebuah Sirah Nabawiyah dari Sisi yang Jarang Terungkap oleh Para Penulis Sira* (*Muḥammad: The Greatest in All the History of the World: A Biography of the Prophet from the Sources That Have Rarely Been Considered by the Compilers of the Sīra*),[12] a translation from an Arabic work, is a readable book that is broken into short sections, each with a catchy heading. It was available at many bookshops, from the major chain store Gramedia to independent sellers and stalls. Sources are cited explicitly, but on examination, they do not actually appear to be so rare after all; however, what the work does offer is a fresh mixture of *ḥadīth* citations and quotes from the Qur'ān, as in the case of Haykal's work. Other compilations of *ḥadīth*s commonly seen in Indonesia in 2008 emphasized even more particularized characteristics of the Prophet. Of this type there were many Arabic works in translation, such as *Nasehat Nasehat Nabawiyyah* (*Prophetic Admonition*), which addresses issues in areas of questionable personal conduct, such as the permissibility of smoking cigarettes.[13]

[12] Syekh Abdullah Najib Salim, *Muhammad: Sang Agung Sepanjang Dunia: Sebuah Sirah Nabawiyah dari Sisi yang Jarang Terungkap oleh Para Penulis Sirah* (Arabic title transcribed as: *Mawaqif an-Insaniyyah fi As-Sirah An-Nabawiyya*), trans. Mahmud Salim and Sholihin (Jakarta: Mirqat Publishing, 2007).

[13] Shaikh Muhammad Bin Jamil Zainu, *Nasehat Nasehat Nabawiyyah* (Arabic title transcribed as: *Kaifa Nurabbi Auladana Wa Ma Huwa Wajibul-Ana' Wal-Abna'*), trans.

This type of religious biography of the Prophet Muḥammad was usually cast in terms of certain roles, particularly the Prophet as a healer, as a diplomat, and especially as an educator. For example, *Rasulullah Sang Dokter* (*The Prophet, the Great Physician*) is a translation of an Arabic work.[14] The author is introduced as an "expert in biology and physiology." It is structured as another topical arrangement of *ḥadīths*, focusing on what has long been considered an autonomous field of Islamic knowledge, Prophetic medical science. Many other works featured the theme of Muḥammad as a healer; some of these were not so much compilations of *ḥadīths* as thematic reflections on illness and healing from an Islamic and Prophetic perspective. This market for books on the theme of Muḥammad as a healer is no doubt driven as vigorously now as it has been for centuries by universal human needs to address conditions of illness and suffering.

Traditional sources that circulate globally have long been received in Muslim Southeast Asia in terms of regional patterns of Islamic tradition and piety. Classical Prophetic religious biography includes recitational texts that praise and venerate the Prophet Muḥammad, especially texts in the *mawlid* cycle.[15] Related devotional genres include collections of prayers and invocations, as well as other materials praising the Prophet as the "Perfect Man." An example of ongoing adaptation of this tradition of religious biography is the contemporary Indonesian work *Kisah-Kisah Hikmat Mukjizat Rasulullah SAW* (*Accounts of the Miracles of the Prophet*).[16] This book presents episodes of the miracles of Muḥammad, some of which have not always been defined by Muslims as miracles (e.g., the defeat of various enemies, the Qur'ānically attested intervention in

Abul-Hasan (Yogyakarta: Maktabah al-Hanif, 2005). Another example of a general work of this type is Sayyid Muhammad Alwy Al-Malıky, *Insan Kamil: Sosok Keteladanan Muhammad SAW*, trans. Hasan Baharun (Surabaya: Bina Ilmu, n.d.). The title translates as "The Perfect Man: A Framework for the Exemplary Model of the Prophet."

14 Muhammad Sayyid Abdul Basith, *Rasulullah Sang Dokter* (Arabic title transcribed as: *Ath-Thib Al-Wisa'i min Al-Qur'an was As-Sunnah*), trans. H. Masnur Hamzah and H. Habiburrahim (Solo: Tiga Serangkai, 2006). Another of many such works popularly available was Mahmud Syalaby, *Muhammad Sang Penyembu Untuk Penyakit Fisik dan Psikis* (Arabic title transcribed as: *Mu'alij ar-Ruh wa al-Jasad*), trans. Muhammad Edy Waluyo (Yogyakarta: Mitra Pustaka, 2007).

15 See Marion Katz's essay in Chapter 7 of this volume. The *mawlid* tradition has been exceptionally strong in the Malay-speaking world, and many of the first Islamic texts in circulation in the early modern era were in fact variants of the principal *mawlid* texts. Today these are bound in volumes of four separate works and are readily available in Islamic bookshops.

16 Samsul Munir Amin, *Kisah-Kisah Hikmat Mukjizat Rasulullah SAW* (Jakarta: AMZA, 2006).

the victorious Battle of Badr). The *hikmah* (wisdom or interpretation) that follows each case takes the form of a short, moralized explanation of the occurrence. This usually focuses on how the event brought others to Islam, and thus propagated the faith, or discusses how it presents an instructive model for personal conduct or reflection. The account's pious theme (e.g., miracles) and its formal features (e.g., the use of *ḥadīth*) allow the book's expression to expand beyond older formats.

A second category of religious biography was formally less *ḥadīth* driven, even as it embraced the authority of the past. This was readable *Sīra* that stretched traditional narrative style toward accessibility and practical application. These materials included many works that were written for children, often with each historicized chapter of the book ending with a summary of main teachings. This would frame the content thematically with a new voice (that of the textbook), which was further reinforced by study and practice questions.[17]

Examples of the Indonesian adaptation of the standard narrative of *Sīra* to make it fun or engaging reading also included a series of books on various Islamic prophets, with the book about Muḥammad being the last among the collection of twenty-five thin volumes. The little book *Nabi Muhammad* (from *Seri Para Nabi*, or the Prophets' Series) had its third printing in 2006 (first edition 2004).[18] It pushes the genre of nonfiction prophetic biography strongly toward narrativity and even a kind of fictionalization in the manner through which it dramatizes episodes reported in *ḥadīth*. It tells the whole story of the Prophet's life engagingly, giving some quotes from the Qur'ān and material known from *ḥadīth*; striking, however, is that much dialogue has also been provided and embellished for the figures in the story. The authority of established source text here is what affords the very process of its own creative embellishment.

For example, on the episode of the courtship of Khadīja and the Prophet Muḥammad, *Nabi Muhammad* reads:

> At that time, Khadīja was already forty years old. Many of the tribe of the Quraysh in Mecca had tried to propose marriage to her. But she had never bothered to consider them at all. She always just said no to them.

17 For example, Hamid Ahmad Al-Thahir, *Sejarah Hidup Muhammad Untuk Anak*, trans. Fathurrahman Abdul Hamid (Bandung: Irsyad Baitus Salam, 2006).

18 Hilmi Ali Sya'ban, *Nabi Muhammad*, 3rd ed. (Arabic title transcribed as: *Muhammad Sallallahu alaihi wa Sallam*), trans. Tholhatul Choir Wafa (Yogyakarta: Mitri Pustaka, 2006).

Contrary to all this, Khadīja felt something entirely different for Muḥammad. Secretly she carried a longing to marry Muḥammad that stirred deep in her heart. She was not outspoken enough to speak the truth [*sejujurnya*] thundering inside her. Finally, she chose "Nafisah binti Muniyah" as the person to convey her wish to Muḥammad.

"What makes you [informal] not want to get married, O Muḥammad?" That was how Nafisah started off right away when she came over to his house.

"How could I [informal] manage it, since at the moment I don't have the money [*bekal*]"?

"You [polite form] are a youth full of charm [*pesona*]. How about if you could get married to a woman [*putri*] who was both rich and beautiful, would you want that?"

"Who is she?"

"She is Khadīja. Khadīja would like very much to marry you, if you would agree. I have been sent here to tell you this."

Muḥammad bent his head down for a moment. He tried to weigh all sides of the offer. Deep in his thoughts, he wanted to marry Khadīja too. It was not long before he had replied yes to the request.[19]

The main outline of the account and even most of the words of the exchange are to be found in the sources. The exchange is not found in the classical *Sīra* by Ibn Isḥāq, however, where Khadīja puts her proposal directly to the Prophet herself.[20] The dialogue instead corresponds to the account given by Muḥammad Ibn Saʿd, a scholar in ninth-century Baghdad. Ibn Saʿd reports that it was Nafīsa who proposed to Muḥammad as an intermediary, and he presents the exchange along the basic lines here.[21]

[19] Hilmi ʿAli Syaʿban, *Nabi Muhammad*, 91–2.

[20] ʿAbd al-Malik Ibn Hishām, *The Life of Muhammad: A Translation of Ibn Ishāq's Sīrat Rasūl Allāh*, 6th ed., trans. Alfred Guillaume (Oxford: Oxford University Press, 1980), 82.

[21] An English-language translation of the relevant passage from the *Ṭabaqāt* of Ibn Saʿd is found in Norman Calder, Jawid Ahmad Mojaddedi, and Andrew Rippin, trans. and eds., *Classical Islam: A Sourcebook of Religious Literature* (London: Routledge, 2003), 31. Other classical variants of the story identify Nafīsa alternatively as Nufaysa and as bint Munabbih or bint Umayyah; many accounts report that the Prophet discussed Khadīja's proposal with his uncle and protector Abū Ṭālib before accepting it.

The dialogue is thus apparently inspired by classical tradition, at least as it had developed by the third century. At the same time, the Indonesian source also diverges completely from Ibn Saʿd's account after the name Khadīja is revealed. The descriptive and emotive material about Khadīja's deep feelings of secret love, as well as the Prophet's consideration and response to her proposal, is a pious, affective addition. Haykal offers a similarly interactive and sentimentalized account in his text, and this may very well have been the direct source for the Indonesian account.[22] In any case, however, this is a relatively long account that is drawn out dramatically in the relatively short Indonesian book *Nabi Muhammad*, ascribing a fictionalized world of feeling to the revered figures of the Prophet Muḥammad and Khadīja.

A third major category of Indonesian religious biography comprises works that are structured entirely around a theme or an idea and do not take the form of a story or a grouping of *ḥadīths*. These materials selectively deploy examples and episodes from the life story of the Prophet for illustration and authentication. This genre tends to develop new and emergent themes and topics of Muslim religious biography. For example, it includes a popular genre of self-help books, which in Indonesia readily spans religious as well as other motivational genres. A more traditional work of this type, in translation from Arabic, is *Bukan Manusia Besi: Sisi Manusiawi Muhammad SAW* (*No Man of Iron: The Human Side of the Prophet Muḥammad*),[23] which features the social and spiritual challenges the Prophet had to overcome. Other works of this type consider, for example, the theme of material wealth, often advising the reader to accept challenging circumstances and limitations (rather than reaching for the "abundance" or "prosperity" that other nonreligious works on money and self-help emphasize).[24]

Reflecting a global trend in nonreligious inspirational materials is the motivational work *Manajemen Hidup Rasulullah* (*The Life*

[22] Haykal, *Life of Muhammad*, 62. Note Haykal's own mention of his use of the source by Ibn Saʿd, cited previously.

[23] Husein Mu'nis, *Bukan Manusia Besi: Sisi Manusiawi Muhammad SAW* (Arabic title-transcribed as: *Al-Tarikh Al-Shihi Al-Rasul*), trans. A. Khotib (Jakarta: Bening Publishing, 2004).

[24] There is, for example, the book published in 2007, Ummi Alhan Ramadhan Mazayasyah, *Mengapa Muhammad Tidak Memilih Kaya Raya: 10 Teladan Rasulullah SAW Menikmati Kesederhanaan* (Semarang: Qudsi Media, 2007). The words of the title mean, "Why the Prophet Was Not Wealthy: Ten Examples of How the Prophet Appreciated Simplicity." It includes traditional material about the asceticism of the Prophet, such as how the Prophet was world rejecting, how he never acted as if he felt sorry for himself, and so on.

Management of the Prophet),[25] a translation of an Arabic title. The book highlights strategies for presenting a winning persona that may result in promotion and opportunities for leadership, as well as the innovative techniques of problem solving for which successful people are recognized. It includes flow charts, worksheets, and bulleted checklists.

Each chapter begins by describing the named characteristic to be cultivated, such as *disiplin* or becoming more *kreatif* and *inovatif*. Then, examples from the life of the Prophet illustrate his exemplary model in the given area. Next come activities for the reader, as if in a workshop breakout session of a corporate seminar, such as hypothetical scenarios for the reader to imagine in his or her own life or workplace, or prompts to list aspects of one's personal or professional life experience that could be more disciplined, creative, and innovative, and so on.

Such idealized characteristics promote new parameters for moral comportment, such as the *motivasi* to work hard, as well as outside-the-box *ijtihad* in solving problems. Throughout the book, the use of *ḥadīth* and episodes from the Prophet's life signals a legitimate Islamic basis, even as the model of the Prophet extends to new areas of behavior and life management. More generally, *Manajemen Hidup Rasulullah* represents contemporary trends in its invitation to embrace the model of the Prophet Muḥammad in all aspects of life, including the workplace. Such processes of global Muslim religious biography are apparent especially in an Indonesian emphasis on teaching, learning, and interaction as religious people reach out to encounter others, Muslim and non-Muslim, as the Prophet would.

THE MODEL OF THE PROPHET IN A PLURAL WORLD

Since at least the era of Muḥammad Haykal, new global genres of the Prophet's religious biography locate Islam in the context of other messages that reflect plurality and difference, including messages that may even take pluralism as their main theme. For example, Karen Armstrong had authored two English-language biographies popularly available in Indonesia in translation in 2008. The first, *Muhammad: A Biography of the Prophet* (1991), is a standard narrative that, like Haykal's work, offers new headings for information. It anticipated questions in non-Muslim settings such as (in this case) the Satanic Verses. At the time of its publication, the Salman Rushdie affair would have been well known

[25] Muhammad Ahmad Abdul Jawwad, *Manajemen Hidup Rasulullah* (Arabic title transcribed as: *Asrar At-Tamayiz Al-Idary wa Al-Mahary fi Hayah Al-Rasul*), trans. H. Nor Hasanuddin (Bandung: Media Qalbu, 2005).

and probably a topic of keen interest among the book's English-language readership.

Armstrong's other work, *Muhammad: A Prophet for Our Time* (published in 2006), was widely promoted in Indonesia in translation in 2008, and it is much shorter. The heavy pages of the English-language edition are bound with uneven edges in a style that is typical of the industry's marketing of edifying and spiritual, nightstand products. The series in which it appears places Muḥammad on the list of "Eminent Lives," not one Prophet among many as in the Islamic tradition but one "eminent life" among many in the tradition of the European Enlightenment. The series list (with works by various authors) includes culture heroes: William Shakespeare, Ludwig van Beethoven and George Balanchine, as well as the American presidents George Washington, Thomas Jefferson, and Ulysses S. Grant.

A modern emphasis in both Muslim and non-Muslim accounts of the Prophet has been a humanizing focus on personal ethics and conduct; in Muslim settings, this trend (if it is indeed to be seen as only a modern one) can be traced back to the works of figures such as Muḥammad ʿAbduh. Tariq Ramadan's two recent works on the life of the Prophet bridge old boundaries of genre and of the symbolic divide of East and West while focusing emphatically on the theme of moral conduct. His reflective book, widely available in Indonesia in 2008, *In the Footsteps of the Prophet: Lessons from the Life of Muhammad*, highlights events from *Sīra* such as the opening of the breast of Muḥammad and his Night Journey and ascent, encompassing the pious tradition of venerating the Prophet in spiritualized modes. Blending long-accepted expectations like these with new global and pluralist sensibilities, the work highlights the Prophet's internal experience (e.g., dreams, hardships, inspirations). The work thus simultaneously presents Muḥammad as the model, perfect man of Islamic tradition and views his as an eminent life that any cultivated global citizen may appreciate, and from which he or she may derive an instructive example.

The final pages of Ramadan's book praise the Prophet, a beloved and old mode that is here expressed in an updated style and language. The following excerpt appears after pages of discussion that consider the life of the Prophet as a model and a guide for social justice, gender relations, and good parenting. Under the subject heading "Freedom and Love," Ramadan writes of the Prophet Muḥammad:

> An elect among the inhabitants of this earth, he concealed neither his fragility nor his doubts; in fact, God had, very early on,

> made him doubt himself so that he should never henceforth doubt his own need for Him, and shown him the reality of his failings so that he should seek His perfect Grace and remain indulgent toward his fellow human beings.... However, absolutely everything in his life was an instrument of renewal and transformation, from the slightest detail to the greatest events. The Muslim faithful, believers of any faith, and all who study Muhammad's life regardless of personal religious belief can derive teachings from this, this reaching toward the message and the light of faith.[26]

Part of the power of the emulative model, as presented here by Ramadan, is that practically anyone (i.e., "all who study Muḥammad's life regardless of personal religious belief") can claim it, regardless of the firmness of his or her faith conviction or even what is his or her own faith community, if any. This universality, with its natural ambiguity, must explain part of the wide appeal of the work.

In Indonesia, other works developed even more significantly the ideal of Prophet as a public diplomat, conflict resolver, and social leader of a plural community. Such a modern biographical theme was established in global circulation by W. Montgomery Watt's work *Muhammad: Prophet and Statesman*, which is still popularly available in Indonesia in translation. In addition, the modern religious biography that was perhaps the most widely available across secular and religious contexts alike in 2008 was titled *Muhammad for the Global Village: Muhammad Chahaya Dunia* (the Indonesian part of the title translates as "Muḥammad, the Light of the World").[27] The book is a translation of an original Arabic work, *Muḥammad li-l-qarya al-ʿalamiya* (*Muḥammad for the Global Village*), by Muhammad al-Hasyimi Al-Hamidi. The book's jacket identifies the author as a radio-show personality, born in Tunis in 1964, with degrees from the School of Oriental and African Studies in London.

The apparent popularity of this title, *Muhammad for the Global Village*, suggests a keen interest in the Muslim-majority world of Indonesia in imagining the whole world to be Muḥammad's global village, as if globalization has been a long process extending and universalizing the original community established in Islamic Medina. Along with the

[26] Ramadan, *In the Footsteps*, 214.

[27] Muhammad al-Hasyimi Al-Hamidi, *Muhammad for the Global Village: Muhammad Chahaya Dunia* (Arabic title transcribed as: *Muhammad lil al-Qaryah al-ʿAlamiyah*), trans. Zulfakar Ali and Alimin Kuto El-Madjid (Jakarta: Rabitha Press, 2006).

Figure 9. Cover art from *Rasul Emang COOL*, by Bambang Q-Anees. Reproduced with permission from Mizan Publishing House.

up-to-date resonance of such a totalizing theme, Indonesians have also been developing for decades distinctive approaches to religious difference among Muslims based on the example of the Prophet. Increasingly, the ideal has developed to try to become like the Prophet in encountering difference. This process has been evident especially in the overlapping areas of Islamic outreach, or *dakwah*, and the closely related field of education.

Dakwah is premised on the awareness that there are choices and alternatives, even within Islam. In fact, the first example presented in this chapter, the book *Rasul Emang COOL*, self-consciously competes with other messages of youth culture. The text on the back jacket ends a reference to high-speed electronic connectivity with these words:

> Just think, wow, if you could put your questions straight to the Prophet [instead of searching the Internet], wow wee [*wuih*]. For sure, that would have to be so much more totally awesome than any computer, even one with a million gigabytes! Could you even imagine that?[28]

[28] The jacket copy ends, "So, the Prophet is *totally* awesome *and cool* ["*emang* hebat *and cool*," emphasis in text], right?!"

In the context of multiple media and mixed messages, here the Prophet is a perfect model of knowledge, engagement, and interaction. This Indonesian work, along with many others, renders the Prophet Muḥammad not just a part of a global or fast-paced interfaith diversity. In *Rasul Emang COOL*, the attempt is actually to become like the Prophet in dealing with religious difference, especially as one reaches out to *ngobrol bareng* ("hang out and chat with") and befriend a secularized, youthful Muslim other. Such tendencies have been all the more evident in recent Indonesian religious biography of the Prophet that is aimed at settings of outreach (*dakwah*) and other knowledge transfer (e.g., education).

TEACHING AND PREACHING LIKE THE PROPHET

Indonesian Muslim religious biography highlights features of the authoritative prophetic model that relate to formal topics like dialogue, interaction, and question and answer. This revitalized interpretation blends classical text and theory with contemporary terms and concepts. Some of the many works of this type that were found popularly available in Yogyakarta came from the field of education, whereas others (like *Rasul Emang COOL*) stand alone as a new genre of religious biography and as *dakwah*. In general, *dakwah* (Ar. *daʿwa*) is a Qurʾānic term that is interpreted and applied in different ways in different global contexts, and it has differed widely even across Indonesia itself in the past decades. Most basically, the term means a call to deepen one's own or to encourage others' Islamic piety. In Indonesia, mainstream *dakwah* has been understood as an invitation to voluntary Islamic piety issued only to Muslims, not to members of other faith communities.

The work of K. H. Zainuddin, M. Z., a well-known orator in Indonesia in the 1980s and 1990s, represented the emergent link between mainstream Indonesian Islamic *dakwah* in the twenty-first century and the model of the Prophet. His book (the title of which translates as *Secrets to the Success of K. H. Zainuddin, M. Z.'s Dakwah*) explains that *dakwah* carries the basic meaning of persuading Muslims to commit to Islamic values and, by extension, to the improvement of all of human existence. When K. H. Zainuddin, M. Z. explains his own method for *dakwah*, he employs the example and rationale of the life of the Prophet Muḥammad while expressing a similar kind of rhymes, rhythm, and speech patterns that a preacher (male or female) might use. In this presentation, the preacher does not just preach about the Prophet; he or she tries to teach or preach like the Prophet, especially by being approachable, engaging, and wise.[29]

Indonesian religious biography that was available a decade later, in 2008, cast material about the Prophet more robustly in terms of themes of dialogue, interaction, and *dakwah*. First, for example, there was the standard work *40 Strategi Pembelajaran Rasulullah* (*Forty Teaching Strategies of the Prophet*), a topical *ḥadīth* collection based on university lectures by a Saudi Arabian professor.[30] The forty strategies are based on a grouping of forty *ḥadīth*s of the Prophet,[31] but the book presents the *ḥadīth* material in terms of nontraditional formal categories under the heading, "Metode-Metode Pengajaran Rasulullah" ("The Teaching Methods of the Prophet"). Instances include the use of analogical examples (*tamthīl*, no. 8), the practice of comparing cases (*tashbīh*, no. 9), and other practices that draw on information reported in *ḥadīth*, such as the following:

- The teaching of the Prophet was *interaktif* ("Dialog," question and answer) (no. 5).
- The Prophet offered his teaching with humor and jokes (no. 22).
- The Prophet was committed to teaching and instructing women (no. 36).
- Rasulullah encouraged his companions to learn foreign languages (no. 39).

Like the precious information that is reported in any *ḥadīth* tradition, the model of the sayings, actions, and approvals of the Prophet is here an example for effective educators to follow.[32]

[29] H. Mahfudh Syamsul Hadi, H. Muaddi Aminan, and Cholil Uman, eds., *Rahasia Keberhasilan Dakwah oleh K. H. Zainuddin M. Z.* (n.p., n.d.), 251. Cited at length and discussed in Anna M. Gade, *Perfection Makes Practice: Learning, Emotion and the Recited Qur'an in Indonesia* (Honolulu: University of Hawaii Press, 2004), 134–5.

[30] Abd al-Fattah Abu Ghuddah, *40 Strategi Pembelajaran Rasulullah* (Arabic title: *Al-Rasul al-mu'allim ṣl'm wa-asalibuhu fī l-ta'līm*, 2nd ed. [Beirut, 1997]), trans. Sumedi and Umi Baroroh (Yogyakarta: Tiara Wacana, 2005).

[31] This genre, a collection of "forty (or four hundred) sayings," is very old in the educational history of Islam.

[32] Another example like this is Ahmad Mudjab Mahalli, *Dialog-dialog Rasulullah* (Yogyakarta: Menara Kudus Yogyakarta, 2003), "Dialogues of the Messenger of God," which presents the life of the Prophet Muḥammad as a model for answering questions of ethics and conduct. Chapters are arranged systematically in terms of the Prophet's purported method, such as "Ethics of Dialogue," with examples provided from his biography. The book's principal theme is the Prophet's method of question and answer (dialogue) for seeking knowledge and for *dakwah* and instruction.

Another work, *Muhammad Sang Pendidik* (*Muḥammad the Noble Teacher/Great Educator*),[33] by the Indonesian author Mohammed Slamet Untung, provides a more imaginative presentation of the teaching method (*metode pendidikan*) of the Prophet. This work relies heavily on contemporary concepts and terms in educational theory and practice. It begins as historiography, opening with chapters on transmission of knowledge with the coming of Islam in the Meccan and Medinan period, and even later after the time of the Prophet. When discussion turns to the subject of the teaching method of the Prophet, the prophetic model is shown to bridge difference that is not just socially external but also psychologically internal, that is, in terms of learners' own experiences.

The book's chapter on modeling opens with the claim that the teaching method of the Prophet was a "balance of aspects that are cognitive and spiritual and the realization of concrete actions from the psychological lives of people (*aspek psikomotorik*)."[34] The religious context, the author explains, provided further *motivasi* to realize the educative principles that were demonstrated by the Prophet Muḥammad in theory and practice. The author states that the fundamental teaching method of the Prophet was to create a transformational experience (*metamorfosis*) for his community, and that this impetus became the psychological basis for the "prinsip-prinsip metodologis" of Islamic educational tradition.[35]

The author highlights the importance of providing concrete examples in teaching and learning. For example, he notes, instruction by way of case studies was modeled by the Prophet himself, exemplifying active teaching and learning (as opposed to passive teaching and learning). The author further observes that the Qur'ān does not instruct in terms of "talk only" with "no action," and likewise the Prophet Muḥammad demonstrated how principles, such as helping the poor, must be acted on.[36]

Mohammed Slamet Untung, the book's author, then explains the theory and practice of modeling itself, as inspired by the moralized and ultimate model of the Prophet Muḥammad's life. A teacher is to become like the Prophet to bring the student to overcome differential internal

33 Moh. Slamet Untung, *Muhammad Sang Pendidik* (Semarang: Pustaka Rizki Putra, 2005).

34 Ibid.,159–60.

35 Ibid.

36 Ibid.,161.

gaps in knowledge, so that students may realize their moral "potential for goodness." According to him, the ideal model may create a "transformative experience" for others (i.e., learners) that is realized concretely in the vocation of a classroom teacher:

> In education, *modeling* represents the most effective method among all others in the area of instructing on morals, spirituality, and social issues. The instructor is a guide to be followed in word and deeds. Pupils are in a state of great potential that is thus under the best influence, and they can thus realize their potential for goodness directly through the example of the goodness and the high moral standards of someone whom they themselves consider to be a model. An ideal teacher is a person who possesses every quality of high morals and intellectual capacity that is unshakable; in addition, it is important that he or she has realized these qualities in the academic life of the classroom as well as in society at large.[37]

On one level of meaning, here is a familiar expression of the idealized guide along the path to knowledge in Islam, one who stands in for the presence of the Prophet as a guide and model. Classroom theory and practice are also expressed in modern terminology and even jargon, with many phrases (from English) rendered in the Indonesian text without translation, such as "the transfer of values/norms."[38]

The introduction to this work, written by a professor at a state-run Islamic university, reflects an institutional and disciplinary impetus to develop materials that correlate the prophetic tradition with the field of education. However, in the context of social pluralism, this sort of religious biography of the Prophet Muḥammad also implies a wider process at work. It is an invitation to bridge difference within the Muslim community itself, as in the case of all *dakwah*, not only through effective knowledge transfer but also and more powerfully through a religious and moral *metamorfosis*.

[37] Ibid.

[38] Ibid., 162. Another work of this type is *Muhammad SAW: Sang Guru Besar Ummat: Keteladanan Bagi Para Pendidik: Panduan Efektif Megemgbangkan Proses Belajar Mengajar Cara Rasul* (*Muhammad: The Great Teacher: Materials for Educators: An Effective Guide for Developing the Process of Teaching and Learning in the Manner of the Prophet*; Arabic title: *Al-Muʿallim al-awwal* [*The First Teacher*] by Syeikh Syahlub), trans. Ikhwan Fauzi (Jakarta: Bina Mitra Press, 2003). This work considers the Prophet's teaching method, reflecting fully modern terminology and systematization with terms in Indonesian such as *relasional, proporsional,* and so on.

CONCLUSION

In a definitional work on religious biography, the historian of religions and Southeast Asianist Frank Reynolds explains "sacred biography" to be

> [T]hose accounts written by followers or devotees of a founder or religious savior. Such documents are an extraordinary form of biography because they both recount the process through which a new religious ideal is established and, at the same time, participate in that process.[39]

Modern accounts of the Prophet Muḥammad in Muslim-majority Indonesia are a part of an ongoing, global biographical process. For example, they have increasingly rendered an image of the Prophet Muḥammad that both selectively presents and narratively enhances received accounts, features that Reynolds identifies as foundational to religious biographical processes in general. These accounts also balance a tension between humanization and spiritualization, evident in modern Muslim accounts of the life of the Prophet from Haykal to Ramadan, another key feature of the biographical process discussed by Reynolds.[40] In contemporary works available in Indonesia, the sacred biography of the Prophet Muḥammad in print form has also supported new textual structures (e.g., the limited citation of *ḥadīth*s in the work *Rasul Emang COOL*). It has also fostered new themes (e.g., successful, corporate prophetic life management), and it continues to be reoriented by global conditions, such as with materials that address the question of religious difference both inside and outside of Islam with the model of the Prophet.

Muḥammad Haykal's *Ḥayāt Muḥammad* signaled the worldwide circulation of biographies of the Prophet Muḥammad in the era of nation-states. Haykal's work was written self-consciously to be modern and was appreciated as a confessionally Muslim account. Religious biographies that followed in the decades of the twentieth and twenty-first centuries have increasingly stretched the traditional contours of genre in the complementary directions of fiction and authenticity. Now, under accelerating conditions of global capitalism and worldwide Islamic awakening, new types of texts circulate in regional context that have both Muslim and non-Muslim origins; and, importantly, they may even seek to blend (or blur) the boundaries among these systems. This has appeared to be

39 Reynolds, "Introduction," in *The Biographical Process*, 3.
40 Ibid., 3–4.

the case, for example, in Armstrong's and Ramadan's popular works that offer the example of the Prophet's life to a religiously plural world.

Popular religious biography in Indonesian literature shows the contextual reception and re-formation of themes and structures like these, shaping them in terms of distinctively regional interests that push and pull. Such Muslim religious biography presents Islam as an option among others. Even in a Muslim-only setting, as is presumed in Indonesian Islamic education and *dakwah*, the example of the life of the Prophet Muḥammad is a powerful model for encountering difference and for transferring knowledge. Religious biography shows how to cross boundaries, whether within Islam or across the wider global village. In Indonesia in the twenty-first century, the illustration of the life of the Prophet Muḥammad no longer merely enhances established practices of *dakwah* or education (as in forty *ḥadīth*s found on the subject). The reverse has also, and far more profoundly, come to be the case: the very understanding of the figure of the Prophet Muḥammad himself and his life story may now be imagined entirely in terms of inspiring connection over distance and difference.

Further reading

Armstrong, Karen. *Muhammad: A Biography of the Prophet*. London: Phoenix, 1991.

Gershoni, Israel. "The Reader: Another Production. The Reception of Haykal's Biography of Muhammad and the Shift of Egyptian Intellectuals to Islamic Subjects in the 1930s." *Poetics Today* 15, no. 2 (1994): 241–77.

Haykal, Muḥammad Ḥusayn. *Life of Muhammad [Arabic title: Ḥayāt Muḥammad]*, 8th ed. Translated by Isma'il al-Faruqi. Plainfield, IN: American Trust Publications, 1997.

Ramadan, Tariq. *In the Footsteps of the Prophet: Lessons from the Life of Muhammad*. Oxford: Oxford University Press, 2007.

Reynolds, Frank, and Donald Capps, eds. *The Biographical Process: Studies in the History and Psychology of Religion*. The Hague: Mouton, 1976.

Watt, William Montgomery. *Muhammad: Prophet and Statesman*. London: Oxford University Press, 1961.

Waugh, Earle. "The Popular Muhammad: Models in the Interpretation of an Islamic Paradigm." In *Approaches to Islam in Religious Studies*, edited by Richard Martin, 41–58. Tucson: University of Arizona Press, 1985.

13 Images of Muḥammad in literature, art, and music

AMIR HUSSAIN

> God and God's angels bless the Prophet. Oh you who have faith, invoke God's peace and blessing upon him.
>
> – Qur'ān 33:56

We live in a world where, as a 1990 advertisement for a camera famously stated, "image is everything." This is certainly true of the study of Islam, particularly after the terrorist attacks of September 11, 2001, on the United States. Prior to that, I would begin my introductory course on Islam with a book about the life of the Prophet Muḥammad. I did this because my students, whether or not they were Muslim, knew very little about the Prophet and the beginnings of Islam. After September 11, my students thought that they knew everything about Islam because of what they had learned through the media, particularly from television news. So I had to begin by teaching them how to understand images, especially images of the Prophet.

This focus on images raises a paradox, as Muslims for the most part have been aniconic with respect to visual images of the Prophet Muḥammad. When Muslim artists seek to represent the Prophet in an image, they face a unique set of issues. Mohamed Zakariya, the most famous American Muslim calligrapher, expresses the paradox in this way on his Web site: "How does one describe the indescribable? How does one form an image of that which cannot be portrayed?" In part, Zakariya is referring to a legal ruling against portrayal of the Prophet, but there is also the larger philosophical problem of encompassing the meaning of Muḥammad in a single image. He answers these questions with a description of the *ḥilya* (in Turkish, *hilye*), a characterization of the Prophet Muḥammad: "That is what the *hilye* does – it gives parameters to the imagination so that one can think about the Prophet with a mental or spiritual image to hang onto, yet not attempt to visualize him or portray him in a painting. But the *hilye* is not an icon in words. As

Figure 10. Traditional *hilye* by calligrapher Mohamed Zakariya, partly reproduced on the front cover of this volume.

impressive and accurate as the many *hilye* texts are, they still remain vague, contrary to the claims of literalists, who would reject these texts as being visual portraits."[1]

SONGS AND CARTOONS

Zakariya's definition of the *ḥilya* points to the fact that Muslims have numerous mental images of the Prophet. Some of these find expression in the visual arts, but Muslims also remember the Prophet Muḥammad with songs of praise. In 2006, Yusuf Islam (the former Cat Stevens) returned to popular music, releasing a CD titled *An Other Cup*. The CD ended with a modern English song in praise of the Prophet Muḥammad, "The Beloved." That song, with back-up vocals by the Senegalese Muslim singer Youssou N'Dour, provided a wonderful example of a contemporary devotional song to the Prophet.

His wisdom flowed from Heaven's Book
Just like threaded pearls,

Just like threaded pearls
He left his self to flee to God

And God sent him back to us
He was born to be the Beloved; a will of the Divine
He was born to be the Beloved; he was born to guide
He prayed all his nights alone
In stars and Angels' sight
And in the day he lit the way, with blazing words so bright

He was born to be the Beloved; a will of the Divine
He was born to be the Beloved; he was born to be kind
He taught the people to worship
Bowing to One God, Bowing to one God
His mercy stretched from East to West
To every man, woman and child

He was born to be the Beloved; a will of the Divine
He was born to be the Beloved; nature – sublime

He opened up the doors of love
For every heart parched with thirst
He was a mercy to the worlds and unto the universe

1 Taken from the Web site http://www.zakariya.net/resources/hilye.html.

He was born to be the Beloved; a will of the Divine
He was born to be the Beloved; he was born to guide[2]

Praise poems to the Prophet Muḥammad follow an ancient lineage, originating with the Qur'ānic command, cited at the beginning of this chapter, to "invoke God's peace and blessing upon him" and his family. Cat Stevens, one of the most popular singer-songwriters of the 1960s and 1970s, became a Muslim in 1977, a year after he received a copy of the Qur'ān from his brother. Famously, he stopped performing after his conversion, an event taken by many non-Muslims to suggest an incompatibility between art and Islam. But as Yusuf Islam explained in an article published in the British magazine *Islamic Voice* in 2005, his reasons were more complex:

> When I embraced Islam in 1977 I was still making records and performing. The chief Imam in the London Central Mosque encouraged me to continue my profession of composing and recording; at no time was there ever an ultimatum for me to have to choose between music or Islam. Nevertheless, there were lots of things about the music industry which contravened the Islamic way of life and I was new to the faith, so I simply decided myself to give up the music business. This helped me to concentrate fully on learning and practising Islam – the five pillars – and striving to get close to Allah through my knowledge and worship. However, it is interesting to quote here part of the first interview I gave to a Muslim magazine back in 1980; when asked about my thoughts with regard to music I said, "I have suspended my activities in music for fear that they may divert me from the true path, but I will not be dogmatic in saying that I will never make music again. You can't say that without adding Insha Allah."[3]

It was through the war in the Balkans in the 1990s that Yusuf Islam found his way back to music, ultimately recording a CD for Bosnian orphan relief. Of that return to music, Islam wrote in the same 2005 magazine article: "It's true that I have gradually softened my objections to the use of music and songs over the years, and there are good reasons. Since the

[2] Yusuf Islam, "The Beloved," from the CD *An Other Cup* (2006). Permission to reprint kindly granted by Yusuf Islam and EMI Records.

[3] Yusuf Islam, "Music: A Question of Faith or Da'wah?" in *Islamic Voice*, March 2005, http://islamicvoice.com/March2005/LivingIslam/index.php#MusicAQuestionofFaithorDawah.

genocide against Bosnia in 1992, I learnt how important motivational songs are in keeping people's spirits high during times of great calamity. One of the things that changed me greatly was listening to the cassettes coming out of the Balkans at that time; these were rich and highly motivating songs (*nasheeds*), inspiring the Bosnians with the religious spirit of faith and sacrifice."[4]

In examining the lyrics to "The Beloved," one sees a deep respect for the Prophet. They are not at all a physical description of the Prophet, but instead a description of his role as one who brings the divine word to the people. The mercy of the Prophet is stressed, echoing a verse from the Qur'ān (21:107): "We did not send you but as a mercy for all of the worlds."

Although the year 2006 saw the release of this devotional hymn, that same year witnessed vigorous debates over a Danish newspaper's publication of a dozen cartoons of the Prophet Muḥammad.[5] The cartoons were discussed in forums as scholarly as the American Academy of Religion and as popular as the animated television show *South Park*. The bitter controversy raised a number of questions, ranging from the role of images in Islam to violence in the contemporary Muslim world.

As a Western Muslim, I deeply appreciated the song but had mixed responses to the cartoons. My Western roots taught me to value freedom of expression and the freedom of the press. Having spent time in certain parts of the Muslim world where the state controls the media, I much prefer the freedoms of North American society. (It is true that six corporations – BMG, Viacom/CBS, Disney/ABC, GE, Time Warner, and News Corporation – control the majority of North American media, but lively independent media are free to bring some balance and objectivity.) My Muslim roots, however, teach me to value the life of the Prophet Muḥammad. He is like a member of my family – a beloved and respected elder. I feel a strange need to protect him from unjust criticism in the same way that I would protect my parents, my siblings, my teachers, or my friends. Many Muslims will not even say his name without adding the formula "May God bless him and give him peace" or "Peace be upon him."

SALMAN RUSHDIE AND STEREOTYPES

When I first saw the controversial cartoons, I thought of the novelist and literary critic Salman Rushdie. Many people know Rushdie only

[4] Ibid.

[5] The cartoons were first published in *Jyllands-Posten* on September 30, 2005, though the controversy reached its zenith months later.

as the author of *The Satanic Verses*, a novel that earned him a death sentence from Iran's Ayatollah Khomeini in 1989 and forced Rushdie into hiding until 1998. In the 1980s, however, Rushdie had also been involved in campaigns against racism in Britain. In an essay titled "The New Empire within Britain," he wrote about how Britain, once a powerful empire, was now colonizing itself by creating ghettos for people of South Asian and African ancestry. In his 1984 essay "Outside the Whale," Rushdie wrote about the "Raj revival" that was taking place in Britain – a wave of nostalgia for the British colonial rule in India. Commenting on the television series *The Far Pavilions* and *The Jewel in the Crown*, he wrote:

> It would be easy to conclude that such material could not possibly be taken seriously by anyone, and that it is therefore unnecessary to get worked up about it.... I would be happier about this, the quietist option... if I did not believe that it matters, it always matters, to name rubbish as rubbish; that to do otherwise is to legitimize it. I should also mind less, were it not for the fact that [it] is only the latest in a very long line of fake portraits inflicted by the West on the East.... Stereotypes are easier to shrug off if yours is not the culture being stereotyped; or, at the very least, if your culture has the power to counterpunch against the stereotype.[6]

Rushdie's words were prescient of the situation, two decades later, when a number of non-Muslim cartoonists would create their own images of the Prophet Muḥammad, ones that would be deeply offensive to Muslims. The media discussions that ensued, usually quite simplistic in nature, revolved around freedom of expression, but what was rarely discussed was that this was simply another in that "very long line of fake portraits." When Muslims became upset, they were termed fanatical and intolerant, even if they expressed their hurt through lawful and peaceful protests.

Connecting Salman Rushdie to the Danish cartoons in this way is perhaps counterintuitive, as a few years after writing these lines, Rushdie would publish *The Satanic Verses* and find himself embroiled in his own controversy over producing an image of the Prophet Muḥammad. I discuss *The Satanic Verses* below in more detail, but we can learn much from the many ways that the Rushdie affair was similar to the cartoon controversy. In both cases, the initial protests were ignored.

6 "Outside the Whale," reprinted in *Imaginary Homelands: Essays and Criticism, 1981–1991* (New York: Viking Penguin, 1991), 88–9.

British Muslims had objected to *The Satanic Verses* already in October 1988, through contact with the publishers and the government. This got them nowhere. On December 2, a small group burned the book in protest, but this also got no media attention. It wasn't until a group in Bradford burned the book on January 14, 1989, that the media began to pay attention, mostly because the group thought to invite them. Also, in both cases, important Muslim voices urged calm and an end to violence. In 2006, major Muslim groups in North America called on Muslims upset by the cartoons to remain peaceful, just as they had urged North American Muslims to remain calm during the Rushdie affair almost twenty years earlier. The Canadian Islamic Congress (CIC), for example, called for a "calm period of healing" after the cartoons sparked worldwide protests.[7] Unfortunately, these Muslim voices for peace were seldom heard in the mainstream media.

A third parallel is that, in each case, some Muslim leaders around the world assumed roles as so-called defenders of Islam, inciting more hatred. In 2006 a Pakistani cleric, for example, reportedly offered a twenty-five-thousand-dollar reward for the killing of one of the cartoonists. However, this action was denounced by other Muslims. Dr. Mohamed Elmasry, the national president of the CIC, commented, "What has been said and done by this irresponsible individual is totally against the teachings of the Qur'ān, which condemns the taking of human lives.... Only God is ultimate arbiter and judge of those who do wrong."[8]

Let me be clear about my own views. Although I disapprove of the cartoons, I defend the right of the press to publish them. I oppose any form of violent protest against the cartoons. I also reject the retaliatory acts of the Muslim media, such as publishing offensive cartoons about the Holocaust. Even so, I wonder what was to be gained in publishing the cartoons, especially because the same newspaper had earlier refused to print offensive cartoons about Jesus. As I discuss later in this chapter, double standards such as these are part of the history of polemical images of Muḥammad.[9]

The Muḥammad in the cartoons is not the beloved Prophet of the Muslim faithful, one of whose attributes is mercy. When Muḥammad came into a position of political power after decades of persecution, his first act was to forgive those who had persecuted him. His heart of mercy

[7] From a Media Communique by the CIC, available from the Web page http://www.icsfp.com/en/contents.aspx?aid=3736.

[8] From a Media Communique by the CIC, available from the Web page http://www.mail-archive.com/muslim@yahoogroups.com/msg00653.html.

[9] See also John Tolan's discussion in Chapter 11 of this volume.

is also illustrated by this *ḥadīth*: "A dying child was once brought to the Prophet Muḥammad (peace be upon him). When, on seeing the child's last breaths, the Prophet began to shed tears, one of his companions asked why he was crying. He replied: 'It is mercy that God has put in the hearts of God's servants, and God is merciful only to those of God's servants who are merciful to others.'"[10] I hope that, in the midst of public debate between Muslims and non-Muslims, we all can be merciful to one another.

LITERARY REPRESENTATIONS BY MUSLIMS

Salman Rushdie's image of Muḥammad in *The Satanic Verses* may be the most (in)famous of literary depictions of the Prophet Muḥammad, but it is hardly the only one. In fact, the twentieth century saw a new trend in literary works that represent the life of the Prophet. In the previous chapter, Anna Gade described the influential biography by Muḥammad Haykal. But at about the time that Haykal was writing his work, his fellow Egyptian, the cultural critic and novelist Ṭāhā Ḥusayn (d. 1973), wrote *On the Margin of the Biography of Muḥammad* from 1933 to 1946. Ḥusayn's work emphasized the cultural heritage of Islam as found in the classical works of *Sīra*. Like Haykal, Ḥusayn stressed the rational elements in Muḥammad's life rather than invoking the miraculous. These literary biographies were not limited to Egypt. For example, the Iranian thinker ʿAlī Dashtī (d. 1982) wrote *23 Years: A Study of the Prophetic Career of Mohammad* in the 1930s as well. His work was an extreme example of the rationalization described earlier, with the Qur'ān seen as bringing nothing new and characterized as a product of Muḥammad's consciousness.

These biographies laid the groundwork for the most prestigious literary take on the Prophet's life by another Egyptian, Naguib Mahfouz (d. 2006), who received the Nobel Prize in Literature in 1988. In 1959, he included an allegory of Muḥammad in his novel *Children of Gabalawi* (Ar. *Awlād ḥāratinā*). The novel chronicled the story of a patriarch with four sons, each of whom was an allegory for the prophets Adam, Moses, Jesus, and Muḥammad. Changed from the historical setting of Arabia to the streets of Cairo, the Muḥammad character (Qāsim, taken from one of the Prophet's nicknames, Abū l-Qāsim) is represented as a deeply

[10] From the *Ṣahih al-Bukhārī*, Vol 2, Book 23, ḥadīth number 373, available from the Web page http://www.usc.edu/schools/college/crcc/engagement/resources/texts/muslim/hadith/bukhari/023.sbt.html

committed man who challenged the secular powers. His goal was frustrated by his later followers. Salman Rushdie's 1988 novel builds on this modern tradition of literary depiction while also exploring the classical *Sīra* tradition.

The main character of *The Satanic Verses*, indeed, the first character introduced in the novel, is Gibreel Farishta (whose name translates out of the Urdu as "the angel Gabriel"). This character assumes the persona of the angel Gabriel ("I mean the real one, or the allegedly real one," as Rushdie remarked when he read from the book in Toronto in October 1988),[11] and in this persona, he has a series of dreams about the founding of a great religious tradition, which is, of course, Islam. In other chapters of the book, Gibreel has a series of encounters with a character known simply as "the Imam," who is, of course, the Ayatollah Ruhollah Khomeini. He also has another dream, this one set in rural India, where an orphaned peasant girl named Ayesha convinces those in her village to make a pilgrimage to Mecca on foot, and he has numerous adventures with the second character introduced in the novel, Saladin Chamcha. These encounters elaborate on themes of migration and identity, including Muslim identity, which is arguably the central issue of the book. But my focus here is on the character that Rushdie calls Mahound.

THE BIOGRAPHY OF THE PROPHET IN *THE SATANIC VERSES*

Rushdie's second chapter, "Mahound," begins with Gibreel Farishta in the arms of his mother: "Little devil, she scolds, but then folds him in her arms, my little farishta [angel], boys will be boys, and he falls past her into sleep."[12] So begin his dreams that he is the archangel Gabriel. But before he dreams of the Prophet, we are told that Gibreel dreamed of much older things. He dreamed about the creation of Satan and his subsequent fall from heaven; about three goddesses worshipped in pre-Islamic Arabia (al-Lāt, al-ʿUzza, and Manāt); about the story of Abraham, Hagar, and their son Ishmael; and about the rediscovery by ʿAbd al-Muṭṭalib (the grandfather of Muḥammad, who is referred to in the novel simply as Muttalib) of the well of Zamzam, which Muslims believe was originally revealed by God to Ishmael and Hagar to keep them alive in

[11] This quote is a transcription of Rushdie's words as they are recorded on TV Ontario video-cassette no. 35112, "Authors at Harbourfront: Salman Rushdie."

[12] Salman Rushdie, *The Satanic Verses* (London: Penguin Books, 1988), 91.

the desert.[13] Finally, Gibreel dreams of "the businessman," who with his tendencies toward asceticism was a "strange manner of businessman."[14] Of course, in the traditional Muslim biographies, Muḥammad was a fairly successful Meccan businessman before his prophetic career began.

We are told that, at times when he is dreaming, Gibreel thinks himself to be mad, and that these thoughts are just what "the businessman . . . felt when he first saw the archangel: thought he was cracked, wanted to throw himself down from a rock, from a high rock."[15] Here again, Rushdie's writing closely parallels a tradition about Muḥammad found in the famous *Sīra* of Ibn Isḥāq (d. 150/767):

> I [Muḥammad] thought, Woe is me poet or possessed – Never shall Quraysh say this of me! I will go to the top of the mountain and throw myself down that I may kill myself and gain rest. So I went forth to do so and then when I was midway on the mountain, I heard a voice from heaven saying, "O Muḥammad! thou art the apostle of God and I am Gabriel." I raised my head towards heaven to see [who was speaking], and lo, Gabriel in the form of a man with feet astride the horizon saying, "O Muḥammad! thou art the apostle of God, and I am Gabriel."[16]

Although the event is historical, Rushdie takes it as an opportunity to discuss doubt, which he considers the opposite of faith. In the novel, doubt is "the human condition" that separates humanity from the angelic order.[17] Again, this observation is based on Islamic tradition, where angels are thought to be bound to the will of God, whereas humans are free to doubt.

Rushdie's focus on the interior life of his characters continues with his observations on the fact that Mahound, like Muḥammad, was an orphan: "Orphans learn to be moving targets, develop a rapid walk, quick reactions, hold-your-tongue caution."[18] Rushdie also describes Mahound as "a fit man, no soft-bellied usurer he."[19] This serves to differentiate

[13] For a traditional Muslim understanding of the stories of Abraham, Hagar, Ishmael, and ʿAbd al-Muṭṭalib's rediscovery of the well of Zamzam, see Martin Lings, *Muhammad* (London: George Allen & Unwin, 1983), 1–2, 10–11. The way Lings recounts his stories is very similar to the way Rushdie mentions them in *The Satanic Verses*.

[14] Rushdie, *Satanic Verses*, 92.

[15] Ibid.

[16] Ibn Isḥāq, *The Life of Muhammad*, trans. Alfred Guillaume (London: Oxford University Press, 1955), 106.

[17] Rushdie, *Satanic Verses*, 92.

[18] Ibid., 93.

[19] Ibid.

Mahound from the rest of the business community around him. Then Rushdie explains the name of his prophet:

> His name: a dream-name, changed by the vision. Pronounced correctly, it means he-for-whom-thanks-should-be-given, but he won't answer to that here; nor, though he's well aware of what they call him, to his nickname in Jahilia down below – *he-who-goes-up-and-down-old-Coney*. Here he is neither Mahomet nor MoeHammered; has adopted, instead, the demon-tag the farangis hung around his neck. To turn insults into strengths, whigs, tories, Blacks all chose to wear with pride the names they were given in scorn; likewise, our mountain-climbing, prophet-motivated solitary is to be the medieval baby-frightener, the Devil's synonym: Mahound.[20]

The foregoing passage requires several comments. First, the translation of *Muḥammad* does mean "praised" or "commendable." However, his Meccan opponents twisted his name into Mudhammam, which translates as "greatly dispraised."[21] Second, the name Mahound was a medieval European name meaning "the 'false prophet' Mohammed; in the Middle Ages often vaguely imagined to be worshipped as a god."[22] The first occurrence of Mahound was in approximately 1290 CE, and it was used by such writers as Edmund Spenser (1596) and Alexander Pope (1735).[23] It is important to note that Rushdie makes explicit that this term of derision has been appropriated by his prophet in the same way that other groups had turned "insults into strengths." The name Mahound, then, is not used as a term of derision for the Prophet Muḥammad in the novel.

The city in which Mahound first preaches is Jahilia. The noun *jāhiliyya* occurs four times in the Qur'ān (3:148, 5:55, 33:33, and 48:26) and means either "pagan ignorance" or the "age of ignorance." *Jāhiliyya* is the usual Muslim term for pre-Islamic Arabia. The heart of the city of Jahilia is described in the novel as the "House of the Black Stone."[24] This is, of course, a reference to the Kaʿba, believed by Muslims to have

20 Ibid.

21 In fact, there is a *ḥadīth* in which the Prophet expressed thanks that the Quraysh cursed and abused Mudhammam while his name was Muḥammad; see Muhammad Muhsin Khan, trans.,*The Translation of the Meanings of Sahih al-Bukhari* (Lahore: Kazi Publications, 1986), 4:482.

22 *The Compact Edition of the Oxford English Dictionary* (New York: Oxford University Press, 1986), 1:1694.

23 Ibid.

24 Rushdie, *Satanic Verses*, 94.

been built by Abraham and Ishmael as the house of worship for the one true God.

There are a number of other Islamic themes and allusions throughout the remainder of the book, including a section in which Mahound recites the Satanic verses. Later in the novel, Salman (one of Mahound's companions but also Rushdie's historical namesake) claims that, in the act of copying, he changed the words of the revelation to Mahound, and Mahound did not immediately detect the changes. When Mahound does discover the changes, Salman flees. After the conquest of Jahilia, Salman is brought before Mahound. Salman is not allowed to convert to "Submission," as Mahound tells him that "Your blasphemy, Salman, can't be forgiven. Did you think I wouldn't work it out? To set your words against the Words of God?"[25] However, Salman's life is spared as a result of the intercession of Bilal.

This scene, with its setting of "Salman's words" against the words of God, seems now to foreshadow the real-life controversy that would ensue, particularly in England.[26] In October 1988, after the book was banned in India, Muslims in England began to protest the novel. Of those protesters, Bhikhu Parekh wrote that what struck him the most was "not so much their intolerance as their timidity, not their feeling of rage but a sense of hurt, not their anger but their distress."[27] As mentioned previously, the initial protests were limited to contact with the publishers and government officials and were either ignored by the British press or not taken seriously. Parekh reported: "Neither the quality nor the quantity papers published the offending passages, or invited Muslim spokesmen to state their case, or themselves made an attempt to read the book with their eyes. Instead they mocked the Muslims, accused them of 'intolerance,' and wondered if a tolerant society should tolerate the intolerant."[28]

[25] Ibid., 374.

[26] For some of the early British reactions (both from Muslims and non-Muslims) to the book, see Jørgen S. Nielson, ed., *The "Rushdie Affair": A Documentation*, Research Papers, Muslims in Europe No. 42 (Birmingham, U.K.: Centre for the Study of Islam and Christian-Muslim Relations, Selly Oak Colleges, 1989). For a more recent reaction, see the chapter by Fred Halliday, "'Islam Is in Danger': Authority, Rushdie and the Struggle for the Migrant Soul," in *The Next Threat: Western Perceptions of Islam*, ed. Jochen Hippler and Andrea Lueg (Boulder, CO: Pluto Press, 1995), 71–81.

[27] Bhikhu Parekh, "The Rushdie Affair and the British Press," in *The Salman Rushdie Controversy in Inter-Religious Perspective*, ed. Daniel Cohn-Sherbok (Lewiston, NY: Edwin Mellen Press, 1990), 75. Originally published in 1990 by the Commission for Racial Equality as a booklet titled *Free Speech*.

[28] Ibid.

Elsewhere in the world, the reaction to the novel that drew the most attention was in Iran. Michael Fischer and Mehdi Abedi wrote:

> The book was published in late September 1988, and was given a dismissive review in Tehran without any special notice or concern. Rushdie was well-known: both *Midnight's Children* and *Shame* had been translated into Persian, the latter even winning the state prize, awarded by President Ali Khamenei, for the best translation of a novel. Both these previous novels contain considerable satire about (mis)uses of Islam. It was only four and a half months later, on 14 February 1989, that Khomeini issued the *fatwā* declaring Rushdie essentially an apostate, *maḥdūr al-dam* (one whose blood may be shed without trial, the term used to facilitate the execution and murder of Baha'is). This *fatwā* was disputed in its legal validity by various Muslim jurisprudents.[29]

Khomeini's *fatwā* was undoubtedly harsh, but its legal implications are generally misunderstood. Fischer and Abedi explain: "Technically, Khomeini's *fatwā* is but an opinion issued in response to questions submitted to him by Muslims in Britain, and is not enforceable unless there is a trial under Islamic due process." They concluded, "The timing of Khomeini's call was not arbitrary: it was a way to seize international leadership for a cause célèbre that others had created in other arenas, and it blocked a series of moves by internal factions to normalize relations with the West."[30] For many Muslims outside of Iran, there was concern over Khomeini's death sentence and the image it created that Khomeini somehow spoke for all Muslims.[31]

Thankfully, Rushdie was not physically harmed and continues to write both fiction and nonfiction. Nor have his experiences prevented other authors from writing about the Prophet Muḥammad, though an increased sensitivity to the impact of images is apparent. Of books written in North America, one of the most interesting is a recent biography for children, *Muhammad*, written and illustrated in 2003 by the award-winning children's author Demi. The cover of the book actually presents an image of the Prophet in a scene from the *miʿrāj*. However, here and

[29] Michael M. J. Fischer and Mehdi Abedi, *Debating Muslims: Cultural Dialogues in Postmodernity and Tradition* (Madison: University of Wisconsin Press, 1990), 388.

[30] Ibid., 398–9.

[31] For example, Mohammad Kamali wrote that the "*fatwā* evoked mixed responses from the *ʿulamāʾ* [religious leaders] and Muslim leaders who expressed reservations over the wisdom of [Khomeini's] verdict addressing the Muslims at large to kill Rushdie without any reference to due judicial process" (*Freedom of Expression in Islam* [Cambridge: Islamic Texts Society, 1997], 296–7).

in the book, he is always presented in gold silhouette, a technique also used by Muslim artists for centuries. Demi's lavishly illustrated book fits securely into the genre of children's picture books but also demonstrates that, in contemporary society, it is hard to tell a story without images, including ones that move.

MUḤAMMAD IN FILM AND MUSIC

Mustapha Akkad (1930–2005) was perhaps the best-known producer-director in the Muslim world. Known to Hollywood audiences as the executive producer of the successful *Halloween* series of films, Akkad's most famous film was *The Message* (1976), which told the story of the revelations to Muḥammad and the beginnings of Islam. The film is one of the rare positive portrayals of Islam and Muslims in cinema, and it still stands up more than three decades later. I was a child when the movie first came out, and my parents took our family to see it when it played at the Indian movie house in Toronto. It was the first Muslim film that I had ever seen, and I walked out of the movie theater with a tremendous pride in my faith. I was also puzzled at the Muslims who were protesting the film and wondered whether they would object to the film had they actually seen it.

Some of the Muslim protests were based on erroneous gossip before the film was released, claiming that an actor would play Muḥammad.[32] In fact, in keeping with Muslim reservations about depicting the Prophet, no actor portrayed him, and his voice was never heard. Instead, in an ingenious directorial decision, the camera point of view was often used for Muḥammad, and actors would speak to the camera as if they were speaking to him (nonetheless controversial for some Muslims). At other times, when Muḥammad was on the move, the camera might focus on his camel instead of on him.

The other Muslim objection was based on the genre, under the assumption that film should not be used to tell the story that was sacred

[32] On March 9, 1977, Hamaas Abdul Khaalis, founder of the Hanafi movement in the United States, took 134 hostages and seized control of the District Building, B'nai B'rith, and the Islamic Center in Washington, D.C. He was seeking revenge for the murder of his family members by Black Muslims (from whom Khaalis had split when he founded the Hanafi movement in 1968) in 1973. Khaalis also was angered about *The Message* and wrongly believed that it depicted the Prophet. One of his demands was that the film be withdrawn. During the hostage situation, a young reporter was killed. Details of the incident are reported by Kareem Abdul-Jabbar, who was mentored and given his name by Khaalis, in Abdul-Jabbar's autobiography *Giant Steps* (New York: Bantam Books, 1983), 260–81.

Figure 11. Poster for Mustapha Akkad's film *The Message* (1976).

to the protestors. However, Akkad was very careful in keeping to the standard hagiographical accounts of Muḥammad's life. The accuracy of the film was approved by both Sunni scholars at Al-Azhar University in Cairo and Shīʿī scholars in Lebanon. The film was also shot back-to-back in both English and Arabic, and it was released in both versions.

The film starred Anthony Quinn as Ḥamza, the uncle of the Prophet, and it is Quinn who is the real protagonist in the film. To this day, his portrayal is one of the most positive Muslim roles in a feature film. For a child of my generation, this was the first Muslim hero whom I ever saw on screen. Another hero in the film was Bilāl, an African slave freed by Muḥammad and portrayed on-screen by the Senegalese actor Johnny Sekka. One scene showed Bilāl being tortured by his owners for converting to Islam and not denouncing his new religion even though it might lead to his death. Bilāl survives and, in a great moment of triumph, gives the first call to prayer when Muḥammad and his community migrate from Mecca to Medina and establish the first mosque there. Another strength of the film was the musical score by Maurice Jarre, which was nominated for an Oscar in 1978.

Another more recent film is the 2002 PBS documentary *Muḥammad: Legacy of a Prophet* (directed by Michael Schwarz). It provides a standard hagiographical account with the use of prominent Muslims and scholars of Islam. The film can be contrasted with more historical-critical accounts and can be used to talk about the ways that contemporary Muslims draw on the life of Muḥammad to make sense of their own lives. The segment with Kevin James, a Muslim fire marshal who helped out at the World Trade Center after it was attacked on September 11, is particularly effective, as is the segment on Muslim American calligrapher Mohamed Zakariya (mentioned previously). Importantly, the film takes advantage of the revolution in media and has an accompanying Web site (http://www.pbs.org/muhammad/) that expands on themes in the film.

Other Internet sites devoted to the life of the Prophet include Muhamed, launched in 2007 in both English and Arabic (http://www.prophet-muhamed.com). In addition to links to the PBS film, the site has links to download two other documentary films, *When the Moors Ruled in Europe* and *Islam: Empire of Faith*. The Web site also has information about famous Muslims in sports and music. The section on music includes, of course, Yusuf Islam, but also the American rappers Mos Def, Ice Cube, and Q-Tip, who are among the many hip-hop artists who are Muslim. Jermaine Jackson is also listed on the Web site, and Jermaine's brother, Michael Jackson, announced his interest in Islam in 2007. However, the King of Pop never formally converted to Islam, nor released any songs that reflected his new religious inquiries. With Jackson's death on June 25, 2009, there was some speculation about his conversion to Islam, and if this would mean a Muslim funeral for him.[33] He was buried in a private ceremony in Los Angeles on September 4, 2009.

Another American Muslim artist is Kareem Salama. Born in Oklahoma to Egyptian parents, Salama is a country singer. On his second album, *This Life of Mine*, released in 2007, he has a song entitled "More Than."[34] While at first listen it appears to be a love song, the third verse gives it away as a song in praise of the Prophet. It is perhaps a

[33] Brad A. Greenberg, "Michael Jackson: Muslim, Christian and Jew?" *The Jewish Journal*. http://www.jewishjournal.com/thegodblog/item/michael_jackson_muslim_christian_and_jew_20090707/.

[34] I am indebted to Barbara von Schlegell for making this song known to me.

mark of the Muslim presence in America that there are even country songs where the Prophet is praised. Of the many other famous Muslim musicians from around the world, perhaps the best known is the late Pakistani singer Nusrat Fateh Ali Khan (1948–97). He was a singer of Qawwālī, the Ṣūfī devotional music associated with the Indian subcontinent. Nusrat sang numerous *naats*, or songs in praise of the Prophet. A new generation of Muslim musicians continues this music, including Sami Yusuf in the United Kingdom and Dawud Wharnsby Ali in Canada. Wildly popular in West Africa is Youssou N'Dour (born in 1959 in Senegal), who represents the Ṣūfī tradition of West Africa. In 2005, he released a CD reflective of his Senegalese Muslim roots that won a Grammy Award for best contemporary world music album. Although known to Western audiences as *Egypt*, the CD was released in Senegal with the title *Thanks to Allah*. On the CD, N'Dour sings in both Wolof and Arabic, and he includes songs of praise to Ahmadu Bamba (d. 1927), the founder of the Mouride order in Senegal.

CONCLUSION: REPRESENTATIONS, DEVOTIONAL AND OTHERWISE

Contrary to popular misconceptions, images and pictures of the Prophet have long been a part of the reverence given to Muḥammad. This is particularly true in the Shīʿī tradition, where to this day in Iran one can buy postcards with images of the Prophet or of his son-in-law, ʿAlī. In both Sunni and Shīʿī forms of Islam, one sees a rich tradition of paintings of Muḥammad's Night Journey to Jerusalem and his ascension to heaven. In some of them, Muḥammad's face is obscured by fire or a veil, but in others it is visible. In Muslim homes, one often sees a written description of the Prophet's features, done in elaborate calligraphy and displayed with great pride.

Unfortunately, non-Muslims have sometimes created negative images of Muḥammad. The Danish cartoon controversy of 2006 is not new in the history of Christian-Muslim polemic. Dante, in his *Divine Comedy*, places both Muḥammad and ʿAlī in the ninth circle of hell, where they are tortured as sowers of "scandal and schism."[35] This is doubly tragic, as Dante's work itself may have been based on the narrative of Muḥammad's ascent to heaven. Dante wrote his work in the Middle Ages, when Islam was understood to be a Christian

35 James Romanes Sibbald, trans. *The Divine Comedy of Dante Alighieri* (Edinburgh: David Douglas, 1884), 211.

heresy and Muḥammad a renegade cardinal who started his own religion after a falling out with the Catholic Church. Such misinformation and hurt continue today. After September 11, for example, one prominent Christian minister referred to the Prophet as a "terrorist," and another described him as "a demon-possessed pedophile."[36]

Thankfully, these are not the only portrayals by Western non-Muslims. The writers Thomas Carlyle, George Bernard Shaw, and James Michener have all portrayed Muḥammad positively, as has the children's author Demi. A number of Christian ministers have reached out to Muslims and borne witness to their own faith without needing to attack Muḥammad. Among them are Rev. Robert Schuller and his son Robert Jr., whose ministry at the Crystal Cathedral is broadcast as the *Hour of Power*. Some journalists have also recognized the positive influence of Muḥammad. Michael Hart, in his book *The 100: A Ranking of the Most Influential Persons in History*, put Muḥammad at the top of his list. "[This choice] may surprise some readers and may be questioned by others," he wrote, "but [Muḥammad] was the only man in history who was supremely successful on both the religious and secular level."[37]

The root of the cartoon controversy was not that Muḥammad was depicted in pictures but that he was depicted as a terrorist, a debauched man possessed by the devil. This, clearly, is an image that causes Muslims to take great offense – just as many Christians raised an outcry at the release of Monty Python's *Life of Brian* or Martin Scorsese's *The Last Temptation of Christ*. The life of Muḥammad is just as important to Muslims as the life of Jesus is to Christians; it should therefore be told in a respectful, if not necessarily reverential, way. The issue is not simply freedom of expression, as it is often made out to be. It is about who has the power to create stereotypes and how those stereotypes affect the way we treat others.

Further reading

Ahmad, Mirza Tahir. *Islam's Response to Contemporary Issues*. Surrey, U: Islam International Publications, 1993.

Cohn-Sherbok, Daniel, ed. *The Salman Rushdie Controversy in Inter-Religious Perspective*. Lewiston, NY: Edwin Mellen Press, 1990.

[36] Reported by Alan Cooperman, "Anti-Muslim Remarks Stir Tempest." *The Washington Post* June 20, 2002, A03. Available at http://www.washingtonpost.com/ac2/wp-dyn/A14499-2002Jun19.

[37] Michael Hart, *The 100* (New York: Citadel Press, 1992), 3.

Hussain, Amir. "Misunderstandings and Hurt: How Canadians Joined World-Wide Muslim Reactions to Salman Rushdie's The Satanic Verses." *Journal of the American Academy of Religion* 70, no. 1 (March 2002): 1–32.
Rosaldo, Renato. *Culture and Truth: The Remaking of Social Analysis*. Boston: Beacon Press, 1993.
Said, Edward. *Covering Islam: How the Media and the Experts Determine How We See the Rest of the World*. New York: Pantheon Books, 1981.
Smith, Wilfred Cantwell. *The Meaning and End of Religion: A New Approach to the Religious Traditions of Mankind*. New York: Macmillan, 1963.

14 Epilogue: Muḥammad in the future

ABDULKADER TAYOB

Typical for any founder of a global religious tradition, the Prophet Muḥammad has enjoyed unusually high attention from friend, foe, and onlooker. From the beginning, his followers were obviously attentive to his words and deeds but also to his demeanor, and their recollections became critical for the meaning and future of Islam. His foes lost no opportunity to make their own conclusions about him, often cast in their familiar frameworks. And we have also occasionally had observers for whom the event of Muḥammad was sufficient inspiration to record. This volume is a rich collection that presents an examination of all three perspectives on the Prophet of Islam. It includes an extensive discussion of the particular identity, emergence, location, and value of these divergent positions. Covering the beginning of Islam through the premodern periods and up to the most recent debates, the chapters provide an overview of the Prophet Muḥammad, particularly how he has been reflected in word, ritual, philosophical concept, and literary novel. In this epilogue, I interrogate these contributions for their representation of modern scholarship on the Prophet Muḥammad. Not surprisingly, the two major concerns that have preoccupied modern scholarship are both clearly evident here, what I term the *history* and *historiography* of the Prophet.

Since the middle of the nineteenth century, when attention to the Prophet Muḥammad came under the influence of the emerging disciplines of history, psychology and the social sciences, a body of literature has grown. On the one hand, there has been greater attention paid to the historicity of the Prophet than at any other time in the past. In this regard, there has been a consistent search for reliable data that could be used to write a definitive biography. This search continues and will continue, even as some feel more reticent than others about the possibility of uncovering the real history of the Prophet.[1] On the other hand, the

[1] Harald Motzki, "Introduction," in *The Biography of Muḥammad: The Issue of Sources* (Leiden: E. J. Brill, 2000), xi–xvi; Andrew Rippin, "Muḥammad in the Qur'ān: Reading Scripture in the 21st Century," in Motzki, *Biography of Muḥammad*, 298–309.

appropriations of the Prophet have also been closely examined. Here, one might speak of a historiography, covering both historical writings and other forms of appropriations and interpretations of the Prophet Muḥammad. The political and cultural presuppositions and motives that lay behind the biographical interpretations have been examined and interrogated. Even though some biographical impressions may fail to meet critical-historical standards, they have revealed something about the authors or cultural groups that turned to the Prophet's life and example. Mirroring these scholarly concerns, some chapters in this volume focus on the historical record, whereas others focus on what may be called the historiography of the Prophet Muḥammad.

ON THE BIOGRAPHICAL PROCESS

Taken as a whole, this book represents an ideal opportunity to reflect on what Reynolds and Capps called the biographical process, as it applies to the writing of a biography of the Prophet Muḥammad.[2] Examining some key approaches in the history of religion, psychology, and anthropology, they concluded that there were some fundamental theoretical approaches for understanding and writing biographies of prominent historical figures. They identified this biographical process as an "interaction between biographical images and individual lives."[3] In religious discourse, this was reflected in the interaction between humanizing and spiritualizing tendencies in the writing of a biography, a desire to show the human side of a prominent figure and to reveal his or her spiritual dimension. In anthropology, it was the mapping of a cultural model against a representative individual. And in psychology, biographies of great men like Gandhi attempted to balance a focus on the individuality of a person in the context of a framework or frameworks. This concept of a biographical process showed that there was a tension between the specific and the ordinary dimensions of religious and cultural figures as well as their model-framing roles. In the life of the Prophet Muḥammad, one may not limit an examination of his life to the humanizing and spiritualization elements. These are clearly present, especially in Muslim literature, but given the political and social dimensions of the life of the Prophet, we can also see the relevance of models and life histories in

[2] Frank E. Reynolds and Donald Capps, "Introduction," in *The Biographical Process: Studies in the History and Psychology of Religion*, ed. Frank E. Reynolds and Donald Capps, *Religion and Reason, Method and Theory in the Study and Interpretation of Religion* (The Hague: Mouton, 1976), 1–33.

[3] Ibid., 15.

anthropological and psychological approaches, respectively, as discussed by Capps and Reynolds. These insights of the biographical process provide a useful perspective on the modern literature on Muḥammad and help us to place our modern predilections in an analytical framework.

The biographical process is basically one of interpretation, and it merits closer attention on more than one level. The interpretative acts of all social actors, not only believers, merit critical assessment. So, too, however, do the interpretative acts of those of us who observe the biographical process. As scholars working in different disciplines, our own work merits some critical self-reflection. The chapters in this book provide an excellent springboard for identifying some distinctive processes in the biographical process of Muḥammad.

The search for the historical Muḥammad is the first of such concerns. An examination of the historical Muḥammad is an utterly secular pursuit that nevertheless attempts to understand the religion of Muḥammad. The frameworks of religion are generally derived from the history of religions, and in this way, we can think of the models used to understand this history. The history of the Prophet, though, also implies a reflection of his statements and his actions conveyed in different forms. This leads us directly into the models and appropriations of the Prophet. I identify at least three such processes in this collection of articles: transcendentalization, personalization, and secularization or sanctification. With these processes, the Prophet is being made as he is being recalled. The two overall concerns – the history of the Prophet as such and the history of his appropriation – stand central in this collection.

THE HISTORICAL PROPHET

In general, the life and biographical record of Muḥammad have presented a challenge to the secular sensibilities of modern historians. For such scholars, the record of a sacred biography cannot be accepted at face value. It has to be translated into a form that explains or at least brackets the claims of divine intervention in earlier Muslim biographies. In keeping with the framework of the biographical process, one might compare this modern naturalization with what Frank Griffel (Chapter 8) notices in the theological and philosophical writings of Muslims in the past. In his analysis, the meaning of revelation was also naturalized in the philosophical discourse of the day. It was interpreted in the framework of models of epistemology explored and developed by premodern philosophers. In the modern context, the search for the historical Muḥammad displays a secular mistrust of religious claims and religious biographies, a familiar mark of the modern age. The naturalization is not presented in a philosophically neutral form of epistemology but in the universal march of history. The modern attempt to link the statements of the Prophet to their perceived antecedents in other traditions (so-called borrowings) might be objectionable to believers, because it seems to confront the belief in the divine nature of revelation. However, the critical historian cannot be satisfied with religious and divine claims and cannot do less than search out the historical connections. In this way, one can speak of the biography of the Prophet as a challenge to modern secular sensibilities: an attempt to write a natural history without recourse to divine interventions.

At the same time, a historical approach to the Prophet also needs to work with models in which the life and career of the Prophet may be deemed reasonable or historically feasible. Such models are markedly different from the religious models that Muslims use or the models that his detractors (past and present) use. They are not immediately apparent, as the search for history is a search for "how it really happened (*wie es eigentlich gewesen ist*)."[4] Suspicious of the historical foundations of the Prophet, Andrew Rippin, for example, has pointed to the need to take a more critical view of the search for sources that has preoccupied scholarship of the Prophet since the nineteenth century. The lack of critical reflexivity in this scholarship, according to Rippin, needs closer examination and might itself be subjected to a hermeneutical reading of modern texts.[5] I propose that one first step in this hermeneutical exercise is to identify models of religions underlying the historical searches. How did the Prophet produce this religion? Or how did it actually emerge? Does it seem to be modeled on similar movements in his time? The biography of the Prophet between the search for history and the employment of models of religion provides an insight into the biographical process of modern scholarship.

In this volume, Michael Lecker and Walid Saleh provide two approaches to the history of the Prophet with which we can begin to examine the search for historical truth as a biographical process. Lecker's essay (Chapter 3) suggests how a careful examination of sources may produce a glimpse of the history behind the images and models that most people are engaged in. The realpolitik of establishing a community with a mission comes into focus, something that appears quite ordinary and human. His presentation of the Prophet Muḥammad does not produce a

4 This is the famous statement from the historian Leopold van Ranke, d. 1886.

5 Rippin, "Muḥammad," 302.

vision of the Prophet distinct from other political leaders embarking on the foundation of a state. In Chapter 1, Saleh also grapples with the history of the Prophet that lies beneath the myth that quickly surrounded him. In his essay, too, the Prophet is thoroughly historicized, and the examination of the context presents a case for counting the Prophet among many similar figures. In comparison with Lecker, though, Saleh is prepared to uncover more than an ordinary political career from the sources. Saleh suggests that the Prophet's extraordinary success calls for an explanation beyond the context and that he might be seen as a classic revolutionary figure. The reference to a revolutionary represented a key to the models that a biographical process implies. The context might reveal the historical nature of the life of Muḥammad, but the motif of a revolutionary connotes a model that one can compare with other similarly extraordinary figures. In contrast, Lecker's implicit model, at least in this essay, seems to be that of an ordinary statesman embarking on achieving mainly political objectives.

This search for history has generally not been as secularist as Lecker's chapter might suggest. In fact, Islam as preached by Muḥammad was a continuation of and final step in the Abrahamic religions. In historical terms, this immediately raised the question of how he had learned about Judaism and Christianity, what he had learned, and how he had formulated a new religion. Hence, since the early nineteenth century, scholars have addressed these questions by examining the religious context of Arabia out of which Islam emerged. Several theories were presented about the historical links of the Prophet Muḥammad to Judaism and Christianity. The proposals were not conclusive, but the search has illuminated the religious context of Arabia and the particular meaning and form of Judaic and Christian strands in the area. This particular approach conveyed the notion of the Prophet Muḥammad as bringing together various elements, Judaic, Christian, and Arab, in the production of a new religion. It is the model of an agent of history who consciously creates a synthesis out of materials available to him or her.[6]

A related model of religion might be gleaned from another group of scholars who examined the history of the Prophet. They, too, seemed to focus on the agency of the Prophet but dwelled more directly on his moral integrity and commitment, invariably comparing those with Christianity. Tor Andrae and W. Montgomery Watt's credulity of Muslim biographies has been questioned and in many cases rejected by critical

[6] For a comprehensive and critical appraisal of these findings, see Irving M. Zeitline, *The Historical Muhammad* (Cambridge: Polity Press, 2007).

revisionists, but their approach to the religious nature of the prophetic message is interesting. Andrae recorded favorably the romanticist's assessment of the Prophet as a man of inspired creativity. He himself concluded that he was sincere and not out to defraud anybody, a simple man who had anguished sometimes over apparently trivial issues.[7] Watt's understanding followed this sentiment, pointing to his sincerity, visionary wisdom as a statesman, and skills as an administrator. From a Christian perspective, Muḥammad should be credited with possessing a creative imagination and, importantly, advancing the religious cause: "not all the ideas he proclaimed are true and sound," wrote Watt, "but by God's grace he has been enabled to provide millions of men with a better religion than they had before they testified that there is no god but God and that Muḥammad is the messenger of God."[8] In both of these influential biographies, another model of the Prophet is brought to the fore. The historical dimension is not ignored, but the Prophet is presented as an ethical religious figure. In particular, he is compared favorably in the Christian perspectives of the authors, who seek to overturn centuries of criticisms of the Prophet as impostor and heretic. Muḥammad is even credited with advancing the cause of religion (which may with reason be interpreted to mean Christianity). Here, the role of the Prophet continues to be that of agent but is informed by ethical standards expected of a Prophet in the biblical tradition.

More historically and sociologically critical scholars have searched for the historical Muḥammad by searching for the directly religious influences that informed him, questioning the biography proposed by the first Muslims. In a recent book that examines these controversies from the nineteenth century to the present, Irving Zeitline builds a theory of the historical Muḥammad on Ibn Khaldun's thesis of the rivalry between nomads and sedentary peoples. This provides him with a sound basis to focus on both the religious and the political dimensions that led to the success of the Prophet Muḥammad. The conflict between Muḥammad and his adversaries was really a conflict between nomads and sedentary peoples, and Islam was a highly successful ideology employed in this enterprise.[9] The agency of the Prophet was also prominent, but now his

[7] Tor Andrae, *Mohammed: sein Leben und sein Glaube* (1932; repr., Hildesheim: Olms, 1977), 176–9 (English trans., *Mohammed: The Man and His Faith* (New York: Harper, 1960). For a recent statement to the same effect, see Christian W. Troll, "Muhammad – Prophet auch für Christen?" *Stimmen der Zeit: Die Zeitschfift für christiche Kultur* 5 (2007): 291–303.

[8] W. Montgomery Watt, *Muhammad: Prophet and Statesman* (London: Oxford University Press, 1961), 232, 236–8, 240, at 240.

[9] Zeitline, *Historical Muhammad.*

decisions seemed to be guided in a sociological model. The Prophet was willing to take chances and risks as they presented themselves. Taking a more literary approach, Angelika Neuwirth also proposed a model of the emergence of a religious community around a book and liturgy. Using the history of the emergence of the Qurʾānic text, she argued that one could identify the formation and development of a religious community around the Prophet Muḥammad. The various references to the book and community in the Qurʾān indicated a development in the sacred text that pointed to the history and formation of a religious cult and community.[10] Between the sociological dimension of Zeitline and the literary reading of Neuwirth, a natural history of early Islam as community, religion, and polity emerges.

The biographical process as a balance between history and models of religion provides a useful framework for understanding the search for the historical Muḥammad. Using the history of religions, one can examine the interpretive dimensions of the search for the historical Muḥammad. Assumptions about religion and its origins provide a base on which the history of Islam and of the Prophet can be mapped. With a few illustrations, I have merely scratched the surface for a more extensive study. Taking a more conscious approach to the religion of early Islam, the sources might reveal something more about early Islam.

MODELS AS PROCESSES

Images and models proposed for the Prophet are more obvious in the biographies and interpretations of his life and career outside the purely historical disciplines. Following Reynolds and Capps, it may be useful to think of representations of the Prophet as distinct processes. The idea of a process implies a series of actions or developments that are evident in the writing of a biography or the representation of the Prophet. The biographies are not given but produced through interpretive movements. Three such processes are immediately noticeable in these essays and highlight some significant ways in which the Prophet has been appropriated: transcendentalization, personalization, and secularization.

[10] Angelika Neuwirth, "Recenzion von J. Wansborough, Quranic Studies," *Die Welt des Islams* 23, no. 4 (1984): 539–42; Neuwirth, "Vom Rezitationstext über die Liturgie zum Kanon," in *The Qur'ān as Text*, ed. Stefan Wild (Leiden: E. J. Brill, 1996), 69–105; Neuwirth, "Some Remarks on the Special Linguistic and Literary Character of the Qurʾān," in *The Qur'ān: Formative Interpretation*, ed. Andrew Rippin (Aldershot: Ashgate, 1999), 253–7.

Some of the contributions provide rich testimony of how the model and image of Prophet were subject to a process of transcendentalization. By "transcendence," I do not refer only to the realms of spirituality. Taking the literal meaning of *transcendence*, I propose that the chapters examine the way in which the Prophet was transposed from his particular social and historical location to another place or toward another purpose. The transcendence was clearly beyond the material world in some cases, as represented in Ṣūfī contexts. Carl Ernst's chapter reminds us that in most periods of history, Muḥammad was taken by Muslims to be the spiritual and cosmic center of reality. The chapter by Marion Katz on the presence of the Prophet in Muslim ritual also illustrates the transcendental dimension. The Prophet was transported from his historical location and brought directly into the ritual practices of Muslims. The closeness of the Prophet was experienced as presence and warmth, in comparison with the rational and textual approaches that appear to dominate modern approaches. Shahzad Bashir's essay also produces something similar, in showing three biographical processes within Iranian Ṣūfī texts in a particularly turbulent period of the fifteenth century. However, one may also examine the transcendence on a material, horizontal level. John Tolan's study of the European images of the Prophet presents a case of transcendence of a very different kind. He traces the extraordinarily complex and changing ways in which the Prophet was located outside Muslim culture. In the West, in particular, the Prophet was taken out of his own cultural meaning and given a completely different one, a process that continues today. Another equally significant example is Frank Griffel's chapter, which links Muslim philosophical and Ṣūfī thinking to the Greek tradition and its search for an ideal ruler. Revelation, as experienced by the Prophet, was taken out of its specific context and given a universal meaning. It was naturalized, both taking it beyond its specific localities and rendering it comprehensible in the general discussion of epistemology. To a limited extent, this was also the process that Saleh suggested in his description of the Prophet as a revolutionary.

A second key process evident in the chapters herein is personalization of the Prophet in one way or another. By this, I mean how the recollection was very closely connected with the individual person recalling or reenacting the Prophet's life. Joseph Lowry's contribution deals with *ḥadīth*, a controversial topic between Western and Muslim scholars as far as its historicity is concerned. While presenting the main arguments of the debate and the ongoing difference of opinion among modern scholars, he also turns to the meaning of *ḥadīth* in Muslim religious values and personal piety. Robert Gleave follows this line by turning to a related and prominent feature of the Prophet's personal example. He shows how this example was debated by Muslim scholarship while providing a powerful source for pietistic movements that continue. Here is an example of the humanizing and spiritualizing tendencies in the heart of Muslim scholarship on the Prophet. Bashir's contribution shows how different Ṣūfī texts appropriate the Prophet. One of them, in particular, establishes a close, personal connection between the Prophet and the founder of a particular Ṣūfī movement. One can identify this motif by considering how Ṣūfīs have sometimes proposed imagining (*taṣawwur*) the Prophet, or the shaykh in place of the Prophet, as a particularly powerful way of personal appropriation. Again, Katz's chapter points us to the personalization in a different direction, showing how women remembered the Prophet through his mother and foster mother. The chapter points clearly to the gendered dimension of the biographical process, which is clearly, though implicitly, present in the other biographies. The military exploits of the Prophet, with their masculine overtones, have been prominent in the historical search since the nineteenth century. As a major corrective to this tendency, biographies of the women around the Prophet address this problem to a remarkable and creative effect. Taking into consideration the dearth of sources but also the very clear references to the role of women in the life of the Prophet, Assia Djebar has used both historical and literary conventions to present a creative reading of the first decades of Islam.[11] And, of course, the very process of incorporating the Prophet Muḥammad in modern novels is beautifully illustrated by Amir Hussain. In his reading of Salman Rushdie's *The Satanic Verses* and other artistic productions, one sees not a polemical portrayal of the Prophet in the tradition of medieval Christianity but a subtle process of working with symbols and antisymbols to uncover the roots of the self and Islam in the modern postcolonial world. This contrasts sharply with most other readings, or rather impressions, of Rushdie's novel. And one may expect more of this to happen as the Prophet becomes the subject of ever divergent and often competing voices.

A third process that can be identified in a number of chapters here seems to me an oscillation between secularization and sanctification.[12] Uri Rubin and Asma Afsaruddin's chapters provide eloquent examples of

[11] Assia Djebar, *Fern von Medina* (Zurich: Unionsverlag, 1994).

[12] Wessels has identified this secular trend among modern Arabic biographies. Antonie Wessels, "Modern Biographies of the Life of the Prophet Muhammad in Arabic," *Islamic Culture* 49, no. 2 (April 1975): 99–105.

these, reminding us that there is no necessary teleology from one direction to the other. Rubin's chapter examines the development of miracles associated with the Prophet. It is insightful on the changing perception of the Prophet in conformity with expectations among Christians, Jews, and other religious groups in the broader religious context of the Near East. Examining the splitting of the moon in its linguistic usage in the Qurʾān, he suggests a meaning that predates the development of a later exegetical interpretation. In the literary meaning of Qurʾān, the splitting (*inshiqāq*) of the moon was easily related to the end of time, to eschatology. Its meaning later expanded and changed, under the influence of exegetical work, to an actual act carried out by the Prophet. The miracle then became associated with the status of Muḥammad rather than with a report of a future eschatological event.

Afsaruddin's chapter can also be read for a similar but interestingly opposite effect. In examining the political literature, she identifies a distinct shift in the meaning associated with the Prophet as a political model for Muslims. The earlier literature emphasized his knowledge and excellence (e.g., generosity), but later, more pragmatic concerns come into play. I read this as a secularization of the image of the Prophet where pragmatic concerns overtake the ethical values that earlier presented a moral benchmark for Muslim leaders. Both Sunnī and Shīʿī sources, according to Afsaruddin, emphasized closeness and fidelity to the Prophet as virtues, later to be translated in more pragmatic political practices. Again, this is a fascinating account of the changing perception of the Prophet as political leader, and it tells us much more about the political models constructed about the Prophet as such. What is also significant, however, when compared with the work of Rubin, is the secularization of the image in the political realm. According to Rubin, the Prophet took on a greater and more personally spiritual dimension over time, in contrast with the desanctification in the political literature. In Afsaruddin's chapter, we are left with an earlier image of the Prophet that has more religious content and meaning. For his early followers, his extraordinary knowledge and character were more prominent, with the Prophet acting as an exemplary leader of a religious community.

The two images are not exclusive of each other. Both chapters, however, come close to telling us something about the earliest recollection of the Prophet that provides a different representation of the past than do the directly historical analyses. Their chapters are not by themselves sufficient to say with a degree of certainty what the original meaning for the early Arabs was. They themselves make no such direct claim. However, they suggest a historical impression that contrasts with the meanings produced in later exegetical works. In this way, one can perhaps look at the chapters as producing a sense of the past even when they do not directly address the past as such. This is not to say that they can be compared to the kind of work that Lecker is engaged in. Nor am I suggesting that one can produce a history from these reflections of Muḥammad in Islamic history. All I am saying is that the chapters indirectly imply an earlier historical representation of the Prophet.

Both Rubin's and Afsaruddin's examinations deal with the premodern period. Secularization, of course, is closely connected with modernity, and some chapters deal directly with this issue. Gade's chapter on Indonesian biographies stands midway between what I have identified as personalization and secularization. The "narrativization" of the Prophet may very much lead to personalization. Taking on a new ideology, however, the narratives of new Islamic groups in Indonesia are pragmatically oriented.[13] In comparison with his presence in the modern novel or in ritual, the Prophet has here become the model of pragmatism and common sense. This result may be compared with the secularization that Tolan records for European Enlightenment thinkers who put forward the idea of the Prophet as the statesperson par excellence. And Katz's chapter explores this same dimension in another way. Tracing the place and presence of the Prophet in the *mawlid*, she records a decline in his presence in more recent times.

There may be more processes identified in the biographical appropriation of the Prophet Muḥammad. However, transcendentalization, personalization, and secularization (sanctification) capture some of the crucial ways in which the Prophet is interpreted for communities and individuals. In these processes, the history of the Prophet neither is the primary concern nor is completely ignored. Greater attention seems to be placed on the moral message, ritual presence, and closeness with the retelling or enactment of the Prophet's life. The emphasis is placed on interpretation and appropriation rather than on a search for the past as it actually happened.

MUḤAMMAD IN THE GLOBAL FLOWS OF LATE MODERNITY

In the past few decades, in the context of both the revival of religion and intense globalization through technology and population migration,

[13] The Prophet at the head of a *dakwah* movement is not limited to Indonesia, as the Prophet as *dāʿī* is a prominent motif in Arab Islamist literature.

the biography of the Prophet has become part of a global popular culture. Through the affair of Rushdie's *Satanic Verses*, the so-called *fatwā* of Khomeini in 1989,[14] and the Danish cartoons of 2005, the image of the Prophet has been literally traded and exchanged over a number of old and new conflicts. As technology facilitates the exchange of images and views at virtual speeds, the prophetic models cannot be confined to their producers. And as people move across the globe, making new homes and communities, they take their models of the Prophet with them. Variant and conflicting models are brought closer together, sometimes more quickly than there is time to process and reconcile them with one another. In terms of the biographical process used herein, it seems that the humanization of the Prophet is gaining the upper hand against his sanctification. Even though one may speak of a continuing competition between the two poles of the process, the public nature of the exchange seems to militate against a private appropriation that favors the Prophet as a model of spirituality.

Given the reality of technological development and the movements of people, this exchange of images of the Prophet might be thought to take place without mediation. In the past two or three decades, though, these exchanges have been framed in very specific contexts of developments in Muslim societies and in global developments. In both cases, the history and image of the Prophet have become a central part of the conflicts. In Muslim societies, the emergence of Islamist and more traditional approaches to Islam and to the earlier sources has rejected the apologetic traditions of the past. Such apologetic approaches, evident in nineteenth- and early-twentieth-century writings of Sayyid Ameer Ali and Muḥammad Ḥusayn Haykal, had been attempting to model the essence of the Prophet in terms of new configurations, not always completely in agreement with modern sentiments but certainly compatible to a considerable degree. In the 1970s, they were replaced with Islamist and traditional approaches that resisted the modernizing tendencies as a matter of principle. Often, these emphasized the image of the Prophet at the head of political states and even militant movements, gleaned from so-called literal and historical, as opposed to mystical and transcendental, readings of the life of the Prophet in past and present biographies. Other pietistic movements have globalized the Prophet as a preeminent model for personal behavior, ritual, and social life. Led by the Tablighi Jamaat from South Asia and Salafiyya from Saudi Arabia,

[14] Although it was later interpreted as a *fatwā*, the original context of Khomeini's statement was quite different. See Mehdi Mozaffari, *Fatwa: Violence and Discourtesy* (Aarhus: Aarhus University Press, 1998).

they have emphasized the Prophet as an externalized model to be imitated rather than to be experienced in mystical thought or practices. At the same time, only partly in response to these developments, many Western journalists and some political scientists created a new image of the balance of powers in the world of nation-states after the collapse of the Soviet Union. The thesis of the clash of civilizations, first presented in 1989, mapped a world of conflicting cultures marked by mutual hostility, mistrust, and incomprehension. In this worldview, the conflict between Islam and the West was a central component of world politics. In such a situation of conflict and increasing contact, the framework of the biographical process still provides useful insights. In this exchange, the humanization of the Prophet seems to tip the balance. And this humanization is driven from different and unlikely sources.

In the most obvious case, this humanization is clearly seen in the number of newspaper articles and books that are published on the so-called real threat posed by Muslims. With a particular focus on what some refer to as the real Muḥammad, it is easy to present the goals of Muslims on the path to world domination that matched the early history of Islam. Those who regarded Islam as the new enemy of Western civilization have turned to the Prophet to display his faults and moral weaknesses. The Danish cartoons of 2005 were a graphic illustration of the images in circulation about the Prophet in popular Western media. Similarly, many books seek to tell the West what Muḥammad was really all about, including Robert Spencer's *The Truth about Muhammad*. The book itself examines the historical record and accepts the conclusion of the scholarship that is critical of Muslim biographical recollection. For Spencer, however, it was sufficient that Muslims believe that the earlier biographies of the Prophet are true. From here, he makes the logical conclusion that the danger of Islam is confirmed and proved.[15] The book promises to be saying something about the Prophet, but it intends to say something more specifically about Muslims. By ignoring the multiple ways that Muslims have appropriated the image and model of the Prophet Muḥammad, Spencer provides a sophisticated example of a general trend: turning to the Prophet to create an impression of the Islamic threat.

The humanization of the Prophet has not only come from clearly defined political groups and institutions. The Danish cartoon debacle originated from the desire of a Danish writer, Kåre Bluitgen, for an image

[15] Robert Spencer, *The Truth about Muhammad: Founder of the World's Most Intolerant Religion* (Washington, D: Regnery Publishing, 2007).

of the Prophet Muḥammad to illustrate children's books on the Prophet and the Qur'ān. The desire to create an image of the Prophet in a children's book to make him accessible to European children was very different from what the cartoons eventually presented. It highlights a process of humanization of the Prophet Muḥammad from a very different perspective. This has more recently been seen in the book by Sherry Jones on the wife of the Prophet, ʿĀ'isha, which created a minor storm on the Internet. Called the *Jewel of Medina*, this romantic depiction of the wife of the Prophet suggests a humanization of a very different kind from that of Spencer and the Danish cartoons.[16]

The antiprophetic literature led by clearly identified political parties and movements in the West has not been the only source of the humanization of the Prophet. Some of the radical Islamist literature on the Internet on the Prophet has also emphasized the role of the Prophet as a political leader par excellence; a leader who does not compromise with his adversaries and is determined to lead the Muslim to dominance.[17] On a subtler and deeper level, the humanization and secularization of the Prophet have been promoted by Muslims who have objected to the negative caricatures and representations in popular literature. In an implicit way, they have popularized these books and images through protests of various kinds. They have used every public forum, and in many cases legal forums as well, to defend the integrity of the Prophet. Often, in their protests at many different levels, they have themselves circulated these images and even cartoons by e-mail, chat rooms, and other forms of public protest. Even as they have been doing so to object to the representations, they have circulated the images and discussions thereof in Internet channels across the globe.[18] On a more explicit level, some of the organized responses to the negative images also revealed a desanctification of the image of the Prophet. The International Union of Muslim Scholars, led by prominent Arab scholars like Yūsuf al-Qaraḍawī, expressed their dismay at the Danish cartoons and regarded them as a deliberate attempt to insult Muslims in Europe and the world. However, its major response

[16] Sherry Jones, *Jewel of Medina* (New York: Beaufort Books, 2008) (originally contracted with Random House but then dropped by the publisher).

[17] See, e.g., http://www.tawhed.ws for a full library of jihadist literature that promotes the Prophet only as a militant leader.

[18] The Internet is not short of discussion of *The Satanic Verses*, the Danish cartoons, and Muḥammad. For some specific points, see Ferial Haffajee, "Faith in an Editor," *Global Journalist*, 2nd quarter 2006, at http://www.globaljournalist.org/magazine/2006–2/journalists-journal.html; and see http://en.wikipedia.org/wiki/Danish_cartoons, for a comprehensive review of the events related to the Danish cartoons.

was to demand an apology from the Danish government and to urge Muslims to boycott Danish goods until such an apology was forthcoming.[19] Such political and economic responses present a desanctification of the Prophet in the global public flow of images.

There is clearly evidence of images of the Prophet in the global flow that moves in the opposite direction. For one, there have been rebuttals to the negative characterization of the Prophet that emphasized his religious character. To mention one prominent example in English, Karen Armstrong's writings on Islam in general and on the Prophet Muḥammad in particular presented a countervoice to Spencer and to the Danish cartoons. At the same time, Web sites set up by Muslims who support the ritual presence of the Prophet have begun to make their presence felt. The Web is not only the home of those who emphasize the political and social dimensions of the Prophet. Many Ṣūfī networks and orders, long closely associated with the sanctification of the Prophet, have also made their presence felt. In a quick search of *mawlid* on YouTube.com, I obtained 1,470 hits.[20] This suggests a very different appropriation from that indicated in many observations of Muslim societies. And yet I do think that the public sphere in general and the Internet in particular promote the desanctification of the Prophet to a remarkable degree. The responses and counterresponses might argue for different images, but they all externalize the appropriation of the Prophet to some extent. To fully appreciate the sanctification of the Prophet, one needs to turn to the personal and communal appropriations in Muslim societies.

CONCLUSION

The biographical process is an interpretive exercise that works at many different levels in popular and academic scholarship. It reveals a struggle to balance a historical view of the Prophet with the models and frameworks of those who approach the Prophet. Here, I have identified the biographical process in the search for the historical Muḥammad and in the search for the religious context of the foundation of Islam. Turning our attention to the later recollection of the Prophet, we find a variety of processes that produced images of the Prophet Muḥammad. In the recent flow of images on the Internet and a global public sphere, a greater

[19] See the Web site (http://www.iumsonline.net) of the International Union of Muslim Scholars in general and the particular statement: Yūsuf al-Qaradawi and Muḥammad Salīm al-ʿAwwā, "Bayān al-ittiḥād ḥawl nashr ṣuwar musīʾa li al-rasūl," January 1, 2006, http://www.iumsonline.net/articls/2006/01/article04.shtml.

[20] Searched on November 26, 2008.

tendency toward desacralization seems to dominate. However, I would not be surprised to find that closer attention to personal appropriations might suggest parallel processes of resanctification.

The hermeneutical challenge presented by Rippin might also lead to some interesting new directions. The literature on the Prophet, in the past and present, also invites deeper readings beyond the contextual readings that we have seen. In thinking about this epilogue, I see possibly new directions in the reinterpretations of Islam that are being presented in the most recent past. For a reexamination of the Prophet, such a search would or should take the historical records, and the multiple readings of Muḥammad in the past and the present, seriously. In addition, though, following the interpretive turns that they are already suggesting, scholars might want to interrogate the meaning of the Prophet in the way developed by Paul Ricoeur in the readings of theological and philosophical texts. From this perspective, I would venture to say that the appropriation of the Prophet would reveal the conflicting features of modernity. On the one hand, in the image of Muḥammad, we see a resistance to the role of great men, particularly religious men, in the production of history and to the founding of religions, as this view of history robs humanity of its freedom and its maturity. On the other hand, Muḥammad might be seen as a response to the confusion of modernity and its dehumanization. Modernity, in this view, is not a sign of liberation but a juggernaut that evokes a desire to control and contain. For many believers, Muḥammad becomes a bulwark against this uncertainty.

We can say, therefore, that the future of Muḥammad is ensured; he is an enduring figure in our common history, both for Muslims and for non-Muslims alike. But writing about Muḥammad remains an important way for many actors to express their attitudes toward modernity, religious conflicts, and the like. Scholarship cannot hope to evade these powerful currents, but it can maintain its integrity by interrogating, and admitting, its relationship to these forces. This book, then, should help many readers begin to establish their own views of Muḥammad in a complex and integrated fashion.

Index of Qur'an verses

General Index

Other titles in the series *(Continued from page iii)*

THE QUR'AN
Edited by Jane Dammen McAuliffe

KARL RAHNER
Edited by Declan Marmion and Mary E. Hines

REFORMATION THEOLOGY
Edited by David Bagchi and David Steinmetz

FREIDRICK SCHLEIERMACHER
Edited by Jacqueline Mariña

ST. PAUL
Edited by James D. G. Dunn

THE TALMUD AND RABBINIC LITERATURE
Edited by Charlotte E. Fonrobert and Martin S. Jaffee

HANS URS VON BALTHASAR
Edited by Edward T. Oakes and David Moss

CLASSICAL ISLAMIC THEOLOGY
Edited by Tim Winter

PURITANISM
Edited by John Coffey and Paul C. H. Lim

JOHN WESLEY
Edited by Randy L. Maddox and Jason E. Vickers